PERCHANCE TO DREAM

ANCIENT NEAR EAST MONOGRAPHS

General Editors
Alan Lenzi
Juan Manuel Tebes

Editorial Board
Reinhard Achenbach
C. L. Crouch
Roxana Flammini
Esther J. Hamori
Christopher B. Hays
René Krüger
Graciela Gestoso Singer
Bruce Wells

Number 21

PERCHANCE TO DREAM

Dream Divination in the Bible and the Ancient Near East

Edited by
Esther J. Hamori and Jonathan Stökl

 PRESS

Atlanta

Copyright © 2018 by SBL Press

All rights reserved. No part of this work may be reproduced or transmitted in any form or by any means, electronic or mechanical, including photocopying and recording, or by means of any information storage or retrieval system, except as may be expressly permitted by the 1976 Copyright Act or in writing from the publisher. Requests for permission should be addressed in writing to the Rights and Permissions Office, SBL Press, 825 Houston Mill Road, Atlanta, GA 30329 USA.

Library of Congress Control Number: 2018934759

Printed on acid-free paper.

Table of Contents

Perchance to Dream   1
    Esther J. Hamori

1. Horn and Ivory: Dreams as Portents in Ancient Mesopotamia and Beyond   9
   Christopher Metcalf

2. Portent Dreams in Hittite Anatolia   27
   Alice Mouton

3. When Even the Gods Do Not Know: El's Dream Divination in KTU 1.6 iii   43
   Koowon Kim

4. Maleness, Memory, and the Matter of Dream Divination in the Hebrew Bible   61
   Scott B. Noegel

5. Dreams in the Joseph Narrative   91
   Franziska Ede

6. Samuel's Theophany and the Politics of Religious Dreams   109
   Stephen C. Russell

7. Daniel and the "Prophetization" of Dream Divination   133
   Jonathan Stökl

8. Agency, Authority, and Scribal Innovation in Dream Narratives of the Aramaic Dead Sea Scrolls   157
   Andrew B. Perrin

9. "All the Dreams Follow the Mouth": Dreamers and Interpreters in Rabbinic Literature   183
   Haim Weiss

Contributors   205

Index   207

List of Abbreviations

AASF	Annales Academiae scientiarum fennicae
AB	Anchor Bible
AGAJU	Arbeiten zur Geschichte des antiken Judentums und des Urchristentums
AEM I/1	*Archives Épistolaires de Mari, I/1.* Jean-Marie Durand. ARM 26.1. Paris: ERC, 1988.
AIL	Ancient Israel and Its Literature
AJP	*American Journal of Philology*
AGJU	Arbeiten zur Geschichte des antiken Judentums und des Urchristentums
AMD	Ancient Magic and Divination
ANEM	Ancient Near Eastern Monographs
AnOr	Analecta Orientalia
Ant.	Josephus, *Jewish Antiquities*
AOAT	Alter Orient und Altes Testament
AOS	American Oriental Series
ARA	*Annual Review of Anthropology*
ARM	Archives royales de Mari
ARM 26	Durand, Jean-Marie and Dominique Charpin. *Archives épistolaires de Mari.* 2 vols. Paris: ERC, 1988.
AS	*Aramaic Studies*
ATD	Altes Testament Deutsch
AThANT	Abhandlungen zur Theologie des Alten und Neuen Testaments
AuOr	*Aula Orientalis*
AYBRL	Anchor Yale Bible Reference Library
b. B. Bat.	Tractate Baba Batra in the Babylonian Talmud
b. ʿErub	Tractate ʿErubin in the Babylonian Talmud
b. Maʿaś. Š.	Tractate Maʿaśer Šeni in the Babylonian Talmud
b. Pes.	Tractate Pesaḥim in the Babylonian Talmud
b. Soṭ.	Tractate Soṭah in the Babylonian Talmud
BAR	*Biblical Archaeology Review*
BEHER	Bibliothèque de l'École des hautes Études: Sciences religieuses
Bib	*Biblica*
BibOr	Bibliotheca et Orientalia
BibSem	The Biblical Seminar
BIFAO	*Bulletin de l'Institut Français d'Archéologie Orientale*

BJS	Brown Judaic Studies
BKAT	Biblischer Kommentar, Altes Testament
BMB	Boston Museum Bulletin
BMW	Bible in the Modern World
BN	*Biblische Notizen*
BWANT	Beiträge zur Wissenschaft vom Alten und Neuen Testament
BZ	*Biblische Zeitschrift*
BZAW	Beihefte zur Zeitschrift für die alttestamentliche Wissenschaft
BZNW	Beihefte zur Zeitschrift für die neutestamentliche Wissenschaft
CAD	Gelb, Ignace J., et al. *The Assyrian Dictionary of the Oriental Institute of the University of Chicago*. Chicago: The Oriental Institute of the University of Chicago, 1956–2010.
CAT	*The Cuneiform Alphabetic Texts from Ugarit, Ras Ibn Hani, and Other Places*. Edited by M. Dietrich, O. Loretz, and J. Sanmartin. Munster: Ugarit-Verlag, 1995.
CBET	Contributions to Biblical Exegesis and Theology
CBS	Museum siglum of the University Museum in Philadelphia (Catalogue of the Babylonian Section)
CBQ	*Catholic Biblical Quarterly*
CDOG	Colloquien der Deutschen Orient-Gesellschaft
CHANE	Culture and History of the Ancient Near East
CIS	Corpus Inscriptionum Semiticarum
CM	Cuneiform Monographs
ConBOT	Coniectanea Biblica: Old Testament Series
COS	*The Context of Scripture*. Edited by William W. Hallow. 3 vols. Leiden: Brill, 2000.
CP	*Classical Philology*
CRRAI	Compte rendu de la Rencontre Assyriologique Internationale
CTA	*Corpus des tablettes en cunéiformes alphabétiques découvertes. Ras Shamra-Ugarit de 1929 à 1939*. Edited by Andrée Herdner. Paris: Geuthner, 1963.
CTH	*Catalogue des textes hittites*. Emmanuel Laroche. Paris: Klincksieck, 1971.
DBH	Dresdner Beiträge zur Hethitologie
DCLY	Deuterocanonical and Cognate Literature Yearbook
DSD	*Dead Sea Discoveries*
DULAT	*A Dictionary of the Ugaritic Language in the Alphabetic Tradition*. Gregorio del Olmo Lete and Joaquín Sanmartín. Translated by W. G. E. Watson. Leiden: Brill, 2004.
EJL	Early Judaism and Its Literature
ErIsr	*Eretz Israel*
ERC	Éditions recherche sur les civilisations
ETCSL	Electronic Text Corpus of Sumerian Literature

Exod. Rab.	Exodus / Shemot Rabbah
FCB	Feminist Companion to the Bible
FB	Forschungen zur Bibel
FOTL	Forms of the Old Testament Literature
FRLANT	Forschungen zur Religion und Literatur des Alten und Neuen Testament
Gen. Rab.	Genesis / Bereshit Rabbah
GMTR	Guides to the Mesopotamian Textual Record
HBM	Hebrew Bible Monographs
HeBAI	*Hebrew Bible and Ancient Israel*
Hist.	Herodotus, *Histories*
HKAT	Handkommentar zum Alten Testament
HSM	Harvard Semitic Monographs
HSS	Harvard Semitic Studies
HTR	*Harvard Theological Review*
HUCA	*Hebrew Union College Annual*
HUCM	Monographs of the Hebrew Union College
Il.	Homer, *Iliad*
IOS	*Israel Oriental Studies*
ISBL	Indiana Studies in Biblical Literature
JAJSup	Supplements to the Journal of Ancient Judaism
JANER	*Journal of Ancient Near Eastern Religions*
JANES	*Journal of the Ancient Near Eastern Society of Columbia University*
JAOS	*Journal of the American Oriental Society*
JBL	*Journal of Biblical Literature*
JCS	*Journal of Cuneiform Studies*
JEOL	*Jaarbericht van het Vooraziatisch-Egyptisch Gezelschap (Genootschap) Ex oriente lux*
JJS	*Journal of Jewish Studies*
JNES	*Journal of Near Eastern Studies*
JNSLMS	*Journal of Northwest Semitic Languages Monograph Series*
JQR	*Jewish Quarterly Review*
JRS	*Journal of Roman Studies*
JSJSup	Supplements to the Journal for the Study of Judaism
JSOT	*Journal for the Study of the Old Testament*
JSOTSup	Journal for the Study of the Old Testament: Supplement Series
JSP	*Journal for the Study of the Pseudepigrapha*
JSS	*Journal of Semitic Studies*
J.W.	Josephus, *Jewish War*
KBo	Keilschrifttexte aus Boghazköi
KBo 11	Güterbock, Hans G. and H. Otten. *Texte aus Gebäude K*. WVDOG 72–73. Berlin: Mann, 1960–61.

KBo 17	Otten, Heinrich. *Insbes. Texte aus Gebäude A*. WVDOG 83. Berlin: Mann, 1969.
KBo 18	Güterbock, Hans G. *Hethitische Briefe, Inventare und verwandte Texte*. WVDOG 85. Berlin: Mann, 1971.
KBo 24	Otten, Heinrich and Christel Rüster. *Insbes. Texte aus Gebäude A*. Berlin: Mann, 1978.
KJV	King James Version
KTU	Dietrich, Manfried, Oswald Loretz, and Joaquín Sanamartín, eds. *Die keilalphabetischen Texte aus Ugarit*. AOAT 24.1. Münster: Ugarit-Verlag, 2013. 3rd enl. ed. of *KTU: The Cuneiform Alphabetic Texts from Ugarit, Ras Ibn Hani, and Other Places*. Edited by M. Dietrich, O. Loretz, and J. Sanmartín. Münster: Ugarit-Verlag, 1995 (= *CAT*).
Lam. Rab.	Lamentations Rabbah
LCL	Loeb Classical Library
LHBOTS	The Library of the Hebrew Bible/Old Testament Series
LSJ	*A Greek-English Lexicon*, 9th ed. with a supplement. Edited by Henry George Liddell, Robert Scott, and Henry Stuart Jones. Oxford: Clarendon, 1968.
LSTS	Library of Second Temple Studies
LXX	Septuagint
MH	Magic in History
NABU	*Nouvelles assyriologiques brèves et Utilitaires*
NICOT	New International Commentary on the Old Testament
NINO	Nederlands instituut voor het nabije oosten
NT	*Novum Testamentum*
OBC	Orientalia Biblica et Christiana
OBO	Orbis biblicus et orientalis
Od.	Homer, *Odyssey*
OIS	Oriental Institute Seminars
OTL	Old Testament Library
PIHANS	Publications de l'Institut historique-archéologique néerlandais de Stamboul
RB	*Revue Biblique*
RDSR	Ritual Dynamics and the Science of Ritual
RelSoc	Religion and Society
RevQ	*Revue de Qumran*
RGRW	Religions in the Graeco-Roman World
RechBib	Recherches bibliques
RIME	The Royal Inscriptions of Mesopotamia, Early Periods
RlA	*Reallexikon der Assyriologie*. Edited by Erich Ebeling et al. Berlin: de Gruyter, 1928–.
SAA	State Archives of Assyria

SAA 2	Parpola, Simo and Kazuko Watanabe. *Neo-Assyrian Treaties and Loyalty Oaths*. Helsinki: Helsinki University Press, 1988.
SAA 16	Luukko, Mikko and Greta van Buylaere. *The Political Correspondence of Esarhaddon*. Helsinki: Helsinki University Press, 2002.
SAAS	State Archives of Assyria Studies
SANER	Studies in Ancient Near Eastern Records
SHCANE	Studies in the History and Culture of the Ancient Near East
SJOT	*Scandinavian Journal for the Old Testament*
SJS	Studia Judaeoslavica
SPAW	*Sitzungsberichte der preussischen Akademie der Wissenschaften*
ST	*Studia theologica*
StBibLit	Studies in Biblical Literature
STDJ	Studies on the Texts of the Desert of Judah
StBoT	Studien zu den Boğazköy-Texten
TAPS	*Transactions of the American Philological Association*
TCS	Texts from Cuneiform Sources THeth Texte der Hethiter
TSAJ	Texte und Studien zum antiken Judentum
TThSt	Trierer theologische Studien
TUAT.NF	*Texte aus der Umwelt des Alten Testaments*. Edited by Bernd Janowski and Gernot Wilhelm. Gütersloh: Gütersloher Verlagsanstalt, 2005–2016.
TWOT	*Theological Wordbook of the Old Testament*. Edited by R. Laird Harris, Gleason L. Archer Jr., and Bruce K. Waltke. 2 vols. Chicago: Moody Press, 1980.
UF	Ugarit-Forschungen
UTB	Universitätstaschenbuch
VT	*Vetus Testamentum*
VTSup	Supplements to Vetus Testamentum
WAW	Writings from the Ancient World
WBC	Word Biblical Commentary
WCAD	Workshop of the Chicago Assyrian Dictionary
WdO	*Die Welt des Orients*
WMANT	Wissenschaftliche Monographien zum Alten und Neuen Testament
ZA	*Zeitschrift für Assyriologie*
ZAW	*Zeitschrift für die alttestamentliche Wissenschaft*

Perchance to Dream

Esther J. Hamori

> That weren't no DJ, that was hazy cosmic jive.
> —David Bowie, "Starman"

Throughout the ancient Near East and eastern Mediterranean, as in so many other places and times, communication from beyond seemed at once ubiquitous and perplexing. Deities communicated with human beings in a variety of ways, from directing the movements of the stars and encoding divine messages on the livers of sacrificial animals to directly addressing selected individuals or sending lesser divine beings to speak for them. While expressions of this differed from one context to another, and the predominant modes of divination, methods of interpretation, and literary reflections were far from uniform, the underlying assumption that the gods spoke to people both directly and indirectly, and both explicitly and obliquely, is reflected in the literature of the regions represented in this volume (and beyond).

Among the many forms of divine-human communication seen in these corpora, dreaming occupied the peculiar sphere of being in some ways and at some times a quite direct mode of communication, akin to prophecy, and in other ways and at other times rather opaque, more like the symbolic "writing" of the gods on the liver. Accordingly, some dreams could be understood by the dreamers themselves—as in ARM 26 232, a letter to Zimri-Lim, king of Mari, from a woman named Zunana, who reports how the god Dagan had spoken to her directly in a dream. She is so confident of the clear meaning of Dagan's words to her (that Zimri-Lim should help Zunana locate her servant girl) that she tells the king that on Dagan's command, he should do so. Other dreams were apparently less clear, requiring interpretation either by technical specialists—sometimes with the help of dream books, used especially in Mesopotamia and Egypt to aid expert dream interpreters in their task[1]—or by those with special insight or privileged access to divine knowledge. This category encompasses widely ranging literary portrayals, from the touching poetic story of the devoted (and divine) Geštinanna interpreting her brother Dumuzi's dream, to the matter-of-fact exchange between two men overheard by Gideon which includes a dream interpretation he takes to be more encouraging than Yahweh's own words to him (Judg 7:9–15), to the talmudic tale of the somewhat sketchy Bar-Hedya interpreting the many dreams of the sages Rava and Abaye (see Weiss's contribution to this volume).[2]

Like messages received through other forms of divination, some dreams were apparently met with more acceptance than others. In ARM 26 238, Addu-duri reports to Zimri-Lim that Iddin-ili, priest of Itur-Mer, had a dream in which Belet-biri said (among other peculiar things) that the king should be careful; Addu-duri therefore advises the king to be careful. On the other hand, in ARM 26 229, a report of the dream of a woman named Ayala, the writer reports having already checked Ayala's dream through bird divination, and confirms that the dream really "was seen," meaning that it was understood to have been sent by a deity.[3] Moreover, the writer has enclosed Ayala's hair and hem for the recipient to check further; apparently substantial verification is needed here.

This shows that not every dream was thought to contain a divine message, even when it seemed so to the recipient. In a world understood to contain reflec-

---

[1] On the use of dream books in Mesopotamia, see A. Leo Oppenheim, *The Interpretation of Dreams in the Ancient Near East: With a Translation of an Assyrian Dream-Book*, TAPS 46.3 (Philadelphia: American Philosophical Society, 1956); and in Pharaonic Egypt, see Kasia Szpakowksa, "Dream Interpretation in the Ramesside Age," in *Ramesside Studies in Honour of K. A. Kitchen*, ed. Mark Collier and Steven Snape (Bolton: Rutherford Press, 2011), 509–17. For later Egyptian dream texts see Luigi Prada, "Oneirocritica Aegyptiaca: Artemidorus of Daldis, Egypt, and the Contemporary Oneirocritic Literature in Egyptian," in *Artemidor von Daldis und die antike Traumdeutung: Texte—Kontexte—Lektüren*, ed. Gregor Weber, Colloquia Augustana 33 (Berlin: de Gruyter, 2015), 263–310, and Luigi Prada, "Dream Books in Ancient Egypt: The Evolution of a Genre from the New Kingdom to the Roman Period; with the Edition of an Unpublished Demotic Dream Book" (DPhil diss., University of Oxford, 2014).

[2] Dumuzi's Dream, ETCSL 1.4.3 [http://etcsl.orinst.ox.ac.uk/cgi-bin/etcsl.cgi?text=t.1.4.3#]. In the Judg 7 story, Yahweh anticipates that even after telling Gideon directly that he will prevail against the Midianites, the hero might still be too afraid to go into battle, and so Yahweh instructs him to go listen to what the men are saying in the camp and be emboldened by it (vv. 9–11); and thus Gideon hears the dream interpretation and prepares for battle (vv. 13–15).

[3] Annette Zgoll, *Traum und Welterleben im antiken Mesopotamien: Traumtheorie und Traumpraxis im 3.–1. Jahrtausend v. Chr. als Horizont einer Kulturgeschichte des Träumens*, AOAT 333 (Münster: Ugarit-Verlag, 2006), 76–77, 234, 353–60.

tions of the divine sphere in the sensory realities of the human plane, sometimes in explicit form (as through prophecy) and sometimes encoded, comprehensible only to specialists (as through astrology or haruspicy), an event might be recognized as communicating a divine message—or not. The sign of the fleece in Judg 6:36–40 is surely unusual, with the relative wetness of a sheep generally being a cosmic non-issue. Like other potentially meaningful events, some dreams were accepted as ordinary occurrences, not containing divine communication. Others were recognized as "significant," warranting attention to the divine message within. These included both "symbolic" and "message" dreams—that is, dreams in which the divine meaning is opaque and requires interpretation, and those in which the meaning is overtly stated.

Aspects of dream interpretation can differ substantially across corpora and cultural contexts and should not be universalized or essentialized. It is therefore not the goal of this volume to draw conclusions about dream divination throughout the ancient Near East and eastern Mediterranean, let alone from the period of the Sumerian king Gudea to that of the Babylonian Talmud. However, certain themes and questions do arise repeatedly. I will point to a few such threads here, and observant readers may notice others.

Consider the Sumerian royal cylinder inscription of Gudea of Lagaš, which begins with praise for the ruler chosen to build Ningirsu's temple, and then goes on to relate Gudea's dreams in which Ningirsu instructs him to build the temple (see Metcalf). A bit like the modern American trope, "God told me he wants me to be President," the message of the dream promotes the authority of the dreamer, and it is not coincidentally the dreamer's own narrative. One might wonder, then, if this mode of revelation had the distinct advantage of its messages being impossible to corroborate—and, to be sure, there are plenty of texts from a range of genres in which people dream something that stands to benefit them. In the Hittite text known as the Apology of Hattušili III, Great King Hattušili III has dreams that demonstrate the goddess Šaušga's support for him (see Mouton). In Gen 37, Joseph's dream of the sheaves indicates his primacy over his brothers (see Ede), and in 1 Sam 3, young Samuel receives communication indicating God's choice of his future leadership, displacing the house of Eli (see Russell). In the Ugaritic Baal Epic, the god El's significant dream serves to bolster his authority among the gods (see Kim).

But in fact, the situation is more complicated than this. As noted above, it was recognized that not all dreams were sent by the gods, and so dreams which appeared to contain divine messages were sometimes "verified" by oracular means—and this was so even in the case of kings reporting their own dreams. This is seen, for instance, in the Hittite report of oracular inquiry after the king dreams that the deity has ordered him not to go to Ankuwa, and the question is posed for ritual verification, "Did the deity forbid the king to go to Ankuwa?" (KBo 24.128 rev. 1–4 [CTH 570]; see Mouton). At other times, the dreams of kings required interpretation by a specialist or someone with privileged knowledge, as when Pharaoh (Gen 41:8; see Ede) and Nebuchadnezzar (Dan 2 and 4; see Stökl) turn to their magicians and wise men to interpret their respective dreams. The rhetorical function in the Israelite texts is to highlight Joseph and Daniel's divine access when the king's usual interpreters fail, but the point at the moment is that even kings relied on dream interpreters. As Metcalf observes, the two dreams of Gudea of Lagaš each necessitated one of these: after his first dream, Gudea turns to Nanše for interpretation, and his second dream requires verification through a liver omen. Metcalf notes that this dual example demonstrates both "the importance and the difficulties of dream interpretation in Mesopotamia" (p. 12 in this volume). When a king has dreams that will benefit him, but they must be interpreted by one type of specialist or verified by another, where does the power lie?

This is not only an issue when the dreamer is royal, though such cases particularly raise the question. The power dynamic between dreamer and interpreter varies enormously. In some instances the reliance on an interpreter actually functions as further support for the dreamer's own power, as in the case of Gudea, where interpretation by a deity, the goddess Nanše, does not only elucidate the meaning of the dream—it also inherently demonstrates divine approval. In other cases, the dependence on a dream interpreter serves to undercut the authority of the dreamer, as in tractate Berakhot of the Babylonian Talmud, where the dreams of the well-known Torah scholars Rava and Abaye are subject to the interpretation—and whims—of the unknown interpreter, Bar-Hedya (see Weiss). These examples fall near the two ends of the spectrum; in between is a significant gray area. The power relationship between dreamer and interpreter is an intriguing dynamic in general, and especially so when the dreamer has political or religious authority that might be tempered by the instrumental role of the interpreter. Many of the essays in this volume address issues related to the locus (or loci) of authority in dream divination in a given corpus or text, such as the Qumran Aramaic texts that reflect a particular interest in revelation through dreams (see Perrin), and the major dream narrative of Homer's *Odyssey* (*Od.* 19.535–69), which includes Penelope's dream, Odysseus's interpretation, and Penelope's thoughtful response (see Metcalf). In one way or another, this tension is present in many of the texts under discussion in this volume, from the earliest, in the Gudea cylinder, to the latest, in tractate Berakhot.

Concern in some texts about the source of a dream is matched elsewhere by concern about the source of interpretation. In some cases, the ancient writers appear attentive to the relationship between human effort or technical skill and divine revelation. It is repeatedly emphasized in the Joseph story that Joseph's interpretations come from God, not from himself (see Ede). In Daniel, each interpretation of a dream is explicitly attributed to divine intervention, a development Stökl refers to as the "prophetization" of dream divination. The concern with the source of divinatory interpretation finds its own expression in some biblical material (differently through various Joseph and Daniel texts), but it is not unique to the Bible. Portrayals in some biblical texts of technical divination as distinct from divine inspiration misrepresent broader ancient Near Eastern views. Technical diviners required specialized knowledge and texts, but these things too were understood to be divinely inspired.[4] Throughout the broader region, the salient question was not whether a certain type of divination was inspired, but whether a certain occurrence represented a message sent by the gods. All forms of divination required divine inspiration—even if this inspiration took different forms, and those engaged in "technical" and "intuitive" methods of divination performed their roles differently (and often occupied different social locations).[5]

The explicit attribution of not only the dream, but also the interpretation, to a divine source plainly bolsters the authority of both dream and interpretation. It can also serve to solidify the authority of the dreamer. As mentioned earlier, this is one of the effects of Nanše's interpretation of Gudea's dream. The role of the *angelus interpres* in some Qumran dream texts has a related function (see Perrin). There is a particularly striking example of this rhetorical maneuver in the Baal Cycle, where, as Kim elucidates, El is in control of every aspect of his own dream divination.

Of course, these essays (like all work on dream divination) are not actually evaluating dreams. What is available to us in each case is a text several steps removed from the dream itself. As Mouton frames it, what we have is a distortion: first was a dream, then the oral account of the dream, and then a written dream account, which itself is shaped by the scribal conventions and agendas of the genre in which the dream account is transmitted. Literary conventions and matters of genre are therefore relevant in all analyses. For example, the use of dreams to promote the dreamer's authority varies with genre. In texts like the Gudea cylinders or the Apology of Hattušili III, the royal statement of divinely supported royal authority is effective in real time—that is, while the king is in

---

[4] See, e.g., Francesca Rochberg, "Continuity and Change in Omen Literature," in *Munuscula Mesopotamica: Festschrift für Johannes Renger*, ed. Barbara Böck, Eva Christiane Cancik-Kirschbaum, and Thomas Richter, AOAT 267 (Münster: Ugarit-Verlag, 1999), 415–27.

[5] On the relationship between "technical" and "intuitive" divination, especially considering the issue of social location, see Martti Nissinen, "Prophecy and Omen Divination: Two Sides of the Same Coin," in *Divination and Interpretation of Signs in the Ancient World*, ed. Amar Annus, OIS 6 (Chicago: University of Chicago Press, 2010), 341–51. See also Jonathan Stökl, *Prophecy in the Ancient Near East: A Philological and Sociological Comparison*, CHANE 56 (Leiden: Brill, 2012), 7–11, and his contribution to this volume; and Esther J. Hamori, *Women's Divination in Biblical Literature: Prophecy, Necromancy, and Other Arts of Knowledge*, AYBRL (New Haven: Yale University Press, 2015), 26–30; also 4–8.

power. In a retrospective story like 1 Sam 3, the tale confirms the dreamer's authority, but within the narrative Samuel needs Eli's help to understand what he is hearing. In the establishing tale of Joseph, in addition to being a retrojected fiction about a time already ancient from the author's perspective, Joseph's dream is verified only through later events and so does not have the function of creating or ensuring his authority before he has it. Several of the essays in this volume explicitly address questions relating to use of the expected form and content of a dream divination text (see Russell, Perrin, and Weiss). How is each text shaped by the forms and needs of its genre, and what do we learn about dream divination from these differing presentations? How do various writers utilize expected forms or adapt familiar tropes and literary conventions in order to suit their own purposes, to achieve their particular religious and political goals?

The majority of papers collected in this volume were first presented in a two-year series on dream divination in the Prophetic Texts and Their Ancient Contexts section of the Society for Biblical Literature at the annual meetings in Baltimore (2013) and San Diego (2014). When we started the process of inviting colleagues to present in this series and to contribute essays we were struck by the relative absence of scholarship on theoretical questions such as those mentioned above. There is ample material for those interested in the interpretation of certain visions or dreams, but less scholarship that addresses how dream divination functioned in various corpora. Each chapter in this volume addresses questions about dream divination itself—such as issues of agency, authority, verification, incubation, or literary and political function—with respect to a specific text or corpus. Together they present a snapshot of current ideas about dream divination in a range of ancient Near Eastern (including biblical), eastern Mediterranean, and early Jewish texts.

Some noteworthy corpora are not represented in this volume, such as texts from Egypt and Mari. This is not due to design, but to the availability of scholars working on dream divination in these sources during the period of production of the volume. The current work does not represent an attempt to be exhaustive. The essays that follow should provide interested scholars and students a window onto an array of issues in dream divination across these ancient texts.

Christopher Metcalf ("Horn and Ivory: Dreams as Portents in Ancient Mesopotamia and Beyond") focuses on Mesopotamian texts that reflect the need to verify the significance of dreams by means of other divinatory techniques, illustrating this primarily through an analysis of the detailed dream episode in the Sumerian Gudea cylinder inscriptions. He compares examples of dream interpretation elsewhere, particularly in Homer's *Odyssey*.

Alice Mouton ("Portent Dreams in Hittite Anatolia") provides an overview and analysis of the Hittite sources dealing with portent dreams, considering a range of genres, including historical records, oracular reports, accounts of vows, and prayers. As she notes, each genre has its own agenda; we can observe through them somewhat different aspects of portent dreams and the reactions they provoked.

Koowon Kim ("When Even the Gods Do Not Know: El's Dream Divination in KTU 1.6 iii") offers a detailed analysis of one text, the presentation of El's dream divination in the sixth tablet of the Baal Cycle. Kim focuses on the literary function of this episode, considering how and why the Ugaritic author uses the device of El's incubation and interpretation of his own dream.

Scott Noegel ("Maleness, Memory, and the Matter of Dream Divination in the Hebrew Bible") explores a connection between dreaming in the Hebrew Bible and conceptions of maleness. He argues that several issues—relating to virility, memory, and more—can be brought together to inform our understanding of Israelite dream divination. This connection would then help to explain why only men dream and interpret dreams in the Hebrew Bible.

Franziska Ede ("Dreams in the Joseph Narrative") offers an analysis of dreams and their functions in Gen 37–45. She observes differences between Gen 37 and Gen 40–41 in the presentations of Joseph and his dream divination, with particular attention to the authors' concerns with the source of Joseph's dream interpretation. Ede points to an increasing emphasis on the importance of divine guidance in the formation of the narrative.

Stephen Russell ("Samuel's Theophany and the Politics of Religious Dreams") compares 1 Sam 3 to the literary depiction of dream theophanies elsewhere in the ancient Near East, considering especially the Sumerian legend about Sargon and Urzababa. He shows how the Samuel text has played with the literary conventions governing the depiction of dream theophanies in order to emphasize Eli's authorization of the house that will displace his. These tropes in 1 Sam 3 thus have primarily a political function, supporting the transfer of power from one house to another.

Jonathan Stökl ("Daniel and the 'Prophetization' of Dream Divination") argues that the early chapters of the book of Daniel present dream interpretation—in a Mesopotamian context a form of "technical" divination—as a form of "intuitive" divination. The latter chapters, however, shy away from this and add the figure of the *angelus interpres*. Both of these strategies would later become part of the genre we know as "apocalypse," and in Daniel we can see them before the genre reached a more fully formed state.

Andrew Perrin ("Agency, Authority, and Scribal Innovation in Dream Narratives of the Aramaic Dead Sea Scrolls") examines the Aramaic writings from Qumran which include instances of dream episodes and interpretation. He focuses on the presentations of dreamers and interpreters, considering the questions of where the writers located agency and authority in dream revelation.

Haim Weiss ("'All the Dreams Follow the Mouth': Dreamers and Interpreters in Rabbinic Literature") analyzes the story of Bar-Hedya in tractate Berakhot in the Babylonian Talmud, in which the unknown interpreter temporarily exerts clear authority over the great sages Abaye and Rava through providing interpretations with the power of performative speech, that is, creating the results in the sages' lives through his spoken interpretation. Weiss considers the narrator's purpose in presenting such a potentially problematic conflict of authority.

As we near the end of a long project—from conversations about dream divination with potential contributors, through two years of conference sessions focused on substantial discussion of themes and questions across corpora, to development of the volume—Jonathan Stökl and I would like to thank this international group of scholars for their continual investment in thinking together about dream divination in our respective corpora.

Bibliography

Hamori, Esther J. *Women's Divination in Biblical Literature: Prophecy, Necromancy, and Other Arts of Knowledge*. AYBRL. New Haven: Yale University Press, 2015.
Nissinen, Martti. "Prophecy and Omen Divination: Two Sides of the Same Coin." Pages 341–51 in *Divination and Interpretation of Signs in the Ancient World*. Edited by Amar Annus. OIS 6. Chicago: University of Chicago Press, 2010.
Oppenheim, A. Leo. *The Interpretation of Dreams in the Ancient Near East: With a Translation of an Assyrian Dream-Book*. TAPS 46.3. Philadelphia: American Philosophical Society, 1956.
Prada, Luigi. "Dream Books in Ancient Egypt: The Evolution of a Genre from the New Kingdom to the Roman Period; with the Edition of an Unpublished Demotic Dream Book." DPhil diss., University of Oxford, 2014.
Prada, Luigi. "Oneirocritica Aegyptiaca: Artemidorus of Daldis, Egypt, and the Contemporary Oneirocritic Literature in Egyptian." Pages 263–310 in *Artemidor von Daldis und die antike Traumdeutung: Texte—Kontexte—Lektüren*. Edited by Gregor Weber. Colloquia Augustana 33. Berlin: de Gruyter, 2015.
Rochberg, Francesca. "Continuity and Change in Omen Literature." Pages 415–27 in *Munuscula Mesopotamica: Festschrift für Johannes Renger*. Edited by Barbara Böck, Eva Christiane Cancik-Kirschbaum, and Thomas Richter. AOAT 267. Münster: Ugarit-Verlag, 1999.
Stökl, Jonathan. *Prophecy in the Ancient Near East: A Philological and Sociological Comparison*. CHANE 56. Leiden: Brill, 2012.
Szpakowksa, Kasia. "Dream Interpretation in the Ramesside Age." Pages 509–17 in *Ramesside Studies in Honour of K. A. Kitchen*. Edited by Mark Collier and Steven Snape. Bolton: Rutherford Press, 2011.
Zgoll, Annette. *Traum und Welterleben im antiken Mesopotamien: Traumtheorie und Traumpraxis im 3.–1. Jahrtausend v. Chr. als Horizont einer Kulturgeschichte des Träumens*, AOAT 333. Münster: Ugarit-Verlag, 2006.

1
Horn and Ivory:
Dreams as Portents in Ancient Mesopotamia and Beyond

Christopher Metcalf

Dreaming is an experience that everyone alive today has in common with the people of antiquity, and modern readers of ancient literature have no difficulty in recognizing the vivid and sometimes unsettling qualities of dreams that are described, for instance, in the Akkadian Epic of Gilgamesh.[1] Dreams often feature in ancient Mesopotamian literary compositions as well as in historical narratives, letters, rituals and technical divinatory texts.[2] The present contribution is

---

[1] See, for example, the dream narratives in Standard Babylonian version i 242–98 and vii 162–254. I am grateful to the editors for their invitation to contribute to this volume, and to Dr. Adrian Kelly for his comments on an earlier draft. The present essay is based on a paper read in January 2015 at a seminar on dreams in ancient Greek literature that was convened by Prof. Christopher Pelling at the Faculty of Classics, University of Oxford. All translations are my own.

[2] The fundamental study of dreams and their interpretation in ancient Mesopotamia is Annette Zgoll, *Traum und Welterleben im antiken Mesopotamien: Traumtheorie und Traumpraxis im 3.–1. Jahrtausend v. Chr. als Horizont einer Kulturgeschichte des Träumens*, AOAT 333 (Münster: Ugarit-Verlag, 2006). See also Annette Zgoll, "Nächtliche Wege der Erkenntnis: Möglichkeiten und Gefahren des Außentraumes," in *Wissenskultur im Alten Orient: Weltanschauung, Wissenschaften, Techniken, Technologien*, ed. Hans Neumann, CDOG 4 (Wiesbaden: Harrassowitz, 2012), 169–82; Annette Zgoll, "Dreams as Gods and Gods as Dreams: Dream-Realities in Ancient Mesopotamia from the Third to the First Millennium B.C.," in *He Has Opened Nisaba's House of Learning: Studies in Honor of Åke Waldemar Sjöberg on the Occasion of His Eighty-Ninth Birthday*, ed. Leonhard Sassmannshausen, CM 46 (Leiden: Brill, 2014), 299–313. Recent overviews include Alice Mouton, "Interprétation des rêves et traités oniromantiques au Proche-Orient ancien," in *Artémidore de Daldis et l'interprétation des rêves*, ed. Christophe Chandezon and Julien du Bouchet (Paris: Les Belles Lettres, 2014), 373–92; and Ulla

concerned with dreams that were thought to be portents, that is, ominous signs that could guide the dreamer in interpreting past or future events. The aim will not be to formulate a retrospective psychological analysis of dreams reported in ancient sources,[3] but rather to examine some aspects of dream interpretation that were seen to be particularly notable in ancient Mesopotamia. As the following discussion will illustrate, Mesopotamian royal inscriptions show that rulers considered it legitimate to base important decisions on dreams that they believed to have been sent by the gods. While this may seem naive from a modern point of view, which sees our dreams as products of our own minds rather than as reliable divine messages, the ancient attitude to dream interpretation was more sophisticated than it has sometimes been presented. Recent scholarship has shown that ancient Mesopotamian sources distinguished between dreams that were to be taken seriously as genuine portents and dreams that were to be dismissed as vain and irrelevant. The interpretation of dreams formed part of the larger system of ancient divination, and techniques were developed in order to test the significance of a given dream. The present contribution will revisit a selection of sources that inform us about such techniques, taking one of the earliest and most detailed Mesopotamian dream narratives, in the Sumerian cylinder inscriptions of Gudea of Lagaš (ca. 2100 BCE), as a starting point. This well-known example will provide an opportunity to review the conclusions of recent scholarship on Mesopotamian dreams, in particular on the concept of message dreams. The Hittite sources from the mid to late second millennium BCE offer much additional evidence on the interpretation of dreams, and thus help to place the Mesopotamian evidence in a broader ancient Near Eastern context. Recent research has shown that some of the best-known passages on the significance of portentous dreams in Hittite religion are in fact translations of Mesopotamian texts, and this fact offers a fresh perspective on the similarities between Hittite and Mesopotamian dream interpretation that past scholarship has identified. Finally, the present contribution will consider the episode of Penelope's dream in the nineteenth book of Homer's *Odyssey*, which engages explicitly with some of the same problems of dream interpretation that are encountered in the Mesopotamian and Hittite evidence.

Susanne Koch, *Mesopotamian Divination Texts: Conversing with the Gods: Sources from the First Millennium BCE*, GMTR 7 (Münster: Ugarit-Verlag, 2015), 296–311, where the work of Zgoll, *Traum und Welterleben*, is however not taken into account.

[3] As attempted by Thomas R. Kämmerer, "Archetypen in sumerischen, babylonischen und assyrischen Traumschilderungen," in *Ex Mesopotamia et Syria lux: Festschrift für Manfried Dietrich*, ed. Oswald Loretz, Kai A. Metzler, and Hanspeter Schaudig, AOAT 281 (Münster: Ugarit-Verlag, 2002), 191–207. See further discussion below.

One of the earliest, most detailed and best-known narratives on portentous dreams in Mesopotamia occurs in the Sumerian cylinder inscriptions of Gudea, a ruler of the state of Lagaš (ca. 2100 BCE).[4] The narrative of the cylinder inscriptions begins with a mythological prologue in which Ningirsu, the city god of the capital Girsu, decrees that his Eninnu temple shall be built by the state's pious ruler. In order to communicate his wishes, Ningirsu speaks to the ruler Gudea in a dream, the contents of which are summarized very briefly (cyl. A i 17–23):

> Gudea then saw his king, the lord Ningirsu in a nighttime vision, and (Ningirsu) spoke to him about the building of his temple. He let the Eninnu, whose divine powers are very great, stand before his eyes. Gudea, whose mind was far-reaching, concerned himself with this utterance.

Yet Gudea fails to grasp its intended meaning (šag, literally "insides," i 28) and therefore proposes to consult a dream interpreter, the goddess Nanše. He reports his dream to Nanše, beginning as follows (iv 14–21):

> There was someone in the dream, surpassingly great like the sky, surpassingly great like the earth. That man, regarding his head he was a god, regarding his arms he was the Anzu-bird, regarding his lower body he was a flood-storm. A lion lay at his right and left sides. He told me to build his house, but I do not understand his intended meaning (šag).

Nanše explains that the god seen by Gudea was Ningirsu and that he was speaking to Gudea about the building of his shrine Eninnu (v 17–18). She interprets further elements of the dream and advises Gudea to present certain gifts to Ningirsu, in return for which Ningirsu would reveal the plan of the temple (v 19–vii 8). Gudea proceeds accordingly, and asks Ningirsu for a favorable ominous sign to confirm his intentions: "My lord, what do I know about you?" (viii 15–ix 4). In a second dream, Ningirsu identifies himself and explains in detail his desire for a temple (ix 7–xii 11). Upon waking, Gudea shudders. He checks the dream-message by means of a liver omen, and the outcome is posi-

---

[4] See especially Zgoll, *Traum und Welterleben*, 318–20 ("Gudea von Lagaš als Paradigma"), and the discussions of Claudia E. Suter, *Gudea's Temple Building: The Representation of an Early Mesopotamian Ruler in Text and Image*, CM 17 (Groningen: Styx Publications, 2000), 84–88, and Richard E. Averbeck, "Temple Building Among the Sumerians and Akkadians (Third Millennium)," in *From the Foundations to the Crenellations: Essays on Temple Building in the Ancient Near East and Hebrew Bible*, ed. Mark J. Boda and Jamie Novotny, AOAT 366 (Münster: Ugarit-Verlag, 2010), 3–34, which include general information on Gudea and on Mesopotamian temple building texts. Text and translation: Dietz Otto Edzard, *Gudea and His Dynasty*, RIME 3.1 (Toronto: University of Toronto Press, 1997), 68–106; new translation: Wolfgang Heimpel, "Die Bauhymne des Gudea von Lagasch," in *Erzählungen aus dem Land Sumer*, ed. Konrad Volk (Wiesbaden: Harrassowitz, 2015), 119–65.

tive: "the intention (šag) of Ningirsu has emerged for him as clearly as daylight" (xii 16–19), and Gudea begins to prepare the construction of the temple.

The two dreams of Gudea illustrate both the importance and the difficulties of dream interpretation in Mesopotamia. Dreams were the means by which the god Ningirsu communicated his wishes for a temple to the ruler, but the figure that Gudea saw at the outset did not amount to the clear description of the city god Ningirsu that might have been expected at this point.[5] Gudea's first dream was not sufficiently intelligible for him to understand on his own: he claimed that he saw a man "surpassingly great like the sky, surpassingly great like the earth," among other apparitions, but could not grasp their intended meaning. An innovative recent analysis has interpreted the reference to a great man as a symbol that has archetypal significance, in the terms of modern psychological research, which could indicate Gudea's need for spiritual guidance.[6] But in the culturally specific terms of Mesopotamian religion, the obvious implication of the description "surpassingly great like the sky, surpassingly great like the earth" is that it identifies its subject as a god: Sumerian and Akkadian religious poems often compare the dimensions of the immortals to the greatness of sky and earth, while a well-attested proverb on the inevitable mortality of mankind states that, conversely, "the tallest man cannot stretch to the sky, the broadest man cannot cover the earth."[7] So the opening line of the first dream, as reported by Gudea, immediately announces the great importance of his vision, since the being that appeared to him must have been divine.[8] Gudea realizes that his god had spoken to him about the construction of a temple, and that this dream demanded careful attention, but it is only with the help of a dream interpreter, who in this case appears in a divine transfiguration as the goddess Nanše, that he is able to confirm the precise intention of the divine message.[9]

---

[5] As noted by Adam Falkenstein, *Die Inschriften Gudeas von Lagaš I: Einleitung*, AnOr 30 (Rome: Pontifical Biblical Institute, 1966), 94–95.

[6] Kämmerer, "Archetypen," 201–4.

[7] See the sources compiled by Christopher Metcalf, "Babylonian Perspectives on the Certainty of Death," *Kaskal* 10 (2013): 257–60.

[8] Alice Mouton, *Rêves hittites: Contribution à une histoire et une anthropologie du rêve en Anatolie ancienne*, CHANE 28 (Leiden: Brill, 2007), 14, writes that "lorsque le roi Gudéa voit en rêve un homme de grande taille, cela est on ne peut plus banal, et seule l'interprétation qui en est faite rend ce songe extraordinaire. Ce n'est qu'au moment de l'interprétation que ce grand homme est identifié à un dieu." In my view, however, no (implied) ancient audience familiar with the conventions of religious poetry could be expected to overlook the implications of the "great as the sky, great as the earth" image.

[9] Gudea's reported visit to the goddess presumably reflects his consultation of a professional dream interpreter in the temple of Nanše, which agrees with the attestation of such an official in roughly contemporaneous administrative records: see Hartmut Waetzoldt, "Die Göttin Nanše und die Traumdeutung," *NABU* 1998: §60 (63–65).

The second dream is more intelligible to Gudea: this time the god seems to identify himself by name ("I, Ningirsu…," ix 20), and gives detailed instructions. Here it is said that Gudea "shuddered" upon waking (xii 12–13). This illustrates, according to one view, the "suddenness of the transition between dream and waking" and describes "the surprise of the dreaming person."[10] But the more specific cause of the shudder is likely to be that Gudea has now realized that he has had a direct experience of the divine sphere,[11] whereas after the first dream this encounter remained rather nebulous to him. The second dream is more easily interpreted, but a new problem now presents itself: while the identity of the god appears to be certain, and his wishes explicit, how was Gudea to know whether this was the kind of dream-message that could be trusted? Gudea checked the message by means of a liver omen, which confirmed that the instructions delivered in the second dream should indeed be carried out, and he could at last begin his work.[12]

The two dreams of Gudea, in particular the latter, belong to a familiar type that has often been called a message dream (*Botschaftstraum*): a deity visits a ruler or a priest in his sleep and communicates its wishes to him. Such dreams are attested in Mesopotamian royal inscriptions from Eanatum of Lagaš in the mid-third millennium BCE to Assyrian and Babylonian rulers such as Assurbanipal and Nabonidus in the first millennium BCE.[13] It has been said that the Mesopotamian sources always present such message dreams as clear and authentic articulations of the divine will that do not require any interpretation on the part of the dreamer.[14] But the example of Gudea contradicts the notion of the

---

[10] A. Leo Oppenheim, *The Interpretation of Dreams in the Ancient Near East: With a Translation of an Assyrian Dream-Book*, TAPS 46.3 (Philadelphia: American Philosophical Society, 1956), 191.

[11] Thus Adam Falkenstein, "'Wahrsagung' in der sumerischen Überlieferung," in *La divination en mésopotamie ancienne*, CRRAI 14 (Paris: Presses universitaires de France, 1966), 58–59; similarly Zgoll, *Traum und Welterleben*, 112–15.

[12] A further confirmatory dream is later very briefly reported (cyl. A xx 7–12): see Zgoll, *Traum und Welterleben*, 115–16, 336–37.

[13] See Zgoll, *Traum und Welterleben*, 97–231, for a detailed overview and analysis of the Sumerian and Akkadian material.

[14] Thus recently Koch, *Mesopotamian Divination Texts*, 300, and Walter Sommerfeld, "Traumdeutung als Wissenschaft und Therapie im Alten Orient," in *Heilkunde und Hochkultur I: Geburt, Seuche und Traumdeutung in den antiken Zivilisationen des Mittelmeerraumes*, ed. Axel Karenberg and Christian Leitz (Münster: Lit Verlag, 2000), 202–4: "Die Authentizität der Botschaft geht einher mit einer eindeutigen, klaren Übermittlungsweise. … Der Kern des Traumberichts ist die Theophanie: Eine Gottheit erscheint und übermittelt dem Menschen eine Botschaft in klarer, verständlicher Form. Wenn der Traum auch bildliche und symbolische Elemente birgt, so schließt sich deren Bedeutung doch von selbst auf. Der Botschaftstraum bedarf keiner Deutung und keines Traumdeuters, die Botschaft leuchtet dem Träumer unmittelbar ein."

intrinsically intelligible and reliable message dream, which can be traced to the Greek dream manual *Oneirocritica* by Artemidorus of Daldis (second century CE), since Gudea not only required help in interpreting and confirming his first dream but also thought it necessary to test the trustworthiness of the second, seemingly more explicit dream in which the god Ningirsu identified himself to him.[15] The inscription of Gudea thus illustrates the difficulties and uncertainties of dream interpretation, since dreams may be both nebulous in content and potentially unreliable, even if they appear to convey a message from a deity. In a detailed study of Mesopotamian dream interpretation, Annette Zgoll has demonstrated that the most important categorical distinction pertaining to dreams in Mesopotamia was between dreams that were considered to be significant, in the sense that they had to be taken seriously as genuine portents, and dreams that were considered to be vain and irrelevant. This distinction can be shown to be implicit in the Sumerian and Akkadian terms that were used to describe dreams and dreaming: in the letters from Mari (ca. eighteenth century BCE), for instance, the Akkadian verb *naṭālum* ("to look") is used when someone has experienced a dream that is regarded as ominous, whereas the verb *amārum* ("to see") was used when the significance of a dream was not yet established.[16] Those message dreams reported in Mesopotamian narratives that were thought by past scholarship to be self-explanatory and evidently true should be seen as retrospectively condensed interpretations that convey the essential message of a portentous dream (not as reports that detail the contents of the actual dream).[17] Thus the first dream of Gudea, as he reports it, is a literal account of what he actually experienced: Gudea has already grasped the essential fact that his god has spoken to him about the building of a temple, but still requires the goddess Nanše to provide him with a fuller explanation that mirrors his description and confirms the details of what he has seen. The second dream, on the other hand,

---

[15] For a history of the concept of the message dream, see Zgoll, *Traum und Welterleben*, 88–93. The relevant passages in the *Oneirocritica* of Artemidorus, now edited and translated, with a full commentary, by Daniel E. Harris-McCoy, *Artemidorus' Oneirocritica: Text, Translation, and Commentary* (Oxford: Oxford University Press, 2012), are 2.69, 4.71–72 (where it is admitted that gods speaking in dreams may also pose riddles). See further Gil H. Renberg, "The Role of Dream-Interpreters in Greek and Roman Religion," in *Artemidor von Daldis und die antike Traumdeutung: Texte—Kontexte—Lektüren*, ed. Gregor Weber, Colloquia Augustana 2 (Berlin: de Gruyter, 2015), 233–62, here 251–56.

[16] Zgoll, *Traum und Welterleben*, 76–77, 234, 353–60.

[17] Zgoll, *Traum und Welterleben*, 247: "'Botschaftsträume' werden nicht gedeutet und müssen nicht gedeutet werden, ganz einfach deshalb, weil sie schon gedeutete Fassungen von Träumen darstellen. In schriftlich fixierter Form, dem auf uns gekommenen Material, liegen uns vornehmlich diese schon gedeuteten Träume vor." See also Annette Zgoll, "Traum, Traumgottheiten A.§2," *RlA* 14:115; Zgoll, "Dreams as Gods," 309–12.

is not narrated as a literal report but as a retrospective interpretation of what Gudea considers to be the essence of what Ningirsu has told him.[18]

Given the importance of distinguishing between significant and irrelevant dreams, it is not surprising that, as Zgoll has also shown, the check that Gudea applied to his second dream was by no means an isolated practice in Mesopotamia: verifications of dreams by means of extispicy, among other oracular techniques, are attested also in Mari and in Kassite and Neo-Assyrian divination records.[19] Since the divine will was able to manifest itself in more than one way, and a variety of divinatory techniques were available, it seemed reasonable to compare a combination of ominous signs in order to arrive at a more plausible conclusion: the practice of interpreting dreams in Mesopotamia therefore illustrates what has recently been called the collaborative "interdisciplinarity" of ancient diviners, in the sense that it was common practice to consult specialists in various types of divination in order to ensure that the information obtained was as reliable as possible.[20]

This "interdisciplinarity" offers a starting point for comparison with the information on dreams and their interpretation provided by the Hittite cuneiform sources from ancient Anatolia (mid to late second millennium BCE). The Hittites likewise saw dreams as a means by which gods communicated directly with mortals, and given the hazards of the medium, they similarly attempted to ensure that the divine instructions were correctly understood. The Hittite corpus has been presented and analyzed in detail by Alice Mouton,[21] who has also contributed to this volume. A particularly valuable feature of the Hittite evidence is that it conserves a large number of technical oracular reports that inform us about actual dreams and the manner of their interpretation at the Hittite royal court.[22] There are also some prominent examples of portentous dreams in Hittite

---

[18] Zgoll, *Traum und Welterleben*, 245.

[19] Zgoll, *Traum und Welterleben*, 353–62. See now also Jack M. Sasson, *From the Mari Archives: An Anthology of Old Babylonian Letters* (Winona Lake: Eisenbrauns, 2015), 285–88, and Dominique Charpin, *Gods, Kings, and Merchants in Old Babylonian Mesopotamia*, Publications de l'Institut du Proche-Orient Ancien du Collège de France 2 (Leuven: Peeters, 2015), 37–42, who shows that at Mari such verifications were also made to test prophetic messages, not only dreams. The Kassite example, adduced by Mouton, *Rêves hittites*, 20 n. 63, is CBS 13517 (cdli.ucla.edu/P268556), on which see F. R. Kraus, "Mittelbabylonische Opferschauprotokolle," *JCS* 37 (1985): 147–50, 160–62 (text no.18), and the presentation in the recent overview by Matthew T. Rutz, "The Text After the Sacrifice: Divination Reports from Kassite Babylonia," in *Texts and Contexts: The Circulation and Transmission of Cuneiform Texts in Social Space*, ed. Paul Delnero and Jacob Lauinger, SANER 9 (Boston: de Gruyter, 2015), 224–29.

[20] Stefan M. Maul, *Die Wahrsagekunst im Alten Orient: Zeichen des Himmels und der Erde* (Munich: Beck, 2013), 277–79 ("Interdisziplinarität der Wahrsager").

[21] Mouton, *Rêves hittites*.

[22] See Mouton, *Rêves hittites*, 18–23.

historical texts and religious poetry, but in the latter case it must now be acknowledged, following the recent identification of new literary corresponddences, that the Hittite passages are actually translated and adapted versions of imported Sumero-Akkadian models of the early second millennium BCE. In the following extract from the Hittite Prayer of Kantuzzili that is cited as "Text 1" by Mouton (in this volume), a human supplicant asks his personal god to inform him, by means of various methods of communication, including portentous dreams, about a sin that the supplicant may have committed in the past and for which (he thinks) the god has punished him:

> Now let my god reveal his innermost soul to me with all his heart, and let him tell me my offenses so that I may know them. Let my god either speak to me in a dream—let my god reveal his soul to me and let him tell me my offenses so that I may know them—or let a female dream interpreter speak to me, or let a diviner of the Sun-god speak to me (upon reading from a liver!) Let my god reveal his innermost soul to me with all his heart, and let him tell me my offenses so that I may know them! (*CTH* 373, 24'–28' = KUB 30.10 obv. 24'–28', Mouton "Text 1," in this volume).

While this passage and further related passages, such as Mouton's "Text 11" (in this volume), are frequently adduced to illustrate the role of dreams as divine messages among the Hittites, their phraseology and the religious concepts that underlie them—including the references to dream interpretation and extispicy—are demonstrably Mesopotamian.[23] This does not mean that the practice of interpreting portentous dreams was borrowed by the Hittites from Mesopotamia; rather, it was the preexisting, shared interest in the ominous significance of dreams that allowed the Sumero-Akkadian literary material to be translated and successfully adapted in a new Anatolian context.

It is beyond doubt, then, that passages in Sumero-Akkadian religious poetry in which portentous dreams were described as a means of divine communication seemed intelligible and relevant to a Hittite audience. This fact is of interest in the context of the present volume, since it lends a certain international (or intercultural) dimension to the concept of portentous dreams in the ancient Near East.[24] And it can indeed be observed that the Hittite sources, too, distinguished

---

[23] For details, see Christopher Metcalf, "Old Babylonian Religious Poetry in Anatolia: From Solar Hymn to Plague Prayer," *ZA* 105 (2015): 42–53.

[24] It also casts doubt on some common generalizations about the supposed differences between Hittite and Mesopotamian divination, as recently articulated, e.g., by Marc Van De Mieroop, *Philosophy before the Greeks: The Pursuit of Truth in Ancient Babylonia* (Princeton: Princeton University Press, 2016), 200–201, especially on the notion that the concern with investigating the past (rather than the future) was a Hittite peculiarity. Another possible illustration of Hittite interest in the Mesopotamian practice of dream interpretation is offered by KUB 43.11 (+) KUB 43.12, a fragment of a technical divina-

between dreams that were genuine portents and dreams that could be dismissed as irrelevant. As Mouton illustrates (in this volume), the oracular reports from the Hittite court show that dreams were tested by means of other divinatory techniques in order to establish their significance, and also to guide the interpretation of significant dreams. The following late Hittite oracle report, of which Mouton cites a very brief extract ("Text 3"), is particularly instructive. The passage begins with a statement that the Hittite queen has seen a dream, followed by two sentences in direct speech that were uttered by a diviner. The diviner first reports the queen's dream, in which she spoke to the Hittite king ("my Sun") about a divine message regarding an individual who is probably to be identified with the Hittite prince Kur(unta); then the diviner reports a second dream that was seen by the king himself and that was apparently considered to be related to the queen's dream:

> The queen saw a dream. "In the dream, she keeps telling my Sun: 'The Sungoddess of Arinna has somehow drawn out again this matter concerning Kur(unta).' But later my Sun saw (another) dream, and in the dream something like smoke was appearing in the city of Arinna." If this dream revealed anything, whatever it was, then let that be put aside. But if the deity has not at all drawn out the matter concerning this Kur(unta), then let the liver-omina first be favorable, but then unfavorable (*CTH* 577.1, ii 12–21 = KUB 5.24+KUB 16.31+ ii 12–21).

The phrase "If this dream revealed anything" probably refers to the king's dream, which the diviner proposed to investigate separately. The verification of the queen's dream was then undertaken by means of a liver omen, which turned out to be favorable and then unfavorable.[25] What is significant for the present discussion is the notion that a dream can have a message to "reveal" (*išiyaḫḫ-*): the conditional phrasing clearly implies that not every dream was considered to be portentous (see further Mouton, in this volume). The passage also illustrates the use of extispicy to verify the perceived dream-message, which in this case was shown to be invalid.

Such verifications in the Hittite sources have been compared to the Mesopotamian practice.[26] As mentioned above, the passage in the Hittite Prayer of Kantuzzili that speaks of dreams as a potential means of divine communication was based on a Mesopotamian (ultimately Sumerian) model that, despite its for-

---

tory manual on dreams that probably represents a translation of an Akkadian model: see Mouton, *Rêves hittites*, 18, 170–71.

[25] In the interpretation of this complex episode, I follow Mouton, *Rêves hittites*, 22–23 and 198–201. See also Volkert Haas, *Hethitische Orakel, Vorzeichen und Abwehrstrategien. Ein Beitrag zur hethitischen Kulturgeschichte* (Berlin: de Gruyter, 2008), 165, on the historical context.

[26] Zgoll, *Traum und Welterleben*, 367, and Mouton, *Rêves hittites*, 20 n.63.

eign origin, seemed intelligible and relevant to a Hittite audience. The shared interest in portentous dreams and the shared practice of divinatory cross-checking as a tool for the interpretation of dreams suggest that there was indeed a common basis that allowed Sumero-Akkadian literary descriptions of dream interpretation to be translated into Hittite and then adapted in subsequent Hittite compositions. It is possible that the variety of techniques enumerated in the Prayer of Kantuzzili (dream seen by supplicant; dream seen by dream interpreter; extispicy by the diviner) were seen as an implicit reference to cross-checking. In later versions of this passage that occur in the prayers of King Mursili II (e.g., Mouton's "Text 11" in this volume), the catalogue of techniques was adapted and expanded in a way that certainly reflected Hittite-Anatolian divinatory practices, including perhaps the principle of collaborative cross-checks.[27]

To summarize the discussion so far: recent scholarship on Mesopotamian dream interpretation has emphasized that a distinction was made between portentous and irrelevant dreams. One illustration of this distinction is the testing of dreams by means of other divinatory techniques, in particular extispicy. Such tests were also carried out by diviners at the Hittite court, whose records similarly speak of dreams that have something significant to reveal, in contrast to others that do not. These commonalities make it easier to understand why Sumero-Akkadian religious compositions that describe portentous dreams as a means of divine communication could be translated and adapted in Hittite prayers.

Perhaps the best-known statement on the difficulties of dream interpretation occurs in a literary source that allows us to place the Mesopotamian evidence into a still broader context: the episode of the dream of Penelope, the wife of Odysseus, at the end of the nineteenth book of Homer's *Odyssey*. The comparison has already been made in passing,[28] and it has even been suggested that Homer's tale was inspired by ancient Near Eastern divinatory practices. A brief review and analysis may therefore prove to be instructive.

Portentous dreams occur frequently in the Homeric epics, most notably perhaps at the opening of the second book of the *Iliad*, where the chief god Zeus sends the Greek leader Agamemnon a deceitful dream that falsely promises the capture of Troy (*Il.* 2.1–40). That episode is foreshadowed at the beginning of the epic, when the hero Achilles suggests that the Greeks, who are suffering under a pestilence inflicted by the god Apollo, should consult a "seer, a priest, or even a dream interpreter" in order to learn the causes of the divine wrath, explaining that "dreams too are from Zeus" (*Il.* 1.62–64). It is plain, therefore, that dreams in the Homeric conception were seen to be a means of communication

---

[27] Metcalf, "Old Babylonian Religious Poetry," 51.
[28] Oppenheim, *Interpretation of Dreams*, 240; Zgoll, *Traum und Welterleben*, 367–68; Christopher Metcalf, *The Gods Rich in Praise: Early Greek and Mesopotamian Religious Poetry* (Oxford: Oxford University Press, 2015), 215–16.

between gods and men, and that in this respect a dream interpreter had a function comparable to that of a diviner (who interpreted ominous signs, such as bird-flight) or a priest (who could speak on behalf of a deity).[29]

The dream of Penelope is the major dream narrative in the *Odyssey* (19.535–69). It occurs shortly before the dramatic climax of the poem, the killing of the suitors by Odysseus and his recognition by Penelope. At this point, Odysseus is still a disguised visitor in his own home whose identity has not yet been realized by his wife. In an earlier conversation, Odysseus announced to Penelope, without revealing himself, the impending return of her husband. Now, as it is soon time to go to sleep, Penelope describes to Odysseus the dilemma that she has been pondering in her waking nights: should she remain in her home and respect her marriage, or should she yield to one of the suitors? Abruptly, Penelope asks Odysseus to interpret a dream that she has had: twenty geese that she enjoyed watching as they ate grain in her home were killed by an eagle. She was distressed, but the eagle returned and informed her in a human voice that what she was seeing was not a dream but a happy reality that was to be fulfilled, since the geese represented the suitors and the eagle himself was her husband who, having arrived, would kill all of them. As she awoke, Penelope explains, she saw the geese feeding on the grain as usual. The disguised Odysseus replies to Penelope's dream narrative that there is only one possible interpretation, since Odysseus himself has spoken in the dream and revealed the outcome: none of the suitors will escape death. Penelope's answer does not confront this interpretation directly. Rather, she states that dreams are in general difficult and their messages obscure: not everything comes to pass. Dreams, says Penelope, are fleeting: some come through the gate of horn and are fulfilled, while others come through the gate of ivory and are treacherous and harmful (if acted upon), since they will not be fulfilled. Penelope assumes, in concluding, that her dream has not come through the gate of fulfillment, welcome though that would be.

This episode is part of a series of ominous apparitions that occur throughout the poem. On the one hand, the dream belongs to a sequence of dreams that relate to the return of Odysseus and are seen by Penelope: an earlier dream sent by Athena reassured her on the fate of her son Telemachus but refused to specify

---

[29] The phrasing and context of Achilles's proposal have often been compared to the extract of the Hittite Prayer of Kantuzzili that was quoted and discussed above: see Metcalf, *Gods Rich in Praise*, 191–220, where a tentative but far from conclusive case for historical influence is proposed. Recent overviews of dreams in Homer are James Redfield, "Dreams from Homer to Plato," *Archiv für Religionsgeschichte* 15 (2013): 5–10, and Christine Walde, *Die Traumdarstellungen in der griechisch-römischen Dichtung* (Munich: Saur, 2001), 19–72. For some general comparative observations, see Martin L. West, *The East Face of Helicon: West Asiatic Elements in Greek Poetry and Myth* (Oxford: Oxford University Press, 1997), 185–90, and Beat Näf, *Traum und Traumdeutung im Altertum* (Darmstadt: Wissenschaftliche Buchgesellschaft, 2004), 19–40.

whether Odysseus was alive or dead (*Od.* 4.795–837); in the night after her dialogue with Odysseus, Penelope experiences another, even more poignant dream, in which her husband seemed to lie next to her in bed (*Od.* 20.87–90). On the other hand, the eagle itself is an obvious symbol that announces her husband: the content of the dream particularly resembles an earlier omen in which two eagles sent by Zeus are interpreted by a local expert in Ithaca to signify the return of Odysseus and death to the suitors (*Od.* 2.146–176), and another omen in which an eagle takes a goose, which is seen by Helen to portend the return and vengeance of Odysseus (*Od.* 15.160–178). Penelope's portentous dream thus contributes to the mounting sense of expectation that the narrative has created from the outset.[30] A modern reader may wonder how Penelope can plausibly reject the message that the dream has so obviously delivered (and which Odysseus is in a unique position to confirm), but her skepticism is in fact consistent with her general reluctance to believe that her husband will eventually return, until the famous test of the marital bed at last persuades her (*Od.* 23.173–206).[31] In narrative terms, the dream-episode therefore foreshadows the climax of the poem but at the same time delays it.

While contributing to the effect of dramatic retardation and to the poet's general characterization of Penelope, the episode also formulates an important statement on the uncertainty of relying on dreams as portents. Compared to a hypothetical situation in which Penelope simply observed a bird omen and asked Odysseus to explain it, the fact that the omen occurred in a dream seems to add an additional element of complexity.[32] The meaning of Penelope's dream cannot be in doubt, since it contains its own interpretation that unequivocally announces the return of Odysseus; so, to dismiss it, Penelope must resort to a generalizing statement that fundamentally questions the significance of dreams. Her image of the gates of horn and ivory, which is founded on Greek wordplay (κέρας

---

[30] While the dream brings no divine message, in contrast, for instance, to the dream of Agamemnon, its content has such obvious ominous significance that it can for present purposes nevertheless be treated as a portent; compare the comments of Walde, *Traumdarstellungen*, 66.

[31] Compare, earlier in the conversation between Penelope and Odysseus, his assurances that her husband will return, and her rejection of this idea, in spite of her hopes (19.308–16, cf. 257–60), and her denials when Eurykleia later tries to deliver the happy news (23.10–24, 58–68, 80–82): see Joseph Russo, "Books XVII–XX," in *A Commentary on Homer's Odyssey* (Oxford: Oxford University Press, 1992), 3:10–11 n. 10; Joseph Russo, "Penelope's Gates of Horn(s) and Ivory," in *La mythologie et l'Odyssée: Hommage à Gabriel Germain*, ed. André Hurst and Françoise Létoublon (Geneva: Droz, 2002), 227; Adrian Kelly, "The Audience Expects: Penelope and Odysseus," in *Orality, Literacy and Performance in the Ancient World*, ed. Elizabeth Minchin (Leiden: Brill, 2012), 3–24.

[32] On this point, see Georg Danek, *Epos und Zitat: Studien zu den Quellen der Odyssee* (Vienna: Österreichische Akademie der Wissenschaften, 1998), 388–89.

["horn"] and κραίνειν ["to fulfill"] versus ἐλέφας ["ivory"] and ἐλεφαίρεσθαι ["to harm"]), clearly articulates that trustworthy portents must be distinguished from dreams that will not come true.³³ Commenting on the passage, E. R. Dodds noted that this distinction is widely attested, also beyond ancient Greece,³⁴ although the tale of Penelope is perhaps its best-known expression. In contrast to the ancient Near Eastern instances that have been considered in this discussion, however, Penelope has no means or desire to verify the dream. Her dismissal of the dream is in keeping with the progression of the narrative and the poem's characterization of Penelope, as has just been outlined, but it is also consistent with the general practice of divination as described by Homer and other early Greek sources, in which the systematic cross-checking of ominous messages for the purpose of verification was not a regular feature.³⁵

It has nevertheless been suggested recently that the tale of Penelope reflects ancient Near Eastern attitudes to divination.³⁶ The argument is based in particular on the claim that Penelope's dream is part of a "narrative program of omen verification," as attested in literary and technical sources from the ancient Near East. In this perspective, the aforementioned earlier omina that resemble Penelope's dream and portend the return of Odysseus (the eagles in Ithaca, *Od.* 2.146–156; the eagle in Sparta, 15.160–165), and also the eagle that speaks in her dream itself, amount to a "verification of one omen with another."³⁷ This interpretation deliberately confuses the narrative technique of foreshadowing with a supposed description of divinatory practice, which seems unwarranted and implausible. While divination is frequently practiced in the Homeric poems,

---

³³ The notion of a gate of dreams occurs also in *Od.* 4.809. The wordplay may explain the choice of horn and ivory, but it is not necessarily the primary inspiration of the image, which may be based on the concept of the gate as an otherworldly threshold, in combination with the common Greek notion of two roads that lead to antithetical goals. See Russo, "Penelope's Gates," 224–27.

³⁴ E. R. Dodds, *The Greeks and the Irrational* (Berkeley: University of California Press, 1951), 106–7 with n.23: "If there was ever a period, before the advent of Freud, when men thought *all* dreams significant, it lies very far back." See also the comments of Oppenheim, *Interpretation of Dreams*, 207–8, and the recent study of Vered Lev Kenaan, "Artemidorus at the Dream Gates: Myth, Theory, and the Restoration of Liminality," *AJP* 137 (2016): 189–218. Roman attitudes are surveyed by William V. Harris, "Roman Opinions About the Truthfulness of Dreams," *JRS* 93 (2003): 18–34.

³⁵ For details, see Metcalf, *Gods Rich in Praise*, 215 with n. 68.

³⁶ Scott B. Noegel, "Dreaming and the Ideology of Mantics: Homer and Ancient Near Eastern Oneiromancy," in *Ideologies as Intercultural Phenomena: Melammu Symposia III*, ed. Antonio Panaino and Giovanni Pettinato (Milan: University of Bologna and IsIAO, 2002), 167–81; Scott B. Noegel, *Nocturnal Ciphers: The Allusive Language of Dreams in the Ancient Near East*, AOS 89 (New Haven: American Oriental Society, 2007), 191–222.

³⁷ Noegel, *Nocturnal Ciphers*, 201–2.

it plainly does not involve systematic cross-checks for the purpose of verification.[38]

Penelope's reaction to her portentous dream should not be compared to the practice of divination in ancient Near Eastern sources, but rather to the dismissive views expressed by other Homeric characters when confronted with an inconvenient omen.[39] For instance, the suitor Eurymachos states, in reaction to the observation of the eagles in Ithaca, that many birds fly about under the sun but not all are portentous (*Od.* 2.181–182); the Trojan hero Hector dismisses a bird omen, and bird omina in general, on the basis of an earlier direct message from Zeus (*Il.* 12.230–243); the Trojan king Priam similarly implies that he would be prepared to ignore the advice of diviners or priests, in contrast to a direct god-sent message (*Il.* 24.217–224); his words echo those of wise Nestor, who stated earlier that he would disregard Agamemnon's dream if it had been reported by any lesser Greek (*Il.* 2.80–82). Such criticism of portents may seem surprisingly radical, but subsequent events usually show that the skeptics are overconfident in their ability to assess the ominous signs[40]—just as Penelope's blunt dismissal of the dream's message (that her husband has returned and will kill the suitors) turns out to be contrary to the facts. In sum, Penelope's com-

---

[38] It is possible, but quite uncertain, that Achilles's proposal to consult "a seer, a priest, or even a dream interpreter" (*Il.* 1.62–63), cited by Noegel, *Nocturnal Ciphers*, 201–2 n. 46, recalls a conventional phrase in Hittite prayers (see above, n. 29), but in the absence of clear Homeric parallels it does not seem safe to assume that this refers to cross-checking by means of different divinatory techniques; see Metcalf, *Gods Rich in Praise*, 215. Nor is any divinatory cross-checking implied by *Il.* 5.149–51 (Metcalf, *Gods Rich in Praise*, 212) or Pindar, *Olympian Odes* 13.60–82 (dreamer consults interpreter), cited by Noegel, *Nocturnal Ciphers*, 201–2 n. 46. Noegel, *Nocturnal Ciphers*, 202 n.49, more plausibly adduces the sign sent by Zeus upon the request of Odysseus in *Od.* 20.102–4 as a counter-example, yet it should be noted that the preceding vision of Penelope that Odysseus has seen is not described as a dream but as a personal impression, and Odysseus does not consider it to be ominous (20.92–94). Another counter-example can perhaps be seen in *Il.* 24.308–21, where Priam requests, and obtains, a sign from Zeus to confirm his earlier verbal instruction, delivered by the messenger Iris (24.171–87), to supplicate Achilles in person; but the context is again not strictly mantic. Clear examples of cross-checking occur in later sources: see the discussion referred to in n.35 (above) and the fuller historical study by Pierre Bonnechere, "Oracles and Greek Mentalities: The Mantic Confirmation of Mantic Revelations," in *Myths, Martyrs, and Modernity: Studies in the History of Religions in Honour of Jan N. Bremmer*, ed. Jitse Dijkstra, Justin Kroesen, and Yme Kuiper (Leiden: Brill, 2010), 115–33.

[39] As noted by Oppenheim, *Interpretation of Dreams*, 240.

[40] For further examples and discussion, see recently Michael A. Flower, *The Seer in Ancient Greece* (Berkeley: University of California Press, 2008), 132–52; Kai Trampedach, "Authority Disputed," in *Practitioners of the Divine: Greek Priests and Religious Officials from Homer to Heliodorus*, ed. Beate Dignas and Kai Trampedach (Washington: Center for Hellenic Studies, 2008), 207–30.

ments may be seen to articulate a distinction that is implicit in the literary and technical sources from the ancient Near East: while some dreams have genuine meaning that can help the dreamer to interpret the future (or the past), others do not. It is implausible to suggest, however, that Penelope's dream itself owes anything to the practice of divination in the ancient Near East.[41]

The dream episodes considered in the present essay illustrate that some basic conceptions were shared by the Homeric poems and ancient Near Eastern literature: dreams were seen as a means of communication between gods and men, and the difficult task of interpretation was to establish their significance and meaning. The wide attestation of dream interpretation no doubt reflects the fact that dreaming is a common human experience, and in this sense its status differs from other more technical forms of divination encountered in the course of the present discussion. Extispicy, for instance, is not clearly attested in Homer, while augury, which is common in Homer and in Hittite sources, does not occur in Sumerian texts. But the means by which dreams were interpreted were not necessarily identical. In the episode of Penelope, the rejection of the dream-message is based on a general statement about the unreliability of dreams, which is consistent not only with Penelope's typical reluctance to believe announcements of her husband's return but also with the practice of divination as described by Homer, where characters may (at their peril) dismiss an inconvenient omen but do not attempt to test it. This is a contrast that cannot fail to strike the reader familiar with ancient Near Eastern sources on dream interpretation, since both technical and literary texts describe the elaborate methods of verification that were developed there. A prayer in Sumero-Akkadian religious poetry that mentions portentous dreams was translated and adapted in Hittite, and the literary borrowing was no doubt facilitated by a common interest in and similar practice of dream interpretation; one further reflection of this prayer can perhaps be perceived in Homer (*Il.* 1.62–64), but this is far from certain. When read in sequence, the selection of texts considered in the present contribution illustrates the common significance of portentous dreams in antiquity, and the variety of means by which the uncertainties of dream interpretation could be articulated and addressed.

---

[41] The further argument of Noegel, *Nocturnal Ciphers*, 204–11, 214–22, relies heavily on the observation that ancient Near Eastern literary dream narratives and technical divinatory sources often use verbal puns as hermeneutic tools, and that puns also occur in and around the Penelopean dream narrative (e.g., κέρας / κραίνειν, see above). This again confuses poetic technique with divinatory practice, and is in my view unconvincing.

Bibliography

Averbeck, Richard E. "Temple Building Among the Sumerians and Akkadians (Third Millennium)." Pages 3–34 in *From the Foundations to the Crenellations: Essays on Temple Building in the Ancient Near East and Hebrew Bible*. Edited by Mark J. Boda and Jamie Novotny. AOAT 366. Münster: Ugarit-Verlag, 2010.
Bonnechere, Pierre. "Oracles and Greek Mentalities: The Mantic Confirmation of Mantic Revelations." Pages 115–33 in *Myths, Martyrs, and Modernity: Studies in the History of Religions in Honour of Jan N. Bremmer*. Edited by Jitse Dijkstra, Justin Kroesen, and Yme Kuiper. Numen 127. Leiden: Brill, 2010.
Charpin, Dominique. *Gods, Kings, and Merchants in Old Babylonian Mesopotamia*. Publications de l'Institut du Proche-Orient Ancien du Collège de France 2. Leuven: Peeters, 2015.
Danek, Georg. *Epos und Zitat: Studien zu den Quellen der Odyssee*. Vienna: Österreichische Akademie der Wissenschaften, 1998.
Dodds, E. R. *The Greeks and the Irrational*. Berkeley: University of California Press, 1951.
Edzard, Dietz Otto. *Gudea and His Dynasty*. RIME 3.1. Toronto: University of Toronto Press, 1997.
Falkenstein, Adam. *Die Inschriften Gudeas von Lagaš I: Einleitung*. AnOr 30. Rome: Pontifical Biblical Institute, 1966.
———. "'Wahrsagung' in der sumerischen Überlieferung." Pages 45–68 in *La divination en mésopotamie ancienne*. CRRAI 14. Paris: Presses universitaires de France, 1966.
Flower, Michael A. *The Seer in Ancient Greece*. Berkeley: University of California Press, 2008.
Haas, Volkert. *Hethitische Orakel, Vorzeichen und Abwehrstrategien: Ein Beitrag zur hethitischen Kulturgeschichte*. Berlin: de Gruyter, 2008.
Harris, William V. "Roman Opinions About the Truthfulness of Dreams." *JRS* 93 (2003): 18–34.
Harris-McCoy, Daniel E. *Artemidorus' Oneirocritica: Text, Translation, and Commentary*. Oxford: Oxford University Press, 2012.
Heimpel, Wolfgang. "Die Bauhymne des Gudea von Lagasch." Pages 119–65 in *Erzählungen aus dem Land Sumer*. Edited by Konrad Volk. Wiesbaden: Harrassowitz, 2015.
Kämmerer, Thomas R. "Archetypen in sumerischen, babylonischen und assyrischen Traumschilderungen." Pages 191–207 in *Ex Mesopotamia et Syria lux: Festschrift für Manfried Dietrich*. Edited by Oswald Loretz, Kai A. Metzler, and Hanspeter Schaudig. AOAT 281. Münster: Ugarit-Verlag, 2002.
Kelly, Adrian. "The Audience Expects: Penelope and Odysseus." Pages 3–24 in *Orality, Literacy and Performance in the Ancient World*. Edited by Elizabeth Minchin. Leiden: Brill, 2012.
Kenaan, Vered Lev. "Artemidorus at the Dream Gates: Myth, Theory, and the Restoration of Liminality." *AJP* 137 (2016): 189–218.
Koch, Ulla Susanne. *Mesopotamian Divination Texts: Conversing With the Gods. Sources from the First Millennium BCE*. GMTR 7. Münster: Ugarit-Verlag, 2015.
Kraus, F. R. "Mittelbabylonische Opferschauprotokolle." *JCS* 37 (1985): 127–218.

Maul, Stefan M. *Die Wahrsagekunst im Alten Orient: Zeichen des Himmels und der Erde*. Munich: Beck, 2013.

Metcalf, Christopher. "Babylonian Perspectives on the Certainty of Death." *Kaskal: Rivista di storia, ambienti e culture del Vicino Oriente Antico* 10 (2013): 255–67.

———. "Old Babylonian Religious Poetry in Anatolia: From Solar Hymn to Plague Prayer." *ZA* 105 (2015): 42–53.

———. *The Gods Rich in Praise: Early Greek and Mesopotamian Religious Poetry*. Oxford: Oxford University Press, 2015.

Mouton, Alice. *Rêves hittites: Contribution à une histoire et une anthropologie du rêve en Anatolie ancienne*. CHANE 28. Leiden: Brill, 2007.

———. "Interprétation des rêves et traités oniromantiques au Proche-Orient ancien." Pages 373–92 in *Artémidore de Daldis et l'interprétation des rêves*. Edited by Christophe Chandezon and Julien du Bouchet. Paris: Les Belles Lettres, 2014.

Näf, Beat. *Traum und Traumdeutung im Altertum*. Darmstadt: Wissenschaftliche Buchgesellschaft, 2004.

Noegel, Scott B. "Dreaming and the Ideology of Mantics: Homer and Ancient Near Eastern Oneiromancy." Pages 167–81 in *Ideologies as Intercultural Phenomena: Melammu Symposia III*. Edited by Antonio Panaino and Giovanni Pettinato. Milan: University of Bologna and IsIAO, 2002.

———. *Nocturnal Ciphers: The Allusive Language of Dreams in the Ancient Near East*. AOS 89. New Haven: American Oriental Society, 2007.

Oppenheim, A. Leo. *The Interpretation of Dreams in the Ancient Near East: With a Translation of an Assyrian Dream-Book*. TAPS 46.3. Philadelphia: American Philosophical Society, 1956.

Redfield, James. "Dreams from Homer to Plato." *Archiv für Religionsgeschichte* 15 (2013): 5–15.

Renberg, Gil H. "The Role of Dream-Interpreters in Greek and Roman Religion." Pages 233–62 in *Artemidor von Daldis und die antike Traumdeutung: Texte—Kontexte—Lektüren*. Edited by Gregor Weber. Colloquia Augustana 2. Berlin: de Gruyter, 2015.

Russo, Joseph. "Books XVII–XX." Pages 1–127 in vol. 3 of *A Commentary on Homer's Odyssey*. Oxford: Oxford University Press, 1992.

———. "Penelope's Gates of Horn(s) and Ivory." Pages 223–30 in *La mythologie et l'Odyssée: Hommage à Gabriel Germain*. Edited by André Hurst and Françoise Létoublon. Geneva: Droz, 2002.

Rutz, Matthew T. "The Text After the Sacrifice: Divination Reports from Kassite Babylonia." Pages 214–50 in *Texts and Contexts: The Circulation and Transmission of Cuneiform Texts in Social Space*. Edited by Paul Delnero and Jacob Lauinger. SANER 9. Boston: de Gruyter, 2015.

Sasson, Jack M. *From the Mari Archives: An Anthology of Old Babylonian Letters*. Winona Lake: Eisenbrauns, 2015.

Sommerfeld, Walter. "Traumdeutung als Wissenschaft und Therapie im Alten Orient." Pages 201–19 in *Heilkunde und Hochkultur I: Geburt, Seuche und Traumdeutung in den antiken Zivilisationen des Mittelmeerraumes*. Edited by Axel Karenberg and Christian Leitz. Münster: Lit Verlag, 2000.

Suter, Claudia E. *Gudea's Temple Building: The Representation of an Early Mesopotamian Ruler in Text and Image*. CM 17. Groningen: Styx Publications, 2000.

Trampedach, Kai. "Authority Disputed." Pages 207–30 in *Practitioners of the Divine: Greek Priests and Religious Officials from Homer to Heliodorus*. Edited by Beate Dignas and Kai Trampedach. Washington: Center for Hellenic Studies, 2008.

Van De Mieroop, Marc. *Philosophy before the Greeks. The Pursuit of Truth in Ancient Babylonia*. Princeton: Princeton University Press, 2016.

Waetzoldt, Hartmut. "Die Göttin Nanše und die Traumdeutung." *NABU* 1998: §60 (63–65).

Walde, Christine. *Die Traumdarstellungen in der griechisch-römischen Dichtung*. Munich: Saur, 2001.

West, Martin L. *The East Face of Helicon: West Asiatic Elements in Greek Poetry and Myth*. Oxford: Oxford University Press, 1997.

Zgoll, Annette. *Traum und Welterleben im antiken Mesopotamien: Traumtheorie und Traumpraxis im 3.–1. Jahrtausend v. Chr. als Horizont einer Kulturgeschichte des Träumens*. AOAT 333. Münster: Ugarit-Verlag, 2006.

———. "Nächtliche Wege der Erkenntnis. Möglichkeiten und Gefahren des Außentraumes." Pages 169–82 in *Wissenskultur im Alten Orient: Weltanschauung, Wissenschaften, Techniken, Technologien*. Edited by Hans Neumann. CDOG 4. Wiesbaden: Harrassowitz, 2012.

———. "Dreams as Gods and Gods as Dreams: Dream-Realities in Ancient Mesopotamia from the Third to the First Millennium B.C." Pages 299–313 in *He Has Opened Nisaba's House of Learning: Studies in Honor of Åke Waldemar Sjöberg on the Occasion of His Eighty-Ninth Birthday*. Edited by Leonhard Sassmannshausen. CM 46. Leiden: Brill, 2014.

———. "Traum, Traumgottheiten A.§2." *RlA* 14:114–18.

2
Portent Dreams in Hittite Anatolia

Alice Mouton

In Hittite Anatolia,[1] as in so many places in the world, a dream was perceived as potentially coming from the gods. For this reason, the inhabitants of the Land of Hatti paid close attention to them. Because of their polymorphic character, dreams both fascinate and frighten, and ancient Anatolians tried to decipher and even control them.

The Hittite texts I am going to comment on date from the fourteenth to the late thirteenth century BCE and were mainly uncovered in Hattuša, the modern site of Boğazkale in Turkey. The majority of my corpus dates from Great King Hattušili III's reign, in the mid-thirteenth century. Although they were found in Hattuša, some Hittite religious texts reflect "provincial" beliefs and practices: I will mention in particular Arzawa, in the Luwian speaking Western part of Anatolia and Kizzuwatna, which is a Luwian and Hurrian region in Southern Anatolia.

According to Hittite cuneiform texts, a dream can be defined as a psychic phenomenon occurring while asleep and composed of visual and auditory elements, although the visual component is predominant. Because they occur only while asleep, dreams should be distinguished from visions, as the latter occur while awake. However, the texts do not always make a clear-cut distinction between the two phenomena. Usually, dreams are not shared: they are thought to be a universal and an intimate experience at the same time (experienced by all, but individually), although ancient Anatolians, like their Near Eastern neighbors, believed that collective dreams could also take place. Dreams could be solicited through an incubation ritual, which sometimes consists of asking a question of the gods and then going to sleep, expecting the answer in a dream. In this case,

---

[1] Many thanks to Gil Renberg who improved the English of this paper.

incubation can be viewed as an oracular technique and is better called divinatory incubation. Unsolicited dreams could also contain a divine message. When we look at the Hittite expressions for describing dreaming, what strikes us is that Hittites did not "dream": they only *saw* dreams, and this means that they did not consider themselves as actors of their dreams but rather as onlookers. The dreamer's passive role is, in my view, a central characteristic of dreamers in ancient Near Eastern societies in general.[2]

PORTENT DREAMS IN CONTEXT

Attestations of Hittite dreams are no longer dreams; they are written narratives of dreams. For a given dream, we only have the written source at our disposal, which should be considered a distortion of the dream's oral account, which in turn is a distortion of the dream experience itself. Furthermore, the written account of a dream is frequently distorted further for many reasons, among which scribal conventions figure. Therefore, I shall start by presenting the Hittite written contexts in which a dream appears, each genre of text having its own agenda.

What we are used to calling historical texts, for instance, usually use dreams for their role as conveyer of a divine message. Great King Hattušili III left an important autobiographic text traditionally called "the Apology of Hattušili III" in which five dreams are reported. All those dreams are presented as the *medium* chosen by the Great King's personal goddess Šaušga for expressing herself. Hattušili, like several other ancient Near Eastern kings, made extensive use of dream accounts as so many proofs of the goddess's support and even special affection toward him. Dreams are an important part of his rhetoric, demonstrating his privileged relationship with the goddess. As both a universal and an individual phenomenon, a dream is a very appropriate ideological tool.

In this paper, I will deal specifically with the way dreams function as conveyers of divine messages. In other words, I will focus on portent dreams. As we have just seen, such dreams are described in historical texts, but they are also present in many other genres, such as oracular reports, accounts of vows, prayers, etc. Unlike historical and mythological texts, those latter genres often display very standardized dream reports. This could be explained by the will to provide accounts as objectively as possible. In those contexts, dreams are seen as important messages to be processed.[3]

---

[2] Alice Mouton, *Rêves hittites. Contribution à une histoire et une anthropologie du rêve en Anatolie ancienne*, CHANE 28 (Leiden: Brill, 2007), 9–10 n. 39.

[3] Mouton, *Rêves hittites*, 16–18.

Portent Dreams in Hittite Prayers

As one of the three media—along with prophecy and visions—through which a god can directly express himself to a mortal, portent dreams are requested by individuals in desperate situations. This is the case, for example, in Text 1 (see the appendix below). Prince Kantuzzili, who addresses this prayer to his god, mentions the dream as his preferred mode of communication, as it would allow the god to detail the reason for his anger. This motive can be found in several other prayers, as we will see in another example later on. Text 2 is a prayer of Great King Muwatalli II in which a dream is considered a simpler way for the god to express himself, whereas other oracular techniques might fail to deliver a clear message.

Portent Dreams in Hittite Oracular Reports

Hittite oracular reports very frequently deal with portent dreams. There are three main reasons to mention a dream in an oracular report:

An oracular inquiry is arranged for checking the portent nature of a dream. This is the case in Text 3, where one asks if "this dream has revealed anything." Text 4 is a second example of the same phenomenon. The meaning of the reported dream is unambiguous, so the oracular inquiry is not about its interpretation. Rather, the question focuses on the portent character of the dream. Instead of asking "Is this dream sent by the deity?," the diviner chose to ask: "In a dream, the deity ordered the king not to go to Ankuwa. Did the deity forbid the king to go to Ankuwa?" This asks the same question implicitly: it is about checking the divine origin of this oneiric message.

An oracular inquiry might serve to interpret a potential portent dream. In this case, someone first suggests an interpretation to the dream and then asks the gods to tell whether this interpretation is correct. Text 5 illustrates this. This text is a small tablet which was most probably written during the oracular inquiry.[4] It refers to a dream seen by Queen Puduhepa about the bewitchment of a woman who might have been a high official's wife. The diviner in charge tries to determine the premonitory meaning of Puduhepa's dream. He suggests that it foretells the woman's death, but the KIN oracle—a kind of lot divinatory technique—invalidates this interpretation by providing a "favorable" answer instead of the expected unfavorable one. Text 6 describes a similar procedure: the chief haruspex suggests that the dream seen by the king, probably in the temple of Kubaba itself, witnesses the goddess's anger. For the record, this brief allusion of the king going to the temple and receiving a dream most probably refers to

---

[4] Alice Mouton, "Au sujet du compte rendu oraculaire hittite KBo 18.142," in *Tabularia Hethaeorum: Hethitologische Beiträge Silvin Košak zum 65. Geburtstag*, ed. Detlev Groddek and Marina Zorman, DBH 25 (Wiesbaden: Harrassowitz, 2007), 551–55.

divinatory incubation that the sovereign undertook in order to communicate with the goddess. What we can also deduce from these texts and others is that there was no specialist in dream interpretation or dream divination in Hittite Anatolia.[5] Any diviner could interpret a dream as well as check its portent character through his usual divinatory technique, be it extispicy, bird oracle, KIN oracle, etc.

An oracular inquiry might also help to gain additional data on the matter revealed by a dream. The first example of this kind of inquiry is Text 7. The bad dreams that were seen gave the diviner the impression that they foretold defeat on the battlefield, but this impression had to be verified through oracular inquiry. The second example is Text 8, in which several paragraphs focus on a Great King's dream. The content of the dream itself is not very clear, although we know for sure that it has something to do with a battle. After the—unfortunately—fragmentary depiction of the dream, the oracular questions begin. The first question (Text 8a) checks both the portent value of the dream and its meaning, asking: "Will the city be destroyed?" The oracle confirms this interpretation by providing the expected unfavorable signs. The second question (Text 8b) basically means: "Will the city be destroyed because of the deity's anger?" Once more, the oracle answers: "Yes." The answer is double-checked by a *piqittum*, a second oracular inquiry on the same question. The *piqittum* confirms the divine "yes": the city will indeed be destroyed as a result of the deity's anger. Later in the same text, we find questions surrounding a fire which is determined to have provoked the deity's anger. In Text 8c, only the last of the paragraphs about the fire is provided here in translation. In the end, the dream is interpreted as a divine message from a god who is thus expressing his anger about a fire.

Portent Dreams in Hittite Vow Accounts

One of the novel aspects of the Hittite corpus is the presence of accounts of vows. We traditionally call them "votive texts," but as these texts are not themselves ex-votos but rather memoranda related to vows, this name is somewhat inappropriate. Whenever a high ranking figure—often the king himself, his wife, or someone close to them—pronounced a vow, that is, whenever he or she promised to offer a gift to a particular deity in exchange for a favor, the Hittite central administration kept a record of that promise and of its fulfillment.

From these records, we realize that many vows were thought to have been pronounced in dreams. This phenomenon is only attested for Hattušili III's reign and maybe the period right before it. It has no known parallel in the rest of the cuneiform literature of the Near East. But what we can say for sure is that a dreamt vow is taken as seriously as a vow pronounced while awake. Many

---

[5] Mouton, *Rêves hittites*, 53 with n. 87.

times, the person who dreams these vows is Queen Puduhepa, who was always very worried about her husband's bad health. Text 9a describes a dream of Queen Puduhepa about her royal husband's throat ache. She promises three different golden items to the goddess Hepat of the city of Uda in exchange for her husband's full recovery.

Sometimes, the dreamt vow involves a short dialogue between a god and the dreamer, like in Text 9b. The deity Kuwaršu promises to help cure the queen's husband, that is, the Great King, and in exchange for this divine help, the queen promises in her dream to offer three vases full of foodstuffs. Text 10 is the last example of a dreamt vow, which, interestingly enough, occurred during a festival. The queen promises to offer a golden soul-figurine to the god Šaumatari if "nothing coming from" her harms her husband, whatever this means. What is most striking in this passage is the context of the dream: the text specifies that it occurred during the torch festival.[6] I believe that we have the key to those puzzling dreamt vows here: they are actually dreams obtained through divinatory incubation during cultic festivals.[7] I would now like to turn my attention to this particular practice.

DIVINATORY INCUBATION

In the Hittite texts, the expression *šuppa/šuppaya šeš-*, "to sleep in a consecrated manner," designates divinatory incubation that most of the time took place during cultic events. The best testimony for this is the famous passage of a Muršili II's plague prayer (Text 11), which mentions all the priests being ordered by the Great King to sleep in a consecrated manner in order to receive the expected message-dream of the angered deity. Several Hittite festival texts quickly refer, in my opinion, to divinatory incubation, a practice that could be performed by the Great King himself and, as we have just seen with the last vow account (Text 10), also by the queen.

Text 12 is, I believe, an example of this. This is the sequence of a festival celebrated in honor of Šaušga of the field of the city of Šamuha. I have suggested elsewhere that this particular goddess's main function is to deal with the Hittite king's military campaigns, and that "field" should be understood here as meaning "battlefield".[8] The festival is to be performed when the king returns from battle and only at that time. The text specifies that it should not be performed if the king did not go to war. At any rate, what interests me here is the

---

[6] Alice Mouton, "Torche et encens en Anatolie et Mésopotamie anciennes," in *Noms barbares I: Formes et contextes d'une pratique magique*, ed. Michel Tardieu, Anna Van den Kerchove and Michela Zago, BEHER 162 (Turnhout: Brepols, 2013), 56.

[7] Mouton, *Rêves hittites*, 45.

[8] Alice Mouton, "Rituels hittites à effectuer avant ou après le combat," *HiMA* 3 (2016): 277–88, here 284–85.

sequence I reproduced below. It shows that at some point during the ceremony, the king is expected to enter the temple and sleep in the temple itself while a group of musicians and ritual experts spend the night sleepless.[9] I believe that the king might be performing a divinatory incubation, maybe trying to get a supportive message from the goddess after returning from battle.

Text 13 is another example of divinatory incubation. Great King Tudhaliya receives a dream in the "temple of the grandfathers," that is, probably a kind of royal mausoleum.[10] Thus, we might call this particular type of divinatory incubation "necromantic incubation": it most probably aimed to establish an oneiric contact with the dead ancestors of the king and/or the Sun goddess of the earth, who is the mistress of the Netherworld.[11]

There are also numerous references to the temple's "inner room" in which a "sacred bed" is mentioned. The king often enters that inner room and he even lies down on the sacred bed from time to time. As I have shown elsewhere,[12] I believe that this is a highly significant rite which involves divinatory incubation: after all, the inner room is the god's own bedroom—the king sleeps in the god's bed!

THERAPEUTIC INCUBATION

In Hittite Anatolia, incubation rituals can also be used for therapeutic reasons. In these cases, we can distinguish two main streams of rituals: the ones that involve only a healing sleep and the ones that include a portent dream as part of the patient's cure.[13] Because of the focus of this volume, I will dwell only on the second group of incubation rituals, namely the ones including a portent dream. The main example of this is Text 14, Paškuwatti's ritual against sexual impotence (a man's sexual behavior has become that of a woman, states the text). In this ritual, the patient performs an incubation in order to receive a particular dream, namely an oneiric—and sexual—theophany; in order to be cured from impotence, he needs to sleep with a particular goddess in his dream. This particular type of dream involving a theophany is the most direct it can get: the deity is willing to be physically present. The text of Paškuwatti's ritual describes the Arzawan ritual procedure of therapeutic incubation:

1. Preparation of the ritual implements comprising food offerings for the goddess Uliliyašši, a *galaktar*-plant (which might be poppy), drinks, clothes, etc.

---

[9] Alice Mouton, "Usages privés et publics de l'incubation d'après les textes hittites," *JANER* 3 (2003): 76.
[10] Magdalena Kapelus, "La 'maison (le palais) des ancêtres' et les tombeaux des rois hittites," *Res Antiquae* 4 (2007): 221–30.
[11] Mouton, "Usages privés," 82.
[12] Mouton, "Usages privés," 79–80.
[13] Mouton, "Usages privés," 83–87.

The patient has washed himself but he does not dedicate the offerings to the goddess, a virgin does. Then everybody goes to an uncultivated place where the patient's impurity will be more easily disposed of.

2. A "magical" gate made of reed is built and the patient crosses it, thus transforming his "behavior" from female back to male. This involves gendered objects that the patient holds right before and after the crossing: first he holds the spindle and distaff, which symbolize his femininity, but after his crossing of the gate, he gets the bow and arrows, illustrating his reacquisition of virility.

3. Then the patient goes home, where he performs the incubation rite. He offers food to the goddess three times in a row. He spreads his clothes on the floor in front of the divine table. This is where he is supposed to sleep and receive a portent dream from the goddess.

4. If the expected dream does not occur, the ritual process cannot move on, and the patient has to repeat the same operations until he gets what he wants.

Two birth rituals from Kizzuwatna attribute great importance to a pregnant woman's dreams. The content of the woman's dreams reflects her state of purity, or to put it otherwise, her relationship with her gods. Text 15 uses the expression "to be pure through (one's) dream," which, I suggest, means: "to be declared pure by the gods through a dream."[14] If the gods are dissatisfied by the woman in any way, they will not communicate their good will through a dream, and the ritual expert will thus understand that the purification rites should be carried on.[15] Text 16 refers to a message-dream the pregnant woman is supposed to receive about the *šinapši*-temple. This temple is a place in which she will be purified if necessary. In other words, if the dream she saw delivered an unfavorable message from the gods, it means that they consider her impure, and she should then go and purify herself and make peace with the gods in the *šinapši*-temple.[16]

Through this short contribution, I have tried to show how important portent dreams were for the ancient Anatolians. They were perceived as unique opportunities to be in direct contact with the gods, if, of course, those gods agreed to show up.

---

[14] Mouton, *Rêves hittites*, 64.

[15] Concerning the relationship between the spatial progression and the woman's purification process, see Alice Mouton, "Temporalité et spatialité dans les rites de passage de l'Anatolie hittite," in *Time and History in the Ancient Near East: Proceedings of the 56th Rencontre Assyriologique Internationale at Barcelona 26–30 July 2010*, ed. Lluís Feliu, Joana Llop, Adelina Millet Albà, and Joaquín Sanmartín (Winona Lake: Eisenbrauns, 2013), 225–40.

[16] Mouton, *Rêves hittites*, 64–65.

Appendix

Text 1 = KUB 30.10 Obv. 24'–28' (CTH 373)

Lit.: Itamar Singer, *Hittite Prayers*, WAW 11 (Atlanta: Society of Biblical Literature, 2002), 31–33.

[kinun]=a=mu=za ammel DINGIR=YA ŠÀ=ŠU ZI=ŠU hūmantet kardit kīnuddu nu=mu wašdul=mit [tēd]du n=e=zan ganiešmi naššu=mu DINGIR=YA zašheya mēmau nu=mu=za DINGIR=YA ŠÀ=ŠU kinuddu [nu=mu wašd]ul=mit tēddu n=e=zan ganiešmi našma=mu ᴹᵁᴺᵁˢENSI mēmau [našma=mu Š]A ᴰUTU ᴸᵁ́AZU IŠTU ᵁᶻᵁNÍG.GIG mēmau nu=mu=za DINGIR=YA hūmantet kardit [ŠÀ=ŠU ZI=ŠU] kīnuddu nu=mu wašdul=mit tēddu n=e=zan ganiešmi

"[Now] let my god open the bottom of his soul to me with sincerity, let him tell me my faults. I will acknowledge them. Either let my god speak in a dream, let him open his heart to me, let him tell [me] my [fa]ults—I will acknowledge them; or let the ENSI female diviner tell me, [or else] let the AZU-man of the Sungod tell [me] through a liver. Let my god open [the bottom of his soul] to me with sincerity; let him tell me my faults. I will acknowledge them."

Text 2 = KBo 11.1 (CTH 382)

Lit.: Singer, *Hittite Prayers*, 84–85.

[UL=ma=a]t=mu šalliš ᴸᵁ́ŠU.GI memai nu=mu DINGIR-*LIM* kūn memian tešhit parkunut

"God, clarify this matter to me through a dream (in case) the great Old Man can[not] tell me."

Text 3 = KUB 5.24+KUB 16.31+ ii 17–18 (CTH 577)

Lit.: Theo van den Hout, *Der Ulmitešub-Vertrag. Eine prosopographische Untersuchung*, StBoT 38 (Wiesbaden: Harrassowitz, 1995), 262–65; Mouton, *Rêves hittites*, 198–202.

nu mān kāš Ù-*TUM* kuit imma kuit išiyahta

"If this dream has revealed anything"

Text 4 = KBo 24.128 Rev. 1–4 (CTH 570)

Lit.: Mouton, *Rêves hittites*, 176–77.

Ù-*an kuit INA* ^{URU}*Anku*[*w*]*a ANA* EZEN$_4$ *ZUNNI* DÙ-*uanzi pai*[*zzi*? *n*=*a*]*š*=*za*=*kan* Ù *IMUR* ^{D}UTU-*ŠI*=*wa INA* ^{URU}*Ankui lē paizz*[*i šar*]*ā pāuwaš* NU.SIG$_5$-*ta nu*=*za mān* DINGIR-*LUM apūš* U$_4$.KAM^H[^{Á}-*uš INA*? ^{UR}]^U*Ankuwa pāuanzi markiyan harta*

"(He/she saw) a dream: (about) the fact that he [*will*] go celebrate the rain festival in Ankuwa, he/she saw a dream (saying): 'My Sun should not go to Ankuwa! Going up (there) has been (determined as) unfavorable!' if the deity has forbidden (the king) to go to Ankuwa during those days, (...)"

Text 5 = KBo 18.142 Obv. 1–7 (CTH 581)

Lit: Mouton, "Au sujet du compte," 551–5.; Mouton, *Rêves hittites*, 220–21.

UH$_7$=*za*=*kan kuin* Ù MUNUS.LUGAL *ANA* DAM ^{ITI_8MUŠEN}.LÚ *anda IMUR* [*n*]=*at*=*ši mān* [S]AG.DU-*aš* ÚŠ-*an nu* KIN NU.SIG$_5$-*du*

"The bewitchment that the queen has witnessed in a dream about Harranaziti's wife, if it (means) death of her person (= Harranaziti's wife), let the KIN oracles be unfavorable."

Text 6 = KUB 22.69 ii 4'–6' (CTH 570)

Lit.: Mouton, *Rêves hittites*, 178.

nu LUGAL *kuwapi INA* É ^{D}*Kupapa pait nu*=*za*=*kan apēdani* Ù(-)[...] *kuin* Ù-*an aušta* GAL $^{LÚ.MEŠ}$HAL *ariyat ŠA* DINGIR-*LIM kuišk*[*i*] TUKU.TUKU-*za nu TE*^{MEŠ} NU.SIG$_5$-*du*

"When the king went to the temple of Kubaba, for that dream [...], the dream that he saw, the chief of the haruspex made an oracular inquiry (asking): (is it about) some anger of goddess's? (If yes), let the exta be unfavorable."

Text 7 = KUB 5.1 iii 48–50 (CTH 561)

Lit.: Ahmet Ünal, *Hattušili III*, THeth 4 (Heidelberg: Winter, 1974), 2:72–73; Mouton, *Rêves hittites*, 172.

uniuš=*za*=*kan kuēš* Ù^{MEŠ} HUL-*luš uškezzi* GISKIM^{HÁ}=*ya*=*za arpuwanta kikištari* DINGIR^{MEŠ} *ANA* KASKAL ^{URU}*Tanizila* MÈ-*aš arpan uškitteni* NU.SIG$_5$-*du*

"Those bad dreams that he/she keeps on seeing and (those) signs of bad luck (that) keep on taking place, (do they mean that) you, gods, (fore)see defeat in battle during the Tanizila military campaign? (If yes), let (the oracle) be unfavorable."

Text 8 = KUB 5.11 (CTH 577)

Lit.: Mouton, *Rêves hittites*, 193–97.

Text 8a = KUB 5.11 i 1–9

[Ù-*TUM* ᴰ]UTU-*ŠI INA* ᵁᴿᵁ*Tiliura IMUR zahhiy*[*a=w*]*a* [...] ᴰUTU-*ŠI šešzi nu=wa memieškezzi* [...]x *ūhhun* INIM ᵁᴿᵁ*HATTI=kan* [...]x ᴰUTU-*ŠI IDI* § (...) *QĀTAMMA=pat aši* URU-*aš harakzi=pat nu* KIN NU.SIG₅-*du* (...) *nu=kan* DINGIRᴹᴱŠ-*aš* NU.SIG₅

"[A dream] (of) my Sun. He saw (a dream) in Tiliura: 'During a battle [...] my Sun lies down and says: 'I saw [...].'" The matter of Hattuša [...] my Sun knew. § (...) Will thus this city be destroyed? (If yes), let the KIN oracle be unfavorable. (...) The gods (said): unfavorable."

Text 8b = KUB 5.11 i 26–29

[*kī k*]*uit* [SIxSÁ]-*at*? <<*ŠA* >> *aši* Ù *ŠA* DINGIR-*LIM kuinki* TUKU.TUKU-*tan* [*išiy*]*ahta nu TE*ᴹᴱŠ NU.SIG₅-*du* (...) [N]U.SIG₅ § [*IŠT*]*U* ᴹᵁᴺᵁˢŠU.GI IR-*TUM QĀTAMMA=pat nu* KIN NU.SIG₅-*du* (...) NU.SIG₅

"So it was determined. Did this dream [re]veal some anger of deity's? (If yes), let the exta be unfavorable. (...) Unfavorable. § The same question (was asked) [b]y the Old Woman. (If yes), let the KIN oracle be unfavorable. (...) Unfavorable."

Text 8c = KUB 5.11 iv 55–62:

INIM IZI *kuit* SIxSÁ-*at nu pānzi* INIM IZI *išhiulahhanzi*

"Because it was determined (that it was related to) the matter of the fire, they will instruct the matter of the fire."

Text 9 = KUB 15.1 (CTH 584)

Lit.: Johan de Roos, *Hittite Votive Texts*, PIHANS 109 (Leiden: NINO, 2007), 88–105; Mouton, *Rêves hittites*, 260–66.

Text 9a = KUB 15.1 i 1–11

^{D}*Hepat* ^{URU}*Uda* Ù-*TUM* MUNUS.LUGAL INIM ^{UZU}GÚ.HAL=*kan* GAM *maniya*[*hta*] *kuwapi anda nu*=*za*=*kan* MUNUS.LUGAL ŠÀ Ù-*TI ANA* ^{D}*Hepat* ^{URU}*Uda kiššan IKRUB mān*=*wa* DINGIR-*LUM* GAŠAN=*YA* ^{D}UTU-*ŠI* TI-*nuan harti* HUL-*ui*=*war*=*an parā UL tarnatti nu*=*wa ANA* ^{D}*Hepat* ALAM KÙ.GI *iyami AYARU* KÙ.GI=*ya*=*wa*=(*š*)*ši iyami nu*=*war*=*at*=*za ŠA* ^{D}*Hepat AYARU halziššan*[*z*]*i* ^{UZU}GABA-*aš*=*ma*=*wa*=*du*=*za TUDITUM* KÙ.GI *iyami nu*=*war*=*at*=*za TUDITUM* DINGIR-*LIM halziššanzi*

"Hepat of Uda: a dream (of) the queen. She *attrib*[*uted*] the matter (of) the throat (to her). At a certain moment, in (her) dream, the queen made the following vow to Hepat of Uda: 'If you, goddess, my Lady, you keep my Sun (= the Hittite Great King) alive, (if) you do not abandon him (in presence of) evil, I will make for Hepat a golden effigy. I will also make a golden rosette for her. They will call it the rosette of Hepat. I will make a golden *TUDITTUM*-pin for your breast and they will call it the *TUDITTUM*-pin of the goddess!'"

Text 9b = KUB 15.1 iii 7'–16'

[Ù-*TUM* MUNUS.LUGA]L INIM ^{D}*Gurwašu*=*kan kuwapi* [*anda* ^{D}*Gu*]*rwašuš*=*kan* GIM-*an* ŠÀ Ù-*TI* [*AN*]*A* MUNUS.LUGAL *IQBI apūn*=*wa kuin ŠA* ^{LÚ}*MUDI*=*KA* INIM-*an* ZI-*za harti nu*=*war*=*aš* TI-*anza* 1 ME MU.KAM^{HÁ}=*ya*=*wa*=(*š*)*ši pihhi* MUNUS.LUGAL=*ma*=*za*=*kan* ŠÀ Ù-*TI kišan IKRUB mān*=*wa*=*mu apēniššuwan iyaši nu*=*wa* ^{LÚ}*MUDI*=*YA* TI-*anza nu*=*wa ANA* DINGIR-*LIM* 3 ^{DUG}*haršiyalli* 1-*EN ŠA* Ì 1-*EN ŠA* LÀL 1-*EN ŠA INBI tehhi*

"[A dream (of) the quee]n: when Kurwašu (has uttered those) words. As, in the dream, [Ku]rwašu said to the queen: '(Concerning) the matter of your husband that you (always) have in mind, he will live. I will grant him one hundred years.' in the dream, the queen has pronounced the following vow: 'If you do that for me so that my husband remains alive, I will deposit (before you), deity, three *haršiyalli*-vases: one of oil, one of honey (and) one of fruits.'"

Text 10 = *KUB 15.19 obv.? 11'–13' (CTH 590)*

Lit.: de Roos, *Hittite Votive Texts*, 176–78; Mouton, *Rêves hittites*, 283–84.

[*zašhiyaz*]*a* MUNUS.LUGAL *ANA* U₄.KAM^(HA) EZEN₄ ^(GIŠ)*zuppari ANA* ᴰ*Šaumatar*[*i arkuwar kišan*] *ēššešta mān=wa ANA* ᴰUTU-*ŠI ammēdaza UL kuē*[*zqa* GÙB-*lišzi nu=wa AN*]*A* ᴰ*Šaumatari* 1 ZI KÙ.GI 20 GÍN *uppahhi*

"During the days of the torch festival, the queen has uttered through [a dream the following prayer] to Šaumatari: 'If nothing coming from me [harms] my Sun, I will send to Šaumatari one golden soul(-figurine) of 20 shekels.'"

Text 11 = *KUB 14.8 Rev. 41'–46' (CTH 378)*

Lit.: Singer, *Hittite Prayers*, 60.

[*namma=m*]*a mān tamētaz=*(*zi*)*ya kuēzqa uddānaz akkiškettari n=at=za=kan naššu tešhit uwallu našma=at ariyašešnaz* [*handay*]*attaru našma=at* ᴸᵁDINGIR-*LIM-nianza=ma memāu našma ANA* ᴸᵁ.ᴹᴱˢSANGA *kuit* [*h*]*ūmandāš watarnahhun n=at=šamaš šuppaya šeškiškanzi*

"[Furthermore], if lots of people are dying because of another matter, either let me see it through a dream, or let it be [determ]ined by an oracle, or let the man of the deity tell it, or else, because I have commanded all the priests (to do so), let them sleep in a consecrated manner."

Text 12 = *KUB 27.1 iv 46–50 (CTH 712)*

Lit.: Ilse Wegner, *Hurritische Opferlisten aus hethitischen Festbeschreibungen: Texte für Ištar-Ša(w)uška*, Corpus der hurritischen Sprachdenkmäler 1/3-1 (Rome: Bonsignori, 1995), 52, 54.

nu LUGAL-*uš INA* É ᴰIŠTAR.LÍL *annalaš* ᵁᴿᵁ*Samūha paizzi nu* LUGAL-*uš uni IŠTU* ᴰᵁᴳ*KUKUB* KÙ.GI GEŠTIN-*it šūwan šipanti* LUGAL-*uš* UŠKEN *nu=*(*š*)*ši kuwapi āššu n=aš apiya šešzi PANI* ᴰIŠTAR.LÍL=*ma eša* ᴸᵁ.ᴹᴱˢNAR ᴸᵁ.ᴹᴱˢAZU=*ya* GE₆-*an laknuwanz*[*i*]

"The king goes to the temple of the old Šaušga of the field of Šamuha. The king libates to this (goddess) with a golden pitcher full of wine. The king bows down. Then he will sleep wherever seems appropriate to him but (before that) he sits in front of Šaušga of the field (while) the musicians and the AZU ritual experts spend the night sleepless."

Text 13 = KUB 43.55 v 6'–13' (CTH 434)

Lit.: Piotr Taracha, *Ersetzen und Entsühnen. Das mittelhethitische Ersatzritual für den Grosskönig Tuthalija (CTH *448.4) und verwandte Texte*, CHANE 5 (Leiden: Brill, 2000), 24–25; Mouton, *Rêves hittites*, 148–49.

uit=man=zan ᴰUTU-*ŠI kuwapi* ¹*Duthaliyaš* [L]UGAL.GAL *taknaš* ᴰUTU-*aš* SÍSKUR ᵁᴿᵁ*Hattuši INA* É *huhhaš tešhan aušta MUTI=ma kī mehur ēšta apēdani* MU.KAM-*ti* ᴰIM-*aš INA* ᵁᴿᵁ*Urwara tethaš* EZEN₄ *tethešnaš=ma*

"When my Sun Tudhaliya happened to see a dream in Hattuša during the ceremony of the Sun goddess of the earth, in the temple of the grandfathers, it was at that time of the year, during that year that the Storm-god thundered in the city of Urwara (and that it was) the thunder festival."

Text 14 = KUB 9.27+ iv 1–9; iv 19–21 (CTH 406)

Lit.: Harry A. Hoffner, "Paskuwatti's Ritual against Sexual Impotence (CTH 406)," *AuOr* 5 (1987): 271–87; Alice Mouton, ed. "Rituel de Paškuwatti d'Arzawa (CTH 406)," hethiter.net/:CTH 406 (INTR 2012-02-23).

nu=za BÊL SÍSKUR *šešzi nu=za=kan mān* DINGIR-*LUM zašhiya tuēkki=(š)ši aušzi katti=(š)š[i] paizzi n=aš=ši katti=ši šešzi kuitman=ma* DINGIR-*LUM INA* U₄.3.KAM *mug[āmi] nu=za=kan zašhimuš kuiēš uškizz*[*i*] *n=aš memiškezzi mān=ši* DINGIR-*LUM* IGI^{ḪÁ}-*wa parā tekkušnuškezz*[*i*] *nu=(š)ši mān* DINGIR-*LUM katti=(š)ši šešzi* (...) § [*mān=ka*]*n tuekki=(š)ši=ma* [*UL aušzi nu*] DINGIR-*LUM zašhiya katti=(š)ši* [*UL šešzi*] *iššiškemi=pat*

"The patient sleeps. (Afterward, he will tell) whether he sees the goddess's incarnation in (his) dream, (whether) she goes to him and sleeps with him. While I invo[ke] the goddess during three days, he describes the dreams he sees (and tells) whether the goddess shows him (her) eyes or (whether) the goddess sleeps with him. (...) § [If he does not see] her incarnation, if the goddess [does not sleep] with him in (his) dream, I will go on performing (the ritual)."

Text 15 = KUB 9.22 (CTH 477)

Lit.: Gary Beckman, *Hittite Birth Rituals*, StBoT 29 (Wiesbaden: Harrassowitz, 1983), 94–97; Alice Mouton, ed., "Rituel de naissance du Kizzuwatna (CTH 477)," hethiter.net/:CTH 477 (INTR 2012-05-07)

[*lu*]*kkatta=ma nu=za* MUNUS *ārri nu mān* MUNUS *tešhaz parkuīš n=an=kan* ᴸᵁ*patiliš harnāui anda pēhutezzi* § *n=aš* UŠKEN *harnāuiy*[*a*]=*ma*=(*š*)*šan QĀTAM dāi* § *mān=aš tešhaz UL parkuiš n=aš PANI* KÁ É.ŠÀ UŠKEN *namma*=(*š*)*šan arahzeni=ya*=(*š*)*šan harnāui QĀTAM parā dāi*

"The day after, the woman washes. If (she is) pure through (her) dream, the *patili*-ritual expert takes her to the birth stool. § She bows down toward the birth stool and places her hand on it. § But if (she is) not pure through (her) dream, she bows down in front the door of the inner room (instead) and then from afar she raises her hand toward the birth stool."

Text 16 = KBo 17.65+ (CTH 489)

Lit.: Beckman, *Hittite Birth Rituals*, 140–41; Francesco Fuscagni, ed., "Rituale di nascita: 'Quando una donna resta incinta (CTH 489),'" hethiter.net/:CTH 489 (INTR 2011-08-30)

nu=za=kan kuit kuit ŠA ᴱ[*šin*]*apši uttar tešhit uwan*[*na paizz*]*i*ʾ *kuit=a*=(*š*)*ši=kan mahhan* ZI-*ni and*[*a*] *nu=za apēd*[*a*]*ni uddan*[*i*] *INA* ᴱ*šinapši* MUŠENᴴᴬ *peran arha* [*wa*]*rnuzi*

"Whatever matter related to the *šinapši*-temple she [*is going to*] see through a dream, when something (comes) to her mind, for this matter she will entirely burn birds in the *šinapši*-temple."

Bibliography

Beckman, Gary. *Hittite Birth Rituals*. StBoT 29. Wiesbaden: Harrassowitz, 1983.
Fuscagni, Francesco, ed. "Rituale di nascita: 'Quando una donna resta incinta (CTH 489).'" hethiter.net/:CTH 489 (INTR 2011-08-30).
Hoffner, Harry A. "Paskuwatti's Ritual against Sexual Impotence (CTH 406)." *AuOr* 5 (1987): 271–87.
van den Hout, Theo. *Der Ulmitešub-Vertrag: Eine prosopographische Untersuchung*. StBoT 38. Wiesbaden: Harrassowitz, 1995.
Kapelus, Magdalena. "La 'maison (le palais) des ancêtres' et les tombeaux des rois hittites." *Res Antiquae* 4 (2007): 221–30.
Mouton, Alice. "Au sujet du compte rendu oraculaire hittite KBo 18.142." Pages 551–55 in *Tabularia Hethaeorum. Hethitologische Beiträge Silvin Košak zum 65. Geburtstag*. Edited by Detlev Groddek and Marina Zorman. DBH 25. Wiesbaden: Harrassowitz, 2007.
———. *Rêves hittites: Contribution à une histoire et une anthropologie du rêve en Anatolie ancienne*. CHANE 28. Leiden: Brill, 2007.
———. "Rituels hittites à effectuer avant ou après le combat." *HiMA* 3 (2016): 277–88.
———, ed. "Rituel de naissance du Kizzuwatna (CTH 477)." hethiter.net/:CTH 477 (INTR 2012-05-07).
———, ed. "Rituel de Paškuwatti d'Arzawa (CTH 406)." hethiter.net/:CTH 406 (INTR 2012-02-23).
———. "Temporalité et spatialité dans les rites de passage de l'Anatolie hittite." Pages 225–40 in *Time and History in the Ancient Near East. Proceedings of the 56th Rencontre Assyriologique Internationale at Barcelona 26–30 July 2010*. Edited by Lluís Feliu, Joana Llop, Adelina Millet Albà, and Joaquín Sanmartín. Winona Lake: Eisenbrauns, 2013.
———. "Torche et encens en Anatolie et Mésopotamie anciennes." Pages 51–66 in *Noms barbares I. Formes et contextes d'une pratique magique*. Edited by Michel Tardieu, Anna Van den Kerchove, and Michela Zago. BEHER 162. Turnhout: Brepols, 2013.
———. "Usages privés et publics de l'incubation d'après les textes hittites." *JANER* 3 (2003): 73–91.
de Roos, Johan. *Hittite Votive Texts*. PIHANS 109. Leiden: NINO, 2007.
Singer, Itamar. *Hittite Prayers*. WAW 11. Atlanta: Society of Biblical Literature, 2002.
Taracha, Piotr. *Ersetzen und Entsühnen: Das mittelhethitische Ersatzritual für den Großkönig Tuthalija (CTH *448.4) und verwandte Texte*. CHANE 5. Leiden: Brill, 2000.
Ünal, Ahmet. *Hattušili III*. 2 vols. THeth 4. Heidelberg: Winter, 1974.
Wegner, Ilse. *Hurritische Opferlisten aus hethitischen Festbeschreibungen: Texte für Ištar-Ša(w)uška*. Corpus der hurritischen Sprachdenkmäler 1/3. Rome: Bonsignori, 1995.

3
When Even the Gods Do Not Know: El's Dream Divination in KTU 1.6 iii

Koowon Kim

It was generally believed in the ancient Near East that the gods spoke to humans through their dreams. These could be either vivid message dreams or enigmatic ones that required interpretation. Although there are traces of the notion that dreams could be caused by the state of mind or body of the dreamer in the wisdom tradition, ancient dream divination depended for its operation on the corporate assumption that dreams are of divine origin and thus of revelatory significance.[1]

Though the paucity of data hinders us from saying anything definitive about the Ugaritic practice of dream divination, it is safe to assume that attitudes to-

---

[1] Not all dreams are ominous. Some dreams relate to the dreamer's psychological or physical state. Oppenheim cites, for instance, a saying from a fragmentary cuneiform wisdom text: "Remove woe and anxiety from your heart, woe and anxiety create dreams!" A. Leo. Oppenheim, *The Interpretation of Dreams in the Ancient Near East: With a Translation of an Assyrian Dream-Book*, TAPS 46.3 (Philadelphia: American Philosophical Society, 1956), 227. According to Gnuse, the phrase "in the manner of a dream" in an Egyptian wisdom text indicates shallowness, reminiscent of the attitude of Job toward dreaming, "He shall fly away as a dream and not be found ($kaḥălō^wm\ yā'ū^wp\ wəlō'\ yimṣā'ū^whū^w$, 20:8)." Robert Karl Gnuse, "The Dream Theophany of Samuel: Its Structure in Relation to Ancient Near Eastern Dreams and Its Theological Significance" (PhD diss., Vanderbilt University, 1980), 55. Gnuse, *Dreams and Dream Reports in the Writings of Josephus: A Traditio-Historical Analysis* (Leiden: Brill, 1996), 101. Biblical wisdom literature shows a similar attitude to dreams: Job 20:8; Eccl 5:2, 6; Pss 73:20, 126:1. See for detailed discussion on these passages Shaul Bar, *A Letter That Has Not Been Read: Dreams in the Hebrew Bible*, HUCM 25 (Cincinnati: Hebrew Union College Press, 2001), 126–32.

ward dreaming in Ugarit are likely to have been similar to those of their contemporary neighbors. That is, the Ugaritians also believed that dreams were a means of divine-to-human communication; dreams were understood as the "words of the gods." This is evidenced not only by the Ugaritic dream book (KTU 1.86)[2] but also by the fact that three major Ugaritic literary texts, the Baal Cycle, the Kirta Epic, and the Aqhat Epic, use dream incidents as structural devices in their plot developments.[3]

This paper will focus on El's dream divination in the sixth tablet of the Baal Cycle (KTU 1.6 iii), and specifically on how and why the Ugaritic author or scribe uses the literary device of El engaging in dream incubation.[4] It is significant that El's incubation is distinct from the other such instances in the Kirta and Aqhat Epics in two main respects. First, it is sought by El, the chief deity of the Canaanite pantheon, and not by a human being. Second, it is a symbolic dream, not a message dream.[5] By analyzing El's dream omen as a quasi-performative utterance, this paper aims to show how El's dream divination functions as the structural key to the plot of the narrative.[6] Further, it will also be shown how El's incubation serves as a literary tool for his characterization: the fact that he is both the recipient and sender of the dream, and thus wholly in control in bring-

---

[2] The distribution of Ugaritic data on dream incidents is uneven. KTU 1.86, the only extant Ugaritic dream manual, is in a poor state of preservation, not permitting any definite conclusion concerning its interpretation. For a detailed study of this text, see Dennis Pardee, *Les textes rituels*, Ras Shamra-Ougarit 12 (Paris: ERC, 2000), 1:457–68. The remaining dream reports come from purely literary texts.

[3] In discussing the use of dream incidents as a literary device, Oppenheim distinguishes the structural use from the non-structural use. The former concerns the dreams that play a crucial role in the development of the story, while the latter entails those that are introduced only for the purpose of preparing the reader for an inevitable plot. Oppenheim, *Interpretation of Dreams*, 215.

[4] Noegel attributes much of Ilimilku's sophisticated craftiness concerning the literary use of dreams to his profession as a diviner. Scott B. Noegel, *Nocturnal Ciphers: The Allusive Language of Dreams in the Ancient Near East*, AOS 89 (New Haven: American Oriental Society, 2007), 108–9.

[5] By "symbolic dreams," I refer to all dream-contents that require interpreting, whether images from everyday life or a surreal world. For a survey of various typologies of dream, see Naphtali Lewis, *The Interpretation of Dreams and Portents* (Toronto: Stevens, 1976), 19–22. Noegel is dubious about the widely cited typology that distinguishes "message dreams" from "symbolic dreams," because there is no difference between message and symbol in the logocentric ideology that informs ancient Near Eastern oneirocritics. Noegel, *Nocturnal Ciphers*, 274–76.

[6] El's dream of the heavens raining down oil and the wadis running with honey is not performative in the traditional sense of the term, but it is presented as part of the incubation type-scene, the version of which in KTU 1.6 iii tinge El's dream omen with a performative effect.

ing about the future, underscores El's authority as the sole arbitrator of divine disputes.[7] Before we discuss El's dream divination in KTU 1.6 iii, some explanation of the use of the term "performative" in relation to El's divination is warranted.

Incubated dreams are usually message dreams.[8] Incubants receive them during an oneiric theophany, either in the form of a command (e.g., Kirta's dream) or a promise (e.g., Danel's dream). Since the oneiric command or promise is given by a favorable deity, incubated dreams are usually performative in the sense that they are to be translated into actions by the incubant to bring about a change in their predicament.[9] El's incubated dream, however, is a symbolic dream, which thus makes us wonder how it could be performative. The answer to this question lies in the broader context of the narrative of El's dream divination in which it is embedded: namely, in the unique configuration of motifs by the author or scribe as he attempts to compose an incubation type-scene.[10] As is

---

[7] Cryer observes a connection in the Hebrew Bible between the literary use of divination and the legitimization or enhancement of the authority of the proponents involved in the process. Cryer, *Divination in Ancient Israel and Its Near Eastern Environment: A Socio-Historical Investigation*, JSOTSup 142 (Sheffield: JSOT Press, 1994), 322.

[8] Oppenheim first proposed that the incubation dream should be considered as the literary prototype for all accounts of ancient Near Eastern message dreams (Oppenheim, *Interpretation of Dreams*, 190). Ann Jeffers goes further to argue that the form-critical structure of the message dream may have originated in the practice of incubation. Jeffers tries to draw a pattern of an incubation scene from some of the reports that Oppenheim categorizes as message dreams (Ann Jeffers, *Magic and Divination in Ancient Palestine and Syria*, SHCANE 8 [Leiden: Brill, 1996], 134–36).

[9] Typologically, incubated dreams may be divided into three kinds. First, an incubant may have a dream that is itself curative. The deity in a dream may directly cure the incubant, who then would return home healthy the next day. Numerous testimonies were written in votive stelae in Asclepius temples in Hellenistic Greece. Second, an incubant may get a series of commands to follow in order to have a problem solved. Although there is a debate as to whether the imperative should be recognized as a performative utterance, it may be considered as such in the sense that the imperative also fits the broader concept of the performative, that is, "doing things with words." So the illocutionary meaning of the dream is to be translated into the actions by the incubant. Kirta's dream provides a case in point. Third, an incubant may receive a prophecy from a deity in a dream. The prophecy will be fulfilled if the dream is genuine. Hence, one may say even in this case that the illocutionary meaning of the dream depends on the actions of the deity. For the latter two kinds, the incubated dreams are usually message dreams, which need no interpreter.

[10] For some of these conventions, see Koowon Kim, *Incubation as a Type-Scene in the Aqhatu, Kirta, and Hannah Stories: A Form-Critical and Narratological Study of KTU 1.14 I–1.15 II, 1.17 I–II, and 1 Samuel 1:1–2:11*, VTSup 145 (Leiden: Brill, 2011), 62–87.

discussed below, El sets up an interpretive mechanism as a preparation for dream divination. The *id'* clause therefore (KTU 1.6 iii 8) elevates the interpretation of El's symbolic dream to a performative utterance, not only through the illocutionary force of informing El of Baal's being alive but also with the perlocutionary effect of making El initiate the actual process of bringing him back.[11] The symbolic reference of El's dream does not exhaust its meaning, but it also creates a structure of desires and hopes upon which to base practical endeavors to ensure Baal's return. Thus, El's dream divination, embedded within the context of the larger narrative, functions at a higher narrative order to advance the plot by creating new dynamics in the behavior of its main characters.

EL'S INCUBATION (KTU 1.6 III–VI)

The narrative of El's dream divination consists of three sections, following the conventional structural pattern of the incubation type-scene: preparation, mantic dream, and its follow-up motifs. Due to the broken state of the tablet, only one motif remains in the preparation section.[12] El's dream is a symbolic one, not a

---

[11] J. L. Austin divided what we do in uttering something into three types: locutionary, illocutionary, and perlocutionary acts. Roughly speaking, the locutionary act refers to denoting things in the world through the "literal" meaning of an utterance, that is, the meaning of the utterance which is carried by the words in the utterance. The illocutionary act refers to what the speaker intends to do with an utterance: for example, in uttering an utterance he states a fact or an opinion, confirms or denies something, makes a prediction, a promise, a request, issues an order, gives advice, names a child, swears an oath. Finally, the perlocutionary effect refers to the effect of an utterance on the hearer: for example, speakers want their opinions to be recognized, their requests to be enacted, their commands to be obeyed, and so forth. Linguists agree that perlocutionary acts are responses to the illocutions in utterances (cf. K. Allan, "Speech Act Theory: Overview," in *Concise Encyclopedia of Philosophy of Language*, ed. Peter V. Lamarque [Oxford: Pergamon, 1997], 454–66). Sanders, citing the problems of Austin's definition of a performative utterance, argues that the performative act is determined both by its social situation and by the verbal, namely, rhetorical or symbolic meaning of an utterance. Sanders, "Performative Utterances and Divine Language in Ugaritic," *JNES* 63 (2004): 166–67.

[12] In theory, the preparation section may include such motifs as the predicament of an incubant, time, place, and preparatory ritual observances. Those motifs relating to preparatory ritual observances such as the offering, the temple, nighttime, etc., may have been missing in the first place, since they are meant for human beings seeking divine help. It would be interesting, however, to ask what the predicament was that led El to resort to dream divination. For a detailed study of the incubation type-scene, see Koowon Kim, *Incubation as a Type-Scene*.

message dream as is usual in an incubation type-scene. The final section consists of two motifs: change of mood and fulfillment of the dream.

Preparatory Ritual: El Sets the Terms for Incubation (1.6 iii 1–9)

[w idʻ k mt aliyn bʻl][13]	[Then I'll know that Mighty Baʻlu is dead,]
(1) k ḫlq . zb[l bʻl . arṣ]	that the Prin[ce, master of the earth], has perished.
(2) w hm . ḥy . a[iyn . bʻl]	But if M[ighty Baʻlu] is alive
(3) w hm iṯ . zbl . bʻ[l arṣ]	and if the Prince, mast[er of the earth], exists,
(4) b ḥlm . lṭpn . il . d pid	(then) in a dream of the Gracious One, the kindly god,
(5) b ḏrt14 . bny . bnwt	In a vision of the Creator of creatures,
(6) šmm . šmn . tmṭrn	The heavens will rain down oil,
(7) nḫlm . tlk . nbtm	The wadis will run with honey.
(8) w idʻ . k ḥy . aliyn . bʻl	So I'll know that Mighty Baʻlu is alive,
(9) k iṯ . zbl . bʻl . arṣ	That the Prince, master of the earth, exists.

El Has a Dream (1.6 iii 10–13)

(10) bḥlm . lṭpn . il d pid	In a dream of the Gracious One, the kindly god,
(11) b ḏrt . bny . bnwt	In a vision of the Creator of creatures,
(12) šmm . šmn . tmṭrn	The heavens rain down oil,
(13) nḫlm . tlk . nbtm	The wadis run with honey.

---

[13] CTA restores [kmt . aliyn . bʻl], and KTU suggests the same. I add [w idʻ] to that reconstruction, seeing that that the space in that line can accommodate a few more letters as in line 8. For my literary justification of adding [w idʻ], see the discussion below.

[14] For the etymological meaning of ḏrt, see Dennis Pardee, "The Baʻlu Cycle," in *Context of Scripture*, ed. William W. Hallo (Leiden: Brill, 1997), 1:271; Mark S. Smith, "The Baal Cycle," in *Ugaritic Narrative Poetry*, ed. Simon B. Parker (Atlanta: Scholars Press, 1997), 157; N. Wyatt, *Religious Texts from Ugarit*, BibSem 53 (London: Sheffield Academic Press, 2002), 136; Manfried Dietrich and Oswald Loretz, "Mythen und Epen in ugaritischer Sprache," in *Weisheitstexte, Mythen und Epen*, ed. Wilhelm H. Ph. Römer and Wolfram von Soden, TUAT.NF 3 (Gütersloh: Gütersloher Verlagshaus, 2005), 1190; André Caquot, Maurice Sznycer, and Andrée Herdner, *Textes ougaritiques: mythes et légendes* (Paris: Cerf, 1974), 261.

Change of Mood: Declaration of Baal's Revival (1.6 iii 14–21)

(14) šmḫ . lṭpn . il . d pid	This brings joy to the Gracious One, the kindly god,
(15) pʿnh . l hdm . yṯpd	He taps his feet on the footstool
(16) w prq . lṣb . w yṣḥq	His brow unfurrows and he laughs.
(17) yšu . gh . w yṣḥ	He raises his voice and cries out:
(18) aṯbn . ank . w anḫn	(now) I can again get some rest,
(19) w tnḫ . b irty . npš[15]	my innermost being can get some rest,
(20) k ḥy . aliyn . bʿl	For mighty Baʿlu is alive,
(21) k iṯ . zbl . bl . arṣ	The Prince, master of the earth, exists.

Fulfillment: El Charts a Series of Actions to Bring Baal Back (1.6 iii 22–iv 5)

(22) gm . yṣḥ . il . l btlt	Ilu calls aloud to Girl Anatu:
(23) ʿnt . šmʿ . l btlt . ʿnt	Listen, Girl Anatu
(24) rgm . l nrt . il[m] . špš	(Go) say to Šapšu, luminary of the gods:
(iv 1) pl . ʿnt . šdm . y špš	Dried up are the furrows of the fields, O Šapšu,
(2) pl ʿnt . šdm[.]il . yštk	Dried up are the furrows of Ilu's fields,
(3) bʿl . ʿnt . mḫrṯt	Baʿlu is neglecting the furrows of the plowland.[16]
(4) iy . aliyn . bʿl	Where is Mighty Baʿlu?
(5) iy . zbl . aliyn . bʿl	Where is the Prince, master of the earth?
......	......

About 40 lines are missing at the beginning of the third column of KTU 1.6.[17] The extant context for El's dream divination is the scene of Anat killing Mot and throwing parts of his mutilated body to birds of prey (KTU 1.6 ii 30–35).[18] It is generally believed that Anat, after killing Mot, went to El and report-

---

[15] For detailed discussion of lines 14–19, see Josef Tropper, "Ugaritic Dreams Notes on Ugaritic ḏ(h)rt and hdrt," in *Ugarit, Religion and Culture: Essays Presented in Honour of Professor John C. L. Gibson*, ed. N. Wyatt, W. G. E. Watson, and J. B. Lloyd, Ugaritisch-Biblische Literatur 12 (Münster: Ugarit-Verlag, 1996), 305–14.

[16] For the discussion of this difficult passage, see Pardee, "The Baʿlu Cycle," 271 n. 62.

[17] CTA, 40; KTU, 26b, n. 1.

[18] The abandonment of corpses without burial amounts to desecration of the dead. This practice is reported several times in the Assyrian material (e.g., The Vassal-Treaties of Essarhadon, cf. SAA 2 4, 6, 15, see Simo Parpola and Kazuko Watanabe, *Neo-Assyrian Treaties and Loyalty Oaths*, SAA 2 [Helsinki: Helsinki University Press, 1988]; see also SAA online: http://oracc.museum.upenn.edu/saao/saa02/corpus) in association with bodily mutilations. Wyatt argues that Anat's failure to bury Mot's corpse is an ad-

ed on the death of Mot.[19] It is also plausible that Anat stayed with El while he undertook the dream divination, judging from the fact that immediately after his successful dream divination, El was able to address Anat without summoning her, and also from the fact that in his address to her (iv 1–5), he does not repeat the interpretation of his dream (cf. lines 20–21). It is less certain, however, whether Anat played any role in the oneiromantic procedure. Suffice it to say that the news of Anat killing Mot must have encouraged El to resort to the dream divination.[20]

Preparatory Ritual: El Sets the Terms for Incubation (1.16 iii 1–9)

In incubation narratives, the preparation scene usually includes various ritual elements, such as offering, fasting, weeping, praying, bathing, etc. All of these rituals are essential for the inducement of a favorable dream in a human being, but the preparation scene under discussion has a different purpose: it aims to set specific terms for the dreams' interpretation. This peculiarity is partly because El is not a human being but a god. Unlike other incubants (cf. Kirta or Danel) who passively wait for a favorable dream, El attempts to control not only the content of his mantic dream, but also its interpretation.[21] In describing El as having control over the anticipated dream oracle, the author's intention may have

---

umbration of Mot's resurrection later in the story. Wyatt, *Religious Texts from Ugarit*, 136 n. 85.

[19] Wyatt, *Religious Texts from Ugarit*, 136 n. 85. Gibson further argues that it is Anat who invites El to dream a dream "whereby he may discover whether Ba'lu can come back to life." See John C. L. Gibson, *Canaanite Myths and Legends* (London: T&T Clark, 2004), 17. Although some scholars, such as Gaster, speculate that it was Anat's dream, not El's, this is not likely. See Theodor H. Gaster, *The Oldest Stories in the World* (Boston: Beacon, 1952), 223. Cf. Dietrich and Loretz, "Mythen und Epen in ugaritischer Sprache," 1190 n. 37; Johannes C. de Moor, *An Anthology of Religious Texts from Ugarit*, Nisaba 16 (Leiden: Brill, 1987), 90.

[20] In Ugaritic mythology death is narrated not only as going down into Mot's underworld domain but also as descending into the throat (*npš*) of, into the stomach (*mhmrt*) of Mot. KTU 1.5 ii 2–5 narrates Baal's death in terms of his entering Mot's insides (*kbd*) after portraying Mot's mouth in the following terms: "[He puts (one) lip to the] earth, (the other) lip to the heavens, [...] (his) tongue to the stars." Thus, Anat's mutilation of Mot's body may signal a hope in Baal's revival, cf. John F. Healey, "Mot," in *Dictionary of Deities and Demons in the Bible*, ed. Karel van der Toorn, Bob Becking, and Pieter W. van der Horst (Leiden: Brill, 1999), 598–602.

[21] Although Dumuzi is another deity who was given a dream, his dream was not incubated, and he had to go to his sister to have it interpreted. Cf. Bendt Alster, *Dumuzi's Dream: Aspects of Oral Poetry in a Sumerian Myth* (Copenhagen: Akademisk Forlag, 1972), 52–83.

been to legitimize or enhance the authority of El, whose role as the arbitrator of divine family disputes becomes very important later in the story.

A binary structure characterizes El's preparation for the dream oracle. This is no surprise as divination is binary in character.[22] The preserved line that begins KTU 1.6 iii may actually be the end of the first part of the binary structure, whereas line 2 begins its second part. The complete form of El's dream divination would look like the following.[23]

[hm . mt . aliyn . bʻl	[if Mighty Baʻlu is dead
whm . ḫlq . zbl . bʻl . arṣ	and if the Prince, master of the earth, has perished,
b ḥlm . lṭpn . il . d pid	In a dream of the Gracious One, the kindly god,
b ḏrt . bny . bnwt]	In a vision of the Creator of creatures,]
[*Dream Content*]	[(then) *Dream Content*]
[w idʻ . k mt . aliyn . bʻl]	[So I'll know that Mighty Baʻlu is dead,]
k ḫlq . zb[l . bʻl . arṣ]	That the Prin[ce, master of the earth,] has perished
w hm . ḥy . a[iyn . bʻl]	if M[ighty Baʻlu] is alive
w hm iṯ . zbl . bʻ[l arṣ]	and if the Prince, mast[er of the earth], exists
b ḥlm . lṭpn . il . d pid	(then,) in a dream of the Gracious One, the kindly god,
b ḏrt . bny . bnwt	In a vision of the Creator of creatures,
šmm . šmn . tmṭrn	*The heavens will rain down oil,*
nḫlm . tlk . nbtm	*The wadis will run with honey.*
w idʻ . k ḥy . aliyn . bʻl	So I'll know that Mighty Baʻlu is alive,
k iṯ . zbl . bʻl . arṣ	That the Prince, master of the earth, exists

The dream content of the first part of the binary structure may be irrecoverable, but we may plausibly assume that it has to do with the symbol of drought, the expected consequence of the disappearance of the bringer of rains.[24] Lines 6–11 in KTU 1.5 iv enumerate the attendants who follow Baal on his way to the netherworld. Since they are all various manifestations of his powers as the bringer of rain—clouds (ʻrpt), wind (rḥ), watering devices (mdl), rain (mṭr), Pidray ("fatty, oily"), daughter of Aru ("a type of dew"), and Ṭallay ("dew"),

---

[22] Oppenheim, *Interpretation of Dreams*, 212–13. Divinatory answers come in binary terms, such as Yes/Success/Good or No/Failure/Bad. For a literary rendition of binary divination, see 1 Sam 6:7–9, especially v. 9; for similar examples from an Assyrian dream book, see Cryer, *Divination in Ancient Israel*, 117; Noegel, *Nocturnal Ciphers*, 95.

[23] Cf. Lewis, *The Interpretation of Dreams*, 16.

[24] Mark Smith says, "The missing section contains the first possible reading of nature: if the rains have not returned, then El will know that Baal remains dead." Smith, "The Baal Cycle," 157. Dietrich and Loretz also write in a similar vein, "Sollen El von einer Trockenheit träumen, so weiß sie [Anatu], daß Baal nicht mehr lebt." Dietrich and Loretz, "Mythen und Epen in ugaritischer Sprache," 1190 n. 37.

daughter of Rabbu ("shower")—one may argue that drought must be the result of his descent into the netherworld.[25]

In any event, the testing of omens by binary divination is not unknown in the Ugaritic mythological literature. For instance, in the birth myth of Šaḥru-wa-Šalimu, El comes up with a handy test for the maturity of the one with whom he is planning to mate (KTU 1.23 39–46). That divinatory test is also couched in a binary structure that is not dissimilar to the reconstructed text of El's dream divination.

hm aṯtm tṣḥn	If, (says he,) the two women cry out:
y mt mt......	O man, man....
a[t]tm aṯt il	(then) the two women (will be) the wives of Ilu,
aṯt il w ʻlmh	Ilu's wives forever.
w hm aṯtm tṣḥn	But if the two women cry out:
y ad ad.......	O father, father...
btm bt il	(then) the two daughters (will be) the daughters of Ilu,
bt il w ʻlm	Ilu's daughters forever.

A comparison between El's tests in KTU 1.23 and KTU 1.6 iii reveals two significant points about his dream divination. First, El's dream test reverses the normal relationship between protasis and apodosis in oneirocritical literature. The apodosis (the "then" clause) in lines 4–7 of KTU 1.6 iii registers the dream content, and the protasis (the "if" clause) in lines 2–3, El's dream interpretation. But in dream manuals, a dream's content is listed in the protasis, while its interpretation comes in the apodosis. El's other divinatory test in KTU 1.23 maintains this normal relationship between protasis and apodosis: the protasis concerns observational data and the apodosis its interpretation. The reversal in El's dream divination in the Baal Cycle represents a sophisticated literary strategy that brings the illocutionary effect of El's dream to the foreground of the narrative. This leads us to the second point, which entails the redundant clause headed by the first-person verb *idʻ* "I (shall) know." The reversal of the protasis and apodosis in El's dream divination in KTU 1.6 iii seems to have necessitated the repetition of what has already been said in the protasis in the *idʻ* clause. If the author or scribe had not reversed the accepted relationship between protasis and apodosis in an omen, the repetition would have been unnecessary. The fact that

---

[25] De Moor, *Anthology of Religious Texts*, 90.

El's test in KTU 1.23 is immediately followed by the motif of fulfillment[26] underscores the redundancy of the *id'* clause in El's dream divination.[27]

What, then, is the literary function of the apparently redundant *id'* clause in lines 8–9? I suggest that by inserting the *id'* clause, which repeats what is said in the protasis, the author or scribe intends to make it a quasi-performative utterance. Notably, many performative utterances are couched in the first person: for instance, "I name this ship the Queen Elizabeth"—as uttered when smashing the bottle against the bow.[28] It is also generally agreed that there is no performative utterance unless it includes "a formula containing a verb in the first person of the present."[29] The only problem with seeing *id'* as a performative verb may be its prefix form, for the grammatical form of a performative in West Semitic is assumed to be a suffix form.[30] But Sanders argues that "recently the situation has been shown to be more complex in West Semitic," and that in Ugaritic texts, "utterances perform actions with a confusing variety of linguistic forms."[31] He illustrates his point with *iqra.ilm.n'[mm]* ("I will invoke the gra[cious] god") (KTU 1.23 1) as an example. Sanders says, "while the *qra*-invocation of the gracious gods is not grammatically performative, it is performed by being nar-

---

[26] (46) *w hn attm tṣḥn y mt mt…*(48) *attm* (49) *att [il] att il w 'lmh.* "The two women do (in fact) cry out: "O man, man…The two women (become) the wives [of Ilu], Ilu's wives forever."

[27] The presence of *w* before *id'* does not necessarily indicate the beginning of the "then" clause. El's test in KTU 1.23 does not mark the beginning of the apodosis, just as El's dream divination does not. It is also worth noting that in the change of mood motif following a dream, the first-person verb *id'* disappears, turning its clausal complement "Mighty Ba'lu is alive" into an independent declaration.

[28] Sanders, "Performative Utterances," 164. Cf. J. L. Austin, *How to Do Things with Words: The William James Lectures Delivered at Harvard University in 1955*, ed. J. O. Urmson (New York: Oxford University Press, 1965), 4–5.

[29] Benveniste emphasizes self-reference ("reflexivity") as a crucial feature of a performative utterance: "a performative utterance must name the spoken performance as well as its performer… There is no performative utterance unless it contains the mention of the act." Emile Benveniste, *Problems in General Linguistics* (Miami: University of Miami Press, 1971), 327. Cited in Sanders, "Performative Utterances," 167.

[30] The biblical example is found in Gen 41:41, *nātattî 'ōtkā 'al kol- 'ereṣ miṣrāyim* "I set you over the whole land of Egypt." This speech of Pharaoh actually accomplishes the transfer of authority. Note the first-person suffix form *nātattî*. The Ugaritic example is found in KTU 1.100 75, *ytt nḥšm mhrk* "I hereby give serpents as your bride price." Note also the suffix form *ytt*. Sanders, "Performative Utterances," 167. The semantics of the verb *id'* "I know" do not disqualify the verb from being performative. Austin acknowledges the possibility of "I know" being a performative. Sanders, "Performative Utterances," 90.

[31] Sanders, "Performative Utterances," 163.

rated in the ritual."³² This seems to show that linguistic form alone is not a sufficient criterion for a performative utterance. As Sanders points out, performativity seems to be only "culturally defined, or, in linguistic terms, lexical, only becoming apparent in attested cultural contexts in which the verb is used."³³ One may apply all this to the verb *id'* in our text. What makes *id'* ("I shall know") performative is not simply its grammatical form but also its narrative role in the literary context. As a performative, the statement "I (shall) know that Mighty Ba'lu is alive, the Prince, master of the earth, exists" does not simply reference or predict the return of Baal, which is its illocutionary force; but it also creates its own narrative context by modeling an act that would result in the return of the rain-bringer onto the earth. That El sends Anat to Šapšu to bring Baal back must be understood from this perspective: it is the perlocutionary effect of El's dream omen.

El's Incubated Dream (1.16 iii 10–13)

El's incubated dream is an exaggerated image from daily life: heavens pouring oil-rains and a river flowing with honey.³⁴ It is a symbolic dream that would require interpretation, were it not for the preceding interpretive context set up by El himself. The possible relationship between El's dream and its interpretation rests on the general system of symbols, to be precise, the literary convention created by Ugaritic scribes.³⁵ The image of Baal as the bringer of rain is known not only within the Baal Cycle, but also in other Ugaritic mythological texts. Smith and Pitard write, "[t]he central importance of Ba'lu's provision of rain is quite clear through the corpus of Ugaritic texts."³⁶ The episode of building Baal's house, for instance, culminates in the moment of window-opening ("aperture," *ḥln*), which is related to Baal's function as rain-bringer (KTU 1.4 vii 25-29).

---

[32] Sanders, "Performative Utterances," 163–65.

[33] Sanders, "Performative Utterances," 177.

[34] Joseph's dreams present scenes from daily life with unrealistic touches. His first dream (Gen 37:5–7) begins with a harvest scene of Joseph and his brothers binding sheaves of grain. Then something unnatural, or even supernatural, occurs. Joseph's sheaf stands up and remains upright. In Joseph's second dream (Gen 37:9), we also find occurrences that are not natural along with naturalistic elements. For details see Bar, *A Letter*, 46–47. See also Franziska Ede's contribution to this volume.

[35] For the role of wordplay in El's dream, see Noegel, *Nocturnal Ciphers*, 109–12.

[36] Mark S. Smith and Wayne T. Pitard, *The Ugaritic Baal Cycle: Introduction with Text, Translation and Commentary of KTU/CAT 1.3–1.4*, VTSup 114 (Leiden: Brill, 2009), 15.

yptḥ ḫln bbhtm	Baʿlu opens an aperture in the house,
urbt bqrb hklm	A window amid the palace.
[yp]tḥ bʿl bdqt ʿrpt	Baʿlu opens a break in the clouds,
qlh qdš bʿ[l y]tn	Baʿlu gives vent to his holy voice.

Also in KTU 1.16 iii 4–8, the drought caused by Kirta's near-death is portrayed in terms of the lack of Baal's provision of rain.

ʿn larṣ mṭr bʿl	Look to the earth for Baʿlu's rain,
wlšd mṭr ʿly	to the field, for the Most High's rain!
nʿm larṣ mṭr bʿl	So good for the earth is Baʿlu's rain,
wlšd mṭr ʿly	and for the field, the Most High's rain!

All these demonstrate the literary connection between Baal and the provision of rain in Ugaritic literature. The image of heavens pouring long-awaited rains is related to the return of Baal. This reading of the dream within the general system of symbols at Ugarit may coincide with the possible mechanism of dream interpretation attested to in the only Ugaritic dream book. Judging from the structure of KTU 1.86, in which several items seen in a dream are combined into one common interpretation, one may presume that the interpretation rests on the general system of symbols.[37] This stands in contrast to Mesopotamian dream omens where symbolic associations as mechanisms of dream interpretation are rare.[38]

El's incubated dream is a symbolic one, unlike most others.[39] But the author or scribe makes it a quasi-performative by crafting it into the incubation narrative where its illocutionary force and perlocutionary effect become evident. As we have discussed above, El sets up an interpretive mechanism as a preparation for dream divination. The *idʿ* clause thus tinges the interpretation of El's symbolic dream with an illocutionary force, namely, a quasi-prophecy, "I shall know...." The symbolic reference of El's dream does not exhaust its performative meaning. In other words, El's dream does more than just predict Baal's re-

---

[37] "Si cela est bien le cas, la science oniromantique propre à Ougarit aurait réduit le grand nombre d'entités et de situations que comportait la science oniromantique mésopotamienne en une petite série de cas et d'interprétations typiques correspondant à chaque catégorie et sous-catégorie de ce sommaire." Dennis Pardee, *Les textes rituels*, 468.

[38] Gnuse, "The Dream Theophany of Samuel," 21.

[39] Most incubated dreams are messages dreams. This explains why scholars like Oppenheim see connection between the form-critical structure of the message dream and the practice of incubation. Of course, not all incubated dreams are message dreams. For instance, Gudea's first dream is symbolic, although it is debatable whether it is incubated or not.

turn.[40] It creates a structure of desires and hopes upon which to base practical endeavors. The motifs following El's oneiric experience are evoked to realizing this perlocutionary effect of El's dream.

Change of Mood: Declaration of Baal's Revival (1.6 iii 14–21)

After describing the climactic event of incubation, namely, the dream, the narrator may register the change of mood motif as a way of confirming the verity of the oneiric experience.[41] This motif may be a literary representation of the Mesopotamian custom of confirming the verity of dreams through other divinatory means such as extispicy.[42] The incubation type-scene in the Aqhat Epics registers Danel's change of mood among the subsequent motifs to the dream. What differentiates it from El's change of mood is the addition to the latter of the *k* clause stating the reason for the change of mood: "For Mighty Baʿlu is alive, the Prince, master of the earth, exists" (KTU 1.6 iii 20–21). Interestingly this *k* clause in the change of mood motif coincides with the clausal complement of the verb *idʿ* in lines 8–9, both interpreting El's symbolic dream. This double duty of the *k* clause—giving the reason for El's change of mood and interpreting El's symbolic dream—tinge the change of mood motif with a performative effect. This is confirmed by the fact that lines 14–19 of KTU 1.6 iii—the description of Baal's physical and psychological reactions to the dream—practically replaces the first-person verb *idʿ* "I shall know."[43] Thus, the change of mood motif may be argued to turn the *k* clause about Baal revival into a performative utterance as the verb *idʿ* does in the preparation section. By stating that Baal is alive, El is not simply giving the reason for his festive mood, but is officially declaring Baal's return. This naturally leads to the fulfillment of dream section where El initiates the chain of events that will bring Baal back into the living.

---

[40] I subscribe to Dilbert Hillers's definition of a performative utterance represented by Sanders: "[the performative] sentence does not refer to a past act but to *an action in the present* that is accomplished, at least in part, by the speaker's pronouncement of utterance under appropriate circumstances." (emphasis added) Sanders, "Performative Utterances," 166. This definition does justice both to the verbal reference of a performative and to its illocutionary effect.

[41] Kim, *Incubation as a Type-Scene*, 80.

[42] According to the Cylinder of Gudea (cyl. A xii 13–19), Gudea, after walking from his dream, turns to extispicy by killing a goat in order to confirm the verity of the oneiric message, cf. COS 2.155.

[43] Interpretive setup: If I should dream of the heavens raining down oil...then I will know (*idʿ*) that Baal is alive; Expected sequence: El dreams of the heavens raining downs oil...now he knows (*idʿ*) that Baal is alive! Actualized sequence: El dreams of the heavens raining downs oil..."Now he is happy (change of mood)" that Baʿlu is alive!

The 'Fulfillment' Section (KTU 1.6 iii 22–iv)

The fulfillment section registers the perlocutionary effect of El's dream divination. It describes the chain of events that bring back the fertility god back from the netherworld. Apparently, the defeat of Mot by Anat did not lead to the immediate revival of Baal. Although it has loosened the realm of the dead's iron grip on Baal, he still needs help in order to return to his place in Ṣapanu from where he will rule over the earth. This scenario fits well with the fact that the author or scribe renders Baal's death in two different ways: death in terms of his body falling on the ground (KTU 1.5 vi 8–9) and the same in terms of Baal's descent into the underworld (KTU 1.5 v 14–15).[44] Correspondingly, Baal's resurrection is also described both in terms of mutilating Mot's body (KTU 1.6 ii 30–35) and in terms of bringing Baal from the realm of the dead (KTU 1.6 iii–vi).

El's message to Šapšu reveals the opposite of El's oneiric symbol; the earth was suffering from severe drought. El's confident proclamation that Baal is alive is the first step to flood the parched fields with water again. This seems to intimate that El's message for Šapšu is not simply to locate the whereabouts of Baal, who had presumably been brought back to life, but to help Baal to return to Ṣapanu from where he is to rule over the earth. In this regard, it bears repeating that El's dream divination is performative and its perlocutionary effect moves the plot of the narrative forward. The import of El's dream does not merely lie in its symbolic reference to Baal's revival, but also in the act of prophetically declaring Baal's revival (illocution) so as to initiate a chain of events that would eventually bring Baal back from the realm of death (perlocution).

Conclusion

As a way of concluding this literary study of El's incubation, I would like to point out how it contributes to articulation of El's character in the narrative. El is the ultimate arbitrator of divine family disputes. The description of his dream divination gives El complete agency over the mantic process: he not only seeks a dream, but also imposes particular terms on the interpretation of his incubated dream. Moreover, El determines even the very dream he will have, since he is recognizably the deity who sends dreams to humans![45] He is thus given full con-

---

[44] Pardee, "The Ba'lu Cycle," 267 n. 30.

[45] For the argument that El is recognized as the source of dreams, see Baruch Margalit, "Studies in NW Semitics Inscriptions," *UF* 27 (1995): 210; Robert Karl Gnuse,

trol of the entire divinatory process. Furthermore, El's performative utterance, "I (shall) know that Mighty Baʿlu is alive," not only makes Baal's revival "official" but also sets in motion the narrative plot of bringing Baal back to the earth and helping Baal gain the upper hand over Mot in the final battle. Arguable, the poet deliberately composed El's dream divination at this crucial juncture of the story; it has the effect of legitimizing and enhancing the authority of El as the arbitrator of divine family disputes. El is not simply an old weakling who is threatened by younger deities. The Baal Cycle presents El as playing an important role in maintaining the balance in the conflicting interests of the divine family.[46] The scene of El's dream divination is one of the moments when El most makes his presence felt in the narrative, by taking full initiative to return nature to a state of equilibrium.

Dreams are a means of divination favored by the gods. Although one may take issues with divine ignorance ("how come the gods do not know!"), the author or scribe has all the literary liberty to describe the gods in whatever human terms that best fit the purpose of his literary work. If there are moments when even the gods do not know what to do, the question then is, how do they discover the hidden knowledge?[47] Do they resort to divination as humans do? The question becomes more pointed when even the highest god does not know. It seems strange that the highest god would resort to divination, namely, other gods' help, as if mantic information would come from yet a higher source of authority. The answer to this question may be found in the reason why the author of the Baal Cycle describes El as resorting to dream divination, rather than some other means of divination. It is partly owing to the notion that dreams may originate in the dreamer himself, a notion found, albeit in a primitive form, in ancient "wisdom" or philosophical texts. If this "subjective" notion of dreams were applied to El's dream, one might argue that dreaming is the most felicitous means of divination for him, because it prevents an ironical situation in which El turns to a source of authority higher than himself. Dream divination enables El

---

"Redefining the Elohist," *JBL* 119 (2000): 201–20. In the Kirta story, it is El who sends dream to Kirta.

[46] Smith and Pitard argue that the story of securing of El's permission to build the palace in KTU 1.3 iii–1.4 emphasizes El's status as the head of the pantheon and the patriarch of the family. The poet of the Baal Cycle is concerned with showing the value and efficacy of proper etiquette in this section, recounting both the breaches of etiquette and the resulting failure and exemplary performance of correct procedures. According to Smith and Pitard, all this underscores the status of El as the head of the divine family. Smith and Pitard, *The Ugaritic Baal Cycle*, 36.

[47] We have several attestations of one deity getting help from another deity in matters of knowledge. For instance, the Sumerian god, Dumuzi, goes to his sister and attempts to have his symbolic dream interpreted by her without success. Cf. Alster, *Dumuzi's Dream*, 52–83.

to get information from within himself. That El favors dreams as his means of divination may be one of the author's literary strategies to enhance El's authority as the highest of all gods. It may also suggest a high appreciation of mantic dreams in Ugarit and more generally in wider Levant. It would be no coincidence that all three major works of Ugaritic mythological literatures use dream incubation as a literary motif that leads to underscoring the piety or the authority of the incubants and that Ilimilku, responsible for at least two of them (the Baal Cycle and the Kirta Epic), was a diviner (*prln*) himself.[48]

BIBLIOGRAPHY

Allan, K. "Speech Act Theory: Overview." Pages 454–66 in *Concise Encyclopedia of Philosophy of Language*. Edited by Peter V. Lamarque. Oxford: Pergamon, 1997.
Alster, Bendt. *Dumuzi's Dream: Aspects of Oral Poetry in a Sumerian Myth.* Copenhagen: Akademisk Forlag, 1972.
Jeffers, Ann. *Magic and Divination in Ancient Palestine and Syria.* SHCANE 8. Leiden: Brill, 1996.
Austin, J. L. *How to Do Things with Words: The William James Lectures Delivered at Harvard University in 1955.* Edited by J. O. Urmson. New York: Oxford University Press, 1965.
Bar, Shaul. *A Letter That Has Not Been Read: Dreams in the Hebrew Bible.* Translated by Lenn J. Schramm. HUCM 25. Cincinnati: Hebrew Union College Press, 2001.
Benveniste, Emile. *Problems in General Linguistics.* Miami: University of Miami Press, 1971.
Bloch, Raymond. *La divination dans l'antiquité.* Paris: Presses universitaires de France, 1984.
Caquot, André, Maurice Sznycer, and Andrée Herdner. *Textes ougaritiqus: mythes et légendes.* Paris: Cerf, 1974.
Contenau, G. *La divination chez les assyriens et les babyloniens.* Paris: Payot, 1940.
Cryer, Frederick H. *Divination in Ancient Israel and Its Near Eastern Environment: A Socio-Historical Investigation.* JSOTSup 142. Sheffield: JSOT Press, 1994.
Dietrich, Manfried, and Oswald Loretz. "Mythen und Epen in ugaritischer Sprache." Pages 1090–316 in *Weisheitstexte, Mythen und Epen.* Edited by Wilhelm H. Ph. Römer and Wolfram von Soden. TUAT.NF 3. Gütersloh: Gütersloher Verlagshaus, 2005.
Gaster, Theodor H. *The Oldest Stories in the World.* Boston: Beacon, 1952.
Gibson, John C. L. *Canaanite Myths and Legends.* 2nd ed. London: T&T Clark, 2004.
Gnuse, Robert Karl. "The Dream Theophany of Samuel: Its Structure in Relation to Ancient Near Eastern Dreams and Its Theological Significance." PhD diss., Vanderbilt University, 1980.

---

[48] For the meaning of *prln*, see W. H. van Soldt, "*'Atn prln*, ''attā/ēnu the Diviner'," *UF* 21 (1989): 356–68.

———. *Dreams and Dream Reports in the Writings of Josephus: A Traditio-Historical Analysis*. Leiden: Brill, 1996.

———. "Redefining the Elohist." *JBL* 119 (2000): 210–20.

Healey, John F. "Mot," Pages 598–602 in *Dictionary of Deities and Demons in the Bible*. Edited by Karel van der Toorn, Bob Becking, and Pieter W. van der Horst. Leiden: Brill, 1999.

Kim, Koowon. *Incubation as a Type-Scene in the 'Aqhatu, Kirta, and Hannah Stories: A Form-Critical and Narratological Study of KTU 1.14 I–1.15 III, 1.17 I–II, and 1 Samuel 1:1–2:11*. VTSup 145. Leiden: Brill, 2011.

Lewis, Naphtali. *The Interpretation of Dreams and Portents*. Toronto: Stevens, 1976.

Margalit, Baruch. "Studies in NW Semitic Inscriptions." *UF* 27 (1995): 177–214.

de Moor, Johannes C. *An Anthology of Religious Texts from Ugarit*. Nisaba 16. Leiden: Brill, 1987.

Noegel, Scott B. *Nocturnal Ciphers: The Allusive Language of Dreams in the Ancient Near East*. AOS 89. New Haven: American Oriental Society, 2007.

Oppenheim, A. Leo. *Ancient Mesopotamia: Portrait of a Dead Civilization*. Chicago: The University of Chicago Press, 1977.

———. *The Interpretation of Dreams in the Ancient Near East: With a Translation of an Assyrian Dream-Book*. TAPS 46.3. Philadelphia: American Philosophical Society, 1956.

Pardee, Dennis. "The Ba'lu Cycle." Pages 241–73 in vol. 1 of *The Context of Scripture*. Edited by William W. Hallo. Leiden: Brill, 1997.

———. *Les textes rituels*. 2 vols. Ras Shamra-Ougarit 12. Paris: ERC, 2000.

Parpola, Simo and Kazuko Watanabe. *Neo-Assyrian Treaties and Loyalty Oaths*. SAA 2. Helsinki: Helsinki University Press, 1988.

Sanders, Seth L. "Performative Utterances and Divine Language in Ugaritic." *JNES* 63 (2004): 161–81.

Smith, Mark S. "The Baal Cycle." Pages 81–176 in *Ugaritic Narrative Poetry*. Edited by Simon B. Parker. Atlanta: Scholars Press, 1997.

Smith, Mark S. and Wayne T. Pitard. *The Ugaritic Baal Cycle: Introduction with Text, Translation and Commentary of KTU/CAT 1.3–1.4*. VTSup 114. Leiden: Brill, 2009.

van Soldt, W. H. "'*Atn prln*,' 'attā/ēnu the Diviner'." *UF* 21 (1989): 356–68.

Tropper, Josef. "Ugaritic Dreams Notes on Ugaritic *ḏ(h)rt* and *hdrt*." Pages 305–14 in *Ugarit, Religion and Culture: Essays Presented in Honour of Professor John C. L. Gibson*. Edited by N. Wyatt, W. G. E. Watson, and J. B. Lloyd. Ugaritisch-Biblische Literatur 12. Münster: Ugarit-Verlag, 1996.

Wyatt, N. *Religious Texts from Ugarit*. 2nd ed. BibSem 53. London: Sheffield Academic Press, 2002.

4
Maleness, Memory, and the Matter of Dream Divination in the Hebrew Bible

Scott B. Noegel

In this essay, I should like to bring together four topics that I contend are reciprocally illuminating for the study of dreams and dream divination in ancient Israel. The first is a relationship between gendered constructions of Israelite diviners and beliefs concerning fertility and the stigma of pollution. The second is an association of dreams with male virility. The third topic is a perceived connection between memory and masculinity. The fourth is the role of the heart as an organ for recording dreams. As I shall argue, the four topics are mutually defined by conceptions of maleness, which, in turn, inform our understanding of the Israelite dream experience, its import, and narratives concerning dreams. In particular, they combine to explain why only men dream and interpret dreams in the Hebrew Bible, unlike elsewhere in the ancient Near East, and how the heart and the phallus became competing loci for inscribing covenantal memory. I shall use the terms prophet, diviner, and mantic interchangeably.[1]

---

[1] In agreement with a number of scholars, e.g., Martti Nissinen, *References to Prophecy in Neo-Assyrian Sources*, SAA 7 (Helsinki: Neo-Assyrian Text Corpus Project; Helsinki University Press, 1980); Martti Nissinen, *Prophets and Prophecy in the Ancient Near East*, with contributions by C. L. Seow and Robert K. Ritner, WAW 12 (Atlanta: Society of Biblical Literature, 2003); Thomas W. Overholt, *Channels of Prophecy: The Social Dynamics of Prophetic Activity* (Minneapolis: Fortress, 1989); Jean-Michel de Tarragon, "Witchcraft, Magic, and Divination in Canaan and Ancient Israel," in *Civilizations of the Ancient Near East*, ed. Jack M. Sasson (New York: Scribner, 1985), 3:2070–81.

I begin with the relationship between gendered constructions of Israelite diviners and beliefs concerning fertility and the stigma of pollution. Scholars long have examined the Hebrew Bible's mantics and their social, historical, and literary contexts, but it is only in recent years that they have turned their attention to the role that conceptions of gender play in defining these contexts.[2] For example, Esther Hamori has shown that biblical portraits of female diviners often place them in non-normative roles in family structures and follow a "widespread association between childless women and access to divine knowledge."[3] This coincides with a pattern that one finds in ancient, medieval, and modern societies of female diviners as virgins, celibate, or postmenopausal. Her biblical examples of female diviners not said to have children include Miriam,[4] Deborah,[5] Huldah, Noadiah, and the wise women of Tekoa and Abel.[6] Inversely, Israelite writers typically portray male prophets in narratives as married or as otherwise part of normative family structures. Her analyses, and those of other scholars,[7] have shown that the Israelite understanding of both male and female prophets was informed largely by constructions of maleness that circumscribed prophetic

---

[2] See especially the essays collected in Deborah W. Rooke, ed., *Embroidered Garments: Priests and Gender in Biblical Israel*, HBM 25 (Sheffield: Sheffield Phoenix Press, 2009); Deborah W. Rooke, ed., *A Question of Sex? Gender and Difference in the Hebrew Bible and Beyond*, HBM 14 (Sheffield: Sheffield Phoenix Press, 2007); Ovidiu Creangă, ed., *Men and Masculinity in the Hebrew Bible and Beyond*, BMW 33 (Sheffield: Sheffield Phoenix Press, 2010); Jonathan Stökl and Corinne L. Corvalho, eds., *Prophets Male and Female: Gender and Prophecy in the Hebrew Bible, the Eastern Mediterranean, and the Ancient Near East*, AIL 15 (Atlanta: Society of Biblical Literature, 2013).

[3] Esther J. Hamori, "The Prophet and the Necromancer: Women's Divination for Kings," *JBL* 132 (2013): 829 n. 9. See also Esther J. Hamori, "Childless Female Diviners in the Bible and Beyond," in *Prophets Male and Female: Gender and Prophecy in the Hebrew Bible, the Eastern Mediterranean, and the Ancient Near East*, ed. Jonathan Stökl and Corinne L. Carvalho, AIL 15 (Atlanta: Society of Biblical Literature, 2013), 169–91.

[4] Josephus (*Ant.* 3.54) gives Hur as the name of Miriam's husband, but the Targum to 1 Chron 2:19, 4:4, and Exod. Rab. 48:3 say Hur is Miriam's son and that Miriam (also known as Ephrath) was Caleb's wife. No tradition concerning a husband for Miriam appears in the Bible.

[5] Deborah is the wife of Lappidoth (Judg 4:4), but she is not said to have children.

[6] I would add here also Samson's mother (Judg 13:2–3). We are told that she was barren when Yahweh's angel contacted her and promised her that she would have a child. The one exception to the pattern is an anonymous woman in Isa 8:3 who bears a child who serves as a portent. As Hamori observes, the account contains no prophecy, song, or speech.

[7] See, e.g., the contributions found in Stökl and Corvalho, *Prophets Male and Female*.

performance, agency, behavior, status, and identity. As Jonathan Stökl and Corinne Corvalho have put it: "Masculinity was an essential element in understanding the gender dynamics of the prophetic phenomena."[8]

While I take their observations to be axiomatic, I find it equally informative to look at these dynamics in association with beliefs concerning fertility and pollution. In his study of disability, Saul Olyan discusses fertility and the stigma of pollution in a way that bears directly upon our understanding of Israelite diviners. His summation is worth citing in full.

> Inclusion of the menstruant and the parturient among the Hebrew Bible's disabled persons also introduces a gender dimension to our discussion for a whole class of women—those of child-bearing age—are stigmatized and periodically marginalized as a result of their construction as severe polluters. Even when such women are not menstruating or giving birth, their potential to pollute and the consequent need to restrict their contact with others at regular intervals is presumably never forgotten, and so their stigmatization as potential polluters is ongoing, even if their marginalization is not. One might even argue that immature girls and postmenopausal women share this stigmatization, given that they will become/once were women of childbearing age. In contrast, males are not subject to such stigmatization as regular, severe polluters. Sexually mature males may pollute through emissions of semen, but such emissions result only in minor impurity, defiling the male, his partner, and anything the semen touches for 1 day (Lev 15:16–18); in addition, emissions of semen are potentially subject to voluntary control, in contrast to menstruation.[9]

Building on Olyan's observation of the androcentric conceptions of fertility and pollution, we may bring into focus the equally androcentric conceptions of Israelite diviners. Like women generally, female diviners carried the stigma of those who will become, or once were, severe and regular polluters. Since disability prohibited one's access to the divine, female diviners occupied a rather paradoxical and potentially liminal place in Israelite society, for they bore the possibility of blurring the boundary between the sacred and profane. Casting them as childless not only placed them in non-normative family structures, it reinforced constructions of masculinity by marking their "disability" and placing their fertility in check.[10] Thus, even if still fertile, non-childbearing women were

---

[8] Stökl and Corvalho, *Prophets Male and Female*, 6.

[9] Saul M. Olyan, *Disability in the Hebrew Bible: Interpreting Mental and Physical Differences* (Cambridge: Cambridge University Press, 2008), 59.

[10] On disability as bolstering constructed forms of masculinity, see Cheryl Strimple and Ovidiu Creangă, "'And His Skin Returned Like a Skin of a Little Boy': Masculinity, Disability, and the Healing of Naaman," in *Men and Masculinity in the Hebrew Bible and*

stigmatized as socially "infertile," and thus "disabled." Inversely, male mantics are depicted as fertile husbands and fathers who enjoy normative reproductive lives. Their opportunities to become polluters are periodic at best.

It is within this broader context of fertility, pollution, and divine access that I now should like to move to the second section of this essay and revisit the Hebrew word for "dream," i.e, חלם, the etymology for which relates not to sleep or sensory phenomena,[11] like expressions for dreaming in other ancient Near Eastern languages, but to male strength and reproductive health.[12] Essentially it means to "be strong, virile, or sexually mature."[13] The root bears this nuance in

---

Beyond, ed. Ovidiu Creangă, BMW 33 (Sheffield: Sheffield Phoenix Press, 2010), 110–26.

[11] Cf. Akkadian *šuttu* ("sleep") and *munattu* ("slumber"), both constructed with *amāru* ("to see"), *tabrît mûši* = Sumerian maš₂-gi₆ ("vision of the night"), *šubrû* ("cause to see [a dream]"), Hittite *tešḫanna* ("appear in a dream"), Egyptian *qd* ("sleep") and *mȝȝ rswt* ("see a dream"), Coptic *nw* ("sleep"), Greek ὄναρ ἰδεῖν ("see a dream"), etc. On the Akkadian *ḫiltu* as a possible exception, see n. 13 below.

[12] Notwithstanding the suggestion that the root *ḥlm* means "see," by A. Leo Oppenheim, *The Interpretation of Dreams in the Ancient Near East: With a Translation of the Assyrian Dream Book*, TAPS 46.3 (Philadelphia: American Philosophical Society, 1956), 226. The root *ḥlm* is found in Ugaritic, Hebrew, Aramaic, Arabic, Syriac, and Ethiopic. On its use in Ugaritic, see n. 17.

[13] See, e.g., Arabic حلم (*ḥalama*; "dream," "experience a seminal emission," "attain puberty," in Edward William Lane, *An Arabic-English Lexicon* [London: Williams & Norgate, 1863], 1.2:631–33 s.v. حلم). The Ugaritic root *ḥlm* also means "dream" and "be a fully grown, mature animal." See *DULAT* 361, s.v. *ḥlm* I and II. Note also the polyglot vocabulary entry *ḫu-ul-ma-tu₄* ("strength, potency, soundness") in John Huehnergard, *Ugaritic Vocabulary in Syllabic Transcription*, HSS 32 (Atlanta: Scholars Press, 1987), 125. Observe the possible similar semantic development of the Akkadian term *ḫiltu, ḫištu* ("dream"), if derived from *ḫâlu* ("seep out," "pollution [during a dream]"). See *CAD* 6:188, s.v. *ḫiltu*. The association of dreams with nocturnal emissions in Jewish tradition continued into later times, hence the existence of a stone amulet in the form of a phallus now in the possession of Museé Saint-Raymond in Toulouse. The amulet is inscribed with the words "accident of sleep" and with the biblical verse "his bow remained firm" (Gen 49:24). The amulet is noted by Joshua Trachtenberg, *Jewish Magic and Superstition: A Study in Folk Religion* (New York: Behrman's Jewish Book House, 1939), 134. On the bow as a phallic symbol, see Harry A. Hoffner, "Symbols for Masculinity and Femininity: Their Use in Ancient Near Eastern Sympathetic Magic Rituals," *JBL* 85 (1966): 327; Sandra Jacobs, "Divine Virility in Priestly Representation: Its Memory and Consummation in Rabbinic Midrash," in *Men and Masculinity in the Hebrew Bible and Beyond*, ed. Ovidiu Creangă, BMW 33 (Sheffield: Sheffield Phoenix Press, 2010), 146–70.

two biblical texts.[14] The first, in Job 39:3–4, parallels the birthing of animals with their own sexual maturity and departure from the herd.

תכרענה ילדיהן תפלחנה חבליהם תשלחנה
יחלמו בניהם ירבו בבר יצאו ולא־שבו למו

They crouch and bring forth their young, they send forth their labor pains.
Their sons become virile and multiply in the field, they go out and do not return.

The second use of חלם in this sense appears in Hezekiah's prayer following his near-death experience: ותחלימני והחיני ("and you invigorated me and you enlivened me," Isa 38:16).

Since such texts appear far from notions of dreaming, the standard dictionaries typically distinguish חלם I ("be strong, virile") from חלם II ("dream"). Yet, as Jean-Marie Husser observes, we should not divorce the two.

> We should remember that the erection of the penis is one of the physiological characteristics of paradoxical sleep at every age in life. The correlation between seeming sexual arousal and dreams may well have been established at a very early period. It could well have led to a semantic link between dreams and virility, without necessarily taking into account the sexual content of dreams.[15]

This link has remained a philological curiosity for those who have studied biblical dreams, and to my knowledge Husser never pursued this line of inquiry further.[16] Nevertheless, I contend that a connection between dreams and male

---

[14] It is possible that the verb appears with this sense also in Ps 126:1, but the passage is ambiguous. Most English translations understand כחלמים to mean "as dreamers" (e.g., Vulgate: *quasi somniantes*), though the LXX reads: παρακεκλημένοι ("comforted ones") and some manuscripts of the Vulgate read *sicut consolati*. The Targum translates: היך מרעיא דאתסיאו ממרעיהון ("like the sick who were healed of their sickness").

[15] Jean-Marie Husser, *Dreams and Dream Narratives in the Biblical World*, trans. Jill M. Munro, BibSem 63 (Sheffield: Sheffield Academic Press, 1999), 88.

[16] Ruth Fidler, *"Dreams Speak Falsely?" Dream Theophanies in the Bible: Their Place in Ancient Israelite Faith and Traditions* (Jerusalem: Hebrew University Magnes, 2005), 17–18 n. 84–85, 20 n. 96 [Hebrew], argues that the root *ḥlm* underwent a semantic development from "be strong" to "attain puberty" to "have sexual dreams" to "dream (generally)." However, such a development is unlikely given a general Near Eastern identification of sexual dreams and nocturnal emissions with demonic attacks and bewitchment. See S. A. L. Butler, *Mesopotamian Conceptions of Dreams and Dream Rituals*, AOAT 258 (Münster: Ugarit-Verlag, 1998), 54–65. Thus, below I account for the semantic overlap (not development) differently.

health and reproduction is central to the Israelite conception of the dream experience and its literary portrayal. Indeed, I aver that we can account for the connection between dreams and virility by positing that the Israelites regarded the dreams of young men as potentially divine only after they reached puberty and entered adult tribal life.[17]

In ancient tribal society, the health of the tribe was inextricably fused with each individual's ability to reproduce and contribute members to the group, as Hector Avalos observes: "The terminology and references to illness in the Bible allow one to characterize illness as a condition with visible symptoms that rendered a human being physically and/or mentally unable to fulfill the normal *social and/or physical* role assigned by society."[18] In ancient Israel, a normal social role required having a family, and so an inability to have children, for both men and women, was considered an "illness" that signaled a sort of "death" to the lineage. Thus, childlessness required healing. This is most apparent in the account of Abimelek's wife and servants, who could not bear children until Yahweh healed both Abimelek *and* the women.

וירפא אלהים את־אבימלך ואת־אשתו ואמהתיו וילדו: כי־עצר עצר יהוה בעד כל־רחם לבית אבימלך על־דבר שרה אשת אברהם

God healed Abimelek, his wife, and his female slaves, so they bore children, for Yahweh had hindered all the women in Abimelek's household from conceiving because of Abraham's wife Sarah. (Gen 20:17–18)

Healing signaled the act of restoring someone to a normal state and role in society.[19] It made them whole again. Insofar as Israelites related normality and wholeness to purity,[20] we may understand the perception of childlessness as an

---

[17] Comparative support comes from the Ugaritic corpus, which similarly restricts the dream experience (*ḥlm*) to young men. Thus, in KTU 1.14 i 40, El addresses Kirtu in his dream as a *ǵlm* ("youth"). Cf. the Arabic cognate غلم (*ġalama*; "be sexually mature, be lustful," in Lane, *An Arabic-English Lexicon*, 6.1:2286–87, s.v. غلم). In KTU 1.4 iii 4, El hopes to see signs that Baal lives in a dream. On El's virility, see KTU 1.4 iv 38–39, 1.23:30–35, and Baruch Margalit, "On Canaanite Fertility and Debauchery," in *"He Unfurrowed His Brow and Laughed": Essays in Honour of Nicolas Wyatt*, ed. W. G. E. Watson, AOAT 299 (Münster: Ugarit-Verlag, 2007), 177–92.

[18] Hector Avalos, *Illness and Health Care in the Ancient Near East: The Role of the Temple in Greece, Mesopotamia, and Israel*, HSM 54 (Atlanta: Scholars Press, 1995), 248. Italics are the author's.

[19] See Avalos, *Illness and Health Care*, 250. Cf. n. 14 above and the Targum's rendering of the root חלם in Ps 126:1.

[20] See most famously, Mary T. Douglas, *Purity and Danger: An Analysis of the Concepts of Pollution and Taboo* (London: Routledge, 1966).

illness, as manifesting purity concerns of the social body. While this concern certainly extended to women as well as men, it is males alone who become the object of reproductive concerns when dreams are involved. This is obvious in accounts of so-called "incubation dreams" that involve a promise of progeny or inheritance to men,[21] such as Jacob's dreams at Bethel (Gen 28:10–22) and at Paddan-Aram (Gen 37:10–13),[22] but it is apparent also by the dread with which dreamers understood enigmatic dreams (e.g., Gen 41:8, Dan 2:3),[23] for they had great potential for portending illness or worse. Indeed, there is more than one account of a dream portending the dreamer's death (e.g., Gen 20:3, 40:22). For this reason, enigmatic dreams required interpretation, a ritual process that we might best qualify as therapeutic or medicinal, not unlike the healing required for childlessness.[24] Thus, in Gen 41:16, Joseph explicitly associates the interpre-

---

[21] Evidence for the practice of incubation in cuneiform sources has been found at Ugarit, at Mari, and in Assyria, Babylonia, and the Hittite world, though these texts have not produced much in the way of specific ritual procedures. For Ugaritic incubation texts, see, KTU 1.14 i 20–ii 5, iii 46–49, in which Kirta asks El for descendants in a dream and is given Lady Huraya as a wife. In KTU 1.17 i 15–ii 15, Baal intercedes with El to promise Danel a son. For Akkadian exemplars, see Jean-Marie Durand, *Archives Épistolaires de Mari I/1*. ARM 26.1 (Paris: ERC, 1988), 461; Oppenheim, *Interpretation of Dreams*, 188; Annette Zgoll, "Die Welt im Schlaf sehen—Inkubation von Träumen im antiken Mesopotamien," *WdO* 32 (2002): 74–101; Alice Mouton, *Rêves hittites: Contribution à une histoire et une anthropologie du rêve en Anatolie ancienne*, CHANE 28 (Leiden: Brill, 2007). For notable exceptions from the first millennium, see Butler, *Mesopotamian Conceptions of Dreams*, 212, and Hermann Hunger, "How to Make the Gods Speak: A Late Babylonian Tablet Related to the Microzodiac," in *Studies Presented to Robert D. Biggs*, ed. Martha T. Roth et al., WCAD 2 (Chicago: Oriental Institute of the University of Chicago, 2007), 141–51. Of course, incubation practices are attested in Egypt and in the Graeco-Roman world. See Kasia Szpakowska, *Behind Closed Eyes: Dreams and Nightmares in Ancient Egypt* (Swansea: Classical Press of Wales, 2003); William V. Harris, *Dreams and Experience in Classical Antiquity* (Cambridge: Harvard University Press, 2009); Gil H. Renberg, *Where Dreams May Come: Incubation Sanctuaries in the Greco-Roman World*, RGRW 184 (Leiden: Brill, 2017).

[22] In the account at Bethel, the dream's import for male virility is underscored by God's threefold mention of Jacob's future offspring (lit. "seed," Gen 28:13, 14 [twice]).

[23] On the use of "enigmatic" over "symbolic," see Scott B. Noegel, *Nocturnal Ciphers: The Allusive Language of Dreams in the Ancient Near East*, AOS 89 (New Haven: American Oriental Society, 2007), 6–9, 274–76.

[24] The Hebrew terms used for interpreting enigmatic dreams, i.e., פשר and פתר, also mean "solve, resolve, absolve." On dream interpretation as a curative, juridical, and crisis ritual of transformation, see Noegel, *Nocturnal Ciphers*, 46–50. For an earlier discussion, see Oppenheim, *Interpretation of Dreams*, 218–20. Akkadian possesses the cognate *pašāru*. The Egyptian term is *wḥꜥ* ("loosen, untie a knot, explain"). Its Coptic form, *woh*, appears in the Sahidic translation of פותר in Gen 41:8.

tations of Pharaoh's dreams with his health and wholeness: אלהים יענה את־שלום פרעה ("God will respond with regard to Pharaoh's well-being").[25] Thus, the Israelite dream experience was intimately connected to male reproductive concerns.

Indeed, it is no accident that all of the figures said to experience a dream and/or to interpret one are men. Moreover, most of them are portrayed as in the prime of their reproductive lives or as having reproductive concerns. This is most clear with regard to Jacob, Joseph, Pharaoh's baker and cupbearer, the Midianite soldier, Solomon, Job, and Daniel.[26] Thus, Jacob's first dream occurs en route to Paddan-Aram on a quest to find a wife. Joseph was seventeen when he recounted his first dream (Gen 37:2). We are not told the ages of Pharaoh's attendants. Nevertheless, cupbearers in Egypt were valued for their youthful beauty in addition to their modesty and trustworthiness.[27] Tomb reliefs and other

---

[25] Moreover, Pharaoh's dreams portended periods of fertility and famine for Egypt. One could argue that the use of the word שלום ("well-being") here denotes notions of fulfillment by way of progeny, as is recalled by the words of Eliphaz to Job: "You will know that your tent is complete (שלום). You will visit your oasis and you will miss nothing. You will know that great is your seed (זרעך), and your progeny (צאצאיך), like the grass of the earth" (Job 5:24–25).

[26] The others include Abimelek, Laban, Pharaoh, and Nebuchadnezzar. We do not know Abimelek's age, but the author does depict him as having a sexual interest in Abraham's wife (Gen 20:3–7). When Laban has his dream, he already has grandchildren (Gen 31:24, 28). Nevertheless, he makes clear that claims of progeny and inheritance are at stake, for as he tells Jacob: "The women are my daughters, the children are my children" (Gen 31:43). We are told of Pharaoh's birthday, but not his age (Gen 40:20). Proposing an age for Nebuchadnezzar is inherently difficult, because of the fictive nature of the story and the distinct possibility that it conflates Nebuchadnezzar's life with that of Nabonidus (Dan 5:20–21). Yet, even if we take the story at face value (i.e., Dan 2:1), then Nebuchadnezzar's dream in the second year of his reign would make him thirty-one years old, young enough to produce children. Nebuchadnezzar II was born in 634 BCE, and he ascended the throne in 605 BCE.

[27] See, e.g., William Kelly Simpson, "A Relief of the Royal Cup-Bearer *Tja-wy*," *BMB* 71 (1973): 69–82. Instructive too is the existence of a cosmetic box containing ointments and a mirror belonging to the cupbearer Kemeni now at the Metropolitan Museum of Art (no. 26.7.1438). Throughout the Near East, cupbearers were young and selected for their beauty. Tobit 1:22 states that the cupbearer Achiacharus was Tobit's nephew. Since Tobit describes himself as young (1:4), his nephew also is likely young. Josephus too describes Herod's cupbearer in terms of his youthful beauty (*Ant.* 16.8.1). Compare Greek and Roman mythology, in which Hebe (= Roman Juventa), the goddess of youth, served as cupbearer to the gods (*Il.* 5.1–5). See also Ganymede (= Roman Catamitus), whom Homer describes as the most beautiful mortal whom Zeus abducted to become his eternal cupbearer (*Il.* 20.232).

pictorial remains of head bakers also show them to be young.²⁸ The Midianite soldier too must be relatively young to be of fighting age.²⁹ When Solomon had his dream (1 Kgs 3:5–14), he was still a נער ("youth," 1 Kgs 3:7). Indeed, he is not explicitly labeled "old" until after he had acquired seven hundred wives and three hundred concubines (1 Kgs 11:4). Job was certainly not a young man, though not as old as his friends (Job 15:10, 32:6), but the loss of his entire family renewed his reproductive needs, as the addition of seven sons and three daughters at the tale's end demonstrates (Job 42:13).³⁰ Daniel's age is unknown, but when the chief official saw he was not eating the food prepared for him, he asked, "Why should he (i.e., the king) see you looking worse than the other young men (הילדים) your age?" (Dan 1:10).³¹ Such evidence further supports the notion that the Hebrew חלום denotes a dream experience that bears directly on the virility and reproductive abilities of a male dreamer.³²

---

²⁸ See, e.g., the images of the royal bakery in the mastaba of Ti at Saqqara and that of Ramesses III in the Valley of the Kings. Depictions of non-royal bakeries too, like that in the tomb of Khnumhotep and Niankhkhnum at Saqqara, and in various Middle Kingdom models, show the work to be grueling, and thus performed primarily by young men. For a treatment of artistic remains of bakeries unrestricted to period, see H. Wild, "Brasserie et panification au tombeau de Ti," *BIFAO* 64 (1966): 95–120.

²⁹ Num 1:3 states that an Israelite soldier must be twenty years of age or older. Presumably military practices were not that different in Midian.

³⁰ Eliphaz states that he and the friends are older than Job's father (Job 15:10). For Job's frightening dreams, see Job 7:14. He lived until he was 140 (Job 42:16). Note too that Job makes reference to his hope for future virility by way of a metaphoric use of the term "bow" (Job 29:20). On this, see Shalom Paul, "The Shared Legacy of Sexual Metaphors and Euphemisms in Mesopotamian and Biblical Literature," in *Sex and Gender in the Ancient Near East: Proceedings of the Forty-Seventh Rencontre Assyriologique Internationale, Helsinki, July 2–6, 2001*, ed. Simo Parpola and Robert M. Whiting (Helsinki: The Neo-Assyrian Text Corpus Project, 2002), 493–94.

³¹ The term appears again in Dan 1:15, 17. The word ילד need not refer to a small child, for it also can be used of a young man (e.g., 1 Kgs 12:8). If the figure whom Ezekiel mentions is our Daniel, and not the Danel known from Ugaritic texts, then he also is said to have children (Ezek 14:20).

³² The account of Abram's oneiric experience in Gen 15:12–15 states that Yahweh promised him future progeny, though it never employs the term חלום. Instead, we read: "and a deep-sleep (תרדמה) fell upon Abram" (Gen 15:12), and it is during this sleep that Yahweh spoke to him. Gen 12:4 informs us that Abram was seventy-five years old when he left Harran. I suggest that Israelite authors distinguished between חלום and תרדמה when conveying a dream experience, associating the latter with older men. Daniel twice employs the verbal form of the root רדם ("sleep") when describing angelic visits (Dan 8:18, 10:9). However, in both cases his slumber takes place within the context of a vision (חזון and מראה respectively), and not as a prelude to the vision. Of course, the term תרדמה does not always denote a dream experience, but rather simply a divine sleep dur-

Moreover, even the passages that employ the verb חלם I, "be strong, virile" refer solely to young males.[33] Note that Job 39:3–4, cited above, refers only to the young male offspring, and that the description of Hezekiah's invigoration in Isa 38:16 follows upon his explicit query concerning his own youth: בדמי ימי אלכה ("Must I go in the prime of my life?" Isa 38:10).

The connection of both חלם I and חלם II to male virility explains why biblical texts accord divine dreams and an ability to interpret them only to men,[34] despite the presence of female prophets in Israel and a wealth of comparative

---

ing which a dream might or might not occur. Thus, God lays a תרדמה on Adam (Gen 2:21) and on Saul and his men (1 Sam 26:12), but their experiences do not include dreams. In fact, Isa 29:10 associates a רוח תרדמה ("spirit of sleep") not with a theophoric experience, but with closing the eyes of prophets and covering the heads of seers. The only other figure who associates a תרדמה with dreaming is Eliphaz, who tells Job: "A word was stolen to me, my ear took a whisper from it. Amid disquieting visions of night, when deep sleep (תרדמה) falls upon men" (Job 4:12–13). We do not know Eliphaz's age, but in Job 32:4, Elihu regards him as one of the elders (i.e., זקנים). Further, the text makes Eliphaz the first respondent, thus portraying him as the eldest of Job's friends by deference. Moreover, Elihu addresses Job's friends as ישישים ("elderly men," Job 32:6). Elihu also refers to a תרדמה in Job 33:15, but not as a personal experience. On Job 4:12–13 as a reference to oneiric punning, see Noegel, *Nocturnal Ciphers*, 185–87.

[33] This is also the case in Ugaritic texts in which we find *ḥlm* II ("be sexually mature"). *DULAT* 361, s.v. *ḥlm*.

[34] Moreover, this generally holds true for Hellenistic Jewish texts as well. Out of the nearly one hundred dreams mentioned in this corpus, only five belong to women: Miriam (Liber antiquitatum biblicarum 9.10), Rebecca (Jub. 27:1, 35:6), Glaphyra (*Ant.* 17.349–53), Stratonica (Josephus, *Against Apion* 1.206–207), and the wife of Pontius Pilate (Matt 27:19). Interestingly, each of the portraits casts a negative light upon the female dreamer, as observed by Frances Flannery-Dailey, *Dreamers, Scribes, and Priests: Jewish Dreams in the Hellenistic and Roman Eras*, JSJSup 90 (Leiden: Brill, 2004), 120–21. With regard to Rebecca's dream in Jub. 27:1, I note that it also constitutes an exegetical gloss on Gen 27:41–42. In the latter text, the narrator informs us that Jacob had considered fratricide "in his heart," but that Rebecca learned of his plans. The Jubilees account explains how she obtained the information by placing it in a dream. In any event, each of the aforementioned dreams represents Graeco-Roman influence. Indeed, one can find many more references to women dreaming in Graeco-Roman literature generally, e.g., Penelope (*Od.* 19.535–53), Atosa (Aeschylus, *Persae* 176–230), Clytaemnestra (Aeschylus, *Choephori* 32–36, 526–54; Sophocles, *Elektra* 417–20), Iphigenia (Euripides, *Iphigeneia at Tauris* 42–45), Polycrates's daughter (Herodotus, *Histories* 1.209), Agarista (Herodotus, *Histories* 6.131), and Perpetua (*Passio Sanctarum Perpetuae et Felicitatis* 4), to name a few. See Patricia Cox Miller, *Dreams in Late Antiquity: Studies in the Imagination of a Culture* (Princeton: Princeton University Press, 1994); Robert K. Gnuse, *Dreams and Dream Reports in the Writings of Josephus: A Traditio-Historical Analysis*, AGAJU 36 (Leiden: Brill, 1996).

evidence for female dream interpreters in Syria and Mesopotamia.³⁵ Again, I contend that we can explain the connection between dreams and male virility by positing that the Israelites regarded the dreams of young men as potentially meaningful only after they reached puberty.³⁶

This brings me to the third portion of this study, on the perceived connection between memory and masculinity. Here again, an androcentric conception of female fertility informs the context. As Baruch Levine observes, the Israelite view represents "an appropriation of the mother's status by the father. The mother, and her 'belly' belong to the father; her womb and what grows in it have become his 'fruit'."³⁷ Moreover, female fertility, like that of crops and livestock, was considered a blessing that God bestowed upon those who kept his covenant (Exod 23:25–26; Deut 7:14–15, 28:1–24; Ps 127:3), and since the covenant was memorialized in flesh by way of circumcision, the covenant represented what Deborah Rooke has called "God's claim over the ordinary Israelite male's fertility."³⁸ In addition, the blessing of fertility, the covenant, and its memory be-

---

³⁵ The great majority of recorded dreams in Mesopotamian literature and omen texts also occur to males, though some female dreamers are known. See Butler, *Mesopotamian Conceptions of Dreams*, 17–19; Annette Zgoll, *Traum und Welterleben im antiken Mesopotamien: Traumtheorie und Traumpraxis im 3.–1. Jahrtausend v. Chr. als Horizont einer Kulturgeschichte des Träumens*, AOAT 333 (Münster: Ugarit-Verlag, 2006).

³⁶ Seeing the root חלם in this context lends greater nuance to Joel's famous prophecy: אשפוך את־רוחי על־כל־בשר ונבאו בניכם ובנותיכם זקניכם חלמות יחלמון בחוריכם חזינות יראו ("I shall pour out my spirit on all flesh, and your sons and your daughters shall prophesy, your old men shall dream dreams, your young men will see revelations," Joel 3:1). This passage has received much attention, especially by scholars of Christianity, since it is quoted in Acts 2:17 as a prediction of the Pentecost experience. However, in the light of the evidence gathered here, we may read Joel's prophecy as even more novel than hitherto recognized. We may see it as proclaiming a future in which, contrary to societal norms, it is the old men, and not solely those in the prime of their reproductive lives, who will dream divine dreams. Indeed, the words "all flesh," imply that, previous to the prophecy's fulfillment, reception of the spirit was selective, and since prophesying women already existed in Israel, the selection must be based on age and not gender. Note too that while Yahweh promises to impart prophecy to males and females alike, both dreams and revelations apparently will remain exclusively male experiences.

³⁷ Baruch A. Levine, "'Seed' versus 'Womb': Expressions of Male Dominance in Biblical Israel," in *Sex and Gender in the Ancient Near East: Proceedings of the Forty-Seventh Rencontre Assyriologique Internationale, Helsinki, July 2–6, 2001*, ed. Simo Parpola and Robert M. Whiting (Helsinki: The Neo-Assyrian Text Corpus Project, 2002), 340.

³⁸ Deborah W. Rooke, "Breeches of the Covenant: Gender, Garments and the Priesthood," in *Embroidered Garments: Priests and Gender in Biblical Israel*, ed. Deborah W. Rooke, HBM 25 (Sheffield: Sheffield Phoenix Press, 2009), 30.

came the privilege of men, as Ilona Rashkow explains: "The Hebrew Bible posits the human penis as the explicit, emblematic and exclusive symbol of religious identity and membership of the communal order. Thus, the penis symbolizes the special link between the society's God and the (male) members of the community."[39]

Moreover, the connection between maleness and memory is not only socially constructed, it is etymological: the words "male" (i.e., זָכָר) and "remember" (i.e., זָכַר) are cognates (both derive from Proto-Semitic *dkr*).[40] Indeed, in the Bible, it is men who typically remember, who are remembered, who erect memorials, and for whom such memorials are erected.[41] Thus, with regard to Joshua's erecting of memorial stones, Ovidiu Creangă remarks:

> The verticality of these commemorative monuments constructs a phallic symbol representing Joshua's masculinity. The idea that masculinity and public commemoration are linked is reinforced by physical monuments. Conversely, physical erasure of memory as a result of complete destruction enters the domain of the 'feminine.'[42]

---

[39] Ilona N. Raskow, *Taboo or Not Taboo: Sexuality and the Family in the Hebrew Bible* (Minneapolis: Fortress, 2000), 75.

[40] See Athalya Brenner, *The Intercourse of Knowledge: On Gendering Love, Desire and "Sexuality" in the Hebrew Bible* (Leiden: Brill, 1997), 11–13.

[41] As a gendered male, God too takes an active role in memorializing his covenant. See Thomas Edward McComiskey, "זָכַר," *TWOT* 1:241–43. On the role of women in memorializing events in song, see Carol L. Meyers, "Miriam the Musician," in *A Feminist Companion to Exodus to Deuteronomy*, ed. Athalya Brenner, FCB 6 (Sheffield: Sheffield Academic Press, 1994), 207–30. For a change in this pattern, see Ovidiu Creangă, "The Silenced Song of Victory: Power, Gender, and Memory in the Conquest Narrative of Joshua (Joshua 1–2)," in *A Question of Sex? Gender and Difference in the Hebrew Bible and Beyond*, ed. Deborah Rooke, HBM 14 (Sheffield: Sheffield Phoenix Press, 2007), 106–23.

[42] Creangă, "The Silenced Song of Victory," 117. On the memorials, see Josh 4:7, 23–24; 7:26; 8:29; 10:27. For texts describing the removal of someone from memory as textual erasure, see Yahweh's command to Moses: "Write this remembrance (זכרון) on a text (בספר) and put (it) in the ears of Joshua, for I verily will erase (מחה אמחה) the memory (זכר) of Amalek from beneath the heavens" (Exod 17:14). See also his remark: מי אשר חטא־לי אמחנו מספרי ("Whoever sins against me, I will erase him from my text," Exod 32:33). Such pronouncements constitute standard curse formulae attested elsewhere, see, e.g., *CAD* 12:249–51, s.v. *pašāṭu* ("efface, erase"). Often these curses include statements concerning one's lack of progeny, thus equating the extension of one's name after death with their offspring. Cf. the losses of the evildoer in Job 18:7–19, which include lack of virility, loss of progeny, and removal from social memory. On the destruc-

It is in this light that we should see Absalom's memorial:

ואבשלם לקח ויצב־לו בחיו [בחייו] את־מצבת אשר בעמק־המלך כי אמר אין־לי בן בעבור
הזכיר שמי ויקרא למצבת על־שמו ויקרא לה יד אבשלם עד היום הזה

And Absalom took and erected to himself, while he was alive, a standing-stone, which is in the Valley of the King, for he said, "I have no son so that he might invoke my name," and he called the standing-stone by his name, and it is called the "hand" of Absalom to this day. (2 Sam 18:18)[43]

The androcentric conception of memory is made apparent in the very name for the memorial, for the "hand" is a euphemism for the penis.[44] Thus, just as

---

tion of texts as ritual acts of power, see Scott B. Noegel, "The Ritual Use of Linguistic and Textual Violence in the Hebrew Bible and Ancient Near East," in *State, Power, and Violence*, ed. Margo Kitts et al., RDSR 3 (Wiesbaden: Harrassowitz, 2010), 33–46.

[43] According to 2 Sam 14:27, Absalom had three sons and a daughter. Since they are unnamed, unlike his daughter Tamar, commentators have assumed they died young. For the various scholarly views, see P. Kyle McCarter, *2 Samuel*, AB 9 (Garden City: Doubleday, 1984), 407. The rite of erecting a stone also appears in Ugaritic texts as one of the duties of an ideal son (KTU 1.17 i 26–34). See Theodore J. Lewis, *Cults of the Dead in Ancient Israel and Ugarit*, HSM 39 (Atlanta: Scholars Press, 1989), 54. R. Gordis, "A Note on the Meaning of יד," *JBL* 62 (1943): 341–44, proposes we read the word יד in the expression יד ושם as "offspring." Sara Japhet, "יד ושם (Isa. 56.5): A Different Proposal," *Maarav* 8 (1992): 69–80, argues that it means "share, portion." Sandra Jacobs, *The Body as Property: Physical Disfigurement in Biblical Law*, LHBOTS 582 (New York: T&T Clark, 2014), 154–78, sees the expression as symbolically representing a man's "name and seed."

[44] The word "hand" means "penis" also in Isa 57:8; Jer 5:31, 50:15; and in Ugaritic texts (KTU 1.4 iv 38–39, 1.23:30–35). For the Hebrew "hand" as "phallic monument," see 1 Sam 15:12 (Saul), 2 Sam 8:3 (David), Isa 56:5 (eunuchs deprived of sons), and Ezek 21:24. See M. Delcor, "The Special Meaning of the Word יד in Biblical Hebrew," *JSS* 12 (1967): 230–44; Paul, "Sexual Metaphors," 491; Stefan Schorch, *Euphemismen in der Hebräischen Bibel*, OBC 12 (Wiesbaden: Harrassowitz, 1999), 127–29. In addition to employing the term "hand" for phallus, I note that the word זכרונך ("your monument") in Isa 57:8 is an allusion to "penis/male." Note similarly that cuneiform lexical traditions show that the root *zakāru* can mean "penis" in addition to "male," "memory," and "image, replica, or concept" (i.e., gi-iš uš = *zi-ka-ru*, *i-šá-ru*, *re-ḫu-ú*, a₂ = *idu* ii 34–36, *CAD* 7:226, s.v. *išaru*). See *CAD* 21:16–22, s.v. *zakāru* A; 112–16, s.v. *zikru* A; 116, s.v. *zikru* B. Bolstering the evocative use of "memorial" and "hand" in Isa 57:8 is the verb גלית meaning "you have departed," which can suggest the "uncovering" of clothing, and the verb ותעל ("you have gone up"), which can mean "you have had sex" (e.g., Gen 31:10, 12; 49:4). Moreover, the expression ותכרת־לך מהם ("you have made a covenant with them"), used in conjunction with reference to the "hand," naturally evokes the rite of

one inscribes one's memory on a stone phallus, so does God inscribe the memory of his covenant on the male member.[45]

Masculinity and memory also combined in the practice of oath taking. Though the exact details of the gesture that accompanied oaths have been debated, it is clear that they involved one man touching, holding, or placing a hand near another man's testicles, which are euphemistically referred to as a "thigh" (Gen 24:2–3, 9; 47:29). Scholars have opined that the act established the power relationship between the two parties,[46] while symbolically threatening the lesser party with sterility or the extinction of his offspring should he dishonor the oath.[47] Thus, male genitalia bore the mark of the divine covenant and served to memorialize the promise of its fulfillment.[48] Indeed, the Israelites well anticipated the later rabbinic correlation between memory and masculinity described by Elliot Wolfson:

---

circumcision, especially when considered in the light of זכרונך at the end of the first stich (cf. Ezek 16:17).

[45] Cf. Jacob's erection of a standing stone (מצבה) following his dream (Gen 28:18). The Ugaritic tale of Aqhat also includes the erection of a stone of an ancestral god as a ritual following an apparent incubation (KTU 1.17 i 44). It is tempting to see the מצבה as phallic in shape and import. Nevertheless, the types of standing stones found in the archaeological record are more diverse. See Ziony Zevit, *The Religions of Ancient Israel: A Synthesis of Parallactic Approaches* (London: Continuum, 2001), 256–62; Elizabeth Bloch-Smith, "Will the Real *Massebot* Please Stand Up: Cases of Real and Mistakenly Identified Standing Stones in Ancient Israel," in *Text, Artifact, and Image: Revealing Ancient Israelite Religion*, ed. Gary Beckman and Theodore J. Lewis, BJS 346 (Providence: Brown University Press, 2006), 64–79.

[46] The link between virility and power perhaps is best seen in the term און, which means both "generative power, virility" and "physical strength." Indeed, male offspring are described as the strength of the father (e.g., Gen 49:3; Deut 21:17), and Job 40:16 locates this strength in the loins.

[47] See John H. Elliott, "Deuteronomy 25:11–12 and Biblical Euphemism," in *Ancient Israel: The Old Testament in Its Social Context*, ed. Philip F. Esler (Minneapolis: Augsburg Press, 2006), 161–76; Meir Malul, "More on the *Paḥad Yiṣḥāq* (Genesis XXXI 42, 53) and the Oath by the Thigh," *VT* 35 (1985): 192–200; R. David Freedman, "'Put Your Hand Under My Thigh'—The Patriarchal Oath," *BAR* 2.2 (1976): 3–4, 42; Howard Eilberg-Schwartz, *God's Phallus and Other Problems for Men and Monotheism* (Boston: Beacon Press, 1994), 110–16. For an exemplar from Mesopotamia, see Meir Malul, "Touching the Sexual Organs as an Oath Ceremony in an Akkadian Letter," *VT* 37 (1987): 491–92. The practice is fossilized in the etymological relationship between "testimony" and "testes," via Latin *testis*, "a witness or evidence of virility." The rabbis later understood the act to be that of circumcision (Gen. Rab. 59:8).

[48] Circumcision also came to mark legitimate possession and ownership. See Jacobs, *The Body as Property*, 28–67.

The special relationship that pertains between the two is suggested by the symbolic identification of the *membrum virile* as the seat of memory. This connection is based ... on a word play between *zakhor*, "to remember," and *zakhar*, "masculine." The play on words suggests an ontological connection between masculinity and memory, that is, that which most singularly marks the male Jew, the circumcised penis, which bears the scar that affords him access to the site of memory in the Godhead.[49]

Moreover, the interconnectedness has its roots in the origin of circumcision as an ancient fertility rite. As a number of scholars have argued, among the world's peoples who still practice circumcision, it primarily is performed at puberty or just before marriage.[50] This fits well the narrative of Gen 17, which depicts circumcision as a fertility rite aimed to guarantee the "semen/seed" of the obedient.[51] As Howard Eilberg-Schwartz espies:

---

[49] Elliot R. Wolfson, "The Cut that Binds: Time, Memory, and the Ascetic Impulse," in *God's Voice from the Void: Old and New Studies in Bratslav Hasidism*, ed. Shaul Magid (Albany: State University of New York Press, 2002), 105. See also Elliot R. Wolfson, "Re/Membering the Covenant: Memory, Forgetfulness and the Construction of Identity in the Zohar," in *Jewish History and Jewish Memory: Essays in Honor of Yosef Haim Yerushalmi*, ed. Elishiva Carlebach, John M. Efron, and David N. Myers (Hanover: Brandeis University Press, 1998), 226; Elliot R. Wolfson, "Circumcision, Vision of God and Textual Interpretation: From Midrashic Trope to Mystical Symbol," in *Circle in the Square: Studies in the Use of Gender in Kabbalistic Symbolism*, ed. Elliot R. Wolfson (New York: State University of New York Press, 1995), 30.

[50] For a convenient discussion and bibliography, see Eric K. Silverman, "Anthropology and Circumcision," *ARA* 33 (2004): 419–45. For the evidence from Ugarit, see N. Wyatt, "The Pruning of the Vine in KTU 1.23," *UF* 24 (1992): 403–24.

[51] The term "seed/semen" (זרע) bears the positive meaning "offspring" in Gen 17:7 (twice), 8, 9, 10, 12, 19. Note the relevant observation of Tarja S. Philips, "Gender Matters: Priestly Writing on Impurity," in *Embroidered Garments: Priests and Gender in Biblical Israel*, ed. Deborah W. Rooke, HBM 25 (Sheffield: Sheffield Phoenix Press, 2009), 48: "Only in Leviticus 12 is circumcision mentioned in the context of impurity, but not the impurity of semen, rather of the parturient's bleeding, thus contrasting in this context impure female blood with fertile male seed."

The connection between circumcision and fertility explains why some commentators have been confused over whether circumcision is the covenant or simply a symbol of it.... Circumcision is a symbol that God will make Abraham fruitful and multiply. At the same time, circumcision is also a fulfillment of that promise since the removal of the foreskin symbolically readies the organ for reproduction.[52]

Based on comparative evidence, Michael Fox similarly argues that in Israel "circumcision was originally and essentially a fertility device associated with puberty and marriage."[53] He bolsters his arguments, *inter alia*, by discussing Gen 34, in which circumcision was required for marriage into the tribe, and Exod 4:24–26, in which the circumcised is called a "bridegroom of blood." He concludes that only in later times did the Israelite priesthood downplay the fertility aspect of circumcision and move the rite from puberty to birth: "Circumcision was preparation for the most important aspect of this turn in the life cycle—reproduction."[54]

If this view is correct, and I contend it is, we are left with a remarkable correlation between the Israelite conception of dreams and the original rite of circumcision. Both marked male virility, the time of puberty and/or marriage, and adult membership in the tribe.[55] The correlation is not fortuitous, for otherwise it would be difficult to explain how one could obtain access to divine knowledge before entering God's covenant.[56] Later, when the ritual of circumcision was moved to the eighth day of life, this correlation was lost, but the tradition that only adult males could receive divine dreams and/or interpret them remained.[57]

---

[52] Howard Eilberg-Schwartz, *The Savage in Judaism: An Anthropology of Israelite Religion and Ancient Judaism* (Bloomington: Indiana University Press, 1990), 148.

[53] Michael V. Fox, "The Sign of the Covenant: Circumcision in the Light of the Priestly 'Ôt Etiologies," *RB* 81 (1974): 591. Suggested also by Jack M. Sasson, "Circumcision in the Ancient Near East," *JBL* 85 (1966): 473–76, who proposes that the practice was in place in Canaan already in the Early Bronze Age, ca. 3200 BCE.

[54] Fox, "The Sign of the Covenant," 593.

[55] I note that the rituals of dream interpretation and circumcision were viewed similarly in later times as acts of performative power that made one whole, the former by (re)solving the divine enigma (Noegel, *Nocturnal Ciphers*, 235–51), and the latter by perfecting the human body (see, e.g., Gen. Rab. 42:3, 46:4, 55:4).

[56] According to Gen. Rab. 47:10, 48:2, circumcision was a prerequisite to theophany.

[57] Moreover, though adult male foreigners can receive divine dreams in the Bible, it takes an Israelite male to interpret them. In Judg 7:14, it is a Midianite who suggests the import of his friend's dream, but significantly, the text never uses the word "interpret" (cf. Gen 40:8, 41:15; Dan 2:16). Nevertheless, it does offer clues to its interpretation. See Noegel, *Nocturnal Ciphers*, 141–46. The case of Abimelek of Gerar is more complicated.

Nevertheless, unlike the memory of circumcision, which was inscribed externally on the phallus and which served to memorialize the covenant, God inscribed dreams internally on another human organ—the heart.[58]

This brings me to my fourth and final section on the role of the heart as an organ for recording dreams. In my monograph *Nocturnal Ciphers*,[59] I examined the Israelite conception of dreams within the context of shared Mesopotamian and Egyptian notions of words, signs, and scripts as tools of illocutionary power. I showed that Israelite literati, like their Near Eastern counterparts, understood a word not merely as a referent, representation, or signifier of an object, but as that object itself in the concentrated form of a word.[60] In essence, the dream as a דבר was both "word" and "object."[61] I also observed that, much like omens in the

---

Genesis 20 depicts him as a Yahwist. He converses with Yahweh in his dream and Yahweh saves him from "sinning" against him (21:6). Since Gen 26:1 identifies him as a king of the Philistines, it would appear that the pattern is not entirely uniform. On the other hand, the text is widely regarded as anachronistic, and even Philistines engaged in circumcision during the monarchy. See Avraham Faust, "The Bible, Archaeology, and the Practice of Circumcision in Israelite and Philistine Societies," *JBL* 134 (2015): 273–90.

[58] Note similarly the view of Husser, *Dreams and Dream Narratives*, 89, who likens Israelite dreams to a place or organ: "More precisely, *ḥălôm* describes the framework in which something takes place. This happening occurs 'in a dream', as if the latter were an objective reality, a space, or an organ, in which something is likely to happen. On the other hand, when it comes to 'telling a dream' ... the hallowed expression *spr (ʾt) ḥlwm* assumes that *ḥălôm* refers to the contents themselves of the oneiric experience." I agree that dreams have a location, but I specify the organ as the heart of the dreamer onto which God inscribes his words.

[59] Noegel, *Nocturnal Ciphers*. See similarly the remark of Husser, *Dreams and Dream Narratives*, 124, "We should be careful about using the term *theophany*, for, contrary to the standard definition of the phenomenon, oneiric manifestations of God are in this context not accompanied by visual images. The recurrent use of verbs like 'to come' (*bwʾ*), 'to stand beside' (*nṣb*, *htyṣb*), 'to appear' (*nrʾh*), seems to describe not so much a visual perception as the sensation of a presence, or a sense of the nearness of the divinity. An oneiric theophany in the Old Testament, is a *theophany without vision* of God." Italics are the author's.

[60] Recently, I have argued that the belief in the illocutionary power of signs derived from perceiving them as miniature embodiments of the objects they represent. See Scott B. Noegel, "Scale Scriptitious: The Concentration of Divine Power in the Ancient Near East," in *The Miniature and the Minor in the Ancient Greek, Roman, and Near Eastern Worlds: An Interdisciplinary Investigation*, ed. Jonathan L. Ready (forthcoming).

[61] Thus, when Abimelek awakes from his dream, the narrator refers to his experience as follows: "And he related all these matters/words (הדברים) in their ears, and they were exceedingly afraid" (Gen 20:8). Similarly, when Joseph angered his brothers by relating his dreams, we are told: "But his father kept the matter/word" (הדבר; Gen 37:11). Note also that after Pharaoh relates his enigmatic dream to Joseph, he is told: "This is the

various ancient Near Eastern compendia, literary accounts of dream divination often demonstrate that interpretations were based on the dream as if it had been put into writing. I thus demonstrated that a dream had the ontological status of a text.[62]

As a number of texts show, the human heart was considered the seat of one's memory.[63] Thus, Jeremiah could say of the ark of the covenant: ולא יעלה על־לב ולא יזכרו־בו ("it will no longer arise upon the heart, and (so) they will no longer remember it," Jer 3:16).[64] Since dreams required one's memory to recall them, they too were naturally conceived as texts inscribed upon the heart. Thus, Jeremiah refers to the heart as a locus for dreams in his denunciation of prophets who falsify their interpretations: עד־מתי היש בלב הנבאים נבאי השקר ונביאי תרמת לבם ("how long will this be in the heart of the prophets who prophesy falsehood, and the prophets of the deceit of their heart," Jer 23:26)?[65] Note similarly that when Daniel tells Nebuchadnezzar that God will interpret his dreams, he identi-

---

word/matter (הדבר) that I spoke to Pharaoh: God is showing Pharaoh what he is doing" (Gen 41:28). Note similarly the view of Husser, *Dreams and Dream Narratives*, 89–89, that a vision "never designates a vision as such, but rather a 'revelation,' the 'vision' of God's word. In spite of the primary meaning of *ḥzh*, therefore, when *ḥᵉlôm* and *ḥāzôn* exist in parallel, it is not so much in order to underline the visual character of the dream, as to draw attention to the capacity that the dreams have of making extra-sensorial perceptions during sleep." The veracity of Husser's observation is apparent in Job 33:15–16: "In dreams, a vision of the night, when deep sleep falls upon men, while they slumber upon a bed. Then I shall reveal (to) the ears of men and seal their instruction." Note how, despite the mention of ears, the dream's contents are not said to be "spoken" or "heard," but rather "revealed" (יגלה). See also how Daniel received word of Nebuchadnezzar's dreams: "In a vision of the night (the) mystery was revealed (גלי) to Daniel" (Dan 2:19).

[62] In Israel, this taxonomy also allowed dream interpreters to distinguish the contents of "theophoric" dreams from the making or conjuring of divine images.

[63] Cf. David M. Carr, *Writing on the Tablet of the Heart: Origins of Scripture and Literature* (New York: Oxford University Press, 2005), who argues that, throughout the ancient Near East, the process of internalizing texts by memorization, i.e., "inscribing them upon the heart," was a male-oriented enterprise that aimed to educate and enculturate elite young men for leadership roles. For Carr, this informs how Israelite textual traditions were shaped to instill a predominantly male gender identity on the elites who acquired them.

[64] The same idiom occurs in Jer 44:21, and in reverse sequence in Isa 65:17. Similarly, one is forgotten "from the heart." Thus, the Psalmist cries: נשכחתי כמת מלב ("I am forgotten from the heart like one who is dead," Ps 31:12), and not, as the KJV renders: "I am forgotten as a dead man out of my mind."

[65] Jeremiah does not denounce oneiromancy generally. In fact, he adds: "Let the prophet whose dream is with him recount the dream, and the one with whom my word is with him speak my word truthfully" (Jer 23:28).

fies them with his heart: ורעיוני לבבך תנדע ("so that you might know the thoughts/pur-poses of your heart," Dan 2:30).

While translators often render the Hebrew לב/לבב as "mind," rather than "heart," in order to convey its function as a place of memory, its description as a writing surface for divine words suggests that we think of it not in the Cartesian sense, but more literally.[66] Indeed, the notion that gods could inscribe their intentions on the internal organs of living creatures is well known to students of Near Eastern extispicy. At least since the Old Babylonian period, Mesopotamian extispicers were examining the hearts of animals and they could refer to their internal organs generally with the cognate term *libbu* ("heart"),[67] or more descriptively as the *ṭuppu ša ilī* ("tablet of the gods").[68]

The notion that the divine could inscribe a message upon the human heart is a logical extension of this widespread belief.[69] Moreover, analogues for this concept exist in a number of later Greek texts that connect human viscera to

---

[66] A more active role for the heart during sleep appears in Song 5:2, in which the lover declares: אני ישנה ולבי ער ("I was sleeping, but my heart was awake"). If the text indeed describes a dream (in accordance with Abraham Ibn Ezra), it is the only place in the Hebrew Bible in which a woman is said to dream, and as such, it represents a reversal of gender roles. Nevertheless, the text does not explicitly refer to dreaming. On gender reversal as a theme in the Song, see Scott B. Noegel and Gary A. Rendsburg, *Solomon's Vineyard: Literary and Linguistic Studies in the Song of Songs*, AIL 1 (Atlanta: Society of Biblical Literature, 2009), 156–57.

[67] See Ulla Jeyes, "Divination as a Science in Ancient Mesopotamia," *JEOL* 32 (1991–92): 33.

[68] See Ulla Koch-Westenholz, *Babylonian Liver Omens: The Chapters Manzāzu, Padānu and Pān Tākaltu of the Babylonian Extispicy Series Mainly from Aššurbanipal's Library*, CNI Publications 25 (Copenhagen: Museum Tusculanum Press, 2000), 13.

[69] In this light it is worth noting that extispicy also was an exclusively androcentric enterprise: both the extispicers and the animals they selected (usually a *puḫādu* ["lamb"] or *immeru* ["ram"]) were invariably male. See Jeyes, "Divination as a Science," 33. Parallels between the Israelite view proposed here and extispicy also include a shared sense of the necessity for purity. Like the extispicers and the animals they selected, the retention of sacred memory in Israel required one to be unblemished. It required a pure heart from which one's sins had been erased. Thus, we hear in Ps 51:11–12: "Remove my sins from your presence, and erase (מחה) all of my iniquity. Create in me a pure heart (לב טהור), and renew in my innards (בקרבי) a steadfast spirit." See similarly Isa 43:25: "I, even I am he who erases (מחה) your transgressions for my own sake, I remember your sins no more." On the purity of extispicers and their animals, see Jeyes, "Divination as a Science," 29–30; W. G. Lambert, "The Qualifications of Babylonian Diviners," in *Festschrift für Rykle Borger zu seinem 65. Geburtstag am 24. Mai 1994*, CM 10, ed. Stefan M. Maul (Groningen: Styx, 1998), 141–58. In Mesopotamia, a close relationship between prognostic dreams and extispicy also existed, the latter often performed to verify the former. See Butler, *Mesopotamian Conceptions of Dreams*, 25–26, 30, 39–41.

divine dreams, such as the Asclepian temple stela at Epidaurus, the Hippocratic treatise *On Regimen*, and Plato's *Timaeus* (all from the fourth century BCE). The stela at Epidaurus shows that patients believed that Asclepius healed them during their dreams by performing invasive operations on their internal organs. Hippocrates argues that dreams of cosmological phenomena, such as falling stars, signify bodily ailments. For him, the dream does not constitute a cure, but a symptom, and while the cosmos here is not a god per se, it bears a trace of divinity. In the *Timaeus*, Plato argues that it is the human liver that facilitates the soul's reception of divine messages through dreams.[70] Though I cannot do justice to the complex ideas that inform each of these sources, they do reveal, despite their obvious differences, a general belief in the interconnectedness of dreams, the divine, and human organs as a locus for memory. In his study of dreams and human viscera, Peter Struck summarizes the Greek view as follows: "Dreams do not stand outside the rather common Mediterranean tendency, exhibited in extispicies of all kinds, to see the divine in the viscera."[71] I submit that we may place the Israelite conception of the heart, whether understood as the specific organ or a general reference to the viscera, in this context.

Moreover, since dreams and the rite of circumcision both marked male virility and the time of puberty and/or marriage, the heart and the phallus naturally were brought into comparison as competing loci for divine memory.[72] It is in this light that I aver we understand periodic references to the human heart in phallic terms. Thus, the heart can be either circumcised (e.g., Deut 10:16, 30:6; Jer 4:4) or uncircumcised (e.g., Lev 26:41, Jer 9:25, Ezek 44:7).[73] Indeed, the

---

[70] On these texts, see Peter Struck, "Viscera and the Divine: Dreams as the Divinatory Bridge Between the Corporeal and the Incorporeal," in *Prayer, Magic, and the Stars in the Ancient and Late Antique World*, ed. Scott B. Noegel, Joel Walker, and Brannon Wheeler, MH 8 (University Park: Pennsylvania State University Press, 2003), 125–36. Interestingly, Plato refers to dream contents as εἴδωλα ("images"), rather than words, even though dreams were put into words to interpret them. On the latter as it pertains to Greek traditions, see Noegel, *Nocturnal Ciphers*, 191–233.

[71] Struck, "Viscera and the Divine," 125.

[72] Of course, the heart also served as a locus for covenantal love. See William L. Moran, "The Ancient Near Eastern Background of the Love of God in Deuteronomy," *CBQ* 25 (1963): 77–87.

[73] The connection between circumcision and fertility also appears in Lev 19:23, which refers to an unpruned plant as uncircumcised. As organs for delivering and receiving memories, the lips and ears also can be considered uncircumcised if they are not ritually prepared for the divine word (e.g., Exod 6:12, Jer 6:10). Herbert B. Huffmon, "Gender Subversion in the Book of Jeremiah," in *Sex and Gender in the Ancient Near East: Proceedings of the Forty-Seventh Rencontre Assyriologique Internationale, Helsinki, July 2–6, 2001*, ed. Simo Parpola and Robert M. Whiting (Helsinki: The Neo-Assyrian Text

heart, like the penis, could be inscribed with God's covenant. See, for example, Jeremiah's prophecy concerning the covenant, נתתי את־תורתי בקרבם ועל־לבם אכתבנה ("I will place my law in their innards, and I will write it upon their heart," Jer 31:33),[74] and similarly his description of Judah's sin as כתובה בעט ברזל בצפרן שמיר חרושה על־לוח לבם ("engraved with an iron tool, inscribed with a flint point upon the tablet of their heart," Jer 17:1).[75] The conception of the heart in phallic terms might also explain the denominative root לבב ("ravish"), which often appears in sexually charged contexts.[76]

Corpus Project, 2002), 250–52, argues that Jeremiah employs the term "circumcision of the heart" as an ideology aimed to include women in Yahweh's covenant.

[74] In Jer 23:16, the prophet also refers to some of his contemporaries by saying: חזון לבם ידברו לא מפי יהוה ("a vision of their heart they speak, not from the mouth of Yahweh"). The statement aims not to invalidate dreaming as a method of obtaining divine knowledge, but to castigate prophets who interpret dreams without divine inspiration. Note that the prophet again characterizes the experience as a word recorded on the "heart."

[75] The idiom "tablet of the heart" also appears in Prov 3:3, 7:3; and with significant variations in Aeschylus, *Prometheus Bound* 788: μνήμοσιν δέλτοις φρενῶ ("recording tablets of [the] mind"). The expression likely has its origins in Mesopotamia. Note that the Egyptian expression ḥtj tp ib ("inscribe upon the heart") makes no reference to tablets, because papyrus was the primary medium for writing. Interestingly, one finds the expanded Greek idiom πλαξὶν καρδίαις σαρκίναις ("fleshy tablets of the heart") in 2 Cor 3:3. Is the use of the term σαρκίναις ("fleshy") evidence for a more literal understanding of the heart as an organ for recording the new covenant? On the meaning "fleshy," see LSJ, 1584, s.v. σάρκειος. Some New Testament scholars suggest that the passage echoes Jer 31:33; Ezek 11:19, 36:26, and that the fleshy heart characterizes its obedient nature in contrast to a heart of stone. Cf. Paul's discussion of circumcision of the heart by spirit, rather than the letter (Rom 2:27–29). On these matters, see Thomas E. Provence, "'Who is Sufficient for These Things?': An Exegesis of 2 Corinthians ii 15–iii 18," *NT* 24 (1982): 54–81; Thomas R. Blanton, "Spirit and Covenant Renewal: A Theologoumenon of Paul's Opponents in 2 Corinthians," *JBL* 129 (2010): 129–51.

[76] See, e.g., Song 4:9: לבבתני אחתי כלה לבבתיני באחד [באחת] מעיניך ("you aroused me, my sister, O bride, you aroused me with but one of your eyes"). On the sexual connotations of לבב, see N. M. Waldman, "A Note on Canticles 4, 9," *JBL* 89 (1970): 215–17. The root also appears in Job 11:12: ואיש נבוב ילבב ועיר פרא אדם יולד ("Can a hollow man be aroused, can the colt of a wild ass give birth to a man?"). The parallel with ילד suggests that לבב relates to reproduction. I thus translate the latter as "aroused" rather than "be mindful" or "be two-hearted." Though exegetes often render נבוב as a "hollow" or "empty-headed" man (based on an Akkadian cognate meaning "play the flute," *CAD* 11.1:8, s.v. *nabābu*), one wonders whether the root נבב suggests a man unable to produce semen. He would then be a "hollow pipe," as it were (à la the vulgar English idiom "shooting blanks"). The verse would then suggest that a man unable to produce semen would share the same chances for reproduction as an ass giving birth to a human.

Furthermore, the notion that the heart could be thought of in phallic terms is not unique to ancient Israel. Indeed, the word "heart" serves as a euphemism for the penis in Babylonian rituals for healing male impotence.[77] These texts bear the Sumerian and Akkadian titles ša₃-zi-ga and *nīš libbi*, respectively, meaning "rising of the 'heart.'"[78] The rabbis adopted this practice and thus, they too

---

Interestingly, b. B. Bat. 12b connects Job 11:12 with the root נוב in Zech 9:17. While נוב usually means "prosper" in the sense of "bearing fruit," the rabbis connect it to נבב, ("hollow") and render it with sexual connotations: "R. Abdimi from Haifa said: 'Before a man eats and drinks he has two hearts, but after he eats and drinks he has only one heart, as it says, "ואיש נבוב ילבב" (Job 11:12) ... "R. Huna the son of R. Joshua said: 'If a man is a wine drinker, even though his heart is closed like a virgin, the wine opens it, as it is said: "New wine shall open (ינובב) the maids""" (Zech 9:17). See also 2 Sam 13:6, in which Amnon makes known his intentions concerning his half-sister Tamar: ותלבב לעיני שתי לבבות ואברה מידה. Translators usually render the verse, "Let her prepare before me two cakes that I may eat from her hand," and certainly her baking shortly afterwards shows that this is its outward meaning. Nevertheless, the use of לבב as "ravish" and its use with "eyes" in the aforementioned passage from Song of Songs, together with the fact that the word "eating" can be a sexual euphemism, suggests that the passage possesses added allusive power. The LXX renders לבבות with δύο κολλυρίδας ("two little cakes"), though the diminutive form κολλυρίδας also can refer to a medicinal salve. See LSJ, 972, s.v. κολλύρα. On the euphemism, see Paul, "Shared Legacy," 495–97. Note that the Akkadian cognate *labābu* only means "rage." See *CAD* 9:7, s.v. *labābu*.

[77] Akkadian texts describe impotence as a *libbu* ("heart") that is *lā išari* ("not straight"). The latter also constitutes an illocutionary pun on *išaru* ("penis"). The idiom comes to denote anything impure, unjust, polluted, or irregular. Thus, here too an inability to reproduce is equated with abnormalcy and pollution. See *CAD* 7:226, s.v. *išaru*. The cognate Hebrew expression ישר לב ("upright of heart") does not bear this meaning. The Akkadian *nīš libbi* ("lift the heart") also finds a cognate in the expression נשא לב, but the Hebrew signifies the will of a person in nonsexual contexts (e.g., Exod 35:21, 36:2). Underscoring the euphemistic nature of the term *libbu* is that, when used in reference to a woman, it can refer to her womb. See *CAD* 9:165–66, s.v. *libbu*. Note also the Sumerian medical expression ša₃ giš₃ = Akkadian *lib išari*, lit. "heart of the penis" (possibly read as *muštinnu*), i.e., "urethra," in *CAD* 9:169, s.v. *libbu*. Cf. the Egyptian *Hymn to Osiris*, recorded on the stele of Amenmose (Paris Louvre C 286), which also uses the word *ib* "heart" for "penis." It describes Isis's successful effort to arouse 'weary' (i.e., deceased) Osiris as follows: *stswi nnw n wrd-ib ḫnp mw=f irwt iw 'w* ("[She] raised the inertia of the weary of 'heart,' [she] received his seed, bore an heir," line 16).

[78] See Robert D. Biggs, *Šà.zi.ga: Ancient Mesopotamian Potency Incantations*, TCS 2 (Locust Valley: Augustin, 1967); Robert D. Biggs, "The Babylonian Sexual Potency Texts," in *Sex and Gender in the Ancient Near East: Proceedings of the Forty-Seventh Rencontre Assyriologique Internationale, Helsinki, July 2–6, 2001*, ed. Simo Parpola and Robert M. Whiting (Helsinki: The Neo-Assyrian Text Corpus Project, 2002), 71–79; Irving L. Finkel, "On Some Dog, Snake and Scorpion Incantations," in *Mesopotamian*

employed the word "heart" euphemistically when describing a cure for impotence.[79] The correlation between the heart and the phallus in Mesopotamian and later rabbinic texts further supports the notion that such an association existed in ancient Israel.

In summary, my examination of dreams and dream divination in ancient Israel has maintained four interrelated theses. First, I have argued that examining the androcentric constructions of Israelite mantics from the perspective of fertility and pollution allows us to see their literary portrayals as registering an equally androcentric correlation between access to divine knowledge and male fertility. The depictions follow a general pattern that identifies male mantics with normative reproductive experiences (individual wholeness and societal health), and female mantics with a lack of reproduction (disability).[80] Second, I have argued

---

Magic: Textual, Historical, and Interpretive Perspectives, ed. Tzvi Abusch and Karel van der Toorn, AMD 1 (Groningen: Styx, 1999), 211–52. On the subject generally, see Leonid Kogan and Alexander Militarev, "Akkadian Terms for Genitalia: New Etymologies, New Textual Interpretations," in *Sex and Gender in the Ancient Near East: Proceedings of the Forty-Seventh Rencontre Assyriologique Internationale, Helsinki, July 2–6, 2001*, ed. Simo Parpola and Robert M. Whiting (Helsinki: The Neo-Assyrian Text Corpus Project, 2002), 311–21. One finds a similar semantic development with the word *kabattu* ("liver, innards, mood, mind"), cf. *šamḫāte lina''â kabtassu* ("let prostitutes amuse his 'mind'"; The Descent of Ištar, 129–130).

[79] B. 'Erub 29b: "If a man suffers from weakness of the "heart" (חולשא דליבא) let him obtain the flesh of the right flank of a male beast and excrements of the shepherd (understand: 'cattle') (produced in the month) of Nisan, and if excrements of cattle are not available, let him obtain some willow twigs, and let him roast it (i.e., the flesh on the twig), eat it, and after that drink diluted wine." For the rabbinic usage and its derivation from Babylonian medicinal practices, see Mark J. Geller, *Akkadian Healing Therapies in the Babylonian Talmud*, Preprint 259 (Berlin: Max-Planck-Institut für Wissenschaftsgeschichte, 2004), 27–28.

[80] The androcentric classification of male and female divinatory abilities according to whether they produce children is just one of several dichotomies that illustrate how constructions of gender (and their inversions) inform conceptions of reproduction, pollution, and access to divine knowledge. Deborah W. Rooke, "The Bare Facts: Gender and Nakedness in Leviticus 18," in *A Question of Sex? Gender and Difference in the Hebrew Bible and Beyond*, ed. Deborah W. Rooke, HBM 14 (Sheffield: Sheffield Phoenix Press, 2007), 35, observes that the portrayals of women in the incest laws of Leviticus 18 "use the bodily terminology of relatedness and nakedness to categorize certain forbidden females as conceptually 'inter-sexed' in relation to the males to whom they are forbidden, thus effectively characterizing the women as 'pseudo-males.' Such women are seen as dangerous, because they blur the category boundaries of male and female." According to Nicole J. Ruane, "Bathing, Status and Gender in Priestly Ritual," in *A Question of Sex? Gender and Difference in the Hebrew Bible and Beyond*, ed. Deborah W. Rooke, HBM 14 (Sheffield: Sheffield Phoenix Press, 2007), 79, the laws of bodily emissions follow a

that this context informs the etymological and textual association of dreams and dream divination with male virility and reproduction. It suggests that the Israelites regarded the dreams of young males as potentially divine only after they reached puberty and entered the covenant. Third, I examined the androcentric conception of memory and memorials, especially as it relates to circumcision, and I raised a number of parallels between circumcision as a fertility rite and the conception of divine dreams. Finally, I turned to the heart as an organ for recording dreams and other memories. I proposed that this function finds parallels in extispicy and in later Greek treatments of dreams and I advanced the possibility that the competing roles of the heart and phallus as loci of memory explain the periodic literary treatment of the heart in phallic terms.

I submit that each of the theses allows us to understand the Israelite dream experience with greater nuance and that when combined, they account for some of the more curious features concerning biblical dreams.[81] They demonstrate

---

gendered pattern in which a woman who has ejaculatory intercourse with a man must follow the same ritual procedures as a man who has had a seminal emission, whereas a man who has had sex with a menstruant must follow the procedures of a menstruant: "The sexual partner contacts the same impurity as the source and has the same ritual treatment. Thus, ritually speaking, intercourse has the power to change a sexual partner into a person of the opposite gender." Gender inversions relating to divine access are known elsewhere in the ancient Near East as well, most famously in the cult of Ishtar. See Zainab Bahrani, *Women of Babylon: Gender and Representation in Mesopotamia* (London: Routledge, 2001), 141–60. Mouton, *Rêves hittites*, 7, also discusses the gendering of ritual objects during Hittite incubation rituals. During the process, the patient holds a spindle and distaff symbolizing the feminine side, but he receives a bow and arrows after passing through a magical gate, thus "illustrating his reacquisition of virility."

[81] Viewing gendered constructions of mantics from the perspective of fertility and pollution also sheds light on some of the variations to the patterns for female diviners noted by Hamori, "Childless Female Diviners," like Rebekah and Rachel. Implicit in the story of Rebekah is the threat that she might have miscarried (Gen 25:22–24). We are told that she did not consult Yahweh until she felt that ויתרצצו הבנים בקרבה ("the sons had crushed each other inside her," Gen 25:22). Her query to Yahweh explicitly identifies her as a potential infertile parturient: "If it is so (i.e., that I am to have a child), why am I this way?" (Gen 25:22). In the story of Rachel's theft of the *teraphim* (Gen 31:34–35), the author embeds Rachel's role as a pollutant in her claim that she was menstruating. In one move, the author casts Rachel as a pollutant while putting the household gods in a contaminated position beneath her. Such texts again allow us to place depictions of female diviners within a wider context of fertility and pollution. Therefore, while biblical narratives do not portray every female with access to divine knowledge as childless or belonging to a non-normative family structure, they do mark their "disability" and place their fertility in check. Indeed, one could argue that the stories of Rebekah and Rachel mark their "disability" in pronounced ways, precisely because they do not fit the societal pattern. This also is apparent in the story of Miriam's attempt to challenge Moses as

that, much like circumcision, literary depictions of dreams marked a liminal moment that registered one's reproductive abilities and fitness for divine access.[82] They too recorded a memory of the divine, but unlike circumcision, which marked it on the phallus, they were recorded on the "fleshy tablets of the heart."[83]

BIBLIOGRAPHY

Avalos, Hector. *Illness and Health Care in the Ancient Near East: The Role of the Temple in Greece, Mesopotamia, and Israel.* HSM 54. Atlanta: Scholars Press, 1995.
Bahrani, Zainab. *Women of Babylon: Gender and Representation in Mesopotamia.* London: Routledge, 2001.
Biggs, Robert D. "The Babylonian Sexual Potency Texts." Pages 71–79 in *Sex and Gender in the Ancient Near East: Proceedings of the Forty-Seventh Rencontre Assyriologique Internationale, Helsinki, July 2–6, 2001.* Edited by Simo Parpola and Robert M. Whiting. Helsinki: The Neo-Assyrian Text Corpus Project, 2002.
———. *Šà.zi.ga: Ancient Mesopotamian Potency Incantations.* TCS 2. Locust Valley: Augustin, 1967.
Blanton, Thomas R. "Spirit and Covenant Renewal: A Theologoumenon of Paul's Opponents in 2 Corinthians." *JBL* 129 (2010): 129–51.
Bloch-Smith, Elizabeth. "Will the Real *Massebot* Please Stand Up: Cases of Real and Mistakenly Identified Standing Stones in Ancient Israel." Pages 64–79 in *Text, Artifact, and Image: Revealing Ancient Israelite Religion.* Edited by G. Beckman and Theodore J. Lewis. BJS 346. Providence: Brown University Press, 2006.

God's primary spokesperson (Num 12). When she and Aaron protest, only she is stricken with leprosy, a punishment that marks her as a severe polluter and removes her prophethood from the social body. Thus, the narrative depicts her attempt to compete with male diviners as a transgression of the social norm deserving of a polluted state above and beyond that marked by her childlessness. Though her pollution did not relate to reproduction, the connection was not lost on Aaron, who describes her state as that of an infertile parturient: "Please do not make her like a stillborn boy who goes out of his mother's womb and his flesh is half eaten away" (Num 12:12). Tarja S. Philips, *Menstruation and Childbirth in the Bible: Fertility and Impurity*, StBibLit 88 (New York: Peter Lang, 2006), 25, argues that that the account of Rachel's *teraphim* emphasizes fertility more than pollution. I suggest the categories are not mutually exclusive.

[82] These findings stand in accord with my previous observation in *Nocturnal Ciphers*, 178: "Insofar as the redactors have accurately preserved the *techne* of dream interpreters, they also have legitimized the divinatory powers of the biblical characters who employ it, and by extension, of those in Israelite society most likely to employ such a hermeneutic—priestly or prophetic authors or redactors. This fits well the legitimating function of biblical narratives that report the so-called 'message dreams.'"

[83] On this expression, see n. 75.

Brenner, Athalya. *The Intercourse of Knowledge: On Gendering Love, Desire and "Sexuality" in the Hebrew Bible*. Leiden: Brill, 1997.
Butler, S. A. L. *Mesopotamian Conceptions of Dreams and Dream Rituals*. AOAT 258. Münster: Ugarit-Verlag, 1998.
Carr, David M. *Writing on the Tablet of the Heart: Origins of Scripture and Literature*. New York: Oxford University Press, 2005.
Creangă, Ovidiu. ed. *Men and Masculinity in the Hebrew Bible and Beyond*. BMW 33. Sheffield: Sheffield Phoenix Press, 2010.
———. "The Silenced Song of Victory: Power, Gender, and Memory in the Conquest Narrative of Joshua (Joshua 1–2)." Pages 106–23 in *A Question of Sex? Gender and Difference in the Hebrew Bible and Beyond*. Edited by Deborah Rooke. HBM 14. Sheffield: Sheffield Phoenix Press, 2007.
Delcor, M. "The Special Meaning of the Word יד in Biblical Hebrew." *JSS* 12 (1967): 230–44.
Douglas, Mary T. *Purity and Danger: An Analysis of the Concepts of Pollution and Taboo*. London: Routledge, 1966.
Durand, Jean-Marie. *Archives Épistolaires de Mari I/1*. ARM 26.1. Paris: ERC, 1988.
Eilberg-Schwartz, Howard. *God's Phallus and Other Problems for Men and Monotheism*. Boston: Beacon Press, 1994.
———. *The Savage in Judaism: An Anthropology of Israelite Religion and Ancient Judaism*. Bloomington: Indiana University Press, 1990.
Elliott, John H. "Deuteronomy 25:11–12 and Biblical Euphemism." Pages 171–76 in *Ancient Israel: The Old Testament in Its Social Context*. Edited by Philip F. Esler. Minneapolis: Augsburg Press, 2006.
Faust, Avraham. "The Bible, Archaeology, and the Practice of Circumcision in Israelite and Philistine Societies." *JBL* 134 (2015): 273–90.
Fidler, Ruth. *"Dreams Speak Falsely?" Dream Theophanies in the Bible: Their Place in Ancient Israelite Faith and Traditions*. Jerusalem: Hebrew University Magnes, 2005 [Hebrew].
Finkel, Irving L. "On Some Dog, Snake and Scorpion Incantations." Pages 211–52 in *Mesopotamian Magic: Textual, Historical, and Interpretive Perspectives*. Edited by Tzvi Abusch and Karel van der Toorn. AMD 1. Groningen: Styx, 1999.
Flannery-Dailey, Frances. *Dreamers, Scribes, and Priests: Jewish Dreams in the Hellenistic and Roman Eras*. JSJSup 90. Leiden: Brill, 2004.
Fox, Michael V. "The Sign of the Covenant: Circumcision in the Light of the Priestly 'Ôt Etiologies." *RB* 81 (1974): 557–96.
Freedman, R. David. "'Put Your Hand Under My Thigh'—The Patriarchal Oath." *BAR* 2.2 (1976): 3–4, 42.
Geller, Mark J. *Akkadian Healing Therapies in the Babylonian Talmud*. Preprint 259. Berlin: Max-Planck-Institut für Wissenschaftsgeschichte, 2004.
Gordis, R. "A Note on the Meaning of יד." *JBL* 62 (1943): 341–44.
Gnuse, Robert K. *Dreams and Dream Reports in the Writings of Josephus: A Traditio-Historical Analysis*. AGAJU 36. Leiden: Brill, 1996.

Hamori, Esther J. "Childless Female Diviners in the Bible and Beyond." Pages 161–91 in *Prophets Male and Female: Gender and Prophecy in the Hebrew Bible, the Eastern Mediterranean, and the Ancient Near East*. Edited by Jonathan Stökl and Corinne L. Carvalho. AIL 15. Atlanta: Society of Biblical Literature, 2013.

———. "The Prophet and the Necromancer: Women's Divination for Kings." *JBL* 132 (2013): 827–43.

Harris, William V. *Dreams and Experience in Classical Antiquity*. Cambridge: Harvard University Press, 2009.

Hoffner, Harry A. "Symbols for Masculinity and Femininity: Their Use in Ancient Near Eastern Sympathetic Magic Rituals." *JBL* 85 (1966): 326–34.

Huehnergard, John. *Ugaritic Vocabulary in Syllabic Transcription*. HSS 32. Atlanta: Scholars Press, 1987.

Hunger, Hermann. "How to Make the Gods Speak: A Late Babylonian Tablet Related to the Microzodiac." Pages 141–51 in *Studies Presented to Robert D. Biggs*. Edited by Martha T. Roth, Walter Farber, Matthew W. Stolper, and Paula von Bechtolsheim. WCAD 2. Chicago: Oriental Institute of the University of Chicago, 2007.

Husser, Jean-Marie. *Dreams and Dream Narratives in the Biblical World*. Translated by Jill M. Munro. BibSem 63. Sheffield: Sheffield Academic Press, 1999.

Jacobs, Sandra. *The Body as Property: Physical Disfigurement in Biblical Law*. LHBOTS 582. New York: T&T Clark, 2014.

———. "Divine Virility in Priestly Representation: Its Memory and Consummation in Rabbinic Midrash." Pages 146–70 in *Men and Masculinity in the Hebrew Bible and Beyond*. Edited by Ovidiu Creangă. BMW 33. Sheffield: Sheffield Phoenix Press, 2010.

Japhet, Sara. "יד ושם (Isa. 56.5): A Different Proposal." *Maarav* 8 (1992): 69–80.

Jeyes, Ulla. "Divination as a Science in Ancient Mesopotamia." *JEOL* 32 (1991–92): 23–41.

Koch-Westenholz, Ulla. *Babylonian Liver Omens: The Chapters Manzāzu, Padānu and Pān Tākaltu of the Babylonian Extispicy Series Mainly from Aššurbanipal's Library*. CNI Publications 25. Copenhagen: Museum Tusculanum Press, 2000.

Kogan, Leonid and Alexander Militarev. "Akkadian Terms for Genitalia: New Etymologies, New Textual Interpretations." Pages 311–21 in *Sex and Gender in the Ancient Near East: Proceedings of the Forty-Seventh Rencontre Assyriologique Internationale, Helsinki, July 2–6, 2001*. Edited by Simo Parpola and Robert M. Whiting. Helsinki: The Neo-Assyrian Text Corpus Project, 2002.

Lambert, W. G. "The Qualifications of Babylonian Diviners." Pages 141–58 in *Festschrift für Rykle Borger zu seinem 65. Geburtstag am 24. Mai 1994*. CM 10. Edited by Stefan M. Maul. Groningen: Styx, 1998.

Lane, Edward William. *An Arabic-English Lexicon*. London: Williams & Norgate, 1863.

Levine, Baruch A. "'Seed' versus 'Womb': Expressions of Male Dominance in Biblical Israel." Pages 337–43 in *Sex and Gender in the Ancient Near East: Proceedings of the Forty-Seventh Rencontre Assyriologique Internationale, Helsinki, July 2–6, 2001*. Edited by Simo Parpola and Robert M. Whiting. Helsinki: The Neo-Assyrian Text Corpus Project, 2002.

Lewis, Theodore J. *Cults of the Dead in Ancient Israel and Ugarit*. HSM 39. Atlanta: Scholars Press, 1989.

McCarter, P. Kyle. *2 Samuel.* AB 9. Garden City: Doubleday, 1984.
McComiskey, Thomas Edward. "זָכַר־." *TWOT* 1:241–43.
Malul, Meir. "More on the *Paḥad Yiṣḥāq* (Genesis XXXI 42, 53) and the Oath by the Thigh." *VT* 35 (1985): 192–200.
———. "Touching the Sexual Organs as an Oath Ceremony in an Akkadian Letter." *VT* 37 (1987): 491–92.
Margalit, Baruch. "On Canaanite Fertility and Debauchery." Pages 177–92 in *"He Unfurrowed His Brow and Laughed": Essays in Honour of Nicolaus Wyatt.* Edited by W. G. E. Watson. AOAT 299. Münster: Ugarit-Verlag, 2007.
Meyers, Carol L. "Miriam the Musician." Pages 207–30 in *A Feminist Companion to Exodus to Deuteronomy.* Edited by Athalya Brenner. FCB 6. Sheffield: Sheffield Academic Press, 1994.
Miller, Patricia Cox. *Dreams in Late Antiquity: Studies in the Imagination of a Culture.* Princeton: Princeton University Press, 1994.
Moran, William L. "The Ancient Near Eastern Background of the Love of God in Deuteronomy." *CBQ* 25 (1963): 77–87.
Mouton, Alice. *Rêves hittites: Contribution à une histoire et une anthropologie du rêve en Anatolie anciennes.* CHANE 28. Leiden: Brill, 2007.
Nissinen, Martti. *References to Prophecy in Neo-Assyrian Sources.* SAA 7. Helsinki: Neo-Assyrian Text Corpus Project; Helsinki University Press, 1998.
———. *Prophets and Prophecy in the Ancient Near East.* With contributions by C. L. Seow and Robert K. Ritner. WAW 12. Atlanta: Society of Biblical Literature, 2003.
Noegel, Scott B. *Nocturnal Ciphers: The Allusive Language of Dreams in the Ancient Near East.* AOS 89. New Haven: American Oriental Society, 2007.
———. "The Ritual Use of Linguistic and Textual Violence in the Hebrew Bible and Ancient Near East." Pages 33–46 in *State, Power, and Violence.* Edited by Margo Kitts, Bernd Schneidmüller, Gerald Schwedler, Eleni Tounta, Hermann Kulke, and Uwe Skoda. RDSR 3. Wiesbaden: Harrassowitz, 2010.
———. "Scale Scriptitious: The Concentration of Divine Power in the Ancient Near East." In *The Miniature and the Minor in the Ancient Greek, Roman, and Near Eastern Worlds: An Interdisciplinary Investigation.* Edited by Jonathan L. Ready. Forthcoming.
Noegel, Scott B. and Gary A. Rendsburg. *Solomon's Vineyard: Literary and Linguistic Studies in the Song of Songs.* AIL 1. Atlanta: Society of Biblical Literature, 2009.
Olyan, Saul M. *Disability in the Hebrew Bible: Interpreting Mental and Physical Differences.* Cambridge: Cambridge University Press, 2008.
Oppenheim, A. Leo. *The Interpretation of Dreams in the Ancient Near East: With a Translation of the Assyrian Dream Book.* TAPS 46.3. Philadelphia: American Philosophical Society, 1956.
Overholt, Thomas W. *Channels of Prophecy: The Social Dynamics of Prophetic Activity.* Minneapolis: Fortress, 1989.
Paul, Shalom. "The Shared Legacy of Sexual Metaphors and Euphemisms in Mesopotamian and Biblical Literature." Pages 489–98 in *Sex and Gender in the Ancient Near East: Proceedings of the Forty-Seventh Rencontre Assyriologique Internationale, Helsinki, July 2–6, 2001.* Edited by Simo Parpola and Robert M. Whiting. Helsinki: The Neo-Assyrian Text Corpus Project, 2002.

Philips, Tarja S. "Gender Matters: Priestly Writing on Impurity." Pages 40–59 in *Embroidered Garments: Priests and Gender in Biblical Israel*. Edited by Deborah W. Rooke. HBM 25. Sheffield: Sheffield Phoenix Press, 2009.

———. *Menstruation and Childbirth in the Bible: Fertility and Impurity*. StBibLit 88. New York: Peter Lang, 2006.

Provence, Thomas E. "'Who is Sufficient for These Things?': An Exegesis of 2 Corinthians ii 15–iii 18." *NT* 24 (1982): 54–81.

Raskow, Ilona N. *Taboo or Not Taboo: Sexuality and the Family in the Hebrew Bible*. Minneapolis: Fortress, 2000.

Renberg, Gil H. *Where Dreams May Come: Incubation Sanctuaries in the Greco-Roman World*. RGRW 184. Leiden: Brill, 2017.

Rooke, Deborah W. "The Bare Facts: Gender and Nakedness in Leviticus 18." Pages 20–38 in *A Question of Sex? Gender and Difference in the Hebrew Bible and Beyond*. Edited by Deborah W. Rooke. HBM 14. Sheffield: Sheffield Phoenix Press, 2007.

———. "Breeches of the Covenant: Gender, Garments and the Priesthood." Pages 19–37 in *Embroidered Garments: Priests and Gender in Biblical Israel*. Edited by Deborah W. Rooke. HBM 25. Sheffield: Sheffield Phoenix Press, 2009.

———, ed. *Embroidered Garments: Priests and Gender in Biblical Israel*. HBM 25. Sheffield: Sheffield Phoenix Press, 2009.

———, ed. *A Question of Sex? Gender and Difference in the Hebrew Bible and Beyond*. HBM 14. Sheffield: Sheffield Phoenix Press, 2007.

Ruane, Nicole J. "Bathing, Status and Gender in Priestly Ritual." Pages 66–81 in *A Question of Sex? Gender and Difference in the Hebrew Bible and Beyond*. Edited by Deborah W. Rooke. HBM 14. Sheffield: Sheffield Phoenix Press, 2007.

Sasson, Jack M. "Circumcision in the Ancient Near East." *JBL* 85 (1966): 473–76.

Schorch, Stefan. *Euphemismen in der Hebräischen Bibel*. OBC 12. Wiesbaden: Harrassowitz, 1999.

Silverman, Eric K. "Anthropology and Circumcision." *ARA* 33 (2004): 419–45.

Simpson, William Kelly. "A Relief of the Royal Cup-Bearer *Tja-wy*." *BMB* 71 (1973): 69–82.

Stökl, Jonathan and Corinne L. Corvalho, eds. *Prophets Male and Female: Gender and Prophecy in the Hebrew Bible, the Eastern Mediterranean, and the Ancient Near East*. AIL 15. Atlanta: Society of Biblical Literature, 2013.

Strimple, Cheryl and Ovidiu Creangă. "'And His Skin Returned Like a Skin of a Little Boy': Masculinity, Disability, and the Healing of Naaman." Pages 110–26 in *Men and Masculinity in the Hebrew Bible and Beyond*. Edited by Ovidiu Creangă. BMW 33. Sheffield: Sheffield Phoenix Press, 2010.

Struck, Peter. "Viscera and the Divine: Dreams as the Divinatory Bridge Between the Corporeal and the Incorporeal." Pages 125–36 in *Prayer, Magic, and the Stars in the Ancient and Late Antique World*. Edited by Scott B. Noegel, Joel Walker, and Brannon Wheeler. MH 8. University Park: Pennsylvania State University Press, 2003.

Szpakowska, Kasia. *Behind Closed Eyes: Dreams and Nightmares in Ancient Egypt*. Swansea: Classical Press of Wales, 2003.

de Tarragon, Jean-Michel. "Witchcraft, Magic, and Divination in Canaan and Ancient Israel." Pages 2070–81 in vol. 3 of *Civilizations of the Ancient Near East*. Edited by Jack M. Sasson. New York: Scribner, 1985.

Trachtenberg, Joshua. *Jewish Magic and Superstition: A Study in Folk Religion.* New York: Behrman's Jewish Book House, 1939.
Waldman, N. M. "A Note on Canticles 4, 9." *JBL* 89 (1970): 215–17.
Wild, H. "Brasserie et panification au tombeau de Ti." *BIFAO* 64 (1966): 95–120.
Wolfson, Elliot R. "Circumcision, Vision of God and Textual Interpretation: From Midrashic Trope to Mystical Symbol." Pages 29–48 in *Circle in the Square: Studies in the Use of Gender in Kabbalistic Symbolism.* Edited by Elliot R. Wolfson. New York: State University of New York Press, 1995.

———. "The Cut that Binds: Time, Memory, and the Ascetic Impulse." Pages 103–54 in *God's Voice from the Void: Old and New Studies in Bratslav Hasidism.* Edited by Shaul Magid. Albany: State University of New York Press, 2002.

———. "Re/Membering the Covenant: Memory, Forgetfulness and the Construction of Identity in the Zohar." Pages 214–46 in *Jewish History and Jewish Memory: Essays in Honor of Yosef Haim Yerushalmi.* Edited by Elishiva Carlebach, John M. Efron, and David N. Myers. Hanover: Brandeis University Press, 1998.
Wyatt, N. "The Pruning of the Vine in KTU 1.23." *UF* 24 (1992): 403–24.
Zevit, Ziony. *The Religions of Ancient Israel: A Synthesis of Parallactic Approaches.* London: Continuum, 2001.
Zgoll, Annette. "Die Welt im Schlaf sehen—Inkubation von Träumen im antiken Mesopotamien." *WdO* 32 (2002): 74–101.

———. *Traum und Welterleben im antiken Mesopotamien: Traumtheorie und Traumpraxis im 3.–1. Jahrtausend v. Chr. als Horizont einer Kulturgeschichte des Träumens.* AOAT 333. Münster: Ugarit-Verlag, 2006.

5
Dreams in the Joseph Narrative

Franziska Ede

The first half of the Joseph narrative is characterized by dreams that foreshadow the future. Over against the majority of dreams within the book of Genesis, the dreams in Gen 37–45 represent image dreams rather than speech dreams (e.g., Gen 46:1–5) and, thus, rely on interpretation. Within Gen 40–41 the interpretation is provided by Joseph and earns him the status of second man in Egypt. In Gen 37, on the other hand, Joseph himself receives two dreams, the meaning of which is not revealed explicitly, but unfolds implicitly within the narrative context of Gen 37 and 42–45. The following analysis will provide a close analysis of the dreams in Gen 37 and 40–41 and inquire into their commonalities, differences and their respective function within the immediate and broader context. As the latter aspect is closely connected with general issues that concern the composition of the Joseph narrative, we will commence our analysis with a brief outline of the conception presupposed in this paper.

THE COMPOSITION GENESIS 37–45

It has long been recognized that chapters 39–41 are distinct from the rest of the Joseph narrative. While the remaining chapters revolve around the fate of Joseph, his brothers, and his father, chapters Gen 39–41 focus exclusively on Joseph's fortune in Egypt. And whereas Gen 37 and 42–50 are dependent on Gen 39–41 as the indespensible narrative bridge between Joseph's sale to Egypt and the brothers' purchase of grain in Egypt, the reverse is not true. Though in its current context Gen 39–41 relies on the introduction in Gen 37, their narrative substance might well go back to traditional folktale material.

In view of the above observations several scholars have suggested that

Gen 39–41 represents formerly independent material that was only secondarily integrated into its current literary context.[1] Notwithstanding any further distinctions, the following analysis presupposes this idea and assumes that one or more authors adopted the material that centers on Joseph's fate in Egypt and preluded it with the introduction in Gen 37. The motif of Joseph as dream interpreter in Gen 40–41 may then have influenced the choice of the dream motif as trigger for the brothers' hatred in Gen 37:4–8, 9. It remains to be verified what purpose the motif serves in the immediate and broader literary context and why the formal presentation of the dream account differs from that in Gen 40–41. A close examination of Gen 37:5–9 in its micro and macro context will provide answers.

JOSEPH'S DREAMS IN GEN 37

At the beginning of the non-Priestly exposition of the Joseph narrative in Gen 37:3–4, the reader learns that Israel loves Joseph more than all his other sons, because he was the son of his old age.[2] When the brothers become aware of their father's love for Joseph, they start to hate their brother. These verses presuppose knowledge of events from the patriarchal narratives, with which the introduction of the Joseph narrative is interrelated explicitly (see below). The author—and reader—need to know: the birth account of Isaac (Gen 21:2, 7), the conflict between Rachel and Leah (Gen 29:30–31), and the renaming of Jacob (Gen 32:29).[3] For only those readers who are aware that Jacob, to whom Rachel had borne Joseph (Gen 30:23–24), was renamed Israel in Gen 32:29, will grasp

---

[1] See Hans Strauss, "Weisheitliche Lehrerzählungen in und um das Alte Testament," *ZAW* 116 (2004), 381; David M. Carr, *Reading the Fractures of Genesis: Historical and Literary Approaches* (Louisville: Westminster John Knox Press, 1996), 289; George W. Coats, "Redactional Unity in Gen 37–50," *JBL* 93 (1974): 15–21; or Reinhard G. Kratz, *Die Komposition der erzählenden Bücher des Alten Testaments: Grundwissen der Bibelkritik*, UTB 2157 (Göttingen: Vandenhoeck & Ruprecht, 2000), 283.

[2] See already Hermann Gunkel, *Genesis*, 4th ed., HKAT (Göttingen: Vandenhoeck & Ruprecht, 1917), 401. Similarly, Gerhard von Rad, *Das erste Buch Mose*, ATD 4 (Göttingen: Vandenhoeck & Ruprecht, 1953), 307; Christoph Levin, *Der Jahwist*, FRLANT 157 (Göttingen: Vandenhoeck & Ruprecht, 1993), 265–73; Lothar Ruppert, *Genesis: Ein kritischer und theologischer Kommentar*, FB 118 (Würzburg: Echter Verlag, 2008), 99–100.

[3] A different view is held by Jakob Wöhrle, *Fremdlinge im eigenen Land: Zur Entstehung und Intention der priesterlichen Passagen der Vätergeschichte*, FRLANT 246 (Göttingen: Vandenhoeck & Ruprecht, 2012), 105; Jörg Lanckau, *Der Herr der Träume: Eine Studie zur Funktion des Traumes in der Josefsgeschichte der Hebräischen Bibel*, AThANT 85 (Zürich: Theologischer Verlag Zürich, 2006), 166.

the familial background presupposed throughout the Joseph narrative.[4] And only those readers who know that Rachel was the beloved wife of Jacob, while Leah is described as שׂנואה, will comprehend the function of Joseph as primus inter fratres.[5] Since he is the oldest son of Jacob's beloved wife Rachel, he becomes the beloved son of Israel, on whose fate chapters 39–41 will focus. The motif of old age fatherhood, again, connects the beginning of the Joseph story with the birth account of Isaac.[6] In this regard, it is noteworthy that the reference to the father's old age bears no reference in Joseph's birth account, while it represents a symbol of God's promise to Abraham in the story surrounding Isaac. Even though Sarah was beyond the age of conception, God kept his promise and let her give birth to Isaac. As the son of the promise Isaac becomes Abraham's successor, even though he is not actually his firstborn son. Within the Joseph story the phrase בן לזקניו might, perhaps, best be explained as a deliberate reference to the birth of Isaac that serves to strengthen Joseph's right to continue the patriarchal lineage. Joseph—as Isaac—is not his father's firstborn. As the son of the "beloved" mother, however, he is granted preference.

Gen 21:2, 7

²ותהר ותלד שׂרה לאברהם בן לזקניו למועד אשר־דבר אתו אלהים:
⁷ותאמר מי מלל לאברהם היניקה בנים שׂרה כי־ילדתי בן לזקניו:

Gen 29:30–31

³⁰ויבא גם אל־רחל וַיֶּאֱהַב גַּם־אֶת־רָחֵל מִלֵּאָה ויעבד עמו עוד שׁבע־שׁנים אחרות:
³¹וירא יהוה כי־שְׂנוּאָה לֵאָה ויפתח את־רחמה ורחל עקרה:

Gen 32:29

²⁹ויאמר לא יעקב יאמר עוד שׁמך כי אם־ישׂראל כי־שׂרית עם־אלהים ועם־אנשׁים ותוכל:

Gen 37:3–4

³וישׂראל אָהַב אֶת־יוֹסֵף מִכָּל־בָּנָיו כִּי־בֶן־זְקֻנִים הוּא לוֹ ועשׂה לו כתנת פסים:
⁴וַיִּרְאוּ אֶחָיו כִּי־אֹתוֹ אָהַב אֲבִיהֶם מִכָּל־אֶחָיו וַיִּשְׂנְאוּ אֹתוֹ ולא יכלו דברו לשׁלם:

In Gen 37:5–8 the motif of fraternal preference is followed by the motif of dreams as a trigger for the brothers' hatred. Verse 5 introduces the motif of Joseph's dream and links it to the preceding motif of preference by resuming use of the root שׂנא. The hatred that already existed in Gen 37:4 is presupposed and heightened: ויוספו עוד שׂנא אתו. Verse 5 further adopts the change in perspective

---

[4] See Bernd Willmes, "Objektive Ereignisse bei textinterner Literarkritik: Einige Anmerkungen zur Subjektivität literarkritischer Beobachtung: Harald Schweizers Studie 'Die Josefsgeschichte,'" *BN* 67 (1993): 58.

[5] See esp. Rüdiger Lux, *Josef: Der Auserwählte unter seinen Brüdern* (Leipzig: Evangelische Verlagsanstalt, 2001), 50. Similarly, Sven Tengström, *Die Hexateucherzählung: Eine literaturgeschichtliche Studie*, ConBOT 7 (Lund: Gleerups, 1976), 42.

[6] See Lanckau, *Träume*, 141.

that can be perceived beween verses 3–4. While verse 3 is written from the perspective of the father, who loves Joseph more "than all his sons," verse 4 shifts to the perspective of the brothers, who realize that their father loves Joseph more "than all his brothers," and as a consequence they start to hate him. This inter-fraternal perspective continues in verses 5–8, where it is emphasized further. According to verses 3–4, the unequal distribution of the father's love triggers the brothers' hatred. In verses 5–8, however, Joseph himself contributes actively to the increase in his brothers' hatred. "Once Joseph had a dream, and when he told it to his brothers, they hated him even more" (Gen 37:5). So much does their hatred increase that they intend to kill him:

> They said to one another, "Here comes the Lord of dreams. Come now, let us kill him and throw him into one of the pits; then we shall say that a wild animal has devoured him, and we shall see what will become of his dreams." (Gen 37:19–20)

The conclusion of the scene surrounding the first dream (v. 8b) and the brothers' decision to kill Joseph (vv. 19–20) are interconnected through the key word חלום (plural). This obvious interrelation reveals that the brothers' decision is the immediate consequence that follows from the events described in Gen 37:4–8.[7]

In order better to comprehend the reason for the brothers' decision to kill Joseph, we will now turn our attention to the content of Joseph's first dream and his brothers' interpretation. In verse 7, Joseph reveals the content of his dream openly to his brothers: "Behold, there we were, binding sheaves in the field. Suddenly my sheaf rose and stood upright; but at the same time your sheaves gathered around it, and bowed down to my sheaf." Following the categorization by Zgoll, the dream represents an intrarelational image dream that is both unverified and uninterpreted.[8]

In her study focusing on ancient Near Eastern dream accounts Zgoll distinguishes between image dreams that remain within the realm of the dream, speech dreams that transcend the realm of the dream and combinations of both. Withtin the mixed pattern of image dreams the addressee of speech is decisive

---

[7] With regard to the framing function see Bob Becking, "They Hated Him Even More: Literary Technique in Genesis 37.1–11," *BN* 60 (1991): 41, 45–46; Peter Weimar, "Die Josefsgeschichte als theologische Komposition: Zu Aufbau und Struktur von Gen 37," in *Studien zur Josefsgeschichte*, ed. Peter Weimar, SBAB 44 (Stuttgart: Katholisches Bibelwerk, 2008), 30–31; Norbert Kebekus, *Die Josefserzählung: Literarturkritische und redaktionsgeschichtliche Untersuchungen zu Gen 37–50* (Münster: Waxmann, 1990), 15–16.

[8] Annette Zgoll, *Traum und Welterleben im antiken Mesopotamien: Traumtheorie und Traumpraxis im 3.–1. Jahrtausend v. Chr. als Horizont einer Kulturgeschichte des Träumens*, AOAT 333 (Münster: Ugarit-Verlag, 2006), 243–48.

for further subdivisions. If a speech is directed towards someone within the dream, it is considered intrarelational. If it is directed towards someone outside the dream, it is considered extrarelational. In sum, Zgoll distinguishes between five different subcategories: (1) intrarelational image dreams; (2) image dreams with intrarelational speech; (3) image dreams with extrarelational speech, (4) extrarelational speech dreams; (5) extrarelational speech dreams with images. Generally speaking, the interrelation of speech dreams and image dreams is such that the extrarelational speech dream represents the verified and interpreted version of an intrarelational image dream.

A possible interpretation of Joseph's image dream is given by the brothers in verse 8. Addressing Joseph in direct speech, they ask: "Are you really to reign over us? Will you really have dominion over us?" (Gen 37:8). Joseph himself neither reacts to the brothers' reproach nor attempts to provide a different explanation. This is all the more striking, since it will be his very ability to reveal the hidden meaning of dreams that will make him overseer of the grain in Gen 41 and, consequently, reunite him with his brothers in Gen 42–45.

The reunion of Joseph and his brothers in Gen 42 is also anticipated by the content of the dream in Gen 37:7. When Jacob learns that there is grain in Egypt, he orders his sons to "go down and buy grain for us" (Gen 42:2). The brothers follow their father's command and come to Joseph, for "Joseph was governor over the land; he sold (grain) to all the people of the land. Joseph's brothers came and bowed down low before him" (Gen 42:6). Joseph recognizes his brothers and remembers "the dreams that he had dreamt about them. He said to them, 'You are spies; you have come to see the nakedness of the land!'" (Gen 42:9).

The correspondence between Joseph's first dream and his reunion with his brothers is evident (see below). What the dream foreshadowed in Gen 37:7 is fulfilled in Gen 42:6–9.[9] The brothers bow down before Joseph, because they intend to buy grain. The hidden meaning of the sheaves is now revealed: they anticipate the grain that the brothers are to buy from Joseph, the overseer over the grain (המשביר לכל־עם). The tables have turned. While the brothers had overpowered Joseph in Gen 37, intending to kill the "Master of dreams" (Gen 37:19) and "see what will become of his dreams" (Gen 37:20), Joseph has become the "master of grain," holding the fate of his brothers in his hands.

---

[9] Cf. Horst Seebass, *Genesis III: Josephsgeschichte (37,1–50,26)* (Neukirchen-Vluyn: Neukirchener Verlagsgesellschaft, 2000), 87; Kebekus, *Joseferzählung*, 97–98. For different views cf. Benno Jakob, *Das erste Buch der Tora: Genesis* (Berlin: Schocken, 1934), 765; Jan-Dirk Döhling, "Die Herrschaft erträumen, die Träume beherrschen: Herrschaft, Traum und Wirklichkeit in den Josefträumen (Gen 37,5–11) und der Israel-Josefsgeschichte," *BZ* 50.1 (2006): 1–30 (29–30); Gordon J. Wenham, *Genesis 16–50*, WBC 2 (Dallas: Word Books, 1996), 406.

In Gen 42:6 (cf. Gen 43:26, 28), the brothers bow to Joseph and unknowingly fulfill the hidden meaning of Joseph's dream. In Gen 45 they implicitly but openly accept his primacy. After Joseph reveals his true identity to his brothers (Gen 45:3–4), Gen 45:15 reads: "he kissed all his brothers and wept; after that his brothers talked with him" (Gen 45:15). This scene of reconciliation evokes Gen 37:4b, where the brothers were unable to speak peaceably to Joseph. Their former hatred is now overcome and Joseph sends his brothers home.[10]

Gen 37:4, 7–8

⁴ויראו אחיו כי־אתו אהב אביהם מכל־אחיו וישנאו אתו וְלֹא יָכְלוּ דַּבְּרוֹ לְשָׁלֹם:
⁷והנה אנחנו מאלמים אלמים בתוך השדה והנה קמה אלמתי וגם־נצבה והנה תסבינה אלמתיכם ותשתחוין לאלמתי:
⁸ויאמרו לו אחיו המלך תמלך עלינו אם־משול תמשל בנו ויוספו עוד שנא אתו על־חלמתיו וְעַל־דְּבָרָיו:

Gen 42:6, 9–10

⁶ויוסף הוא השליט על־הארץ הוא המשביר לכל־עם הארץ ויבאו אחי יוסף וישתחוו־לו אפים ארצה:
⁹ויזכר יוסף את החלמות אשר חלם להם ויאמר אלהם מרגלים אתם לראות את־ערות הארץ באתם:
¹⁰ויאמרו אליו לא אדני ועבדיך באו לשבר־אכל:

Gen 45:4, 15

⁴ויאמר יוסף אל־אחיו גשו־נא אלי ויגשו ויאמר אני יוסף אחיכם אשר־מכרתם אתי מצרימה:
¹⁵וינשק לכל־אחיו ויבך עליהם וְאַחֲרֵי כֵן דִּבְּרוּ אֶחָיו אִתּוֹ:

From a literary-critical perspective, the first dream discussed above likely needs to be distinguished from the second dream in verse 9. This assessment is based on various observations: the construction of the second dream in the form of one lengthy participial phrase differs distinctly from the grammatical construction of the first dream.[11] Additionally, the symbolic presentation is lacking a metaphor for Joseph, who is presented unencrypted as himself. As in the first dream he is surrounded by his brothers, who are now depicted as stars and specified as eleven (ואחד עשר כוכבים). Over against the first dream, the second dream also mentions the sun and moon as symbol for Joseph's parents.[12] The imagery of the sun and moon and the parental prostration it symbolizes are found no-

---

[10] Kratz, *Komposition*, 284.

[11] For grammar and syntax see Ron Pirson, *The Lord of the Dreams: A Semantic and Literary Analysis of Gen 37–50*, JSOTSup 355 (New York: Sheffield Academic Press, 2002), 43.

[12] See Benjamin D. H. Hilbert, "Joseph's Dreams, Part One: From Abimelech to Saul," *JSOT* 35 (2011): 260. Too far-fetched seems the assumption offered by Pirson, *Lord*, 57–58, that the eleven stars, the sun, and the moon are meant to represent periods of time: 1+1+11= 13 for the period of time that Joseph spends in Egypt before he is promoted by Pharaoh, and 1+1×11=22 for the time when Joseph and his brothers meet again.

where else in the broader narrative. Moreover, the inclusion of mother and father in the dream represents a departure from the fraternal conflict on which verses 4b–8 focus. Neither in the immediate nor the wider context does their mentioning contribute to the unfolding narrative of the brothers' conflict. In the immediate context of Gen 37, the second dream comes too late after the summarizing statement of verse 8, which already presupposes a plural number of dreams (ויוספועוד שנא אתו על־חלמתיו).[13] In view of these observations it seems likely that the second dream constitutes a secondary expansion, which may have been inspired by the two dreams in Gen 40–41 and which unfolds the plural "dreams" of verse 8b.[14]

What conclusions can be drawn from the above observations? First, the choice of the dream motif in Gen 37:4b–8 seems to have been influenced by the traditional material included in Gen 40–41. However, the dream accounts show certain differences. While all dreams in Gen 37 and 40–41 are presented as intrarelational symbolic dreams that are neither verified nor interpreted, only the meaning of the dreams by the royal officials and Pharaoh in Gen 40–41 is revealed explicitly.[15] Joseph interprets the dreams for the respective recipient. And just as he interprets, so it comes to pass. The hidden meaning of Joseph's dream in Gen 37:4b–8, on the other hand, is only disclosed implicitly in the greater context of the Joseph narrative.[16] This difference might, perhaps, best be explained by the purpose of Gen 37:4b–8 within the wider context of the Joseph narrative.

In the course of our analysis of Gen 37:3–8 we have seen that the motif of the father's preference in Gen 37:3–4a harkens back to passages from the patriarchal narratives. These references both explain and legitimize Joseph's function as *primus inter fratres* and successor of the patriarchal lineage, whose fate is discussed over the following chapters (Gen 39–41). In Gen 37:4b–8 the focus

---

[13] For a different assessment see Wilhelm Rudolph, "Die Josefsgeschichte," in *Der Elohist als Erzähler: Ein Irrweg der Pentateuchkritik? An der Genesis erläutert*, ed. Wilhelm Rudolph and Paul Volz, BZAW 63 (Gießen: Töpelmann, 1933), 152.

[14] See Levin, *Jahwist*, 272; Harald Schweizer, *Die Josefsgeschichte: Konstituierung des Textes* (Tübingen: Mohr Siebeck, 1991), 1:128–32; Ruppert, *Genesis*, 99. For a different assessment cf. Hugo Gressmann, "Ursprung und Entwicklung der Joseph-Sage," in *Eucharisterion: Studien zur Religion und Literatur des Alten und Neuen Testaments*, ed. Hans Schmidt, FRLANT 36 (Göttingen: Vandenhoeck & Ruprecht, 1923), 19, who believed that the first dream was based on the second one.

[15] Cf. Nili Shupak, "A Fresh Look at the Dreams of the Officials and of Pharaoh in the Story of Joseph (Genesis 40–41) in the Light of Egyptian Dreams," *JANES* 30 (2006): 137.

[16] If we take the context of Gen 42:6, 9 seriously, this is true even for Joseph: "Now Joseph was governor over the land; it was he who sold to all the people of the land. And Joseph's brothers came and bowed themselves before him with their faces to the ground. ... Joseph also remembered the dreams that he had dreamt about them. He said to them, 'You are spies; you have come to see the nakedness of the land!'"

shifts from the father's greater love for Joseph to the fraternal conflict it triggers. The brothers' hatred is now also linked to Joseph's own actions: Joseph dreams himself as the first amongst his brothers and through his action increases their hatred. Consequently, they decide to kill him (Gen 37:19–20). The fraternal conflict unfolds and reaches its denouement in Gen 42–45. Further, the context of Gen 42–45 is explicitly anticipated by the prostration of the brothers' sheaves (Gen 37:7, cf. Gen 42:6, 9) and the statements of verses 4b and 8b. While the brothers were not able to speak peaceably with Joseph (Gen 37:4b) and hated him because of his dreams and his words (Gen 37:8b), they overcome their hatred in Gen 45:15 and start speaking with him again.

In sum, we might conclude that the dream account in Gen 37:4b–8 seems to serve a literary—and theological—purpose within the context of Gen 37–45. The choice of the dream motif in Gen 37 may have been inspired by the traditional material in Gen 40–41. It connects Gen 37 to the chapters about Joseph's fate in Egypt (Gen 39–41) and to those about Joseph and his brothers (Gen 42–45). In the context of the wider narrative, the meaning of the dream must stay hidden until the dream is fulfilled. It is not until then that Joseph—himself a capable dream interpreter—realizes the impact of his dream(s) (Gen 42:9). What his brothers perceived as a presumptuous, symptomatic dream constitutes divine foreshadowing of future events. Even though the deity is never explicitly mentioned in this scenario, the idea of divine guidance underlies the entire chain of events. The brothers were supposed to misread the signs that Joseph received in his dreams and thus hate him even more, for Joseph reaches Egypt only as a consequence of their hatred.[17] In Egypt he rises to a high office and is in a position to save his family by providing them with grain. The fulfillment of the dream speaks to the divine providence of the dream, which, in turn, adds to Joseph's authority as *primus inter fratres*. While Gen 37:3–4a refers to passages from the patriarchal narratives to explain Joseph's primacy over his brothers, the dream motif underscores the divine authority with which Joseph's role is sanctioned.[18]

---

[17] See Hilbert, "Dreams," 435. However, Shupak, "Dreams," 137, states that Joseph's dreams "are understood by the dreamer and his hearers and need no explanation."

[18] The theme of divine guidance already implicit in the dream account and its fulfillment seems to have been made explicit only by a later hand that expressly interprets the brothers' misdeed in Gen 37 as an act of divine providence. "And now do not be distressed, or angry with yourselves, because you sold me here; for God sent me before you to preserve life" (Gen 45:5). It would go too far to present a detailed analysis of the literary-critical observations that led to this diachronic differentiation. We thus confine ourselves to referring the reader to Franziska Ede, *Die Josefsgeschichte: Redaktionsgeschichtliche und literarkritische Untersuchungen zur Entstehung von Gen 37–50*, BZAW 485 (Berlin: de Gruyter, 2016), 285–340, 469–512. With regard to possible diachronic distinctions in Gen 45:4–7* cf. also Levin, *Jahwist*, 298–99; with regard to a diachronic distinction in Gen 50:19–21*, see Levin, *Jahwist*, 307–12; Ruppert, *Genesis*, 523–33.

Dreams in Genesis 40–41

As mentioned above, the dream accounts in Gen 40–41 seem to go back to traditional material that was connected secondarily with the events narrated in Gen 42–45 through the dream motif in the exposition of Gen 37. Genesis 40–41 centers on Joseph's fate. He is brought to Egypt where he turns out to be an exceptional mantic capable of interpreting dreams. Before addressing the conceptualization of mantic wisdom underlying Gen 40–41, I will present some literary-critical observations that are significant for the development of theological thought perceptible in these chapters.

In Gen 40:6 the reader learns that Joseph comes to the cupbearer and the baker in the morning and sees that they are troubled. He asks them: "Why are you downcast today?" (Gen 40:7) The royal officials answer Joseph, "Each of us had a dream, and there is no one to interpret it" (Gen 40:8a). In the narrative context of Gen 40 the reference to the lack of other interpreters is rather incongruous. Verse 6 mentions Joseph meeting with the officials "in the morning," suggesting that not much time had passed since they dreamt their dreams. Moreover, the officials are held in custody, which would make it quite difficult for them to consult any diviners other than Joseph.[19]

An almost verbatim reference to the other interperters appears in Gen 41:8, where Pharaoh summons the wise men and the mantics to interpret his dreams. However, there is no one able to reveal the meaning of the dream to him: ואין פותר אותם. The motif of the incapable mantics is only briefly resumed in Gen 41:15, 24b, when Pharaoh first addresses Joseph and reveals the images of his dream to Joseph: "I have had a dream, and there is no one who can interpret it. ... When I told it to the magicians, none of them could explain it to me" (Gen 41:15, 24b).

Beyond Gen 40–41 the motif of the incapable mantics is important for Dan 2, where Nebuchadnezzar is troubled by an uninterpreted dream. He summons the wise men and mantics of Babylon. In Dan 2 the mantics of Babylon play a significant role. They communicate directly with the Babylonian king, who threatens to punish them should they not obey his commands and reveal the dream and its meaning to him. "This is a public decree: if you do not tell me both the dream and its interpretation, you shall be torn limb from limb, and your houses shall be laid in ruins" (Dan 2:5). In order to save himself and the other

---

[19] See already Jacob, *Genesis*, 735; cf. more recently Victor P. Hamilton, *The Book of Genesis: Chapters 18–50*, NICOT (Grand Rapids: Eerdmans, 1995), 476.

wise men of Babylon, Daniel prays to his God, who lets him know the dream and its interpretation. For no "wise men, enchanters, magicians, or diviners can show to the king the mystery that the king is asking; but there is a God in heaven who reveals mysteries, and he reveals to the king ... what is to be" (Dan 2:27–29).

While the motif of the incapable interpreters thus determines the narrative progression in Dan 2, the same cannot be said for Gen 41. Even though Pharaoh, too, summons the mantics and wise men in order to reveal the meaning of his dreams to him, no direct interaction between him and the diviners takes place. Furthermore, their failure to reveal the interpretation of the dreams to him has no consequences of any kind.[20] Altogether, they bear no pivotal significance in the storyline of Gen 41.[21] On the contrary, they are only loosely connected to the context.

The same applies to Gen 40, where the motif of the mantics leads to inconsistencies in the narrative logic. Logical tensions further arise within the context of Gen 40:8, 16, 22. In Gen 40:8a the reader learns that the royal officials are unable to find an interpreter for their dreams. Joseph reacts to their statement with a theological reservation clothed in the form of a rhetorical question: "Do not interpretations belong to God?" Seemingly unaware of his own reservation, he immediately encourages the officials to tell him their dreams: "Please tell them to me."[22] The cupbearer is the first to obey.

> The chief cupbearer told his dream to Joseph, "In my dream there was a vine before me, and on the vine there were three branches. As soon as it budded, its blossoms came out and the clusters ripened into grapes. Pharaoh's cup was in my hand; I took the grapes and pressed them into Pharaoh's cup, and placed the cup in Pharaoh's hand." (Gen 40:9–11)

---

[20] See Seebass, *Genesis*, 67; Ruppert, *Genesis*, 218. See further the observation made by Maren Niehoff, *The Figure of Joseph in Post-Biblical Jewish Literature*, AGAJU 16 (Leiden: Brill, 1992), 19, that "[l]ittle attention is ... paid to the magicians' unsuccessful attempts at interpreting Pharaoh's dreams. Nine words describe how they were called and five more are used for Pharaoh's report to them (*Gen 41:8*). By comparison, the description of Joseph's call is much fuller. In five words Pharaoh's request is related, but nine more are used to depict the details of Joseph's preparation and only then is the king's address communicated" (emphasis in the original).

[21] See Ruppert, *Genesis*, 218.

[22] See especially Schweizer, *Josefsgeschichte*, 152. Similarly, Michael V. Fox, "Joseph and Wisdom," in *The Book of Genesis: Composition, Reception, and Interpretation*, ed. Craig A. Evans, Joel N. Lohr, and David L. Petersen, VTSup 152 (Leiden: Brill, 2012), 245, who thinks that the question is "a pious disclaimer but not exactly a modest one, for even as Joseph denies that he has special skills he is claiming to possess a very significant power: divine guidance. This is the source of Joseph's self-confidence, but the disclaimer has tactical value too."

Joseph's interpretation follows in verses 12–13. He reveals to the cupbearer the meaning of the images and numbers, letting him know that in three days time Pharaoh will restore him to his office. Verse 16 resumes the motif of dream interpretation: "When the chief baker saw that Joseph interpreted (פתר) favorably, he said to Joseph...." Unlike Daniel, of whom we hear that he makes interpretations known to others (אמר, ידע, חוה + פֶּשֶׁר), Joseph is mentioned explicitly as the subject of the active, finite verb פתר.[23] Joseph interprets the dream. Even though the programmatic position of the theological reservation in verse 8 suggests that dream interpretation is dependent on God, the immediate connection of Joseph with the act of interpretation remains puzzling. Why would the narrator have Joseph put such emphasis on the divine origin of dream interpretations in verse 8 and then fail to clarify that it is, indeed, not Joseph who interprets the cupbearer's dream (פתר v. 16; cf. v. 22)?

Gen 40:8, 16, 22:

⁸ויאמרו אליו חלום חלמנו <u>ופתר אין אתו</u> ויאמר אלהם יוסף <u>הלוא לאלהים פתרנים ספרו־</u>
<u>נא לי</u>:
¹⁶וירא שר־האפים <u>כי טוב פתר</u> ויאמר אל־יוסף אף־אני בחלומי והנה שלשה סלי חרי על־
ראשי:
²²ואת שר האפים תלה <u>כאשר פתר להם יוסף</u>:

The immediate context of Gen 40 does not answer the question of how the relation between divine and human agency is to be understood. We will, therefore, turn our attention to Gen 41. In Gen 41:9–12 the cupbearer remembers his encounter with Joseph in Gen 40. After Pharaoh is troubled by his dreams (Gen 41:1–8), the cupbearer addresses him in direct speech referring to Joseph, who acts as subject of the verb פתר: "A young Hebrew was there with us, a servant of the captain of the guard. When we told him our dreams, he interpreted (ויפתר־לנו) them for us, telling each the interpretation (פתר) of his dream" (Gen 41:12). Because Joseph was able to interpret the dreams of the royal officials correctly, he is now brought before Pharaoh (Gen 41:14), who speaks to him: "I have had a dream and no one can interpret it. I have heard of you that when you hear a dream you can interpret it" (Gen 41:15). The latter statement draws on the information provided by the cupbearer, who had told Pharaoh that Joseph was able to interpret his dream. This assumption is met with

---

[23] חוה Dan 2:4, 6–7, 9, 16, 24; 5:7, 12, 15; ידע Dan 2:9, 25–26; 4:3–4, 15; 5:8, 15–17; 7:16; אמר Dan 4:6. The only two instances where (nominal) verbs of the root פשר occur are Dan 5:12 and 14. That it is not Daniel who interprets the dreams, however, is emphasized by the immediate literary context, in which Daniel is characterized as being endowed with the spirit of God (Dan 5:11, 14), which enables him to make interpretations known to others.

a vehement rejection by Joseph: "It is not I; God will give Pharaoh a favorable answer" (Gen 41:16). Just as in Gen 40:8, Joseph declares that dream interpretation belongs to God. Unlike in Gen 40, however, where the interrelation of divine and human agency remains unclear, Joseph emphasizes that his interpretation is divinely provided (אלהים יענה את־שלום פרעה). Even though he might make the interpretation known to Pharaoh, the interpretation itself is given by God. Pharaoh picks up quickly on Joseph's explanation. In Gen 41:38–39 he exclaims: "Can we find anyone else like this—one in whom resides the spirit of God? ... Since God has shown you all this, there is no one so discerning and wise as you."

While the interrelation between human participation and divine agency is thus clarified within the greater context of Gen 40–41, the ambiguity with regard to the active, finite use of the verb פתר remains. It becomes particularly obvious in the narrative context of Gen 40, yet it is also noticeable in the context of the cupbearer's speech in Gen 41:9–12 as the following comparison will show.

In Gen 40:5a the reader learns that the royal officials had a dream—each his dream in one night (אִישׁ חֲלֹמוֹ בְּלַיְלָה אֶחָד). Gen 40:5b repeats the words אִישׁ חֲלֹמוֹ, while expanding them with the information that each of the officials dreamt a dream according to the interpretation of his dream (אִישׁ כְּפִתְרוֹן חֲלֹמוֹ). The accent thus shifts from the temporal coincidence of two separate dreams to the exact meaning of each dream. The phrase איש כפתרון חלמו also occurs in the context of the cupbearer's speech in Gen 41:11. There, the cupbearer recalls the events from Gen 40 as follows: "We dreamt in the same night, he and I, each according to the meaning of his dream we dreamt (איש כפתרון חלמו)". In Gen 41:11, again, the temporal coincidence of two separate dreams is supplemented by the exact interpretation of each dream. A reference to the exact interpretation is missing, however, in the interpretation given by Joseph in Gen 41:12. Rather, verse 12 merely resumes the motif of the temporal coincidence from Gen 40:5a (איש חלמו בלילה אחד) and states that the meaning of the dreams was revealed to the officials by Joseph: ויפתר־לנו את־חלמתינו איש כחלמו פתר.

It follows that in the context of Gen 41:12, the emphasis is put on the fact that both men received their dreams the same night, and Joseph was able to interpret both of them. In contrast, Gen 40:5b and Gen 41:11b stress that the meaning of the dreams was inherent to the dream itself. The nominal phrases (איש כפתרון חלמו) thus clarifies that—even though Joseph might act as the subject of the verb פתר—he is not the interpreter of the dream, but only provides the interpretation that was inherent to the dream all along.

In view of the entirety of observations described above it seems worth considering whether a later hand felt obliged to explain exactly how human participation and divine agency relate to each other.[24] The trigger for this development

---

[24] See Levin, *Jahwist*, 281, 287–88.

might be seen in the active, finite use of the verbal root פתר, in which the divine origin of dream interpretation—though implied—is not made explicit. This is revised by a later hand. In the course of this reworking the divine origin of both dream and interpretation is underlined. The statement of Gen 41:12 seems to have provided a docking point. The authors of the reworking explicitly draw on the phrase וַיִּפְתָּר־לָנוּ אֶת־חֲלֹמֹתֵינוּ אִישׁ כַּחֲלֹמוֹ פָּתָר, which they re-interpret: אִישׁ כְּפִתְרוֹן חֲלֹמוֹ חָלָמְנוּ (Gen 41:11b; cf. Gen 40:5b). The nominal phrase separates the act of interpretation from Joseph and fixes the content of interpretation (cf. Gen 40:12, 18), which is associated directly with the process of dreaming. When the dream is dreamt it already includes its פתרון. This interpretation is (pre-) determined by Elohim, for he is the sole interpreter. The same purpose is pursued by the introduction of the other interpreters, who are only loosely integrated into the context of Gen 40–41. Their incapability in Gen 41 mirrors the omnipotence of Elohim, who alone can interpret dreams. "Joseph answered Pharaoh: 'It is not I; God will give Pharaoh a favorable answer'" (Gen 41:16).

The idea that dream interpretation was essentially subject to the deity, of course, underlies the older narrative as well. In the ancient Near East the conception of mantic wisdom cannot be separated from the divine realm. What distinguishes the older material from the younger reworking is that the once self-evident seems to have become problematic: the immediate or direct relationship of the human to God. Therefore, the authors of the reworking distinguish explicitly between human participation and divine agency. They, too, believe that Joseph has a special relationship to the deity through the רוח אלהים. Yet this relationship needs to be addressed explicitly in order to guarantee that the act of dream interpretation not be mistaken for a human accomplishment.

With the distinction between the divine interpreter and the human mediator, the reworking in Gen 41 corresponds closely with Dan 1–6, where Daniel makes interpretations known to King Nebuchadnezzar (Dan 2; 4; cf. also Dan 5). For Daniel, just as Joseph, is endowed with the spirit of God, and enlightenment, understanding and excellent wisdom are found in him (Dan 5:16, cf. Gen 41:33, 38–39). The distance between human beings and God becomes even farther in the dream accounts of Dan 7–12, where Daniel no longer communicates directly with the deity. Instead, he himself depends on the *angelus interpres*, who assumes Daniel's function from Dan 1–6 and acts as a mediator between the human being, Daniel, and God.

The tendency of an increasing distance towards the deity or deities can also be perceived in Mesopotamian dream accounts:

A diachronic comparison shows that the god of dreams appears more frequently in later texts. To conclude that in earlier texts a deity always brings their message themselves would be to oversimplify matters, as the position of a dream's addressee also plays an important part. But as a general tendency the distance between humans and deities appears to increase over the course of Mesopotamian history.[25]

In sum, it seems that the theological reworking of the older material in Gen 40–41 needs to be understood against the background of the continually increasing distance between the divine and human realms. The clear distinction between human participation and divine agency was introduced into the context of Joseph's dream interpretations in Gen 40–41 to account for this. By contrast, human participation and divine agency had not yet become separate in the older narrative context, but naturally coincided in the human Joseph. Joseph is portrayed as a mantic who interprets dreams. His role in this older text stratum resembles the function of Mesopotamian dream specialists:

> According to Mesopotamian texts, dream specialists can have different functions. Some focused on receiving dreams containing divine messages addressed to other humans, while others specialized on interpreting the dreams of others ("dream interpreter").[26]

We might then conclude that in an older version of Gen 40–41 Joseph was portrayed as a dream specialist who interpreted the dreams of baker, cupbearer, and Pharaoh by himself. Owing to his exceptional mantic abilities, he was promoted into high offices. Only in a later reworking was this mantic ability explicitly linked to the deity. Because Joseph is endowed with the spirit of God, is he able to provide the divine answer that reveals the dream interpretation. The younger reworking thus verbalizes what the older narrative perceived as self-evident.

---

[25] "Der diachrone Vergleich zeigt, daß der Traumgott erst im Lauf der Zeit häufiger erwähnt wird. Nun wäre es zu vereinfacht, zu sagen: Je früher ein Text, desto eher überbringt eine Gottheit selbst ihre Botschaft. Denn der Rang des Adressaten eines Traumes spielt ebenfalls eine Rolle. Doch die Tendenz trifft zu. Es zeigt sich, daß der Abstand zwischen Mensch und Gott im Lauf der mesopotamischen Geschichte größer wird." Zgoll, *Traum und Welterleben*, 295.
[26] "Traumspezialisten können nach Auskunft der mesopotamischen Texte verschiedene Funktionen haben. Während die einen vornehmlich versuchten, für einen anderen Menschen Gottesbotschaften im Traum zu erlangen, also sich darauf spezialisierten, Träume für andere Menschen zu empfangen, hatten andere die Aufgabe, die Bedeutung von Träumen anderer zu erklären (Traumdeuter)." Zgoll, *Traum und Welterleben*, 401. For commonalities with Egyptian dream accounts see Shupak, "Dreams," 137.

Conclusion

The above analysis has shown that Gen 40–41 likely represent the oldest dream material within Gen 37–45. These chapters are concerned with the fate of Joseph, the Israelite mantic, who interprets the intrarelational symbolic dreams of two Egyptian officers and Pharaoh.[27] Joseph's role within this narrative context resembles that of Mesopotamian dream specialists, who were frequently consulted to reveal the hidden meaning of symbolic dreams.[28]

The portrayal of Joseph as a capable mantic seems to have been expanded by explicit references to the divine origin of dream interpretations,[29] which explain what seems to have been self-evident for the authors of the older accounts: that Joseph's ability to communicate to others the interpretations of dreams is directly related to his exceptional relation with the deity. This development might best be understood against the conceptual background of an ever-increasing distance between human beings and God.[30]

The first dream in Gen 37 presupposes the dream material in Gen 40–41—*sans* the reworking—that may have served as a source of inspiration for the author(s) of Gen 37:4b–8.[31] As in Gen 40–41, Joseph's dreams are presented as intrarelational symbolic dreams. In the context of Gen 37 they juxtapose the motif of the father's preference for Joseph and represent a second trigger for the brothers' hatred. In the greater context of the Joseph narrative the account of the first dream in Gen 37:4b–8 prepares the unfolding and denouement of the fraternal conflict in Gen 42–45, which the content of the first dream (Gen 37:7→Gen 42:6; cf. Gen 43:26, 28) and the key word דבר (Gen 37:4b, 8b and Gen 45:15b) anticipate explicitly.[32] From a theological perspective, the fulfillment of the dream as realized in the narrative context of Gen 42–45 underscores both the divine guidance of the entire chain of events commencing with Gen 37 and the authority with which Joseph's role as *primus inter fratres* is sanctioned.

---

[27] See Zgoll, *Traum und Welterleben*, 243–48.

[28] See, e.g., Zgoll, *Traum und Welterleben*, 401; Lanckau, *Träume*, 30.

[29] Levin, *Jahwist*, 280–86.

[30] For the increasing distance between the human and divine realms in Mesopotamian texts see Zgoll, *Traum und Welterleben*, 295.

[31] For the secondary character of the second dream see Levin, *Jahwist*, 272; Schweizer, *Josefsgeschichte*, 128–32; Ruppert, *Genesis*, 99.

[32] Levin, *Jahwist*, 284.

Bibliography

Becking, Bob. "They Hated Him Even More: Literary Technique in Genesis 37.1–11." *BN* 60 (1991): 40–47.
Carr, David M. *Reading the Fractures of Genesis: Historical and Literary Approaches.* Louisville: Westminster John Knox Press, 1996.
Coats, George W. "Redactional Unity in Gen 37–50." *JBL* 93 (1974): 15–21.
Döhling, Jan-Dirk. "Die Herrschaft erträumen, die Träume beherrschen: Herrschaft, Traum und Wirklichkeit in den Josefträumen (Gen 37,5–11) und der Israel-Josefsgeschichte." *BZ* 50.1 (2006): 1–30.
Ede, Franziska. *Die Josefsgeschichte: Redaktionsgeschichtliche und literarkritische Untersuchungen zur Entstehung von Gen 37–50.* BZAW 485. Berlin: de Gruyter, 2016.
Fox, Michael V. "Joseph and Wisdom." Pages 231–62 in *The Book of Genesis: Composition, Reception, and Interpretation.* Edited by Craig A. Evans, Joel N. Lohr, and David L. Petersen. VTSup 152. Leiden: Brill, 2012.
Gressmann, Hugo. "Ursprung und Entwicklung der Joseph-Sage." Pages 1–55 in *Eucharisterion: Studien zur Religion und Literatur des Alten und Neuen Testaments.* Edited by Hans Schmidt. FRLANT 36. Göttingen: Vandenhoeck & Ruprecht, 1923.
Gunkel, Hermann. *Genesis.* HKAT. 4th ed. Göttingen: Vandenhoeck & Ruprecht, 1917.
Hamilton, Victor P. *The Book of Genesis: Chapters 18–50.* NICOT. Grand Rapids: Eerdmans, 1995.
Hilbert, Benjamin D. H. "Joseph's Dreams, Part One: From Abimelech to Saul." *JSOT* 35 (2011): 259–83.
Jacob, Benno. *Das erste Buch der Tora: Genesis.* Berlin: Schocken, 1934.
Kebekus, Norbert. *Die Josefserzählung: Literarturkritische und redaktionsgeschichtliche Untersuchungen zu Gen 37–50.* Münster: Waxmann, 1990.
Kratz, Reinhard G. *Die Komposition der erzählenden Bücher des Alten Testaments: Grundwissen der Bibelkritik.* UTB 2157. Göttingen: Vandenhoeck & Ruprecht, 2000.
Lanckau, Jörg, *Der Herr der Träume: Eine Studie zur Funktion des Traumes in der Josefsgeschichte der Hebräischen Bibel.* AThANT 85. Zürich: Theologischer Verlag Zürich, 2006.
Levin, Christoph. *Der Jahwist.* FRLANT 157. Göttingen: Vandenhoeck & Ruprecht, 1993.
Lux, Rüdiger. *Josef: Der Auserwählte unter seinen Brüdern.* Leipzig: Evangelische Verlagsanstalt, 2001.
Niehoff, Maren. *The Figure of Joseph in Post-Biblical Jewish Literature.* AGJU 16. Leiden: Brill, 1992.
Pirson, Ron. *The Lord of the Dreams: A Semantic and Literary Analysis of Gen 37–50.* JSOTSup 355. London: Sheffield Academic Press, 2002.
von Rad, Gerhard. *Das erste Buch Moses.* ATD 4. Göttingen: Vandenhoeck & Ruprecht, 1953.
Rudolph, Wilhelm. "Die Josefsgeschichte." Pages 143–83 in *Der Elohist als Erzähler: Ein Irrweg der Pentateuchkritik? An der Genesis erläutert.* Edited by Wilhelm Rudolph and Paul Volz. BZAW 63. Gießen: Töpelmann, 1933.

Ruppert, Lothar. *Genesis: Ein kritischer und theologischer Kommentar*. FB 118. Würzburg: Echter Verlag, 2008.
Schweizer, Harald. *Die Josefsgeschichte: Konstituierung des Textes*. 2 vols. Tübingen: Mohr Siebeck, 1991.
Seebass, Horst. *Genesis III: Josephsgeschichte (37,1–50,26)*. Neukirchen-Vluyn: Neukirchener Verlagsgesellschaft, 2000.
Shupak, Nili. "A Fresh Look at the Dreams of the Officials and of Pharaoh in the Story of Joseph (Genesis 40–41) in the Light of Egyptian Dreams." *JANES* 30 (2006): 103–38.
Strauss, Hans. "Weisheitliche Lehrerzählungen in und um das Alte Testament." *ZAW* 116 (2004): 379–95.
Tengström, Sven. *Die Hexateucherzählung: Eine literaturgeschichtliche Studie*. ConBOT 7. Lund: Gleerups, 1976.
Weimar, Peter. "Die Josefsgeschichte als theologische Komposition. Zu Aufbau und Struktur von Gen 37." Pages 27–60 in *Studien zur Josefsgeschichte*. Edited by Peter Weimar. SBAB 44. Stuttgart: Katholisches Bibelwerk, 2008.
Wenham, Gordon J. *Genesis 16–50*. WBC 2. Dallas: Word Books, 1996.
Willmes, Bernd. "Objektive Ereignisse bei textinterner Literarkritik: Einige Anmerkungen zur Subjektivität literarkritischer Beobachtung: Harald Schweizers Studie 'Die Josefsgeschichte.'" *BN* 67 (1993): 54–86.
Wöhrle, Jakob. *Fremdlinge im eigenen Land: Zur Entstehung und Intention der priesterlichen Passagen der Vätergeschichte*. FRLANT 246. Göttingen: Vandenhoeck & Ruprecht, 2012.
Zgoll, Annette. *Traum und Welterleben im antiken Mesopotamien: Traumtheorie und Traumpraxis im 3.–1. Jahrtausend v. Chr. als Horizont einer Kulturgeschichte des Träumens*. AOAT 333. Münster: Ugarit-Verlag, 2006.

6
Samuel's Theophany and the Politics of Religious Dreams

Stephen C. Russell

First Samuel 3 describes how, after three cases of mistaken identity, the young Samuel received in the temple and delivered to his master Eli a prophetic word concerning the overthrow of Eli's house.[1] Scholars have analyzed the story as a call narrative comparable to texts describing the divine commissioning of biblical prophets or as a dream theophany comparable to the descriptions of auditory dream messages in biblical and other ancient Near Eastern literature.[2] Admitted-

---

[1] I am grateful to Robert S. Kawashima, who provided very helpful comments on a written draft of this paper. The narrative uses נער to describe Samuel, a term applicable to wide range of ages. Josephus suggests that Samuel had just completed his twelfth year (*Ant.* V 10.4). See S. Goldman, *Samuel: Hebrew Text and English Translation with an Introduction and Commentary* (London: Soncino Press, 1949), 16. On the meaning of נער here, see Peter R. Ackroyd, *The First Book of Samuel* (Cambridge: Cambridge University Press, 1971), 42–32. Evidently, Samuel was asleep in the sanctuary proper, where the ark was located, while Eli slept within the temple complex but outside the doors to the sanctuary, perhaps in the vestibule. Cf. P. Kyle McCarter, *1 Samuel: A New Translation, with Introduction, Commentary, and Notes*, AB 8 (Garden City: Doubleday, 1980), 98–99.

[2] On 1 Sam 3 as a prophetic call narrative, see Murray Newman, "The Prophetic Call of Samuel," in *Israel's Prophetic Heritage: Essays in Honor of James Muilenburg*, ed. Bernhard W. Anderson and Walter J. Harrelson (New York: Harper, 1962), 86–97; Gerhard von Rad, *Old Testament Theology* (New York: Harper, 1962–65), 2:55; Hans Wilhelm Hertzberg, *1–2 Samuel: A Commentary*, trans. John S. Bowden (Philadelphia: Westminster Press, 1964), 41; McCarter, *1 Samuel*, 99–100. For a critique of the view that the text represents a call narrative see Wolfgang Richter, *Die sogenannten vorprophetischen Berufungsberichte: Eine literaturwissenschaftliche Studie zu 1 Sam 9,1–*

ly, as I note further below, the narrative initiates Samuel into a new role and the description of this revelatory experience shares literary motifs with depictions of ancient Near Eastern dream theophanies. These characterizations of the narrative's form, however, overlook important features of the narrative that are crucial to understanding how it functions in the books of Samuel. In what follows, I argue that compared to the literary conventions characterizing depictions of dream theophanies, one feature of our narrative stands out—Samuel is unable here to perceive the divine nature of the theophanic voice. He requires instruction from Eli in order to receive the word of Yahweh. This unusual feature of the narrative's conception of prophetic revelation, I suggest, allows the character Eli to come to terms with the divine origin of the word against his house and to authorize the house that will replace his. The story of Eli's authorization of Samuel

---

10,16, Ex 3f. und Ri 6,11b–17, FRLANT 101 (Göttingen: Vandenhoeck & Ruprecht, 1970), 174–75. Serge Frolov observes that of the six features that Norman Habel identifies as integral to a call narrative—divine confrontation, introductory word, commission, objection, reassurance, and sign—only two are present in 1 Sam 3: divine confrontation and introductory word. See Norman Habel, "The Form and Significance of the Call Narratives," *ZAW* 77 (1965): 298–301; Serge Frolov, *The Turn of the Cycle: 1 Samuel 1–8 in Synchronic and Diachronic Perspectives*, BZAW 342 (Berlin: de Gruyter, 2004), 110–11. On this question, see also Uriel Simon, "1 Samuel III: A Youth's Call to Prophecy," in *Proceedings of the Seventh World Congress of Jewish Studies, Held at the Hebrew University, Jerusalem, 7–14 August, 1977: 2 Studies in the Bible and the Ancient Near East*, ed. Yisrael Gutman (Jerusalem: World Union of Jewish Studies, 1981), 85–93 [Hebrew]; Uriel Simon, "Samuel's Call to Prophecy: Form Criticism with Close Reading," *Prooftexts* 1 (1981): 119–32; Philippe de Robert, "1 Samuel 3: une vocation prophétique?" *Foi et vie* 83 (1984): 4–10. On 1 Sam 3 as a dream theophany, see Robert Karl Gnuse, *The Dream Theophany of Samuel: Its Structure in Relation to Ancient Near Eastern Dreams and Its Theological Significance* (Lanham: University Press of America, 1984); Peter Mommer, *Samuel: Geschichte und Überlieferung*, WMANT 65 (Neukirchen-Vluyn: Neukirchener Verlag, 1991), 24; Ruth Fidler, "The Shiloh Theophany (1 Samuel 3): A Case Study of the Liminal Report," in *Proceedings of the Twelfth World Congress of Jewish Studies, Jerusalem, July 29–August 5, 1997, Division A* (Jerusalem: World Union of Jewish Studies, 1999), 99–107 [Hebrew]; Ruth Fidler, *"Dreams Speak Falsely"? Dream Theophanies in the Bible: Their Place in Ancient Israelite Faith and Traditions* (Jerusalem: Hebrew University Magnes, 2005), 314–15 [Hebrew]. Compare Ivan Hylander's characterization of 1 Sam 3 as containing an "incubation oracle" (*Der literarische Samuel-Saul-Komplex (1 Sam. 1–15): traditionsgeschichtlich untersucht* [Uppsala: Almquist & Wiksell, 1932], 45–46, cited in Frolov, *Turn of the Cycle*, 111 n. 151. On Hittite parallels to the revelation of God's word in 1 Sam 3 and other biblical texts, see Manfred Hutter, "Bemerkungen über das "Wort Gottes" bei den Hethitern," *BN* 28 (1985): 17–26. I do not find convincing Peter E. Lewis's suggestion that the author of 1 Sam 3 intentionally modeled the narrative on the sixth chapter of the Egyptian Book of the Dead, which he had before him as he worked ("Is There a Parallel between 1 Samuel 3 and the Sixth Chapter of the Egyptian Book of the Dead?" *JSOT* 31 [2007]: 365–76).

is best understood in the social context of competition between priestly families in ancient Israel and Judah, which required both differentiation from and continuity with the past. Finally, I show how scribes have shaped 1 Sam 2 so as to foreshadow the rejection of the house of Saul in favor of the house of David in 1 Sam 15. In these ways, I offer here a political reading of the narrative within its ancient literary contexts.

1 SAMUEL 3 AND THE LITERARY PORTRAYAL OF RELIGIOUS DREAMING

Comparing and contrasting 1 Sam 3 with the many forms of prophetic activity in the ancient world lies well beyond my goals here, but given the focus of this volume, I would like to point out some shared motifs and distinctive features of 1 Sam 3 with respect to literary portrayals of dream theophanies. Robert Karl Gnuse has made the strongest case for understanding the text as depicting a dream theophany.[3] To my mind, the language of the text is too vague to determine definitively whether or not, within the narrative world of the text, the character Samuel experiences a dream theophany or some other form of theophanic experience.[4] Nevertheless, in my judgment, 1 Sam 3 shares much in common with the literary depiction of dream theophanies in biblical and other ancient Near Eastern literature.[5] I would define this literary tradition—whether expressed in narratives, or letters, or some other genre—on the principle of family resemblance.[6] These texts contain identifiable common features, but a given text need not contain every feature in order to be compared meaningfully with other texts that utilize the convention.

---

[3] For a summary, see Gnuse, *Dream Theophany*, 140–52.

[4] Jack M. Sasson traces the motif of seeing in the narratives about Samuel's rise and argues, "awake, Samuel actually saw God." See Jack M. Sasson, "The Eyes of Eli: An Essay in Motif Accretion," in *Inspired Speech: Prophecy in the Ancient Near East, Essays in Honor of Herbert B. Huffmon*, ed. Louis Stulman and John Kaltner, JSOTSup 378 (London: T&T Clark, 2004), 171–90.

[5] In distinguishing between experience and literary convention, I am indebted here to Koowon Kim, *Incubation as a Type-Scene in the 'Aqhatu, Kirta, and Hannah Stories: A Form-Critical and Narratological Study of KTU 1.14 I–1.15 III, 1.17 I–II, and 1 Samuel 1:1–2:11*, VTSup 145 (Leiden: Brill, 2011).

[6] The notion of "family resemblance" was developed in particular by Ludwig Wittgenstein, for example in his posthumously published *Philosophical Investigations*. On "family resemblance," see already Chapter 8 of Book 1 in John Stuart Mill's *A System of Logic*. On sets defined on this principle, see, for example, Rodney Needham, "Polythetic Classification," in *Against the Tranquility of Axioms* (Berkeley: University of Calirofnia Press, 1983), 36–55.

Gnuse highlights points of family resemblance between 1 Sam 3 and the literary depiction of theophanic dreams in other ancient texts. He treats two groups of such features: those related to the setting of the dream theophany and those related to the theophanic experience itself. With regard to setting, Gnuse observes that Samuel's theophany takes place in a sacred location, beside the ark of Yahweh in the temple of Shiloh—compare Solomon's dream theophany at Gibeon where there was a shrine (1 Kgs 3:4–5), Jacob's dream at Beersheba where he had previously offered sacrifice (Gen 46:1), the dream of Kirta in a private chamber (KTU 1.14 i 26–27), the dream of Danel at a site where he offered food to the gods (KTU 1.17 i 2–16), and the dream of Thutmose IV beside the great god, that is, the sphinx (Dream Stele of Thutmose IV).[7] Gnuse also contends that Samuel is asleep in 1 Sam 3:3—compare the textual indications that Danel lies down (KTU 1.17 i 13–14) and Kirta sleeps (KTU 1.14 i 31–35) before their dream theophanies, and the mention of sleep in Thutmose IV's Dream Stele. But the verb שכב is more ambiguous in this regard than Gnuse acknowledges.[8] It may refer here to a prostrate position without sleep.[9] Finally in terms of setting, the theophany apparently occurs at night as suggested by the fact that Samuel lies in place until morning (v. 15)—compare Nabonidus's dream from Sin at night (Harran Inscriptions of Nabonidus H2 i 11) and the nocturnal dreams mentioned in the opening section of Ludlul-bel-nemeqi Tablet iii.[10] With regard to setting, then, 1 Sam 3 shares with other ancient depictions of dream theophanies a sacred setting, perhaps an allusion to sleep, and an indication of nighttime.[11]

Gnuse notes further points of family resemblance between the theophanic encounter proper in 1 Sam 3 and ancient theophanic dream narratives. The narrative depicts Yahweh as initiating the theophany and calling to Samuel—compare Yahweh coming to Abimelech in a dream (Gen 20:3), El approaching

---

[7] The precise term, "ark of god," in 3:3 occurs elsewhere in the Hebrew Bible only in 4:11. There Hophni and Phinehas are killed, in fulfillment of the prophecies against the house of Eli. The closely related term, "ark of the god of Israel," is used in 1 Sam 5:7, 8, 10, 11; 6:3. Compare also "ark of our god" in 1 Chr 13:3. The phrase stitches chapter 3 to the narratives about the ark that follow in chapters 4 through 6.

[8] On the verb here, cf. Sasson, "Eyes of Eli," 177. Frances Flannery-Dailey notes, "In antiquity dreams and visions exist on a continuum and do not always neatly fall into categories of 'sleeping' or 'waking' states, although some individual cases do" (*Dreamers, Scribes, and Priests: Jewish Dreams in the Hellenistic and Roman Eras*, JSJSup 90 [Leiden: Brill 2004], 17).

[9] Gnuse also argues that ancient Near Eastern dream narratives often depict the dreamer as semi-conscious or awake and that if the hallmarks of a dream theophany are present, then ancient dream reports need not use the word "dream" to depict a dream theophany. See Gnuse, *Dream Theophany*, 140.

[10] Sasson, "Eyes of Eli," 177.

[11] Gnuse, *Dream Theophany*, 144.

Kirta (KTU 1.14 i 35–37), and Amun-Re coming before Amenhotep II (Memphis Stele of Amenhotep II 20b–22a).[12] Gnuse contends that Samuel is awoken by the deity to hear the message—compare the priest of Ishtar being aroused in order to receive a message for Ashurbanipal (Rassam Prism [BM 91026] v 50).[13] But the text is more ambiguous in this regard than Gnuse concedes since the narrative does not state explicitly that Samuel was asleep. Gnuse further observes that according to 1 Sam 3:10, "Yahweh came and stood"— compare Yahweh standing beside Jacob (Gen 28:13), Ningirsu standing beside the head of Eanatum in the Vulture Stele, and the god Khnum standing before Djoser in the Famine Stele.[14] Samuel receives a message about imminent destruction of someone else that will pave the way for his own ascendancy—compare the promise of kingship to the young Thutmose IV in his Dream Stele. To sum up, then, while I disagree with some of the claims made by Gnuse, he has demonstrated that 1 Sam 3 shares a sufficient density of literary features in common with ancient Near Eastern descriptions of dream theophanies to be compared profitably to them.[15]

The impression that 1 Sam 3 draws on the literary convention of dream theophanies is strengthened by a consideration of the nature of the religious traditions associated with Shiloh.[16] C. L. Seow has shown that the biblical traditions

---

[12] Gnuse observes, "Dream theophanies of the ancient Near East and the Bible stress the active communication of the deity in a verbal fashion, which then overshadows the visual aspect of the theophany" (*Dream Theophany*, 144–45).

[13] On waking, compare also the Standard Babylonian version of Gilgamesh iv 92–98, where after being startled by his dream, Gilgamesh asks Enkidu, "My friend, did you not call me? Why am I awake? Did you not touch me? Why am I in confusion? Did a god not pass by? Why is my flesh benumbed?" (translation from A. R. George, *The Babylonian Gilgamesh Epic: Introduction, Critical Edition and Cuneiform Texts* [Oxford: Oxford University Press, 2003], 1:593). Despite this rhetoric, Gilgamesh's descriptions of the content of the dream suggest that it was not a theophany proper but rather a symbolic message dream.

[14] On the motif of standing, especially at the head of the dreamer, see A. Leo Oppenheim, *The Interpretation of Dreams in the Ancient Near East: With a Translation of the Assyrian Dream-Book*, TAPS 46.3 (Philadelphia: American Philosophical Society, 1956), 189, 212.

[15] Gnuse also observes some differences between 1 Sam 3 and ancient Near Eastern literary depictions of dream theophanies (*Dreams*, 148–149). Some dream reports contain dialogue between the dreamer and the deity, while 1 Sam 3 contains only Samuel's initial response to being called. The notice that Samuel slept until morning differs from the more typical description of the dreamer awaking suddenly. But compare Jacob and Balaam arising in the morning in Gen 20:8; Num 22:13, 21.

[16] So also Mark Leuchter, *Samuel and the Shaping of Tradition* (New York: Oxford University Press, 2013), 35.

about Shiloh indicate that it housed a cult of El, head of the regional pantheon.[17] The narratives contain a density of El-based theophoric names in Samuel's family tree—his own name, his father Elkanah, and his grandfather Yerohamel (see the LXX to 1 Sam 1:1).[18] The theme of barrenness in 1 Sam 1 is shared by Ugaritic texts in which El bestows children on Kirta and Danel. The tradition of a tent of assembly at Shiloh (Ps 78:60, 1 Sam 2:22) parallels the motifs of the divine assembly over which El presides (e.g., KTU 1.2 i 14–16, 19–24) and the tent where El dwells (KTU 1.1 iii 21–24, 1.3 v 5–9, 1.4 iv 20–24, 1.6 i 32–36, 1.17 vi 46–49). Psalm 78 repeatedly associates Shiloh with El (vv. 7, 8, 18, 19, 34, and 41), Elyon (vv. 17, 56), and El Elyon (v. 35). El, as Seow notes, appears in dream theophanies to Kirta and Danel in the Ugaritic texts, and he himself receives a symbolic dream that heralds Baal's return.[19] As such, the literary motif of a nighttime theophany in 1 Sam 3 may be understood against the background of these connections between Shiloh and El. Seow's exploration of the history of traditions associated with Shiloh thus corroborates Gnuse's arguments about literary convention.

In sum, then, whether the character Samuel experienced a dream theophany or not, the scribes who produced 1 Sam 3 told this story about him by drawing on literary conventions governing the depiction of dream theophanies in the ancient Near East. As such, we might profitably ask: How does 1 Sam 3 play with this literary tradition? In its ancient literary context, one feature of 1 Sam 3 is particularly jarring—Samuel's initial failure to recognize the theophanic message. S. A. L. Butler's classification of Akkadian prognostic dreams into three types is relevant in this regard.[20] Butler distinguishes between message dreams

---

[17] C. L. Seow, *Myth, Drama, and the Politics of David's Dance*, HSM 44 (Atlanta: Scholars Press, 1989), 11–54.

[18] Seow also argues that the name of Shiloh's priest, Eli, is best understood as an abbreviated form of a theophoric name based on Elyon, a title for the head of the pantheon. The head of the pantheon may be understood here as El.

[19] See also C. L. Seow, "The Syro-Palestinian Context of Solomon's Dream," *HTR* 77 (1984): 141–52.

[20] S. A. L. Butler, *Mesopotamian Conceptions of Dreams and Dream Rituals*, AOAT 258 (Münster: Ugarit-Verlag, 1998), 15–24. A very large number of surveys treat the topic of dreaming in biblical and other ancient Near Eastern literature. In his landmark work, A. Leo Oppenheim distinguished within ancient Near Eastern literary evidence three planes of dreaming: dreams that contain a message from the deity, dreams that are symptomatic of the physical or mental state of the dreamer, and dreams that contain prognostications of the future (*Interpretation of Dreams*, 184). Jean-Marie Husser offered a revised taxonomy with more types, including message dreams, symbolic dreams, premonitory dreams, prophetic dreams, and judgment dreams. In developing this taxonomy, Husser observes the distinction between inspired and deductive divination proposed by Plato and the distinction between theorematic and allegorical dreams proposed by Artemis of Daldis. Husser is careful to note, however, the diversity of dream

from a deity or a deity's envoy that are straightforward and have no need of interpretation, symbolic message dreams that require decoding, and dream omens that must be interpreted from a dream-book. The dream theophanies I have been discussing here belong to Butler's first category. Routinely in biblical and other ancient Near Eastern literature, Butler's second and third categories—symbolic message dreams and dream omens—require for their interpretation the assistance of individuals with specialized knowledge. To cite but a few examples, Gudea consults Nanše (cyl. A i 22–ii 3), Dumuzi his sister Geštinanna (Dumuzi's Dream, 20–25), Gilgamesh his mother (i 245), and Pharaoh's officials Joseph (Gen 40:8) in order to determine the meanings of their dreams. In contrast, and by definition, dreams in the first category do not require the help of those with specialized knowledge. Their source and meaning are transparent.[21] In none of the dream theophanies that I have been discussing here does the dreamer mistake a divine voice for a human one.[22] Oppenheim notes, "the scene

---

reports from the ancient Near East. See Jean-Marie Husser, *Dreams and Dream Narratives in the Biblical World*, trans. Jill M. Munro, BibSem 63 (Sheffield: Sheffield Acadmeic Press, 1999), 19–26. The former distinction is evidenced, for example, in the discussion of intuitive and deductive oneiromancy in Jean Bottéro, *Mesopotamia: Writing, Reasoning, and the Gods*, trans. Zainab Bahrani and Marc Van De Mieroop (Chicago: The University of Chicago Press, 1992), 109–16. For surveys of ancient Near Eastern depictions of religious dreaming, see Joel Sweek, "Dreams of Power from Sumer to Judah: An Essay on the Divinatory Economy of the Ancient Near East" (PhD diss., University of Chicago, 1996); Flannery-Dailey, *Dreamers*, 17–56; Annette Zgoll, *Traum und Welterleben im antiken Mesopotamien: Traumtheorie und Traumpraxis im 3.–1. Jahrtausend v. Chr. als Horizont einer Kulturgeschichte des Träumens*, AOAT 333 (Münster: Ugarit-Verlag, 2006); Kim, *Incubation as a Type-Scene*, 27–60.

[21] In fact, dream reports sometimes contain a divine self-identification formula after the initial apparition but prior to the message proper. Thus, for example, the message to Jacob in Gen 28:13 begins, "I am Yahweh, the god of your father Abraham, the god of Isaac" (cf. Gen 31:12; 46:3); the deity tells Thutmose IV, "I am your father Horemakhet-Khepri-Ra-Atum" (Dream Stele); and the god tells Djoser, "I am Khnum, your fashioner" (Famine Stele). See related comments in Gnuse, *Dream Theophany*, 146.

[22] Yet, 1 Sam 3 shares with certain texts describing what Esther J. Hamori has called the *'îš* theophany the assumption that a god could appear in a form that left room for uncertainty and ambiguity. See Esther J. Hamori, *"When Gods Were Men": The Embodied God in Biblical and Near Eastern Literature*, BZAW 384 (Berlin: de Gruyter, 2008). In Gen 18:1–15, Abraham entertains three strangers who turn out to be Yahweh and his messengers. In Gen 32, Jacob wrestles with a man who turns out to be a divine figure. Hamori argues that both texts reflect divine embodiment with anthropomorphic realism. Hamori shows how this form of divine embodiment differs from forms of anthropomorphism in other ancient Near Eastern literature. In general, where the gods are depicted in realistic anthropomorphic terms in Mesopotamian, Egyptian, and Ugaritic literature, they do not interact with humans in that form, and where they are shown interacting with humans, it is not in anthropomorphically realistic form. Although Greek mythology depicts

and the actor(s) of the 'message dream' are rigidly restricted. The 'messenger' appears and is *immediately recognized*."[23] But in our narrative, Samuel three times fails to recognize the source of the theophanic message and must receive the help of a professional, Eli, in order to experience the theophany.[24]

---

the gods as sometimes appearing in human or other forms on earth, such appearance is intentionally a form of disguise. On this last point, see also Benjamin D. Sommer, *The Bodies of God and the World of Ancient Israel* (Cambridge: Cambridge University Press, 2009), 30–36, 194–95 n. 145. Jean-Pierre Vernant notes, "The second type of incognito appearance occurs when a god gives his or her body a strictly human appearance. This frequently used trick, however, has its limits. As well camouflaged as a god may be in the skin of a mortal, there is something 'off,' something in the otherness of the divine presence that remains strange and disconcerting even when the god is in disguise" ("Mortals and Immortals: The Body of the Divine" in *Mortals and Immortals: Collected Essays*, ed. Froma I. Zeitlin [Princeton: Princeton University Press, 1991], 43). See also H. J. Rose, "Divine Disguisings," *HTR* 49 (1956): 63–72. Even if one does not accept Hamori's thesis, the struggle of the biblical and interpretive traditions to find adequate language to describe the beings portrayed in Gen 18 and 32—are they human? are they angelic? are they divine?—points to the possibility of ambiguity and uncertainty in the theophanic experience in biblical literature. While 1 Sam 3 reports a dream rather than an *īš* theophany, the narrative shares with the texts Hamori discusses an assumption that the divine could be perceived as human.

[23] Oppenheim, *Dreams*, 192. Emphasis added. Oppenheim cites as the sole exception the case of a dream of Pharaoh Djoser in which the god appears in disguise. The god is nevertheless recognized by Djoser. He prays to him and is awarded the privilege of seeing his face.

[24] An account in Greek sources of a dream by Ptolemy Soter contains the motif of misrecognition, though not the kind of misrecognition found in 1 Sam 3. According to Plutarch (*De Iside* 28), Ptolemy saw a dream of the colossus of the god Pluto in Sinope commanding him to relocate the image to Alexandria. Ptolemy, however, did not recognize the form because he had not seen the image before. It was only by consulting friends and, through them, a well-travelled man, that Ptolemy was able to identify the form as Pluto's image in Sinope. The account is elaborated by Tacitus (*Historiae* 4:83), who adds flourishes of various kinds—the figure who appeared to Ptolemy was extraordinarily beautiful, after issuing instructions the figure ascended to heaven in a blaze of fire, Ptolemy consulted Egyptian priests experienced in dream interpretation, Ptolemy's failure to obey the divine message necessitated a second more terrifying dream. Tacitus is quite clear that Ptolemy had no difficulty recognizing the dream as a theophany. He only needed the help of dream interpreters because he could not identify precisely which deity had appeared to him. This is also the most straightforward way to interpret Plutarch's account, which is far terser. These Greek texts, then, assume that it was possible to have doubts about which deity appeared in a dream theophany, but neither suggests that it was possible to misrecognize a god for a human.

The Politics of Religious Dreams in the Ancient Near East

This peculiar feature of the literary depiction of Samuel's theophany draws the reader's attention to the relationships of power between the characters in the narrative. Dream reports often serve a legitimating function by lending divine sanction to existing powers or to those overthrowing them. Thus Paul Friedrich notes, "Homer and the Bible focus on political dreams and largely ignore all others; from a Homeric and biblical point of view, dream interpretation should be a subfield of the art of government, and of the discipline of political science."[25] Below, I will highlight the artistry with which motifs of power are developed in 1 Sam 3 and how they connect to the larger political story of the House of David in Samuel–Kings and in particular to 1 Sam 15. To set that discussion in context, I wish first to draw attention to a few ancient Near Eastern texts that contain particularly close parallels to the political themes of 1 Sam 3.

There are thematic similarities between 1 Sam 3 and ARM 26 234 (=ARM 13 112). In this letter, Kibri-Dagan informs the king of Mari of a boy's dream warning that a ruined house should not be rebuilt.[26] The dreamer, it emerges, had initially kept the dream to himself and had only come forward to report it after receiving the same dream on a second night. Abraham Malamat argues that ARM 26 234, like 1 Sam 3, depicts the failure of an inexperienced boy to recognize the divine source of a message.[27] Nowhere in this terse report, however, does Kibri-Dagan indicate that the dreamer misunderstood who spoke to him. In fact, in recounting both dreams, Kibri-Dagan explicitly identifies the speaker as a god.[28] The content of both dreams likewise implies a speaker with supernatural

---

[25] Paul Friedrich, "The Poetry of Language in the Politics of Dreams," in *The Language Parallax: Linguistic Relativism and Poetic Indeterminacy* (Austin: University of Texas Press, 1986), 81, cited in Sweek, "Dreams of Power," 58. Sweek observes, "For rhetorical purposes, which is frankly to say for their political purposes, published dream narratives possess a certain peerless economy in at least three principal features: divine initiative, interpretability, and immediacy of contact" ("Dreams of Power," 55).

[26] On the historical background to the incident, see Frans Van Koppen, "Seized by the Royal Order: The Households of Sammêtar and Other Magnates at Mari," in *Florilegium marianum VI: Recueil d'études à la mémoire d'André Parrot*, ed. Dominique Charpin and Jean-Marie Durand, Mémoires de N.A.B.U. 7 (Paris: SEPOA, 2002), 324. Following Durand, *AEM I/1*, 458, Van Koppen argues that the text has in mind the same situation reflected in ARM 26 243.

[27] Abraham Malamat, "Prophetic Revelations in New Documents from Mari and the Bible," in *Volume du Congrès: Geneva, 1965*, VTSup 15 (Leiden: Brill, 1966), 223–25.

[28] The term dingir-*lum-ma* is clearly visible in 8' and is to be reconstructed also in 1'. See Durand, *AEM I/1*, 476; Martti Nissinen, *Prophets and Prophecy in the Ancient Near East*, with contributions by C. L. Seow and Robert K. Ritner, WAW 12 (Atlanta:

powers: "I will make [the house] collapse into the river." Thus, although the text gives no explicit reason for the boy's failure to deliver the dream message after the first night, one can read ARM 26 234, like 1 Sam 3:15–17, as reflecting instead the motif of a messenger who is reluctant to bear bad news to an authority figure.[29]

The requirement that dreams, even those of ill portent, be reported to those in authority can be understood in the context of the loyalty expected by ancient Near Eastern monarchs. Victor Hurowitz points to related themes in a diviner's oath taken at Mari (ARM 26 1 = *AEM I/1*, 13).[30] Hurowitz summarizes, "According to this text, which is phrased entirely in the first-person singular, the diviner affirms to the king that he will report to the king any and all relevant omens taken for the king (lines 1–6), that he will not reveal to anyone else any negative omens about the king (7–10), that he will guard with secrecy omens of colleagues which he overhears (11–16), that he will report immediately to the king any extispicy performed for rebellious purposes (17–30), and that he will not falsify any omens."[31] This Mari text from the Old Babylonian period requires loyalty from the individual with divinatory experience. The Neo-Assyrian treaties of Esarhaddon required those swearing loyalty to report news to the king, including anything detrimental to the crown spoken by someone else, whether a prophet, ecstatic, or dream interpreter (SAA 2 6:108–122).[32] Failure

---

Society of Biblical Literature, 2003), 65; Jack M. Sasson, *From the Mari Archives: An Anthology of Old Babylonian Letters* (Winona Lake: Eisenbrauns, 2015), 286–87.

[29] Fear is also a motivating factor in Naramsin's refusal to discuss with anyone a dream he had foretelling his downfall (The Curse of Agade, line 87 and 93a, ETCSL 2.1.5). Sasson notes, "XIII:112 ... reveals the price paid by those who fail to communicate a dream to the proper authorities. When a man saw a dream in which a god [read in l. 1': AN^{lum}-*ma*, as in 8'] delivers an ukase, then fails to transmit it, the same dream is repeated the next night [but slightly accented on the active role to be played by the message's ultimate recipients ... the man was stricken ill" ("Mari Dreams," *JAOS* 103 [1983]: 285 n. 12).

[30] Victor Hurowitz, "Eli's Adjuration of Samuel (1 Samuel III 7–18) in the Light of a 'Diviner's Protocol' from Mari (*AEM I/1*, 1)," *VT* 44 (1994): 483–97. Hurowitz also points to the discussion of loyalty oaths in Jean-Marie Durand, "Précurseurs syriens aux protocoles néo-assyriens: considérations sur la vie politique aux Bords-de-l'Euprate," in *Marchands, Diplomates et Empereurs: Études sur la civilisation mésopotamienne offertes à Paul Garelli*, ed. Dominique Charpin and Francis Joannès (Paris: ERC, 1991), 13–71, esp. 14–15.

[31] Hurowitz, "Eli's Adjuration," 489.

[32] So Sweek, "Dreams of Power," 140. See also Joel Sweek, "Inquiring for the State in the Ancient Near East: Delineating Political Location," in *Magic and Divination in the Ancient World*, ed. Leda Jean Ciraolo and Jonathan Lee Seidel (Leiden: Brill, 2002), 49–50. The relevant section of VTE reads, "If you hear any evil, improper, ugly word which is not seemly nor good to Assurbanipal, the great crown prince designate, son of Esar-

to disclose such information was considered treason. This principle of loyalty is also known in a letter from Šamaš-šumu-ukin, crown prince of Babylon, to Esarhaddon (SAA 16 21).[33] The letter summarizes two reports received by Šamaš-šumu-ukin, the first of which concerns divinatory activity directed against the crown.[34] Along related lines, the king of Israel makes the prophet Micaiah son of Imlah swear to speak the truth about the revelations he receives from Yahweh (1 Kgs 22:16).[35] Texts such as these provide a context for understanding Eli's oath, "So may god do and so may he add if you keep from me a single word of all that he said to you!" (1 Sam 3:17). The oath is unique in biblical literature in so far as it is the only time this formula is used to imprecate someone other than the speaker.[36] Its use here draws the reader's attention to the relationship of power between Samuel and Eli. Although clearly depicted as a priest in 1 Sam 3, Eli behaves in this moment like an ancient Near Eastern royal figure by demanding that Samuel disclose the divine message to him.

To my mind, within the corpus of extant Near Eastern literature, the text with the closest parallels to the power dynamics described in 1 Sam 3 is the Su-

---

haddon, king of Assyria, your lord, either from the mouth of his enemy or from the mouth of his ally, or from the mouth of his brothers or from the mouth of his uncles, his cousins, his family, members of his father's line, or from the mouth of your brothers, your sons, your daughters, or from the mouth of a prophet, an ecstatic, an inquirer of oracles, or from the mouth of any human being at all, you shall not conceal it but come and report it to Assurbanipal, the great crown prince designate, son of Esarhaddon, king of Assyria" (translation from Parpola and Watanabe, SAA 2 6). For a discussion of the text, see Martti Nissinen, *References to Prophecy in Neo-Assyrian Sources*, SAAS 7 (Helsinki: Neo-Assyrian Text Corpus Project; Helsinki University Press, 1998), 156–62.

[33] Mikko Luukko and Greta Van Buylaere, *The Political Correspondence of Esarhaddon*, SAA 16 (Helsinki: Helsinki University Press, 2002), 18–19. See also Simo Parpola, "A Letter from Šamaš-šumu-ukīn to Esarhaddon," *Iraq* 34 (1972): 21–34.

[34] Parpola, "Letter," 31–32.

[35] See Hurowitz, "Eli's Adjuration," 491 n. 28. Biblical prophets sometimes declare their intention to speak the truth (Num 22:8) and not to withhold anything (Jer 42:4; cf. Jer 26:2). See Waldemar Janzen, "Witholding the Word," in *Traditions in Transformation: Turning Points in Biblical Faith*, ed. Baruch Halpern and Jon D. Levenson (Winona Lake: Eisenbrauns, 1981), 97–114.

[36] Yael Ziegler, "'So Shall God Do...': Variations of an Oath Formula and Its Literary Meaning," *JBL* 126 (2007): 65–68. Anne Marie Kitz has recently offered a study of Sumerian, Akkadian, Hittite, and Hebrew curses. For Kitz, the curse in 1 Sam 3:17 represents a type of ancient curse in which "an individual or authorized body [enjoins] a conditional imprecation on someone else." She observes, "Eli's command over the matter probably derives from his priestly office." See Anne Marie Kitz, *Cursed Are You! The Phenomenology of Cursing in Cuneiform and Hebrew Texts* (Winona Lake: Eisenbrauns, 2014), 96, 107. Other examples of this type of imposed conditional curses, though pronounced with different formulae than the curse in 1 Sam 3:17, include 1 Sam 11:6–7 and 1 Sam 14:24, 26–28. On these imposed curses, see Kitz, *Cursed Are You!*, 108–14.

merian legend of Sargon published by Jerrold S. Cooper and Wolfgang Heimpel (ETCSL 2.1.4).[37] According to the account, the cupbearer Sargon receives a dream in which Inanna, for Sargon's benefit, drowns his master Urzababa in a river of blood. The dream greatly disturbs Sargon and he cries out in the temple of Ezinu. Hearing his cry, Urzababa summons him and demands of him the contents of the dream. The structure of the relationships of power here parallel those in 1 Sam 3. In both texts, a servant is told in a theophany experienced in a temple that his master will be overthrown.[38] In both texts, the master compels the servant to tell him the divinely delivered message. In neither text does the servant's theophanic vision imply that he will be directly responsible for his master's overthrow. Yet, in both texts, the servant goes on to displace his master. The Sumerian legend also hints that Urzababa had previously received a dream message with the same news, which would parallel an earlier revelation to Eli concerning the downfall of his house.[39] At the same time, there are two fundamental differences between the texts. First, Sargon has no difficulty recognizing who speaks to him, while Samuel only recognizes Yahweh's voice with Eli's help. Second, Urzababa does not acquiesce and instead seeks to kill Sargon, while Eli resigns himself to the message of judgment delivered through Samuel. These two differences, I suggest, are related to one another and are at the crux of how 1 Sam 3 has played with the ancient Near Eastern literary tradition of dream theophanies.

---

[37] Jerrold S. Cooper and Wolfgang Heimpel, "The Sumerian Sargon Legend," *JAOS* 103 (1983): 67–82. The connections between this Sumerian text and 1 Sam 3 are discussed in Moshe Eilat, *Samuel and the Foundation of Kingship in Ancient Israel* (Jerusalem: Magnes, 1997), 30–31 [Hebrew]; Shaul Bar, *A Letter That Has Not Been Read: Dreams in the Hebrew Bible*, trans. Lenn J. Schramm, HUCM 25 (Cincinnati: Hebrew Union College Press, 2001), 178. Jerrold S. Cooper compares the Sumerian account to narratives about dreams in the Joseph story. See Jerrold S. Cooper, "Sargon and Joseph: Dreams Come True," in *Biblical and Related Studies Presented to Samuel Iwry*, ed. Ann Kort and Scott Morschauser (Winona Lake: Eisenbrauns, 1985), 33–39.

[38] As noted above, the Hebrew term נער used to describe Samuel covers a wide range of ages. Both Sargon and Samuel are evidently old enough to render vital service to their respective masters.

[39] The hint comes in lines 3–4, before Sargon receives his dream in lines 12–15. Cooper and Heimpel translate, "He (Urzababa) having lain down in the holy bedchamber, his holy residence, he understood, but would not articulate it, nor speak about it with anyone" ("Sargon Legend," 76).

1 SAMUEL 3 IN ITS LITERARY-HISTORICAL CONTEXT

Reading 1 Sam 3 in its ancient Near Eastern literary context highlights the centrality of political themes to the narrative's arc. The chapter has very cleverly deployed the structure of three failed attempts followed by a successful one in order to bring the character Eli to the realization, and acceptance, of the divine origin of the judgment against his ruling priestly house.[40] Three times, Samuel comes to Eli in the night although he did not call him (vv. 4–8). Eli, despite his fading eyesight, is the first to perceive what is transpiring. The narrative makes explicit his moment of realization, "And Eli understood that Yahweh was summoning the lad" (v. 8b). By giving instructions to Samuel on how to respond, Eli unwittingly authorizes the word of judgment against his own house. The words, "Speak, Yahweh, for your servant is listening" (v. 9), come first from Eli's mouth and, though intended for Samuel, reflect Eli's disposition. It is this act that prepares Eli later in the narrative to accept the divine message. Following Samuel's disclosure of divine judgment, Eli again affirms the divine source of the message. "It is Yahweh," he acknowledges (v. 18), echoing his earlier identification. "Let him do what is good in his eyes," he continues, as though his acquiescence to the judgment follows logically from his acknowledgment of the source of this word (v. 18). The two main points of contrast between our narrative and the Sumerian legend of Sargon are thus related to one another. Within the narrative structure of the episode, Samuel's failure to recognize Yahweh's voice leads Eli to authorize the word against his ruling priestly house and to accept its overthrow.[41] In this way, the narrative depicts Samuel and his house as displacing Eli and his house with Eli's full support.

The political themes of our chapter are in turn related to political themes in 1 Sam 1–3, which describe Samuel's displacement of the house of Eli and Eli's acceptance of this regime change.[42] First Samuel 3:1a, which notes that the lad

---

[40] First Samuel 3 emphasizes Eli's role as the head priest of Shiloh—his authority appears largely confined to the temple. In the larger narrative, however, that authority appears to extend over all Israel in various ways. According to 1 Sam 4:18, Eli judged Israel for forty years. And the eternal promise to Eli alluded to in 1 Sam 2:30 resembles divine promises of royal succession with its use of בית, עד עולם, לפני, and הלך* (cf. 1 Sam 13:13; 2 Sam 7:13, 16, 25–26; 1 Kgs 2:4, 3:6, 8:25, 9:4). On the pattern of three similar elements followed by a distinctive one, see Frolov, *Turn of the Cycle*, 112.

[41] The narrative's description of the change of regime is also emphasized, though in different terms, by Newman, "Prophetic Call of Samuel," 86–97.

[42] The chapter is now embedded in the larger Deuteronomistic History. However, the distinctive language of the Deuteronomistic school is potentially found only in the dream message itself, in v. 11. See Timo Veijola, *Die Ewige Dynastie: David und die*

Samuel ministered before Yahweh, forms part of a structuring refrain within chapters 2–3.[43] Closely related notices are found in 2:11, 2:18, and 3:1. The first notice, in 2:11, serves as a framing device to close Hannah's speech, which is given in the high language of poetry. The second use of the phrase, in 2:18, closes the section about the behavior of Eli's sons. The narrative does not describe their actions with a sequence of *wayyiqtol* verbs. Rather, two sequences of verbs in verses 13–14 and verses 15–16 are used to portray their conduct as habitual.[44] They repeatedly show contempt for the sanctity of sacrificial custom. This explanation of the evil done by Eli's sons differs from that offered in 2:22–25. There, they are rebuked by Eli for abusing their power by having sex with women who come to the sanctuary. The third and final notice that the young

---

Entstehung seiner Dynastie nach der deuteronomistischen Darstellung, AASF B/193 (Helsinki: Academia Scientarum Fennica, 1975), 38–39; McCarter, *1 Samuel*, 98. The phrase, "both ears of anyone who hears about it will tingle," appears here and also in 2 Kgs 21:12 and Jer 19:3, which are sometimes regarded as Deuteronomistic. Moshe Weinfeld includes the phrase in his list of distinctive Deuteronomistic phraseology. See Moshe Weinfeld, *Deuteronomy and the Deuteronomic School* (Winona Lake: Eisenbrauns, 1992), 351. On these texts, see A. Graeme Auld, "Jeremiah-Manasseh-Samuel: Significant Triangle? or Vicious Circle?" in *Prophecy in the Book of Jeremiah*, ed. Hans M. Barstad and Reinhard G. Kratz, BZAW 388 (Berlin: de Gruyter, 2009), 1–9. The entire episode in 1 Sam 3 is predicated on the existence of a dream message with some content. It may be, then, that an existing dream message has been revised by a Deuteronomistic editor in order to draw connections with other Deuteronomistic prophecies of destruction. The precise limits of any Deuteronomistic revision are difficult to determine, however. There are no grammatical shifts that would allow definitive differentiation between the original message and a Deuteronomistic hand. Furthermore, the phrase, "both ears of anyone who hears about it will tingle," is attested only three times in the Bible and is therefore too rare to be considered diagnostic of the Deuteronomistic School. Anthony F. Campbell does not accept the phrase here as indicating Deuteronomistic revision (*1 Samuel*, FOTL 7 [Grand Rapids: Eerdmans, 2003], 55). Tsumura likewise doubts that a later editorial hand is at work in our text. See David Toshio Tsumura, *The First Book of Samuel* (Grand Rapids: Eerdmans, 2007), 179. I share their skepticism. Nevertheless, the oracle may have undergone multiple stages of editorial development. The shift in address between v. 12 and v. 13 is jarring. Verse 12 may be a gloss intended to harmonize the prophecy against the house of Eli given here with the message from the man of god against Eli given in 2:27–36. See Acroyd, *First Samuel*, 43.

[43] Tsumura, building on H. Van Dyke Parunak's work on transitional links in the Bible, notes, "The first clause *the boy Samuel was ministering to the Lord* functions as a link to the preceding chapter, repeating the key words 'boy' and 'ministering' from 1 Sam. 2:11 and 18." See H. van Dyke Parunak, "Transitional Techniques in the Bible," *JBL* 102 (1983): 525–48; Tsumura, *First Book of Samuel*, 53. On this refrain, see also Sasson, "Eyes of Eli," 172–74.

[44] See related comments in Robert S. Kawashima, *Biblical Narrative and the Death of the Rhapsode*, ISBL (Bloomington: Indiana University Press, 2004), 138–39.

Samuel ministered before Yahweh, in 3:1, frames the judgment by the man of God against the house of Eli in 2:27–36.[45] This oracle, especially verses 27–33, appears to be from the hand of a single scribe and is not characterized by Deuteronomistic phraseology.[46] It may be intended to grant further substance to the charges brought against the house of Eli in chapter 3.[47] The three notices about Samuel in 2:11, 2:18, and 3:1 thus provide a syntactical framework that has the effect of painting alternating and contrasting portraits of the progress of Samuel in the service of Yahweh and the sacrilegious behavior of the sons of Eli.[48] This structure, in turn, forms part of the larger narrative of Samuel's rise in chapters 1 through 3.[49]

In our narrative of Samuel's theophany, this contrasting portrait of the development of Samuel and the decline of the house of Eli reaches a climax. The

---

[45] Graeme Auld notes, "The whole paragraph about the wickedness of Eli's house has been interspersed with brief reminders of young Samuel's development. And it nears its end with another (3:1a)" (*1–2 Samuel: A Commentary* [Louisville: Westminster John Knox, 2011], 52).

[46] On the absence of Deuteronomistic language, see Campbell, *1 Samuel*, 54. On the unity of the oracle, see Matitiahu Tsevat, "Studies in the Book of Samuel," *HUCA* 32 (1961): 212–13.

[47] Ackroyd regards the oracle as later insertion (*First Samuel*, 38).

[48] Compare related comments in Robert P. Gordon, *1–2 Samuel* (Sheffield: JSOT Press, 1984), 24; Moshe Garsiel, *The First Book of Samuel: A Literary Study of Comparative Structures, Analogies and Parallels* (Ramat-Gan: Revivim Publishing House, 1985), 37–41; Miscall, *1 Samuel*, 17–19; Robert Polzin, *Samuel and the Deuteronomist: A Literary Study of the Deuteronomistic History, Part Two, 1 Samuel* (San Francisco: Harper & Row, 1989), 40–44; David Jobling, *1 Samuel* (Collegeville: Liturgical Press, 1998), 54; Campbell, *1 Samuel*, 36, 46; Kawashima, *Biblical Narrative*, 139. Campbell notes, "The text from 2:12–26 is scarcely a literary genre in its own right. At best it is a composite account, built up from a series of notices and establishing contrasts between the Elides and Samuel" (*1 Samuel*, 50). For a detailed examination of the alternating vignettes of Samuel and the sons of Eli, see J. T. Willis, "An Anti-Elide Narrative Tradition from a Prophetic Circle at the Ramah Sanctuary," *JBL* 90 (1971): 288–308. See also J. T. Willis, "Cultic Elements in the Story of Samuel's Birth and Dedication," *ST* 26 (1972): 33–61; J. P. Fokkelman, *Narrative Art and Poetry in the Books of Samuel: A Full Interpretation Based on Stylistic and Structural Analyses, Volume IV, Vow and Desire (1 Sam. 1–12)* (Assen: Van Gorcum, 1993), 112–55. Compare also Sasson, "Eyes of Eli," 172–74.

[49] On the structure of 1 Sam 1–3, see Tsumura, *First Book of Samuel*, 103–4. J. Gerald Janzen has observed linguistic connections between chapters 1 and 3 and has argued that chapter 3 describes the "re-birth" of Samuel ("'Samuel Opened the Doors of the House of Yahweh' [1 Samuel 3.15]," *JSOT* 26 [1983]: 89–96). P. Segal has traced the connections between 1 Sam 1–3 and the ancestor narratives in Genesis and has argued that Samuel is presented as a leader like Joseph ("The Succession of Eli," *Beth Mikra* 33 [1988]: 179–83 [Hebrew]).

confrontation between Eli and Samuel in verses 15–18, which follows the theophany in the temple, is integral to the plot.[50] It is tied to the description of the theophany proper by the language of call and response (compare v. 16 with vv. 4, 6, 8, 10). Roles are reversed, however. This time, the caller seeks to receive a message from Samuel, rather than to offer one to him. Roles are also reversed in the oath of confrontation (v. 17), with the oath swearer imprecating someone else.[51] In placing responsibility for the oath on Samuel, Eli contributes to the reader's impression that Samuel is acquiring a greater and greater role, while Eli and his house are on the decline.[52] Samuel and his house displace Eli and his house.

In describing this transfer of power from Eli to Samuel, 1 Sam 3 has played with the literary tradition of dream theophanies in order to emphasize Samuel's displacement of Eli and Eli's authorization of Samuel. This literary theme in our narrative can be understood against the background of competition between priestly families in ancient Israel and Judah. Jeremy M. Hutton and Mark Leuchter have traced the history and social structures of Israelite priestly families in more detail than can be recounted here.[53] By comparing Morocco's Ahansal,

---

[50] At the same time, 3:20–4:1a builds a bridge between Samuel's revelation of the judgment of Yahweh against the house of Eli and the episodes concerning the ark of Yahweh that follow. The verses contain several statements, some of which read like glosses. The susceptibility of this bridging section to repeated editorial supplementation is illustrated by a comparison of the Masoretic Text to the Septuagint. On the additions in the Septuagint here, see Stephen Pisano, *Additions or Omissions in the Books of Samuel: The Significant Pluses and Minuses in the Massoretic, LXX and Qumran Texts*, OBO 57 (Göttingen: Vandenhoeck & Ruprecht, 1984), 29–34. See also McCarter, *1 Samuel*, 97; James R. Adair, *An Inductive Method for Reconstructing the Biblical Text: Illustrated by an Analysis of 1 Samuel 3*, JNSLMS (Stellenbosch: Department of Ancient Studies, University of Stellenbosch, 2000).

[51] Ziegler, "'So Shall God Do,'" 65–68.

[52] Ziegler notes, "Perhaps this oath in which Eli adjures Samuel should be seen as part of the initiation of Samuel into his new role. The thrusting of responsibility upon the young Samuel by the experienced priest, as indicated by the unique second-person imprecation, appears to highlight this theme in the narrative. In this schema, Eli is not simply trying to induce Samuel to speak but rather is impelling Samuel toward his new role" ("'So Shall God Do,'" 67).

[53] Jeremy M. Hutton, "The Levitical Diaspora (I): A Sociological Comparison with Morocco's Ahansal," in *Exploring the Longue Durée: Essays in Honor of Lawrence E. Stager*, ed. David Schloen (Winona Lake: Eisenbrauns, 2009), 223–34; Jeremy M. Hutton, "The Levitical Diaspora (II): Modern Perspectives on the Levitical Cities Lists (A Review of Opinions)," in *Levites and Priests in Biblical History and Tradition*, ed. Mark Leuchter and Jeremy M. Hutton, AIL 9 (Atlanta: Society of Biblical Literature, 2011), 45–81; Jeremy M. Hutton, "All the King's Men: The Families of the Priests in Cross-Cultural Perspective," in *"Seitenblicke": Literarische und historische Studien zu Nebenfiguren im zweiten Samuelbuch*, ed. Walter Dietrich, OBO 249 (Fribourg: Academic

Hutton points to processes of fission and fusion as priestly families in ancient Israel competed for prestige and a limited supply of "saintly function."[54] According to Leuchter, "At least in the early period, Levites could become full-blown priests by virtue of advantageous circumstances where no other priestly family was dominant in a particular area (what Hutton has termed 'fission') or, as in Samuel's case, displacing an extant priestly family and proclaiming typological equivalency with their founding saintly ancestor."[55] One dynamic at play between these social processes of fission and fusion in Iron Age Israel and Judah and what Hutton calls their "literary emplotment," in the Hebrew Bible is the portrayal of competing priestly families as ultimately belonging to the same authoritative lineage.[56] Our narrative portrays Samuel as deriving his authority in large measure from Eli even as he has also displaced Eli's family. Thus, although our narrative might describe fictitious events, it reflects social structures and processes that would have been familiar to the story's ancient audience.

Finally, the political themes in 1 Sam 3 that I have been discussing can be understood in the context of the larger story about David. The motif of Yahweh's words connects 1 Sam 3 to 1 Sam 15, which describes Yahweh's rejection of Saul.[57] The motif first appears in chapter 3 in verse 1b. The narrative sequence of *wayyiqtol* verbs in 3:2–6 is separated from the narrative action in chapter 2 by a digression in verse 1.[58] Verse 1b serves as an introduction intended to clarify the narrative logic of the episode to follow.[59] This introductory note about the scarcity of prophetic vision explains Samuel's failure to immediately

---

Press; Göttingen: Vandenhoeck & Ruprecht, 2011), 121–51; Mark Leuchter, *Samuel and the Shaping of Tradition*, 22–40; Mark Leuchter, *The Levites and the Boundaries of Israelite Identity* (New York: Oxford University Press, 2017), esp. chapter 3.

[54] Hutton, "Levitical Diaspora (I)," 227–28.

[55] Leuchter, *Samuel and the Shaping of Tradition*, 40.

[56] On literary emplotment, see Hutton, "All the King's Men," 121–22.

[57] On the place of chapter 15 in the traditions about Saul, see Hertzberg, *1–2 Samuel*, 123–24; Auld, *1–2 Samuel*, 180–81.

[58] Cf. Frolov, *Turn of the Cycle*, 72.

[59] Graeme Auld suggests that the notice looks both forward and backward, referring to the oracle to come and the one that has just been given in 2:27–36 (*1–2 Samuel*, 52). This may be true in the present arrangement of the material, but the notice is surely provoked by what is to follow in the narrative. Goldman notes, "The statement is intended to account for the fact that Samuel was unaware of the meaning of his experience when God called to him" (*Samuel*, 16). Robert Alter observes, "Samuel's thrice-repeated error in this regard reflects not only his youthful inexperience but, as the sixteenth-century Hebrew exegete Yosef Karo has proposed, the general fact that 'the word of the Lord was rare,' revelation an unfamiliar phenomenon" (*The David Story: A Translation with Commentary of 1 and 2 Samuel* [New York: Norton, 1999], 17).

recognize Yahweh's voice.[60] The *wayyiqtol* narrative sequence is broken again in verse 7 with another editorial note excusing Samuel.[61] The repeated references in verses 1, 7 to "the word of Yahweh" connects the motifs of power at the narrative core of 1 Sam 3 to larger themes in Samuel–Kings, especially to 1 Sam 15. "The word of Yahweh" serves as a *leitmotif* in both chapter 3 and chapter 15.[62] It is used eight times in these two chapters—3:1, 7, 21; 15:1, 10, 13, 23, 26; note also "speak, Yahweh!" in 3:9 and "Yahweh spoke" in 15:16—but elsewhere in the books of Samuel only in 2 Sam 7:4, 12:9, and 24:11.[63] This clustering of uses of the phrase in these two chapters invites the reader to interpret chapter 15 in light of chapter 3, which the reader encounters first.

Graeme Auld has argued that "all of 1 Samuel but the final chapter was written in stages as a new preface to the story of the house of David in 2 Samuel–2 Kings."[64] In Auld's view, one such preface had begun with the introduction of Saul in 1 Sam 9, and another preface, 1 Sam 1–8, had been added later.[65] These new prefaces, written in stages, served as interpretive lenses that framed the story of the house of David in the chapters to follow. An evaluation of Auld's thesis lies well beyond my aims here.[66] At a minimum, the repeated use

---

[60] On the use of יקר and פרץ in the narratives about Saul and David, see Auld, *1–2 Samuel*, 52–53. פרץ here evidently signals some kind of divine irruption, as it does in 2 Sam 5:20 and 2 Sam 6:8.

[61] Both notes serve the same end and both contain a peculiarly repetitive structure that borders on poetic parallelism. Tsumura classifies v. 1b as "semi-poetic" (*First Book of Samuel*, 174). In my assessment, Peter D. Miscall is mistaken when he draws a sharp distinction in 3:1 between "word" and "vision" (*1 Samuel: A Literary Reading* [Bloomington: Indiana University Press, 1986], 24). Anthony F. Campbell notes, "Word and vision are mentioned as though almost synonymous; here, God's word is received in visionary experience" (*1 Samuel*, 54). Given their repetitive structure, which is stylistically different from the main narrative description of events, it is possible that these notes come from a later editorial hand. The double note about Eli's blindness in v. 2b may also be from the same hand, though its intent is less transparent.

[62] Alter comments on "listen to the voice of the words of Yahweh" in 15:1, "This redundant phrasing is a little odd, but is dictated by the pressure of the thematically fraught key phrase, 'listen to the voice,' that defines the entire episode" (*David Story*, 87).

[63] The closely related expression "all the words of Yahweh" is used in 1 Sam 8:10.

[64] Auld, *1–2 Samuel*, 19.

[65] Johannes Klein, who argues that a pre-Deuteronomistic Saul-David narrative began in 1 Sam 9, has offered a helpful chart summarizing various proposals for the extent of that Saul-David narrative. See Johannes Klein, *David versus Saul: Ein Beitrag zum Erzählsystem der Samuelbücher*, BWANT 158 (Stuttgart: Kohlhammer, 2002), 137–38.

[66] Several scholars posit an independent History of David's Rise, 1 Sam 15(16)–2 Sam 5(8), and an independent Succession Narrative, 2 Sam 9–1 Kgs 2, that served as sources for Samuel–Kings. The seminal work in this regard was Leonhard Rost, *Die Überlieferung von der Thronnachfolge Davids*, BWANT 3.6 (Stuttgart: Kolhammer,

of "the word of Yahweh" in chapters 3 and 15 draws the reader's attention to other themes shared between these texts. As such, chapter 3 provides an interpretive lens that colors the reader's understanding of 1 Sam 15.

Samuel's displacement of the ruling priestly house of Eli, particularly as narrated in chapter 3, foreshadows and shapes the reader's interpretation of David's displacement of the ruling royal house of Saul, particularly as narrated in chapter 15. First Samuel 3, and 1 Sam 1–3 more broadly, introduces the motif of the rejection of an established family line that will be revisited in 1 Sam 15. As such, chapters 1–3 make clear that Yahweh's rejection of the house of Saul was not a suspiciously unique event in Israel's history but an unquestionable principle of divinely commissioned government.[67] First Samuel 3 also indirectly strengthens the case against Saul. Chapter 15 indicts Saul for failing to obey prophetic words delivered by Samuel. Chapter 3 strengthens that indictment by making clear that Samuel is authorized to speak Yahweh's words. The narratives also oppose Eli and Saul. While Eli accepts the word of Yahweh against his house, Saul does not come to terms with his rejection. Desperately clinging to Samuel's robe and accidentally tearing it, Saul only offers a prophetic image of Yahweh's tearing of the kingdom away from him (15:27–28).[68] Just as Urzababa is described as seeking Sargon's life, Saul is portrayed as making repeated attempts on David's. Finally, Eli's words—"He is Yahweh. Let him do what is good in his eyes!" (v. 18)— not only apply to the judgment against his own house but also portend Yahweh's intervention in the future history of the monarchy. Because Saul will do "evil in the eyes of Yahweh" (15:19), Yahweh will reject him as king.

In sum, the narrative of Samuel's theophany has at its core political themes. Read in the context of ancient Near Eastern literary depictions of dream theophanies, and especially when compared to the Sumerian Legend of Sargon, 1 Sam 3 is principally concerned with the transfer of power from one house to another.[69] The narrative's political nature is in turn best understood in the literary con-

---

1926). For a thorough recent treatment of the History of David's rise, see Sung-Hee Yoon, *The Question of the Beginning of the So-Called History of David's Rise: A Methodological Reflection and Its Implications*, BZAW 462 (Berlin: de Gruyter, 2014).

[67] Note how Hannah's song lets slip that its real referent is the monarchy: "He will give strength to his king, And exalt the horn of his anointed one!" (2:10). First Samuel 1–3 was evidently composed with the story of the Davidic monarchy already in mind.

[68] The word cloak (מְעִיל) last appeared in the books of Samuel in 1 Sam 2:19, according to which Hannah annually brought a little cloak for Samuel to wear as he served Yahweh in the temple at Shiloh.

[69] Others have argued that the narrative intends to portray the supremacy of prophetic ministry and leadership, embodied in Samuel, over priestly ministry and leadership, embodied in Eli. See I. L. Seeligmann, "Problems in the History and Character of Israelite Prophecy," *ErIsr* 3 (1954): 125–32 [Hebrew]; Y. Amit "The Story of Samuel's Con-

text of Samuel–Kings. It contains particularly strong thematic links to 1 Sam 15 and frames the reader's interpretation of that chapter. In describing the passing of divinely authorized priestly leadership from the house of Eli to the house of Samuel, 1 Sam 3 foreshadows, and contrasts with, the passing of divinely authorized royal leadership from the house of Saul to the house of David.

BIBLIOGRAPHY

Ackroyd, Peter R. *The First Book of Samuel*. Cambridge: Cambridge University Press, 1971.
Adair, James R. *An Inductive Method for Reconstructing the Biblical Text: Illustrated by an Analysis of 1 Samuel 3*. JNSLMS 2. Stellenbosch: Department of Ancient Studies, University of Stellenbosch, 2000.
Alter, Robert. *The David Story: A Translation with Commentary of 1 and 2 Samuel*. New York: Norton, 1999.
Amit, Y. "The Story of Samuel's Consecration to Prophecy in Light of Prophetic Thought." Pages 29–36 in *Sefer Moshe Goldstein: Mehqarim ba-Miqra uve-Mahshevet Yisrael*. Edited by Ben-Tsiyon Lurya. Jerusalem: Kanna, 1987 [Hebrew].
Auld, A. Graeme. *1–2 Samuel*: A Commentary. Louisville, Westminster John Knox, 2011.
———. "Jeremiah-Manasseh-Samuel: Significant Triangle? or Vicious Circle?" Pages 1–9 in *Prophecy in the Book of Jeremiah*. Edited by Hans M. Barstad and Reinhard G. Kratz. BZAW 388. Berlin: de Gruyter, 2009.
Bar, Shaul. *A Letter That Has Not Been Read: Dreams in the Hebrew Bible*. Translated by Lenn J. Schramm. HUCM 25. Cincinnati: Hebrew Union College Press, 2001.
Bottéro, Jean. *Mesopotamia: Writing, Reasoning, and the Gods*. Translated by Zainab Bahrani and Marc Van De Mieroop. Chicago: The University of Chicago Press, 1992.
Butler, S. A. L. *Mesopotamian Conceptions of Dreams and Dream Rituals*. AOAT 258. Münster: Ugarit-Verlag, 1998.
Campbell, Anthony F. *1 Samuel*. FOTL 7. Grand Rapids: Eerdmans, 2003.

---

secration to Prophecy in Light of Prophetic Thought," in *Sefer Moshe Goldstein: Mehqarim ba-Miqra uve-Mahshevet Yisrael,* ed. Ben-Tsiyon Lurya (Jerusalem: Kanna, 1987), 29–36 [Hebrew]. In chapter 3, however, both Samuel and Eli are imagined as carrying out priestly functions in the temple at Shiloh. Furthermore, in so far as Eli instructs Samuel in how to receive prophetic revelation, both are imagined to be capable of prophetic activity. And in the same vein, the implicit indictment of Eli in 3:1 rests on the assumption that his leadership should involve prophetic activity. This thesis is therefore difficult to accept.

Cooper, Jerrold S. "Sargon and Joseph: Dreams Come True." Pages 33–39 in *Biblical and Related Studies Presented to Samuel Iwry*. Edited by Ann Kort and Scott Morschauser. Winona Lake: Eisenbrauns, 1985.
Cooper, Jerrold S. and Wolfgang Heimpel. "The Sumerian Sargon Legend." *JAOS* 103 (1983): 67–82.
Durand, Jean-Marie. *Archives Épistolaires de Mari, I/1*. ARM 261. Paris: ERC, 1988.
———. "Précurseurs syriens aux protocoles néo-assyriens: consid.érations sur la vie politique aux Bords-de-l'Euprate." Pages 13–71 in *Marchands, Diplomates et Empereurs: Études sur la civilisation mésopotamienne offertes à Paul Garelli*. Edited by Dominique Charpin and Francis Joannès. Paris: ERC, 1991.
van Dyke Parunak, H. "Transitional Techniques in the Bible." *JBL* 102 (1983): 525–48.
Eilat, Moshe. *Samuel and the Foundation of Kingship in Ancient Israel*. Jerusalem: Magnes, 1997 [Hebrew].
Frolov, Serge. *The Turn of the Cycle: 1 Samuel 1–8 in Synchronic and Diachronic Perspectives*. BZAW 342. Berlin: de Gruyter, 2004.
Fidler, Ruth. "The Shiloh Theophany (I Samuel 3): A Case Study of the Liminal Report." Pages 99–107 in *Proceedings of the Twelfth World Congress of Jewish Studies, Jerusalem, July 29–August 5, 1997, Division A*. Jerusalem: World Union of Jewish Studies, 1999 [Hebrew].
Fidler, Ruth. *"Dreams Speak Falsely"? Dream Theophanies in the Bible: Their Place in Ancient Israelite Faith and Traditions*. Jerusalem: Hebrew University Magnes, 2005 [Hebrew].
Flannery-Dailey, Frances. *Dreamers, Scribes, and Priests: Jewish Dreams in the Hellenistic and Roman Eras*. JSJSup 90. Leiden: Brill 2004.
Fokkelman, J. P. *Narrative Art and Poetry in the Books of Samuel: A Full Interpretation Based on Stylistic and Structural Analyses, Volume IV, Vow and Desire (1 Sam. 1–12)*. Assen, The Netherlands: Van Gorcum, 1993.
Friedrich, Paul. "The Poetry of Language in the Politics of Dreams." Pages 65–83 in *The Language Parallax: Linguistic Relativism and Poetic Indeterminacy*. Austin: University of Texas Press, 1986.
Garsiel, Moshe. *The First Book of Samuel: A Literary Study of Comparative Structures, Analogies and Parallels*. Ramat-Gan: Revivim Publishing House, 1985.
George, A. R. *The Babylonian Gilgamesh Epic: Introduction, Critical Edition and Cuneiform Texts*. 2 vols. Oxford: Oxford University Press, 2003.
Gnuse, Robert Karl. *The Dream Theophany of Samuel: Its Structure in Relation to Ancient Near Eastern Dreams and Its Theological Significance*. Lanham: University Press of America, 1984.
Goldman, S. *Samuel: Hebrew Text and English Translation with an Introduction and Commentary*. London: Soncino Press, 1949.
Gordon, Robert P. *1–2 Samuel*. Sheffield: JSOT Press, 1984.
Habel, Norman. "The Form and Significance of the Call Narratives." *ZAW* 77 (1965): 297–323.
Hamori, Esther J. *"When Gods Were Men": The Embodied God in Biblical and Near Eastern Literature*. BZAW 384. Berlin: de Gruyter, 2008.
Hertzberg, Hans Wilhelm. *1–2 Samuel: A Commentary*. Translated by John S. Bowden. Philadelphia: Westminster Press, 1964.

Hurowitz, Victor. "Eli's Adjuration of Samuel (1 Samuel III 7–18) in the Light of a 'Diviner's Protocol' from Mari (AEM I/1, 1)." *VT* 44 (1994): 483–97.
Husser, Jean-Marie. *Dreams and Dream Narratives in the Biblical World*. Translated by Jill M. Munro. BibSem 63. Sheffield: Sheffield Academic Press, 1999.
Hutter, Manfred. "Bemerkungen über das "Wort Gottes" bei den Hethitern." *BN* 28 (1985): 17–26.
Hutton, Jeremy M. "The Levitical Diaspora (I): A Sociological Comparison with Morocco's Ahansal." Pages 223–34 in *Exploring the Longue Durée: Essays in Honor of Lawrence E. Stager*. Edited by David Schloen. Winona Lake: Eisenbrauns, 2009.
———. "The Levitical Diaspora (II): Modern Perspectives on the Levitical Cities Lists (A Review of Opinions)." Pages 45–81 in *Levites and Priests in Biblical History and Tradition*. Edited by Mark Leuchter and Jeremy M. Hutton. AIL 9. Atlanta: Society of Biblical Literature, 2011.
———. "All the King's Men: The Families of the Priests in Cross-Cultural Perspective." Pages 121–51 in *"Seitenblicke": Literarische und historische Studien zu Nebenfiguren im zweiten Samuelbuch*. Edited by Walter Dietrich. OBO 249. Fribourg: Academic Press; Göttingen: Vandenhoeck & Ruprecht, 2011.
Hylander, Ivan. *Der literarische Samuel-Saul-Komplex (I Sam. 1–15): Traditionsgeschichtlich untersucht*. Uppsala: Almquist & Wiksell, 1932.
Janzen, J. Gerald. "'Samuel Opened the Doors of the House of Yahweh' (I Samuel 3.15)." *JSOT* 26 (1983): 89–96.
Janzen, Waldemar. "Witholding the Word." Pages 97–114 in *Traditions in Transformation: Turning Points in Biblical Faith*. Edited by Baruch Halpern and Jon D. Levenson. Winona Lake: Eisenbrauns, 1981.
Jobling, David. *1 Samuel*. Collegeville: Liturgical Press, 1998.
Kawashima, Robert S. *Biblical Narrative and the Death of the Rhapsode*. ISBL. Bloomington: Indiana University Press, 2004.
Kim, Koowon. *Incubation as a Type-Scene in the 'Aqhatu, Kirta, and Hannah Stories: A Form-Critical and Narratological Study of KTU 1.14 I–1.15 III, 1.17 I–II, and 1 Samuel 1:1–2:11*. VTSup 145. Leiden: Brill, 2011.
Kitz, Anne Marie. *Cursed Are You! The Phenomenology of Cursing in Cuneiform and Hebrew Texts*. Winona Lake: Eisenbrauns, 2014.
Klein, Johannes. *David versus Saul: Ein Beitrag zum Erzählsystem der Samuelbücher*. BWANT 158. Stuttgart: Kohlhammer, 2002.
Leuchter, Mark. *Samuel and the Shaping of Tradition*. New York: Oxford University Press, 2013.
———. *The Levites and the Boundaries of Israelite Identity*. New York: Oxford University Press, 2017.
Lewis, Peter E. "Is There a Parallel between 1 Samuel 3 and the Sixth Chapter of the Egyptian Book of the Dead?" *JSOT* 31 (2007): 365–76.
Luukko, Mikko and Greta Van Buylaere. *The Political Correspondence of Esarhaddon*. SAA 16. Helsinki: Helsinki University Press, 2002.
Malamat, Abraham. "Prophetic Revelations in New Documents from Mari and the Bible." Pages 207–227 in *Volume du Congrès: Geneva, 1965*. VTSup 15. Leiden: Brill, 1966.
McCarter, P. Kyle. *1 Samuel: A New Translation, with Introduction, Commentary, and Notes*. AB 8. Garden City: Doubleday, 1980.

Miscall, Peter D. *1 Samuel: A Literary Reading*. Bloomington: Indiana University Press, 1986.
Mommer, Peter. *Samuel: Geschichte und Überlieferung*. WMANT 65. Neukirchen-Vluyn: Neukirchener Verlag, 1991.
Newman, Murray. "The Prophetic Call of Samuel." Pages 86–97 in *Israel's Prophetic Heritage: Essays in Honor of James Muilenburg*. Edited by Bernhard W. Anderson and Walter J. Harrelson. New York: Harper, 1962.
Nissinen, Martti. *References to Prophecy in Neo-Assyrian Sources*. SAAS 7. Helsinki: Neo-Assyrian Text Corpus Project; Helsinki University Press, 1998.
———. *Prophets and Prophecy in the Ancient Near East*. With contributions by C. L. Seow and Robert K. Ritner. WAW 12. Atlanta: Society of Biblical Literature, 2003.
Oppenheim, A. Leo. *The Interpretation of Dreams in the Ancient Near East: With a Translation of the Assyrian Dream-Book*. TAPS 46.3. Philadelphia: American Philosophical Society, 1956.
Parpola, Simo. "A Letter from Šamaš-šumu-ukīn to Esarhaddon." *Iraq* 34 (1972): 21–34.
Pisano, Stephen. *Additions or Omissions in the Books of Samuel: The Significant Pluses and Minuses in the Massoretic, LXX and Qumran Texts*. OBO 57. Göttingen: Vandenhoeck & Ruprecht, 1984.
Polzin, Robert. *Samuel and the Deuteronomist: A Literary Study of the Deuteronomistic History, Part Two, 1 Samuel*. San Francisco: Harper & Row, 1989.
von Rad, Gerhard. *Old Testament Theology*. 2 vols. New York: Harper, 1962–65.
Richter, Wolfgang. *Die sogenannten vorprophetischen Berufungsberichte: Eine literaturwissenschaftliche Studie zu 1 Sam 9,1–10,16, Ex 3f. und Ri 6,11b–17*. FRLANT 101. Göttingen: Vandenhoeck & Ruprecht, 1970.
de Robert, Philippe. "1 Samuel 3: une vocation prophétique?" *Foi et vie* 83 (1984): 4–10.
Rose, H. J. "Divine Disguisings." *HTR* 49 (1956): 63–72.
Rost, Leonhard. *Die Überlieferung von Thronnachfolge Davids*. BWANT 3.6. Stuttgart: Kolhammer, 1926.
Sasson, Jack M. "Mari Dreams." *JAOS* 103 (1983): 283–93.
———. "The Eyes of Eli: An Essay in Motif Accretion." Pages 171–90 in *Inspired Speech: Prophecy in the Ancient Near East, Essays in Honor of Herbert B. Huffmon*. Edited by Louis Stulman and John Kaltner. JSOTSup 378. London: T&T Clark, 2004.
———. *From the Mari Archives: An Anthology of Old Babylonian Letters*. Winona Lake: Eisenbrauns, 2015.
Seeligmann, I. L. "Problems in the History and Character of Israelite Prophecy." *ErIsr* 3 (1954): 125–32 [Hebrew].
Segal, P. "The Succession of Eli." *Beth Mikra* 33 (1988): 179–83 [Hebrew].
Seow, C. L. "The Syro-Palestinian Context of Solomon's Dream." *HTR* 77 (1984): 141–52.
———. *Myth, Drama, and the Politics of David's Dance*. HSM 44. Atlanta: Scholars Press, 1989.
Simon, Uriel. "1 Samuel III: A Youth's Call to Prophecy." Pages 85–93 in *Proceedings of the Seventh World Congress of Jewish Studies, Held at the Hebrew University, Jerusalem, 7–14 August, 1977: 2 Studies in the Bible and the Ancient Near East*. Edited by Yisrael Gutman. Jerusalem: World Union of Jewish Studies, 1981 [Hebrew].

Simon, Uriel. "Samuel's Call to Prophecy: Form Criticism with Close Reading." *Prooftexts* 1 (1981): 119–32.
Sommer, Benjamin D. *The Bodies of God and the World of Ancient Israel*. Cambridge: Cambridge University Press, 2009.
Sweek, Joel. "Dreams of Power from Sumer to Judah: An Essay on the Divinatory Economy of the Ancient Near East." PhD diss., University of Chicago, 1996.
———. "Inquiring for the State in the Ancient Near East: Delineating Political Location." Pages 41–56 in *Magic and Divination in the Ancient World*. Edited by Leda Jean Ciraolo and Jonathan Lee Seidel. Leiden: Brill, 2002.
Tsevat, Matitiahu. "Studies in the Book of Samuel." *HUCA* 32 (1961): 1991–216.
Tsumura, David Toshio. *The First Book of Samuel*. Grand Rapids: Eerdmans, 2007.
Van Koppen, Frans. "Seized by the Royal Order: The Households of Sammêtar and Other Magnates at Mari." Pages 289–372 in *Florilegium marianum VI: Recueil d'études à la mémoire d'André Parrot*. Edited by Dominique Charpin and Jean-Marie Durand. Mémoires de N.A.B.U. 7. Paris: SEPOA, 2002.
Veijola, Timo. *Die Ewige Dynastie: David und die Entstehung seiner Dynastie nach der deuteronomistischen Darstellung*. AASF 193. Helsinki: Academia Scientarum Fennica, 1975.
Vernant, Jean-Pierre. "Mortals and Immortals: The Body of the Divine." Pages 27–49 in *Mortals and Immortals: Collected Essays*. Edited by Froma I. Zeitlin. Princeton: Princeton University Press, 1991.
Weinfeld, Moshe. *Deuteronomy and the Deuteronomic School*. Winona Lake: Eisenbrauns, 1992.
Willis, J. T. "An Anti-Elide Narrative Tradition from a Prophetic Circle at the Ramah Sanctuary." *JBL* 90 (1971): 288–308.
Willis, J. T. "Cultic Elements in the Story of Samuel's Birth and Dedication." *ST* 26 (1972): 33–61.
Yoon, Sung-Hee. *The Question of the Beginning of the So-Called History of David's Rise: A Methodological Reflection and Its Implications*. BZAW 462. Berlin: de Gruyter, 2014.
Zgoll, Annette. *Traum und Welterleben im antiken Mesopotamien: Traumtheorie und Traumpraxis im 3.–1. Jahrtausend v. Chr. als Horizont einer Kulturgeschichte des Träumens*. AOAT 333. Münster: Ugarit-Verlag, 2006.
Ziegler, Yael. "'So Shall God Do...': Variations of an Oath Formula and Its Literary Meaning." *JBL* 126 (2007): 65–68.

7
Daniel and the "Prophetization" of Dream Divination

Jonathan Stökl

Dreams were seen as potentially significant in most societies of the ancient Near East and eastern Mediterranean.[1] While many forms of divination appear to be condemned in the texts of the Hebrew Bible, dream divination has two promi-

---

[1] Scott B. Noegel, "Dreams and Dream Interpretation in Mesopotamia and in the Hebrew Bible (Old Testament)," in *Dreams: A Reader on Religious, Cultural and Psychological Dimensions of Dreaming*, ed. Kelly Bulkeley (New York: Palgrave, 2001), 45–71 and Jean-Marie Husser, *Dreams and Dream Narratives in the Biblical World*, trans. Jill M. Munro, BibSem 63 (Sheffield: Sheffield Academic Press, 1999) offer a good overview of dreams and dream interpretation. On ancient Near Eastern dream divination, that is, the interpretation of someone else's significant dreams, see generally, e.g., A. Leo Oppenheim, *The Interpretation of Dreams in the Ancient Near East: With a Translation of an Assyrian Dream-Book*, TAPS 46.3 (Philadelphia: American Philosophical Society, 1956), 179–373; Francesca Rochberg, *The Heavenly Writing: Divination, Horoscopy, and Astronomy in Mesopotamian Culture* (Cambridge: Cambridge University Press, 2004), esp. 81–86. That dreams and dream divination remained significant in Judaism can be seen in the contribution to this volume by Haim Weiss. Another good example can be seen in text Mosseri VI.5 from the Cairo Geniza (http://www.lib.cam.ac.uk/Taylor-Schechter/fotm/december-2014/index.html [last accessed on 12 January 2016]). For a brief overview of dreams in many world religions and cultures, see Kelly Bulkeley, *Dreaming in the World's Religions: A Comparative History* (New York: New York University Press, 2008). I would like to thank the members of the panel and attendees for the discussion at the Prophetic Texts and Their Ancient Contexts session of the SBL in Baltimore, 2013. I would also like to thank Carly Crouch, Madhavi Nevader, Paul Joyce, and Esther Hamori for commenting on earlier drafts of this essay.

nent heroes, Joseph and Daniel, who are portrayed very positively.[2] In this essay I put dream divination in the book of Daniel in the context of current understandings of the way that various forms of divination function in the ancient Near East. I will argue that as it is constructed in Daniel, dream divination is characterized by a mixture of more intuitive and more "technical" aspects of divination.[3]

I will discuss the Danielic chapters in a slightly unusual order, starting with Dan 4–5, then moving on to Dan 6–7 (and 8–12), finishing with Dan 2, where Daniel acts with the most prowess and the least help of angelic figures.

FORMS OF DIVINATION AND DREAMING

The Hebrew Bible distinguishes sharply between what it regards as permissible forms of communicating with the divine and other forms of communication that it regards as impermissible (e.g., Deut 13 and 18). Traditionally, the distinction has been understood to lie between permissible prophecy—and dreaming—and impermissible "divination", which is portrayed as the consequence of partaking in "foreign" practices. This distinction is partly the consequence of translations of Hebrew terms such as קסם as "divination". As a result, readers—and listen-

---

[2] On Joseph see the contribution by Franziska Ede in this volume, as well as—albeit with a rather different interpretation of the evidence—Michael Segal, "From Joseph to Daniel: The Literary Development of the Narrative in Daniel 2," *VT* 49 (2009): 123–49.

[3] The question of the origin of the apocalyptic genre in general and its relationship to certain dream narratives and other ancient Near Eastern texts is of less interest to me here, as I am not looking at the evolution of genre more widely but at the depiction of divination in the various chapters of the book of Daniel. For the evolution of the genre see John J. Collins, *The Apocalyptic Imagination: An Introduction to Jewish Apocalyptic Literature*, 2nd ed., Biblical Resource Series (Grand Rapids: Eerdmans, 1998), 1–42 (the third edition, 2016 was not available to me). Questions of authorship and literary growth are also largely put aside in this essay. The evidence from the Hebrew and Greek texts overwhelmingly argues for the continued literary development of the text(s) of the book far into the late Hellenistic and Roman periods. See, e.g., John J. Collins, *Daniel: A Commentary on the Book of Daniel*, Hermeneia (Minneapolis: Fortress Press, 1993), 38; Klaus Koch, *Daniel (1–4)*, BKAT 22/1 (Neukirchen-Vluyn: Neukirchener Verlag, 2005); Reinhard G. Kratz, "Die Visionen des Daniel," in *Schriftauslegung in der Schrift: Festschrift für Odil Hannes Steck zu seinem 65. Geburtstag*, ed. Reinhard G. Kratz, Thomas Krüger, and Konrad Schmid, BZAW 300 (Berlin: de Gruyter, 2000), 219–36 (English version published as "The Visions of Daniel," in *The Book of Daniel: Composition and Reception*, ed. John J. Collins and Peter W. Flint, VTSup 83 [Leiden: Brill, 2001], 1:91–113).

ers—of biblical texts have encountered "divination" as something that is proscribed and prophecy as good and permissible. It is only in the past forty years that this distinction has been systematically questioned. Frederick Cryer's studies of magic and divination have been influential in questioning the distinction between Israelite prophecy and "foreign" divination, showing instead that many forms of what is commonly understood as "divination" are at home in ancient Israel and Judah.[4]

More recently still scholars such as Lester Grabbe, Cancik-Kirschbaum, Martti Nissinen and Pongratz-Leisten have questioned the biblical distinction between divination and prophecy.[5] Instead these scholars have argued that prophecy is a form of divination and that divination should be understood as the system by which humans gain information from the supra-human or divine spheres by a variety of means.

Martti Nissinen and I have continued to argue for the use of a distinction between "intuitive" and "technical" divination. This distinction is based not on the way that a divine message is received, as people used learned techniques in order to make themselves more receptive to receiving a divine message. A good example of this is dream incubation, by which a person underwent a ritual before going to sleep, often in a special location, all to make it more likely that they would receive a divinely sent dream. Instead the distinction is between types of divination where a divine message is readily understood, and those where the message has to be "translated" from the mode in which it has appeared—as, for instance, the particular constellation of stars or the shape of a

---

[4] See Frederick H. Cryer, "Der Prophet und der Magier: Bemerkungen anhand einer überholten Diskussion," in *Prophetie und geschichtliche Wirklichkeit im alten Israel: Festschrift für Siegfried Herrmann zum 65. Geburtstag*, ed. Rüdiger Liwak and Siegfried Wagner (Stuttgart: Kohlhammer, 1991), 79–88; Frederick H. Cryer, *Divination in Ancient Israel and Its Near Eastern Environment: A Socio-Historical Investigation*, JSOTSup 142 (Sheffield: JSOT Press, 1994).

[5] Lester L. Grabbe, *Priests, Prophets, Diviners, Sages: A Socio-Historical Study of Religious Specialists in Ancient Israel* (Valley Forge: Trinity, 1995), 124, 139–41; Eva Cancik-Kirschbaum, "Prophetismus und Divination—ein Blick auf die keilschriftlichen Quellen," in *Propheten in Mari, Assyrien und Israel*, ed. Matthias Köckert and Martti Nissinen, FRLANT 201 (Göttingen: Vandenhoeck & Ruprecht, 2003), 33–53; Martti Nissinen, "Prophecy and Omen Divination: Two Sides of the Same Coin," in *Divination and Interpretation of Signs in the Ancient World*, ed. Amar Annus, OIS 6 (Chicago: University of Chicago Press, 2010), 341–51. See also my *Prophecy in the Ancient Near East: A Philological and Sociological Comparison*, CHANE 56 (Leiden: Brill, 2012), 7–11; and Esther J. Hamori, *Women's Divination in Biblical Literature: Prophecy, Necromancy, and Other Arts of Knowledge*, AYBRL (New Haven: Yale University Press, 2015), 4–11.

liver must be "translated" into a human language understandable to someone who has not learned the specific ways of decoding such signs.

This latter form of divination is understood as "technical divination" by Martti Nissinen and myself. Other forms of divination, such as prophecy, some message dreams, and others are communicated by the gods in a form that does not require further translation, and Nissinen and I refer to them as "intuitive divination." Messages sent in both forms of divination may require interpretation and possibly reinterpretation, and no value judgment is intended by the distinction. Instead it attempts to capture a difference that appears to have been operational in ancient Mesopotamia, according to the majority of texts that have been preserved. This distinction between "technical" and "intuitive" forms of divination should not be misunderstood to indicate that only intuitive forms are divinely inspired. Indeed, Mesopotamian haruspices, astrologers and other diviners regarded their art and its literature as divinely inspired.

Dreaming itself has a good reputation in the Hebrew Bible. Deuteronomy 13:2–4 and Num 12:6–8 connect dreaming and prophecy as legitimate forms of divine-human communication. Both texts expect Yhwh to speak to prophets in a dream.[6] However, dream interpretation, which in later texts is mostly the domain of the interpreting angel (*angelus interpres*), operates in a different domain than dreaming itself. Dream interpretation, just like other forms of "technical" divination, is a form of divine-human communication in which the human expert understands the divine message in the medium in which it was given, and "translates" it into their own language. This is precisely where "message dreams" and "symbolic dreams" differ: a dream containing a message that needs no translation does not require an expert interpreter, as the divine message is already in a human language. Dreams containing symbols but no direct message require the dream interpreter to translate the divine message contained in the dream so that the addressee of the dream can understand it—even if it may require further interpretation, as the language may be mysterious and imprecise. Indeed, some interpreters, chief among them John J. Collins, have read the book of Daniel as a polemic against "technical" divination.[7]

---

[6] In his recent monograph, Andrew Perrin argues that because dreaming is regarded so positively in these two texts, later Second Temple tradition regarded dreaming as a good way of having God communicate with patriarchs such as Abraham and Levi (*The Dynamics of Dream-Vision Revelation in the Aramaic Dead Sea Scrolls*, JAJSup 19 [Göttingen: Vandenhoeck & Ruprecht, 2015], 139–43).

[7] E.g., Collins, *Commentary*, 50; Collins, *Apocalyptic Imagination*, 91–92, but see also David P. Melvin, *The Interpreting Angel Motif in Prophetic and Apocalyptic Literature*, Society of Biblical Literature Emerging Scholars Series (Minneapolis: Fortress Press, 2013), 153–56.

Dream interpretation is more similar to the reading of a sheep's entrails (hepatoscopy) than it is to dreaming a dream. The dreamer could be understood to be parallel to the sheep's entrails in that a deity could "write" the dream, just as they "write" their message in the path of the stars or the entrails of a sheep. Dream interpretation is thus much closer to other forms of divination that are regarded as suspect by the biblical text, but both Daniel's and Joseph's dream interpretation is depicted as entirely positive in the Hebrew Bible.

Dreams play an important part in the book of Daniel. In the first half of the book, no part of which likely predates the second century BCE by much, Daniel appears as the interpreter of Nebuchadnezzar's dreams.[8] By contrast, the second half of the book mostly contains Daniel's own dreams, which he does not interpret on his own; instead an interpreting angel provides the interpretations. Clearly, this is not the only feature which distinguishes the two parts of the book of Daniel from each other, but with regard to the conceptualization of dreams and their interpretation the distinction is significant and therefore of most interest here.

---

[8] See Collins, *Commentary*, 38, who dates the construction and combination of Dan 1–12 as we know it to the period between 167–164 BCE, notwithstanding the fact that the narratives in Dan 1–6 would have previously circulated independently from each other. The book-internal dating, which puts the events in Dan 2 in the second year of Nebuchadnezzar's reign, makes little historical sense. If Daniel had trained for three years at this point, he would have had to have started his training in the first year of Nebuchadnezzar's reign. Any search for historical verisimilitude in connection to the book of Daniel is, in my view, misguided. In their discussion of the origin of chapters 2–6 Carol Newsom and Brennan Breed rely on the argument brought forward, that the core of Dan 2–6 goes back to the sixth century or shortly thereafter, because of similarities with Nabonidus material (Carol A. Newsom and Brennan Breed, *Daniel: A Commentary*, OTL [Louisville: Westminster John Knox, 2014], 6–12, 128–30; Carol A. Newsom, "Why Nabonidus? Excavating Traditions from Qumran, the Hebrew Bible, and Neo-Babylonian Sources," in *The Dead Sea Scrolls: Transmission of Traditions and Production of Texts*, ed. Sarianna Metso, Hindy Najman and Eileen M. Schuller, STDJ 92 [Leiden: Brill, 2010], 57–79). However, Caroline Waerzeggers shows that the available material is "historical literature" from the late Achaemenid, Seleucid or even Parthian period suggesting interest in Nabonidus material at a much later point in time (Caroline Waerzeggers, "Facts, Propaganda, or History? Shaping Political Memory in the Nabonidus Chronicle," in *Political Memory in and after the Persian Empire*, ed. Jason M. Silverman and Caroline Waerzeggers, ANEM 13 [Atlanta: Society of Biblical Literature, 2015], 95–124; Caroline Waerzeggers, "The Prayer of Nabonidus in the Light of Hellenistic Babylonian Literature," in *Jewish Cultural Encounters in the Ancient Mediterranean and Near Eastern World*, ed. Mladen Popović, Myles Schooner, and Marijn Vandenberghe [Leiden: Brill, 2017], 64–75). There is no need to go into the sixth century BCE for an origin of a Jewish Nabonidus narrative that was later moved to Nebuchadnezzar.

According to Leo Oppenheim dream interpreters had three ways of interpreting a "symbolic" dream: intuitive interpretation of the various parts, consultation of dream omina, and asking the deity who sent the dream to provide an interpretation.[9] There is no question that the first can be found in the book of Daniel (e.g., Dan 2). The second category is not found explicitly, although it is always possible to imagine the knowledgeable expert deriving his information from the standard divinatory reference works without having to look the information up in each individual case. In some sense, the first two categories could be grouped together as relying on human knowledge rather than divine knowledge to interpret dreams (and other omens). The third category, requesting help from the deity, occurs in Daniel as well. Annette Zgoll identifies two kinds of "dream specialists" (*Traumspezialisten*): one who tries to receive divine messages for another through the medium of dreams, and a second who interprets the dreams of others. Interestingly, she sees the second kind—the dream-interpreter—not primarily as a divinatory specialist but as a medical professional who helps a client come to terms with the omina which refer to their future.[10] Her view is partly based on the use of the verb bur$_2$ / *pašāru* ("to solve, untie") in dream interpretation.[11] However, as the verb *pašāru* is also used for the interpretative action of other omen specialists, this argument does not appear to me to be very strong. The specialist who dreams for others, *šabru* (lit.: "show-er"), is broadly attested in Neo-Assyrian texts.[12]

---

[9] Oppenheim, *Interpretation of Dreams*, 221–22. Benjamin L. Gladd, *Revealing the Mysterion: The Use of Mystery in Daniel and Second Temple Judaism with Its Bearing on First Corinthians*, BZNW 160 (Berlin: de Gruyter, 2008), 23–24 argues that in the ancient Near East the gods inspire the original divine message as well as its interpretation. Gladd slightly misrepresents Lawson ("'The God Who Reveals Secrets': The Mesopotamian Background to Daniel 2.47," *JSOT* 74 [1997]: 61–76), but the fact that the divinatory arts trace their own origin to divine intervention is nonetheless important. Whether or not each individual act of interpretation of an ominous sign—be that the flight of birds, the position of the stars, the physical disposition of a liver or, indeed, a dream—was considered inspired is uncertain, but the art of divinatory interpretation itself was.

[10] Annette Zgoll, *Traum und Welterleben im antiken Mesopotamien: Traumtheorie und Traumpraxis im 3.–1. Jahrtausend v. Chr. als Horizont einer Kulturgeschichte des Träumens*, AOAT 333 (Münster: Ugarit-Verlag, 2006), 401–37; Annette Zgoll, "Die Welt im Schlaf sehen–Inkubation von Träumen im antiken Mesopotamien," *WdO* 32 (2002): 74–101.

[11] The professional titles for dream interpreters are ensi (Sumerian) and *šā'ilu*, *šā'iltu* (Akkadian). They are equated in lexical lists and often named together with other divinatory experts; see Zgoll, *Traum und Welterleben*, 401–11.

[12] Zgoll, *Traum und Welterleben*, 413–15.

In the introduction to the book, Daniel is implicitly included in the group of people described as "of royal descent and of the nobility" (מזרע המלוכה ומן הפרתמים; Dan 1:3)[13] and as being without "blemish" (מום). While these words are put into the mouth of King Nebuchadnezzar, it is clear that the author is appealing to his Judean audience who presumably would not have been aware of the Persian origin of the term פרתמים but who would have connected the term מום with the priesthood (see, e.g., the limitations for temple service in Lev 21:16–18). The fact that the youths are taught the language of the Chaldeans also helps to establish the image of Daniel as an elevated, wise and mysterious individual: the royal prince, priest and wise man trained in the Chaldean arts.[14] Following the dating of at least the introduction to the book and chapters 7–12 to the second century, we may safely assume that the writing (or knowledge; ספר ולשון; γράμματα καὶ διάλεκτον) of the Chaldeans refers to the divinatory arts, as was the common understanding of this terminology in Graeco-Roman literature.[15] Indeed, Dan 1:17 makes this abundantly clear even for readers who may

---

[13] This expression betrays a date no earlier than the Persian period—פרתמים is a well-known Persian loan into Hebrew; see, e.g., Edward Lipiński, "Review of André Lacocque, *Le livre de Daniel*, Commentaire de l'Ancien Testament 15b (Delachaux et Niestlé: Neuchâtel & Paris), 1976," *VT* 28 (1977): 233–39, 236–37; Koch, *Daniel*, 3–4. The use of the Late Biblical Hebrew term מלוכה in the sense of "royal" is also a strong indication of the late date of this text.

[14] If this interpretation is correct, this implies that the idea of the wise Chaldean dream interpreter would have had to develop into a recognizable literary trope before Dan 1 was composed. On the composition of Daniel see Collins, *Commentary*; Koch, *Daniel*; Kratz, "Die Visionen des Daniel;" Kratz, "The Visions of Daniel."

[15] I agree with Newsom and Breed, *Daniel*, 41–44, that this scene is likely fictitious. Like others, however, Newsom and Breed argue that access to cuneiform reading and writing skills would have been easy for non-Babylonians under Persian rule. Newsom and Breed give some good examples from Old Babylonian texts, based on Dominique Charpin's important work *Reading and Writing in Babylon* (Cambridge: Harvard University Press, 2010). However, their assumption seems to me unlikely to be correct for the latter half of the first millennium BCE. For cuneiform writing as protected cultural heritage in the second half of the first millennium BCE see, e.g., Philippe Clancier, "Cuneiform Culture's Last Guardians: The Old Urban Notability of Hellenistic Uruk," in *The Oxford Handbook of Cuneiform Culture*, ed. Eleanor Robson and Karen Radner (Oxford: Oxford University Press, 2011), 752–73. Basic knowledge of reading and writing may have been more widespread than we used to think, but the level of understanding and training for the divinatory arts is considerably further advanced. It seems unlikely that it would have been easily available to non-Babylonians. It may be important also to point out here that the *Al Yahudu* tablets are not a good example of Judeans writing cuneiform as all scribes mentioned in the documents have Babylonian names. The archive is clearly

not have picked up the hint in verses 2–4: "Daniel had understanding of visions and dreams of all kinds" (ודניאל הבין בכל-חזון וחלומות), as given by God (והילדים האלה ארבעתם נתן להם האלהים מדע והשׂכל בכל-ספר וחכמה; Dan 1:17). These verses foreshadow what we see later in chapters 2–12: that Daniel's ability to interpret dreams is not only something that he learned from his "Chaldean" teachers, but, more importantly, that God provided him with his skill as well as the concrete interpretation. In this sense, Daniel's form of dream divination is inspired—closer to intuitive divination than technical.[16]

DREAMING AND OMEN DIVINATION IN DANIEL 4–5

The book of Daniel contains a number of different dreams and visions. The most "normal" of these significant dreams is part of the narrative in Dan 3:31–4:34.[17] As is well known, Dan 4–6 is preserved in two substantially different versions. One is preserved by the Masoretic Text, the Peshiṭta and Theodotion (version 1), while the Septuagint (version 2) contains the other. It is clear that both texts are versions of the same narrative, but they differ in some important details.[18] In version 1 Nebuchadnezzar dreams of a huge tree which provides for all living in its shadow. By divine command the tree is cut down and transformed into a wild beast for seven years. None of his advisors can interpret it for him.[19] After their unsuccessful attempts, Daniel is summoned—using his Babylonian name—and he interprets the dream for Nebuchadnezzar (Dan 4:5–24). Nebuchadnezzar de-

---

about Judeans, but whether it was written by Judeans or even owned by Judeans are different questions.

[16] See, e.g., Newsom and Breed, *Daniel*, 43–45.

[17] With "significant dream" I use terminology from Annette Zgoll's work on dreaming that distinguishes between dreams that are "just" dreams and dreams that contain a divine message.

[18] For my current purposes finding a redaction-critical solution to this matters little. Newsom and Breed, *Daniel*, 127–30 offer a good summary of the state of the question and the new consensus that both textual forms go back to a lost Aramaic version; see, e.g., Collins, *Commentary*, 216–21.

[19] Koch argues that it is likely that the version attested in MT and others added the Babylonian advisors following the example of Dan 2 and to some extent Dan 5 (Koch, *Daniel*, 392). The observation that this is a "blasse Wiederholung ..., um die Überlegenheit Daniels herauszustreichen" ("a bland repetition ... in order to underline Daniel's superiority") strikes me both as true and pointless. The point of the Babylonian advisors surely is to show Daniel's superiority, but they are no more "bland" in Dan 4 than in either Dan 2 or 5.

scribes Daniel's ability to interpret dreams as linked to the "spirit of the holy God" being in him (Dan 4:15).

In version 2, Nebuchadnezzar has the dream in the eighteenth year of his reign while sitting on his throne.[20] The eighteenth year of his reign is the year of the campaign against Judah. This suggests that even the destruction of Jerusalem is likely regarded by the authors of the text as one of the ways in which Nebuchadnezzar's hubris manifested. When Nebuchadnezzar says of himself that "[he] was living at peace in [his] home and prospering on [his] throne" (OG Dan 4:1), he is saying that all is well, not that he was sitting on the throne at the moment that he was having the dream.[21] However, the setting in OG is different in that Nebuchadnezzar does not check with his other advisors but goes straight to Daniel, who is not addressed by his Babylonian name, but by his West Semitic name. And instead of the "spirit of the holy God" (MT Dan 4:15) being invoked, Nebuchadnezzar describes Daniel as "the leader of the wise and the leader of those who decide dreams" (OG Dan 4:15).

In version 2, Daniel is presented as a typical ancient Near Eastern dream interpreter. The most famous example of such a figure is probably Gilgamesh's mother Ninsun, who interprets his dreams before meeting Enkidu (Gilgamesh i 244–98).[22] Dream divination in both Dan 4 (version 2) and in Gilgamesh clearly follows Oppenheim's first model: in both literary works, the dream interpreter is able to offer an interpretation of the dream without consulting weighty tomes or tablets, or indeed without first offering a prayer to their deity/deities.[23]

In version 1, Nebuchadnezzar's identification of the "spirit of the holy God" enabling Daniel as dream interpreter indicates that what I call the "prophetization" of dream divination is already visible. The authors of the text are uncomfortable with the possibility that Daniel may be able to decipher his king's

---

[20] Koch, *Daniel*, 391–401.

[21] Εἰρηνεύων ἤμην ἐν τῷ οἴκῳ μου, καὶ εὐθηνῶν ἐπὶ τοῦ θρόνου μου.

[22] A. R. George, *The Babylonian Gilgamesh Epic: Introduction, Critical Edition and Cuneiform Texts* (Oxford: Oxford University Press, 2003), 1:552–557. Similarly, Enkidu fulfills the function of dream interpreter for Gilgamesh on their joint journey to the cedar forest (Gilgamesh ii 9–33; George, *Gilgamesh*, 1:588–591). Ninsun is herself divine and thus her access to the interpretation of Gilgamesh's dreams is easier to understand, but Enkidu has thus far in the narrative not excelled in the scholarly traditions of Babylonian sages.

[23] Phoebe Makiello, "Daniel as Mediator of Divine Knowledge in the Book of Daniel," *JJS* 60 (2009): 18–31, regards Daniel's oneirocritical abilities as increasing throughout the Aramaic section of the book. The evaluation presumably depends on whether one believes Daniel's dream visions in chapter 7 to outshine his interpretative powers in chapters 2 and especially 4. I understand Daniel as a channel for divine interpretation in Dan 7, while in Dan 4, he appears in his most learned guise.

dreams simply through the correct use of the knowledge and training that he has undergone. By having Nebuchadnezzar himself recognize God's input into the interpretative act, the authors/editors of this version of the text move interpretative dream divination closer to the intuitive divinatory arts of prophecy, visions and dreaming—as approved by texts such as Deut 13 and 18—and away from more technical forms of divination, which are condemned in those chapters from Deuteronomy.

Daniel 5 does not contain a dream. Instead, Nebuchadnezzar's son Belshazzar, as afflicted by hubris as his father, has a big party during which a disembodied hand draws or writes various signs on the wall that neither Belshazzar nor any of his advisors can read. However, the queen needs to remind Belshazzar of Daniel's existence—and of Nebuchadnezzar's appointment of Daniel to be the chief of the magicians, exorcists, Chaldeans and diviners.[24] Enter Daniel, who, naturally, not only is able to read the text itself, but also has the hermeneutic skills necessary to understand the message.[25] Here again, he does not consult heavy tomes or tablets to figure out its meaning, but this does not mean that he has not acquired his knowledge from such hermeneutic treasure troves previously.

In version 1 of the narrative, the queen describes Daniel as possessing "illumination, understanding, and wisdom like that of the gods" (MT Dan 5:11); a few verses further on, Belshazzar tells Daniel that he has the "spirit of the gods/God" in him (MT Dan 5:14). In version 2, the queen says that "the/a holy spirit is in him" (OG Dan 5:12); there is no direct equivalent to MT Dan 5:14 in the OG. In both versions, Daniel's ability to interpret omina is attributed to divine intervention, at least in the eyes of the Babylonian aristocracy. Daniel's interpretation of the famous writing on the wall leads King Belshazzar to pay Daniel handsomely—just before the predicted future takes place and the Persians and Medes take over the kingdom.

Again, in neither version of Dan 4–5 does Daniel consult any reference

---

[24] Thus version 1; version 2 only notes that he explained omens to Nebuchadnezzar. Narratively this makes considerably more sense, as it is unlikely that Daniel would not have been summoned immediately if he really were the head of the magicians, exorcists, Chaldeans and diviners.

[25] John J. Collins, "The Court-Tales in Daniel and the Development of Apocalyptic," *JBL* 94 (1975): 218–34; Karel van der Toorn, "Scholars at the Oriental Court: The Figure of Daniel against Its Mesopotamian Background," in *The Book of Daniel: Composition and Reception*, ed. John J. Collins and Peter W. Flint, VTSup 83 (Leiden: Brill, 2001), 1:37–54. See also Holger Gzella, "The Scribal Background of the 'Menetekel' in Daniel 5," *Bible and Interpretation* (2016), http://www.bibleinterp.com/articles/2016/04/gze408029.shtml (last accessed 17 May 2016) on the scribal aspects of the underlying hermeneutics of the vision.

works, nor does he have to explicitly ask his deity to help provide the solution to the question. Yet both versions of these chapters associate Daniel's ability to interpret dreams and other signs with the spirit of God, and with Daniel's direct interaction with God. It is somewhat puzzling why this ability is always acknowledged by a member of the Babylonian royal family, rather than by either Daniel himself, another onlooker or, indeed, the narrator.[26]

DANIEL 7 AND 8 (AND 9–12)

The book of Daniel also contains narratives of Daniel himself dreaming, rather than interpreting the dreams of others such as Nebuchadnezzar (Dan 4), or interpreting the writing on the wall (Dan 5). The first such occasion is in Dan 2, in which Daniel dreams in response to Nebuchadnezzar's dream (see further below). In both chapters 7 and 8, Daniel has a vision or dream.[27] In both cases it

---

[26] While divination was linked to the divine, possession or inspiration by a divine spirit was not a requirement nor especially well regarded in ancient Near Eastern divination. It is clear that this connection is made by the Judean/Jewish authors and redactors of the book of Daniel, presumably in order to give authority of some kind to the statement. It is less obvious why the Babylonian royal family should have particular authority in knowing in whom the spirit of God is active. Perhaps it is linked to the Chaldean fame for divination in the Graeco-Roman period.

[27] Daniel 7 describes the vision as a dream and a vision (וחזוי ... חלם; Dan 7:1) and as a night vision (חזוי ליליא; Dan 7:13). According to Dan 8:1 (and vv. 2, 13, 15, 17 and 26) a vision came to Daniel (חזון; vv. 16, 26 and 27 use מראה), and in Dan 8:2 the same term is used to refer to the vision of chapter 7. The fact that the root חלם is not employed in these two chapters may be significant: they contain visions, not dreams. See James E. Miller, "Dreams and Prophetic Visions," *Bib* 71 (1990): 401–4. Elsewhere, it appears that the two Aramaic terms are used almost interchangeably, see, e.g., Perrin, *Dynamics of Dream-Revelation*, 92–94. For a form-critical distinction of dreams and visions in ancient Near Eastern dreams, see Zgoll, *Traum und Welterleben*, 164. It is tempting to draw a line of comparison also to Nabonidus's dreams in one of his royal inscriptions, in which Nebuchadnezzar asks Nabonidus to tell him what he dreamt, but the obvious difference here is that Nebuchadnezzar does not interpret the dream for Nabonidus (see Hanspeter Schaudig, *Die Inschriften Nabonids von Babylon und Kyros' des Grossen samt den in ihrem Umfeld entstandenen Tendenzschriften: Textausgabe und Grammatik*, AOAT 256 [Münster: Ugarit-Verlag, 2001], no. 3.3a, vi 1'–36', 514–25). It is, of course, very difficult to distinguish clearly and unambiguously between visions and dreams—the night-visions in Zech 1–6 are a case in point. However, the absence of the root חלם appears to me to be significant, so that contrary to, e.g., Karin Schöpflin, I think that there is a difference between the literary constructions of religious experience in Zechariah and Daniel ("God's Interpreter: The Interpreting Angel in Post-Exilic Prophetic Visions of the

144 DANIEL AND THE "PROPHETIZATION" OF DREAM DIVINATION

appears as if Daniel's powers of dream interpretation are sufficient only for interpreting the dreams of others—sometimes with direct divine intervention. His interpretative skill does not extend to understanding his own dreams.[28] In Dan 7:16 he asks one of those attending (קאמיא / ἑστώτων) to help him understand the "true meaning" of this dream vision. In chapter 8, Gabriel, in human form (כמראה־גבר), fulfills the function of the interpreting angel (Dan 8:15–16). This interpreting angel is famously significant in second temple literature.

According to David Melvin, the "elaborate symbolism" of the vision necessitates the presence of an angelic interpreter as Daniel can no longer rely simply on the basic hermeneutical framework with which to understand his visions.[29] However, it seems to me that the identity of the dreamer (Daniel himself) is more important in this regard than the lack of Daniel's divinatory abilities—literary dream interpreters virtually always interpret the dreams of others. In Daniel's case, his ignorance is required to build up the tension that can then be released by divine intervention. Daniel's initial ignorance also emphasizes the underlying "prophetization" of dream divination: divine revelation, rather than

---

Old Testament," in *Angels: The Concept of Celestial Beings—Origins, Development and Reception*, ed. Friedrich V. Reiterer, Tobias Nicklas and Karin Schöpflin, DCLY 2007 [Berlin: de Gruyter, 2007)] 189–203, esp. 190–95). This holds true irrespective of the nature of any potential underlying religious experiences; see, e.g., Lena-Sofia Tiemeyer, "Through a Glass Darkly: Zechariah's Unprocessed Visionary Experience," *VT* 58 (2008): 573–94.

[28] This may reflect the fact that in ancient Near Eastern dream divination, the diviner (interpreter) and the dreamer (medium) are usually not the same person. This was already observed by Susan Niditch, *The Symbolic Vision in Biblical Tradition*, HSM 30 (Cambridge: Harvard Semitic Museum; Missoula: Scholars Press, 1983), 185. There are potential counter examples, such as the *Erra Epos* which is revealed to its author, Kabti-ilani-Marduk, during the "sleep of night" (*ina šāt mūši*) by Išum (Erra v 43). However, the text does not claim that Išum's words were not spoken. Kratz, "Die Visionen des Daniel," 224; Kratz, "The Visions of Daniel," 97, expresses this changed role in different words: "The role which Daniel once played for the king is now played for Daniel himself by someone from the heavenly scene." But there is a difference in that within the world of the narrative, Nebuchadnezzar was the final addressee of the previous messages, while Daniel is not, as such, the final addressee; instead the audience of the book is.

[29] Melvin, *Interpreting Angel*, 157. On prophetic hermeneutics in the Hebrew Bible and the ancient Near East see, e.g., Michael Fishbane, *Biblical Interpretation in Ancient Israel* (Oxford: Clarendon Press, 1985), 441–524; Jonathan Stökl, "Prophetic Hermeneutics in the Hebrew Bible and Mesopotamia," *HeBAI* 4 (2015): 267–92. Fishbane's distinction between aural and oral on the one side and visual on the other seems to me not to work. In the world within the text, a vision is seen but expressed in words, just as an oracle would be. In the world in which the texts came to be, their written nature determines their development, irrespective of whether an oral or a visual experience is described.

human divinatory expertise, is required. The vision's complexity is hardly sufficiently fundamental to make overcoming Daniel's ignorance the book's overall point. Otherwise we could conceive of a wiser dream interpreter than Daniel overcoming the interpretative challenge. But the book suggests that this is a problem to be overcome only with direct and immediate divine support—after all, Daniel and his friends are ten times better at interpreting signs than all the other wise men and diviners (Dan 1:20).

The construction of chapter 8 supports this view, as God does not even wait for Daniel to ask what the meaning of the vision may have been—he commissions Gabriel to act as a divine messenger to provide the vision's interpretation to Daniel (Dan 8:16). That means that, of course, Gabriel performs the task normally assigned to a diviner. Curiously, this construction of dream divination in Daniel's vision seems to show that dream divination as such is slightly absurd. There is no need for God to first send the vision and then for Gabriel to explain what it actually means. God might as well have sent Gabriel straight away. The use of the vision appears to be solely for the gratification of the reader in that it offers the reader not simply the message but also the images connected to it.[30]

In chapter 9, Daniel consults "the books" regarding the "number of years"

---

[30] Melvin, *Interpreting Angel Motif*, 165–67, discusses the importance of the *apkallū* as transmitters of divine knowledge to humanity. In my view his discussion slightly misses the important observation that is made very well in Seth L. Sanders, *From Adapa to Enoch: Scribal Culture and Religious Vision in Judea and Babylonia*, TSAJ 167 (Tübingen: Mohr Siebeck, 2017): the point is not so much whether the *apkallū* are diviners and whether Hellenistic diviners aimed to emulate them, but that the *apkallū* are wise; the fact that they are the ancestral founding fathers of the scribal arts underlies their importance to Mesopotamian divination as a fundamentally scribal activity. And this is also where scribal art and divination meet in Daniel, which, as has recently been pointed out by Gzella, "Scribal Background," is also fundamentally scribal. See also Collins, *Apocalyptic Imagination*, 91–92; Hans-Peter Müller, "Mantische Weisheit und Apokalyptik," in *Congress Volume, Uppsala, 1971*, ed. P. A. H. de Boer, VTSup 22 (Leiden: Brill, 1972), 268–93. Similarly, the close connection between prophetic writing and scribes can be observed in much of the textual development of prophetic literature in the Second Temple period; see, e.g., M. H. Floyd and R. D. Haak, ed. *Prophets, Prophecy, and Prophetic Texts in Second Temple Judaism*, LHBOTS 427 (London: T&T Clark, 2006); Odil Hannes Steck, *Gott in der Zeit entdecken: Die Prophetenbücher des Alten Testaments als Vorbild für Theologie und Kirche*, Biblisch-theologische Studien 42 (Neukirchen-Vluyn: Neukirchener Verlag, 2001). For the late Second Temple period see, e.g., Martin Goodman, "Texts, Scribes and Power in Roman Judaea," in *Literacy and Power in the Ancient World*, ed. Alan K. Bowman and Greg Woolf (Cambridge: Cambridge University Press, 1994), 99–108.

in Jeremiah (Jer 25:11–12 and 29:10).[31] This pericope is interesting for a number of reasons. As in chapter 5, Daniel is interpreting a text, with the difference being that here the text to be interpreted is a "biblical" text.[32] Unlike in chapter 5, but like in chapters 7–8, Daniel needs help to understand correctly what is going on. Fortunately, the angel Gabriel comes to the rescue once again to explain the "precise" meaning of Jeremiah's seventy years (Dan 9:20–27).

While this chapter does not contain a dream to be interpreted and is, therefore, of tangential importance to the subject matter of this essay, it does contain a sophisticated understanding of the divinatory interpretation of reality. Thus Daniel, a trained interpreter of divine signs, can fail in his attempts to understand correctly the Jeremianic passage he is reading. But as Daniel is not simply any interpreter of texts, Gabriel is on hand to help correct his mistaken interpretation. Thus, this chapter shows the awareness of the potentially problematic nature of textual interpretation by the scribes who composed chapter 9.[33]

The image of dream/vision-based divination in chapters 10–12 is mostly straightforward: Daniel has a long vision in which he interacts with heavenly beings who speak to him very clearly. From the point of view of a classical system of divination, Daniel is the recipient of a divine message that is brought to

---

[31] On Dan 9 see, e.g., Newsom and Breed, *Daniel*, 283–320; Paul L. Redditt, "Daniel 9: Its Structure and Meaning," *CBQ* 62 (2000): 236–49; Antti Laato, "The Seventy Yearweeks in the Book of Daniel," *ZAW* 102 (1990): 212–25; Gerald H. Wilson, "The Prayer of Daniel 9: Reflection on Jeremiah 29," *JSOT* 48 (1990): 91–99.

[32] It is likely that the books referred to in Dan 5:2 are indeed part of a nascent collection of books. It is less likely that Daniel is using external written sources—essentially an omen list—in order to understand Jeremiah. However, the latter possibility cannot be entirely excluded. If we allow for the possibility that Daniel is consulting not just Jeremiah but other biblical books (thus, e.g., Hansjörg Rigger, *Siebzig Siebener: die "Jahrwochenprophetie" in Dan 9*, TThSt 57 [Trier: Paulinus-Verlag, 1997], 182–83), he may well be consulting even nonbiblical books. I agree with Newsom and Breed, *Daniel*, 290, that in the depiction of Daniel in 9:2 as a "scribe ... reading and studying, we probably have a close description of the activities of the authors of Dan 7–12 themselves." Based on the note in Dan 7:1 that Daniel has written the dream down, Fishbane (*Biblical Interpretation*, 447) suggests that the dream report is based on a written text. However, it seems unlikely to me that the dream report existed as a written text without the angel's interpretation, in either the world within the text or the world in which Dan 7 was written.

[33] I do not share the view of Newsom and Breed, *Daniel*, 287, that the similarities between chapters 8 and 9 indicate that chapter 9 is not a later addition. Indeed, these similarities argue in favor of a later date for chapter 9, as a reaction to chapters 7–8 (and probably chapters 10–12). Chapter 9 uses the surrounding chapters for its argument that textual interpretation needs to rely not only on the skill of the human interpreter but also on divine help, whether in the form of inspiration or an *angelus interpres*.

him by angelic intermediaries who are performing the prophetic function. Within the construction of the text, the message is not aimed at any audience apart from Daniel, although it is clear that the readers of the text are the ultimate addressees.

DANIEL 2

In Dan 2 we have Nebuchadnezzar's first dream, and the language changes from Hebrew to Aramaic with the response of the Chaldeans within verse 4. Neither the Masoretic nor the Greek text of Daniel make it explicit quite what it is that Nebuchadnezzar asks his diviners to do (Dan 2:1–3): whether he asks them to interpret his dream or to tell him what he dreamt. The former would be an entirely standard approach to royal dream divination in ancient Near Eastern literature. Gilgamesh tells his mother his dream and she interprets it (Gilgamesh i 244–98). Similarly, the baker and the cupbearer tell Joseph their respective dreams (Gen 40:9–11, 16–17), whereupon Joseph interprets them (Gen 40:12–15, 18–19). The first time the topic is introduced, Nebuchadnezzar appears to be doing just this (Dan 2:1–3). However, Dan 2:7–9 indicates that Nebuchadnezzar was testing his diviners even further by asking them not only to interpret his dream but also to divine what his dream was in the first place.

Nebuchadnezzar's test is patently unfair to the diviners, as their knowledge and skill enables them to read divine messages in observed phenomena, not to know what the phenomena would be in the first place. They rightly complain about the request (Dan 2:10–11). When Daniel, who had not been previously consulted in this matter, hears that he and the other wise men are to be executed (Dan 2:13–15), he asks for an audience with the king in order to tell the king the interpretation of the dream without yet knowing the dream itself. Daniel and his friends pray to the God of Heaven for help and, in a night-vision—possibly another dream—God reveals the secret (רז) to Daniel. Daniel goes to the king and tells him both why he had the dream and why Daniel knows about it—and, for the readers' sake, Daniel also kindly relates the dream itself (Dan 2:16).[34]

Daniel 2 is a fruitful chapter for the task of understanding the construction

---

[34] As Lawson ("The God Who Reveals Secrets") rightly points out, much of the portrayal of Daniel's divinatory art in the book works well within a Mesopotamian understanding of divination. I disagree with Lawson, however, that the biblical book's message is that Mesopotamian divination does not work because it is idolatrous. Instead, the other diviners fail in order to aggrandize the single hero Daniel, who prevails where all others fail. See also Alan Lenzi, "Secrecy, Textual Legitimation, and Intercultural Polemics in the Book of Daniel," *CBQ* 71 (2009): 330–48.

of dream divination in second century BCE Yehud/Judaea. In the story, different people dream different kinds of dreams: Nebuchadnezzar dreamt a significant dream, but does not know what it means. In order to find that out he goes and asks his experts without providing them with the dream itself, thereby keeping from them the divine text they were meant to interpret. Only Daniel seems to have direct access to a deity who can reveal to him the original dream, which he can then interpret.

Daniel 2 thus requires the diviner to divine the dream itself as well as its meaning. Nebuchadnezzar's dream requires decoding; just as with a constellation of stars or a sheep's liver, an expert interpreter needs to be consulted to interpret it. Nebuchadnezzar does the logical thing and asks his diviners to interpret, but does not mention the actual contents of his dream. I dare say that few hepatoscopers would have been able to read the divine will in a sheep's liver they had neither seen nor heard described. While there is some evidence that astrologers were amenable to adapting the hermeneutic traditions in the light of royal propaganda, it is likely that most of their observations were partially based on observed phenomena, or at least scholarly extrapolations based on such observations.[35] They also could predict (calculate) celestial phenomena on which they could then base horoscopes.[36] This phenomenon can be understood as similar to Daniel divining Nebuchadnezzar's dream as the Babylonian astrologers divined the future sky before interpreting it. However, I am not aware of similar occurrences in either hepatoscopy or dream interpretation.

Not even among the letters from Old Babylonian Mari do we find evidence for a model of dream divination similar to that of Dan 2. There is some evidence that dream oracles were double-checked by means of other forms of divination. Thus in ARM 26 225 the diviners (dumu-meš máš-šu-gíd-gíd) are called in to verify whether the dream was a significant dream, and in ARM 26 229 bird divination is used to inquire whether a woman called Ayala really did see a significant dream. ARM 26 229 then goes on to mention that Ayala's "hair and hem" are included in the missive so that Zimri-Lim "may inquire about her" (lines 20–21). It is unlikely that Daniel's dream, elicited through the joint prayers of Daniel and his three friends, was intended to check the veracity of Nebuchadnezzar's claim that he had had a significant dream. Instead, it is meant to show Daniel's superiority to other diviners at the Persian court.

What could be the reason for integrating Daniel's interpretative dream into the wider story of Daniel interpreting Nebuchadnezzar's dream? On the one

---

[35] See, e.g., Jeffrey L. Cooley, "Propaganda, Prognostication, and Planets," in *Divination, Politics and Ancient Near Eastern Empires*, ed. Alan Lenzi and Jonathan Stökl, ANEM 7 (Atlanta: Society of Biblical Literature, 2014), 7–31.

[36] See, the discussion in, e.g., Rochberg, *Heavenly Writing*, 297–99.

hand, we could see this as a way of bolstering Daniel's reputation, giving him access to the divine word not only through other people's dreams that he can interpret, but through direct prophetic activity ("When a prophet of YHWH arises among you, I make myself known to him in a vision, I speak with him in a dream," Num 12:6). On the other hand, this could also be read as the careful subordination of Daniel's skill and wisdom to the direct authority of God. If the story ever existed without Daniel's dream, it seems likely that it would have been important to integrate Daniel and his ability into a framework in which God was visibly the source of Daniel's information. The solution found by the author is clever, because a dream is interpreted through a dream, and at the same time somewhat clumsy from a literary point of view, as it does not operate within the common framework for ancient Near Eastern dream interpretation, but that may have been part of the point.

John J. Collins and others have long argued that the portrayal of divination in the book of Daniel can be read as a polemic against "technical" divination.[37] Such a reading is eminently possible: after all, Daniel, who relies on direct divine revelation, and therefore "intuitive" divination, is the only one who can help. But many a Mesopotamian diviner might have protested that "technical" divination is also based on divine inspiration, through the divine inspiration of their art and the literature it produced, such as omen lists. But the internal logic of biblical texts need not rely on Mesopotamian perceptions and realities. This can be easily illustrated by biblical idol polemics, which do not take seriously Mesopotamian understandings of the *mīš pî* and *pit pî* rituals, which represented an attempt to solve the question of the relationship between the divine statue and the deity.[38] In a similar vein, it is likely that the authors and compilers of the book of Daniel were not concerned about misrepresenting Mesopotamian divination to their readers.

In my view, however, another reading of the texts brings us further. Rather than denying the possibility of dream interpretation and other forms of technical divination, or polemicizing against them, the book of Daniel "domesticates" them, at least in its earlier chapters, thereby permitting their use in the communi-

---

[37] E.g., Collins, *Commentary*, 50; Collins, *Apocalyptic Imagination*, 91–92, but see also Melvin, *Interpreting Angel Motif*, 153–56.

[38] On this question, see, e.g., Angelika Berlejung, *Die Theologie der Bilder: Herstellung und Einweihung von Kultbildern in Mesopotamien und die alttestamentliche Bilderpolemik*, OBO 162 (Göttingen: Vandenhoeck & Ruprecht, 1998); Angelika Berlejung, "Washing the Mouth: The Consecration of Divine Images in Mesopotamia," in *The Image and the Book: Iconic Cults, Aniconism, and the Veneration of the Holy Book in Israel and the Ancient Near East*, ed. Karel van der Toorn, CBET 21 (Leuven: Peeters, 1997), 45–72.

ty of the faithful in the second century BCE. This is achieved through explicit references to divine intervention each time Daniel or one of the angels interprets the relevant dream. While dream interpretation is not directly condemned in the Deuteronomic proscriptions of "technical" divination (Deut 13 and 18), elsewhere (e.g., Num 12, Jer 23) dreaming—not dream interpretation—is regarded as a prophetic activity. The book of Daniel, and to a lesser extent the Jacob novella, therefore cover new ground here.

The difference between chapters 2–6 and 7–12 in the way that dream divination is constructed may be significant here. The authors and editors of the later chapters may have felt some unease with the way that Daniel interacted with the deity directly, such that they needed to introduce the *angelus interpres* to distance Daniel from the deity. At the same time, this offered them the opportunity to turn Daniel, who in the earlier chapters had interpreted the dreams of others—a form of technical divination—into a much less controversial prophetic figure by having the angel do the interpreting for Daniel, who is now the dreamer. This latter Daniel does not rely on his human knowledge in the least, but is dependent on divine revelation just like any other prophet. It is possible that the authors of the later chapters were afraid that the strategy in the earlier chapters may not convince their contemporaries, so they brought Daniel in from the cold, so to speak, and characterized him in a way more compatible with Deuteronomic understandings of divination in general and prophecy in particular.

The earlier chapters of the book, however, present dream divination as compatible with being a good prophet and a good Jew, like Daniel. In other words, Dan 2–6 domesticates dream divination by introducing an element of intuitive divination back into the process, by requiring direct divine input in the interpretation. One could say that these chapters "propheticize" dream divination and bring it into the fold of what is acceptable within the various forms of Judaism at the time, at least in the context of a diasporic life such as that of the literary Daniel. The depiction of Daniel as "of royal descent and of the nobility ... without blemish (מום), handsome, proficient in all wisdom, knowledgeable and intelligent, and capable of serving in the royal palace" (Dan 1:3–4) indicates that the book's authors depict him as part of the Jewish establishment, fit to be a priest. This in turn makes his actions as a technical interpreter even more significant. They are the actions of a prophet and of someone who is fit to be a priest—*and* he carries out his divinatory tasks with divine approval. God declares dream interpretation acceptable, so long as it is carried out in his name and he is consulted.

Bibliography

Berlejung, Angelika. "Washing the Mouth: The Consecration of Divine Images in Mesopotamia." Pages 45–72 in *The Image and the Book: Iconic Cults, Aniconism, and the Veneration of the Holy Book in Israel and the Ancient Near East*. Edited by Karel van der Toorn. CBET 21. Leuven: Peeters, 1997.

———. *Die Theologie der Bilder: Herstellung und Einweihung von Kultbildern in Mesopotamien und die alttestamentliche Bilderpolemik*. OBO 162. Göttingen: Vandenhoeck & Ruprecht, 1998.

Bulkeley, Kelly, ed. *Dreams: A Reader on Religious, Cultural and Psychological Dimensions of Dreaming*. New York: Palgrave, 2001.

———. *Dreaming in the World's Religions: A Comparative History*. New York: New York University Press, 2008.

Cancik-Kirschbaum, Eva. "Prophetismus und Divination—ein Blick auf die keilschriftlichen Quellen." Pages 33–53 in *Propheten in Mari, Assyrien und Israel*. Edited by Matthias Köckert and Martti Nissinen. FRLANT 201. Göttingen: Vandenhoeck & Ruprecht, 2003.

Charpin, Dominique. *Reading and Writing in Babylon*. Cambridge: Harvard University Press, 2010.

Clancier, Philippe. "Cuneiform Culture's Last Guardians: The Old Urban Notability of Hellenistic Uruk." Pages 752–73 in *The Oxford Handbook of Cuneiform Culture*. Edited by Eleanor Robson and Karen Radner. Oxford: Oxford University Press, 2011.

Collins, John J. "The Court-Tales in Daniel and the Development of Apocalyptic." *JBL* 94 (1975): 218–34.

———. *Daniel: A Commentary on the Book of Daniel*. Hermeneia. Minneapolis: Fortress Press, 1993.

———. *The Apocalyptic Imagination: An Introduction to Jewish Apocalyptic Literature*. 2nd edition. Biblical Resource Series. Grand Rapids: Eerdmans, 1998.

Cooley, Jeffrey L. "Propaganda, Prognostication, and Planets." Pages 7–31 in *Divination, Politics and Ancient Near Eastern Empires*. Edited by Alan Lenzi and Jonathan Stökl. ANEM 7. Atlanta: Society of Biblical Literature, 2014.

Cryer, Frederick H. "Der Prophet und der Magier: Bemerkungen anhand einer überholten Diskussion." Pages 79–88 in *Prophetie und geschichtliche Wirklichkeit im alten Israel: Festschrift für Siegfried Herrmann zum 65. Geburtstag*. Edited by Rüdiger Liwak and Siegfried Wagner. Stuttgart: Kohlhammer, 1991.

———. *Divination in Ancient Israel and Its Near Eastern Environment: A Socio-Historical Investigation*. JSOTSup 142. Sheffield: JSOT Press, 1994.
Fishbane, Michael. *Biblical Interpretation in Ancient Israel*. Oxford: Clarendon Press, 1985.
Floyd, Michael H. and Robert D. Haak, eds. *Prophets, Prophecy, and Prophetic Texts in Second Temple Judaism*. LHBOTS 427. New York: T&T Clark, 2006.
George, A. R. *The Babylonian Gilgamesh Epic: Introduction, Critical Edition and Cuneiform Texts*. 2 vols. Oxford: Oxford University Press, 2003.
Gladd, Benjamin L. *Revealing the* Mysterion: *The Use of* Mystery *in Daniel and Second Temple Judaism with Its Bearing on First Corinthians*. BZNW 160. Berlin: de Gruyter, 2008.
Goodman, Martin. "Texts, Scribes and Power in Roman Judaea." Pages 99–108 in *Literacy and Power in the Ancient World*. Edited by Alan K. Bowman and Greg Woolf. Cambridge: Cambridge University Press, 1994.
Grabbe, Lester L. *Priests, Prophets, Diviners, Sages: A Socio-Historical Study of Religious Specialists in Ancient Israel*. Valley Forge: Trinity Press International, 1995.
Gzella, Holger. "The Scribal Background of the 'Menetekel' in Daniel 5." *Bible and Interpretation* (2016). http://www.bibleinterp.com/articles/2016/04/gze408029.shtml (last accessed 17 May 2016).
Hamori, Esther J. *Women's Divination in Biblical Literature: Prophecy, Necromancy, and Other Arts of Knowledge*. AYBRL. New Haven: Yale University Press, 2015.
Husser, Jean-Marie. *Dreams and Dream Narratives in the Biblical World*. Translated by Jill M. Munro. BibSem 63. Sheffield: Sheffield Academic Press, 1999.
Koch, Klaus. *Daniel (1–4)*. BKAT 22/1. Neukirchen-Vluyn: Neukirchener Verlag, 2005.
Kratz, Reinhard G. "Die Visionen des Daniel." Pages 219–36 in *Schriftauslegung in der Schrift: Festschrift für Odil Hannes Steck zu seinem 65. Geburtstag*. Edited by Reinhard G. Kratz, Thomas Krüger, and Konrad Schmid. BZAW 300. Berlin: de Gruyter, 2000.
———. "The Visions of Daniel." Pages 91–113 in vol. 1 of *The Book of Daniel: Composition and Reception*. Edited by John J. Collins and Peter W. Flint. 2 vols. VTSup 83. Leiden: Brill, 2001.
Laato, Antti. "The Seventy Yearweeks in the Book of Daniel." *ZAW* 102 (1990): 212–25.
Lawson, Jack N. "'The God Who Reveals Secrets': The Mesopotamian Background to Daniel 2.47." *JSOT* 74 (1997): 61–76.

Lenzi, Alan. "Secrecy, Textual Legitimation, and Intercultural Polemics in the Book of Daniel." *CBQ* 71 (2009): 330–48.
Lipiński, Edward. "Review of André Lacocque, *Le livre de Daniel*, Commentaire de l'Ancien Testament 15b (Delachaux et Niestlé: Neuchâtel & Paris), 1976." *VT* 28 (1977): 233–39.
Makiello, Phoebe. "Daniel as Mediator of Divine Knowledge in the Book of Daniel." *JJS* 60 (2009): 18–31.
Melvin, David P. *The Interpreting Angel Motif in Prophetic and Apocalyptic Literature*. Society of Biblical Literature Emerging Scholars Series. Minneapolis: Fortress Press, 2013.
Miller, James E. "Dreams and Prophetic Visions." *Bib* 71 (1990): 401–4.
Müller, Hans-Peter. "Mantische Weisheit und Apokalyptik." Pages 268–93 in *Congress Volume, Uppsala, 1971*. Edited by P. A. H. de Boer. VTSup 22. Leiden: Brill, 1972.
Newsom, Carol A. "Why Nabonidus? Excavating Traditions from Qumran, the Hebrew Bible, and Neo-Babylonian Sources." Pages 57–79 in *The Dead Sea Scrolls: Transmission of Traditions and Production of Texts*. Edited by Sarianna Metso, Hindy Najman, and Eileen M. Schuller. STDJ 92. Leiden: Brill, 2010.
Newsom, Carol A. and Brennan Breed. *Daniel: A Commentary*. OTL. Louisville: Westminster John Knox, 2014.
Niditch, Susan. *The Symbolic Vision in Biblical Tradition*. HSM 30. Cambridge: Harvard Semitic Museum; Missoula: Scholars Press, 1983.
Nissinen, Martti. "Prophecy and Omen Divination: Two Sides of the Same Coin." Pages 341–51 in *Divination and Interpretation of Signs in the Ancient World*. Edited by Amar Annus. OIS 6. Chicago: University of Chicago Press, 2010.
Noegel, Scott B. "Dreams and Dream Interpretation in Mesopotamia and in the Hebrew Bible (Old Testament)." Pages 45–71 in *Dreams: A Reader on Religious, Cultural and Psychological Dimensions of Dreaming*. Edited by Kelly Bulkeley. New York: Palgrave, 2001.
Oppenheim, A. Leo. *The Interpretation of Dreams in the Ancient Near East: With a Translation of an Assyrian Dream-Book*. TAPS 46.3. Philadelphia, American Philosophical Society, 1956.
Perrin, Andrew B. *The Dynamics of Dream-Vision Revelation in the Aramaic Dead Sea Scrolls*. JAJSup 19. Göttingen: Vandenhoeck & Ruprecht, 2015.
Redditt, Paul L. "Daniel 9: Its Structure and Meaning." *CBQ* 62 (2000): 236–49.
Rigger, Hansjörg. *Siebzig Siebener: die "Jahrwochenprophetie" in Dan 9*. TThSt 57. Trier: Paulinus-Verlag, 1997.

Rochberg, Francesca. *The Heavenly Writing: Divination, Horoscopy, and Astronomy in Mesopotamian Culture.* Cambridge: Cambridge University Press, 2004.

Sanders, Seth L. *From Adapa to Enoch: Scribal Culture and Religious Vision in Judea and Babylonia.* TSAJ 167. Tübingen: Mohr Siebeck, 2017.

Schaudig, Hanspeter. *Die Inschriften Nabonids von Babylon und Kyros' des Grossen samt den in ihrem Umfeld entstandenen Tendenzschriften: Textausgabe und Grammatik.* AOAT 256. Münster: Ugarit-Verlag, 2001.

Schöpflin, Karin. "God's Interpreter: The Interpreting Angel in Post-Exilic Prophetic Visions of the Old Testament." Pages 189–203 in *Angels: The Concept of Celestial Beings—Origins, Development and Reception.* Edited by Friedrich V. Reiterer, Tobias Nicklas, and Karin Schöpflin. DCLY 2007. Berlin: de Gruyter, 2007.

Steck, Odil Hannes. *Gott in der Zeit entdecken: Die Prophetenbücher des Alten Testaments als Vorbild für Theologie und Kirche.* Biblisch-theologische Studien 42. Neukirchen-Vluyn: Neukirchener Verlag, 2001.

Stökl, Jonathan. *Prophecy in the Ancient Near East: A Philological and Sociological Comparison.* CHANE 56. Leiden: Brill, 2012.

———. "Prophetic Hermeneutics in the Hebrew Bible and Mesopotamia." *HeBAI* 4 (2015): 267–92.

Tiemeyer, Lena-Sofia. "Through a Glass Darkly: Zechariah's Unprocessed Visionary Experience." *VT* 58 (2008): 573–94.

van der Toorn, Karel. "Scholars at the Oriental Court: The Figure of Daniel against Its Mesopotamian Background." Pages 37–54 in vol. 1 of *The Book of Daniel: Composition and Reception.* Edited by John J. Collins and Peter W. Flint. 2 vols. VTSup 83. Leiden: Brill, 2001.

Waerzeggers, Caroline. "Facts, Propaganda, or History? Shaping Political Memory in the Nabonidus Chronicle." Pages 95–124 in *Political Memory in and after the Persian Empire.* Edited by Jason M. Silverman and Caroline Waerzeggers. ANEM 13. Atlanta: Society of Biblical Literature, 2015.

Waerzeggers, Caroline. "The *Prayer of Nabonidus* in the Light of Hellenistic Babylonian Literature." Pages 64–75 in *Jewish Cultural Encounters in the Ancient Mediterranean and Near Eastern World.* Edited by Mladen Popović, Myles Schoonover and Marijn Vandenberghe. JSJSup 178. Leiden: Brill, 2017.

Wilson, Gerald H. "The Prayer of Daniel 9: Reflection on Jeremiah 29." *JSOT* 48 (1990): 91–99.

Zgoll, Annette. "Die Welt im Schlaf sehen—Inkubation von Träumen im antiken Mesopotamien." *WdO* 32 (2002): 74–101.

———. *Traum und Welterleben im antiken Mesopotamien: Traumtheorie und Traumpraxis im 3.–1. Jahrtausend v. Chr. als Horizont einer Kulturgeschichte des Träumens*. AOAT 333. Münster: Ugarit-Verlag, 2006.

8
Agency, Authority, and Scribal Innovation in Dream Narratives of the Aramaic Dead Sea Scrolls

Andrew B. Perrin

The Aramaic writings among the Dead Sea Scrolls include copies of twenty-nine literary compositions, approximately two-thirds of which feature instances of dream episodes and interpretations. This new suite of Aramaic texts with an accentuated interest in dream revelation provides fresh comparative context for other early Jewish Aramaic dream narratives, such as those in Dan 2–7, and starkly contrasts with the larger collection of Hebrew texts in the Qumran library, which includes minimal references to dream activity and interpretation.[1] While a comprehensive exploration of all of the questions engendered by these Aramaic dream texts is unattainable within the confines of a single essay, it is possible to look behind the curtains of their dream narratives to consider the core interrelated issues of authority and agency in literary portrayals of revelation. Following a brief orientation to the revelatory dynamics of the Dead Sea Scrolls as a whole, this study tours through a sampling of the Qumran Aramaic dream texts, paying particular attention to interfaces between dreamers and oneirocritics as a means of defining where the writers of these compositions located agency in the revelation of dream content and discerning the strategies by which

---

[1] This treatment is developed out of a larger project, Andrew B. Perrin, *The Dynamics of Dream-Vision Revelation in the Aramaic Dead Sea Scrolls*, JAJSup 19 (Göttingen: Vandenhoeck & Ruprecht, 2015). While I argued in the aforementioned study that the booklet of Aramaic Dan 2–7 is an essential component of the constellation of Jewish Aramaic literature from the mid-Second Temple period, since the dream traditions of the book of Daniel are treated separately in the present volume, I will not include direct treatment of them here. See Jonathan Stökl's contribution to this volume.

they laid claim to authority in their paired inspired interpretations. In view of these issues, I will conclude with a reflection on the ways in which the scribal creators of these texts optimized literary dream divination in historical fictive settings from a time past as a tool for extending inherited, authoritative traditions.

DREAMS AMONG THE REVELATORY REPERTOIRE OF THE QUMRAN COLLECTION

The discovery of the Dead Sea Scrolls added appreciably to our understanding of thought and practice in Judaism during the third to first centuries BCE. Among the finds of some 930 fragmentary manuscripts penned or preserved by the ancient community of Qumran were copies of nearly every book of what became the Hebrew Bible, a robust collection of community-specific writings tailored to the worldview and halakhah of the Qumran group, as well as a sizable cross section of texts that were received within this collection but originated elsewhere. While the keepers of this library seem to have been members of, or associated with, an Essene-like movement, scholars have duly noted both consistencies and tensions between the descriptions of the Essenes in the classical sources and reconstructions of the community's lifestyle, outlooks, demographics, and practices from Qumran literature and archaeology.[2] One such potential disconnect or difference pertains to Essene proficiencies in dream revelation and interpretation. For example, while dream divination is not a hallmark of the more complete portrayals of the Essenes in Josephus's treatments, his writings include parallel versions of a court tale featuring an intriguing symbolic dream episode of the ethnarch Archelaus, the cryptic meaning of which is successfully deciphered by one "Simon the Essene" (*J.W.* 2.111–13, *Ant.* 17.345–48).[3] In view of this portrayal, it may be reasonable to infer that this episode

---

[2] See, for example, the introduction and comparative synopsis by Geza Vermes and Martin D. Goodman, *The Essenes According to the Classical Sources* (Sheffield: JSOT Press, 1989). For a recent treatment of the description and situation of the Qumran community in Second Temple Judaism, see John J. Collins, *Beyond the Qumran Community: The Sectarian Movement of the Dead Sea Scrolls* (Grand Rapids: Eerdmans, 2010).

[3] Other named Essenes in Josephus with the purported ability to foretell the future include Menahem, who prophesied the rise of Herod (*Ant.* 15.373–379), and Judas, who foretold the death of Antigonus (*J.W.* 1.78–80, *Ant.* 13.311–313). VanderKam discussed these and other representations of Essene prognostication in Josephus in view of select divinatory practices evidenced in the Qumran library (James C. VanderKam, "Mantic Wisdom in the Dead Sea Scrolls," *DSD* 4 [1997]: 336–53).

"indicates that Josephus considered the Essenes adept at dream interpretation as a means of predicting the future."[4]

In a recent study on esotericism and applications of mystery terms across the Qumran collection, Sam Thomas uncovered that in many regards the Hebrew "sectarian" literature and the Aramaic compositions exhibit interests in hidden knowledge and transmission of traditions.[5] Features such as sealed books, patriarchal instruction, and "mystery" language (i.e., רז) are described as "esoteric knowledge," which Thomas deduces "was constitutive of the Yahad's own social and religious self-understanding."[6] He further concludes that "in many of the Aramaic compositions we find the kind of material that corresponds with what the Qumran group(s) apparently understood to be within its own special epistemological domain."[7] While I agree in their converging interests on such items highlighted above, dream divination and interpretation do not appear to have played a significant role in the Hebrew literature closely associated with the Qumran community.[8] Rather, it seems that revelation was sought through other innovations and secured by different means.

---

[4] Joan E. Taylor, "The Classical Sources on the Essenes and the Scrolls Communities," in *The Oxford Handbook of the Dead Sea Scrolls*, ed. Timothy H. Lim and John J. Collins (Oxford: Oxford University Press, 2010), 173–99, here 179. For a similar conclusion, see also Solomon Zeitlin, "Dreams and Their Interpretation from the Biblical Period to the Tannaitic Time: An Historical Study," *JQR* 66 (1975): 1–18. Gray's treatment of instances of Essenes in various prophetic roles in the writings of Josephus determined that he associated the group broadly with "esoteric knowledge of an all-encompassing sort" (Rebecca Gray, *Prophetic Figures in Late Second Temple Jewish Palestine: The Evidence from Josephus* [New York: Oxford University Press, 1993], 110). Gnuse described Archaelaus's dream narratives in Josephus in light of compositional patterns for dream episodes in biblical sources (Robert K. Gnuse, "The Jewish Dream Interpreter in a Foreign Court: The Recurring Use of a Theme in Jewish Literature," *JSP* 7 [1990]: 29–53).

[5] Samuel I. Thomas, *The "Mysteries" of Qumran: Mystery, Secrecy, and Esotericism in the Dead Sea Scrolls*, EJL 25 (Atlanta: Society of Biblical Literature, 2009).

[6] Thomas, *"Mysteries,"* 125.

[7] Thomas, *"Mysteries,"* 125.

[8] Considering the library as a whole, one should also take into account the heritage of dream episodes and perspectives on dream revelation in the books that would become the Hebrew Bible. On this referential background, see Jean-Marie Husser, *Dreams and Dream Narratives in the Biblical World*, trans. by Jill M. Munro, BibSem 63 (Sheffield: Sheffield Academic Press, 1999); and Shaul Bar, *A Letter That Has Not Been Read: Dreams in the Hebrew Bible*, trans. Lenn J. Schramm, HUCM 25 (Cincinnati: Hebrew Union College Press, 2001). The issue of what qualifies a text as sectarian—if that is the most appropriate term—is ongoing and one that I acknowledge here but defer to the expert and insightful treatments on the topic by Carol Newsom ("'Sectually Explicit' Literature from Qumran," in *The Hebrew Bible and Its Interpreters*, ed. William Henry Propp, Baruch Halpern, and David Noel Freedman [Winona Lake: Eisenbrauns, 1990],

There are at least four facets of the revelatory profile of the Qumran Hebrew texts, including: figures esteemed in community memory for their divine endowments, the trajectory of prophecy toward text-based interpretive activity, exegetical models in a trajectory from traditional divinatory practices (i.e., the pesharim), and rhetorical jibes at "seers" and "visions."[9] A necessarily brief overview of these items will allow for a preliminary framework in which to consider the striking concentration of literary dreams in the Aramaic texts discovered at Qumran.

First, the interpretive authority looming over some of the insider, group-specific literature of Qumran harkens back to the memory of a founding figure, the "Teacher of Righteousness," who laid claim to some special revelation deemed determinative for Torah interpretation and application. For example, Pesher Habakkuk reflects on this figure and asserts that Hab 2:1–2 referred to "the Teacher of Righteousness, to whom God revealed all the mysterious words of his servants, the prophets (מורה הצדק אשר הודיעו אל את כול רזי דברי עבדיו הנבאים)" (1QpHab VII, 1–5).[10] While the medium of this individual's purported revelation is not entirely clear and the experiential authenticity behind such claims is unverifiable, the espoused locus of social and religious authority for the group is in some way linked to this figure's divine endowment.

Second, increasing attention has been paid to the contribution of the Qumran finds to the textualization of prophecy in ancient Judaism. The Hebrew Scriptures already attest to this development, with the exegesis of omens moving into the scribal domain more than being retained as part of the performative prophetic office.[11] As Jassen has demonstrated, the prophetic activities and writings

---

167–87) and, more recently, Eyal Regev (*Sectarianism in Qumran: A Cross-Cultural Perspective*, Religion and Society 45 [Berlin: de Gruyter, 2007]).

[9] In a similar treatment, Najman and Hilton included prayer and liturgy in the revelatory profile of the collection on account of the Qumranites' views on angelic encounters (Hindy Najman and Nicole Hilton, "What Constitutes Revelation at Qumran?" in *T&T Clark Companion to the Dead Sea Scrolls*, ed. George J. Brooke and Charlotte Hempel [London: Bloomsbury T&T Clark, forthcoming]).

[10] Cf. 1QpHab II, 7–10 and CD VI, 7–8. For a recent survey of the issues related to recovering glimpses of the so-called "Teacher of Righteousness" in the origins of the Qumran community and movement, see Collins, *Beyond the Qumran Community*, 34–39. Hebrew and Aramaic texts in this essay derive form the Accordance Bible Software module by Martin G. Abegg, Jr., "Qumran Sectarian Manuscripts," 2015, save for the original language text of Genesis Apocryphon, which I draw from Daniel A. Machiela, *The Dead Sea Genesis Apocryphon: A New Text and Translation with Introduction and Special Treatment of Columns 13–17*, STDJ 79 (Leiden: Brill, 2009). All translations of Qumran texts are my own.

[11] See, for example, Martti Nissinen, "Spoken, Written, Quoted, and Invented: Orality and Writtenness in Ancient Near Eastern Prophecy," in *Writings and Speech in Israelite and Ancient Near Eastern Prophecy*, ed. Ehud Ben Zvi, and Michael H. Floyd,

of the Qumran community indicate awareness of the distinction between (more) ancient forms of prophecy and their related contemporary counterparts, as well as evince the understanding that the group's own prophetic contributions were in some way commensurate with the earlier heritage of prophetic practice.[12]

Third, the defining terminology and prophetic outlook achieved by the lemma-plus-commentary style of interpretation of the pesharim is on some level indebted to ancient divination approaches. In a similar way that many dream interpretation manuals or omen lists catalogued protases alongside interpreted apodoses, and dream narratives in Israelite scriptural tradition parcelled out dream content into smaller units to be correlated with their interpreted equivalents, the writers of the pesharim lemmatized select portions of authoritative religious literature and expounded upon them in turn, with a unique focus on the contemporized meaning in the author's present day.[13]

Fourth, there are a limited number of Hebrew texts at Qumran that either nod to the language of dreams and visions or include rewritten scriptural narratives on the basis of pre-existing references to revelation in the source text. Mention of "seers" using nouns or substantive participles of common roots associated with visionary activity (e.g., חזה or רוא) and various terms for "vision(s)" (חזיון, חזון, or מחזה) dot the landscape of the texts.[14] At times, such language is deployed for rhetorical purposes, as in the loosely paralleled references to a "vision of knowledge (חזון דעת)" and "seers of error (חוזי תעות)" in the Hodayot

---

SBLSymS 10 (Atlanta: Society of Biblical Literature, 2000), 35–71; and Martti Nissinen, "How Prophecy Became Literature," *SJOT* 19 (2005): 153–72.

[12] Alex P. Jassen, "Prophecy after 'the Prophets': The Dead Sea Scrolls and the History of Prophecy in Judaism," in *The Dead Sea Scrolls in Context: Integrating the Dead Sea Scrolls in the Study of Ancient Texts, Languages, and Cultures*, ed. Armin Lange, Emanuel Tov, and Matthias Weigold, VTSup 140 (Leiden: Brill, 2011), 2:577–93.

[13] This is not to say, however, that the lemmatic commentary of the pesharim is a direct outgrowth of oneirocriticism, as similar approaches are found in other representative texts and traditions. For these interpretive patterns and their potential literary-cultural precursors see the following: Asher Finkel, "The Pesher of Dreams and Scriptures," *RevQ* 4 (1963): 357–70; Isaac Rabinowitz, "'Pēsher/Pittārōn': Its Biblical Meaning and Its Significance in the Qumran Literature," *RevQ* 8 (1973): 219–32; Maren Niehoff, "A Dream Which is Not Interpreted is Like a Letter Which is Not Read," *JJS* 43 (1992): 58–84; and Daniel A. Machiela, "The Qumran Pesharim as Biblical Commentaries: Historical Context and Lines of Development," *DSD* 19 (2012): 313–62.

[14] References to "seers" may be found in the following: 1QH[a] X, 17; XII, 11; XII, 21; CD II, 12; 1QM X, 10; XI, 8; 4QCurses (4Q280) 2, 7; 4QpapUnclassified[d] (4Q517) 15, 1; and 4QpapUnclassified[e] (4Q518) 2, 1. Mention of "vision(s)" include: 1QH[a] VI, 18; XII, 19; 4QH[d] (4Q430) 1, 6; 4QMysteries[b] (4Q300) 1 a ii, 2, 3, 6; 8, 1; 4QNarrative and Poetic Composition[a] (4Q371) 1a–b, 4; 4QNarrative and Poetic Composition[b] (4Q372) 1, 7; 4QVision and Interpretation (4Q410) 1, 9; and 4QInstruction[c] (4Q417) 1 i, 16, 22.

(1QH^a XXII, 19, 21). While terminology is not the only gauge for determining the perspective and prominence of dream revelation at Qumran, the apparent lack of full-blown episodes or interpretations in the sectarian literature is notable. At a minimum, it seems Qumran thought on dreams was informed in part by the Deuteronomic heritage, evidenced by the re-presentation of the classic circumscription of prophetic dreamers in Deut 13:2–6 with little revision in the Temple Scroll (11QT^a [11Q19] LIV, 8–15).

A slightly better representation of dream accounts in Second Temple Jewish literature is found in the nonsectarian Hebrew literature. Presuming both Daniel and Jubilees were known in some complete form at Qumran, these texts would have also provided important examples of Hebrew dream episodes and interpretations among the Qumran library.[15] In addition to these, visionary revelation is a core component of the previously unknown compositions of 4QPseudo-Ezekiel^{a-d} (4Q385, 4Q385b, 4Q386, 4Q388) and 4QpapPseudo-Ezekiel^e (4Q391). A harmonization of Jacob's dream from Gen 31:10–13 is also found in 4Q(Reworked) Pentateuch^b (4Q364) 4b–e ii, 21–26. Beyond these, the advanced state of decay of 4QVision and Interpretation (4Q410) provides an insufficient amount of text to determine the scope of either element represented in the text's proposed modern title.

Yet for all these revelatory expressions, and there are certainly more one could discuss, there is a disproportionate number of new dream episodes, allusions, or interpretations among the Hebrew literature of the Qumran collection when compared with those writings penned in Aramaic. Among those writings that originated before and beyond the Qumran community is a suite of some twenty-nine literary Aramaic texts, representing between 10–13% of the overall Qumran finds.[16] With dream revelations and their inspired interpretations occurring in at least twenty (approximately two-thirds) of these Aramaic compositions, this model of revelatory divination is the most widespread literary *topos* in the Aramaic Dead Sea Scrolls corpus. Dreams, dreamers, and oneirocritics are found in the following Aramaic materials represented at Qumran: Book of Watchers, Astronomical Enoch, Book of Dreams, Epistle of Enoch, Book of

---

[15] Dan 8, 9:20–12:13 and Jub. 14:1–17; 27:21–25; 32:1–2, 16–26; 39:16–18; 40:1–5.

[16] While composition in Aramaic does not immediately disqualify a text from association with the Qumran group, most would agree that the scribal community attached a certain religious and ideological gravitas to the Hebrew language, which seemed to be the preferred idiom of the group-specific compositions. See Ben Zion Wacholder, "The Ancient Judaeo-Aramaic Literature (500–164 B.C.E.): A Classification of Pre-Qumranic Texts," in *Archaeology and History in the Dead Sea Scrolls: The New York University Conference in Memory of Yigael Yadin*, ed. Lawrence H. Schiffman, JSPSup 8 (Sheffield: JSOT Press, 1990), 257–81; Steve Weitzman, "Why Did the Qumran Community Write in Hebrew?" *JAOS* 119 (1999): 35–45; and William M. Schniedewind, "Qumran Hebrew as an Antilanguage," *JBL* 118 (1999): 235–52.

Giants,[17] Words of Michael, Genesis Apocryphon, Testament of Jacob, New Jerusalem, Aramaic Levi Document, Apocryphon of Levi, Visions of Amram, Dan 2–7, Aramaic Apocalypse, Four Kingdoms, Prayer of Nabonidus, 4QVision^a (4Q557), 4QpapVision^b (4Q558), 4QVision^d (4Q575), and 4QpapApocalypse (4Q489).

From the outset, it is essential to point out that none of the texts listed above are personal accounts from individuals, refer to dream manuals of catalogued symbols, omens or portents from verifiable dream experiences, or presuppose a revelatory experience on the part of the author. That is, unlike the example of the Aramaic dream account related in personal correspondence in a fifth- to third-century BCE sherd from Elephantine (CIS 2.137), those from Qumran are purely literary in nature.[18] While many of the dream narratives among the Qumran Aramaic texts are couched in the first person, the "I" addresses that pervade these narratives are not authorial but connote a compositional mechanism whereby "the real authors of these works were assuming a fictional identity embedded in a traditional theme or storyline analogous to their own circumstances."[19] The first-person narratives are either pseudepigraphic in the technical sense (e.g., the assumption of the first-person voice of Abram in Genesis Apocryphon) or are developed in the domain of time past, accessible only through memory (e.g., the first-person dream and oneirocritical accounts of Daniel in the

---

[17] While there is some evidence for the clustering of select Enochic booklets at an early time (e.g., 4QEnoch^c contained material from previously known Enochic booklets as well as content of the Aramaic Book of Giants), the amalgamation of the corpus of Enochic texts that eventually comprise Ethiopic 1 Enoch is a development that did not occur for several centuries. While our knowledge of the transmission between the early Aramaic texts, Greek translations, and eventual rendering in Ethiopic (Ge'ez) is not as complete as it might be, the full corpus in Ethiopic 1 Enoch seems to have emerged between the fourth and sixth centuries CE (George W. E. Nickelsburg, *1 Enoch: A Commentary on the Book of 1 Enoch, Chapters 1–36; 81–108*, Hermeneia [Minneapolis: Fortress Press, 2001], 15. For a codicological list of the content of each Qumran Enoch manuscript, see page 21).

[18] The above dates represent the range proposed in various publications and discussions on the Egyptian Aramaic text. See Julius Euting, "Epigraphische Miscellen. Zweite Reihe," *SPAW* (1887): 407–8; Baruch A. Levine, "Notes on an Aramaic Dream Text from Egypt," *JAOS* 84 [1964]: 18–22); Baruch A. Levine and Anne Robertson, "An Aramaic Dream Report from Elephantine," COS 3.88 (p. 218); and Joseph A. Fitzmyer and Stephen A. Kaufman, *An Aramaic Bibliography: Part I: Old, Official, and Biblical Aramaic* (Baltimore: Johns Hopkins University Press, 1992), 109–10.

[19] Loren T. Stuckenbruck, "Pseudepigraphy and First Person Discourse in the Dead Sea Documents: From the Aramaic Texts to Writings of the *Yaḥad*," in *The Dead Sea Scrolls and Contemporary Culture: Proceedings of the International Conference Held at the Israel Museum, Jerusalem (July 6–8, 2008)*, ed. Adolfo D. Roitman, Lawrence H. Schiffman, and Shani Tzoref, STDJ 93 (Leiden: Brill, 2011), 295–326, here 296.

Babylonian exile). The literary quality of these Aramaic dream accounts is evidenced further by their formal and philological structures, which reflect many of the well-worn patterns established by Oppenheim and extended into the domain of Second Temple period Jewish writings by Flannery-Dailey.[20] These strategically crafted and couched first-person dream accounts, therefore, are closely linked to the predominant narrative settings of the wider Qumran Aramaic corpus, which, as Dimant, Tigchelaar, and García Martínez have observed, revolve around two poles of Israelite history: the distant past in the antediluvian and patriarchal days or the more recent past in the exilic diaspora.[21]

With this background in place for the Qumran library in general, and Aramaic texts among it in particular, we may now proceed to consider the different ways authority and agency are configured in dream narratives across the Aramaic corpus.

CONFIGURING INTERPRETATION: HUMANS, ANGELS, KINGS, AND BASTARDS

Portrayals of dream revelations and oneirocriticism in the Aramaic texts involve a variety of characters in diverse narrative settings and of varying social statuses. Most of these interactions may be illustrated through case studies on three general structures that exist between dreamers and interpreters. The first are examples where the capacities to receive and discern the meaning of revelations are bound up in the same individual. The second are representations of interpretations offered through an angelic intermediary or another otherworldly channel within the dream account itself. The third pertains to instances where a Jewish courtier comes to the divinatory aid of a foreign king. Under these headings, the descriptions and analyses offered below integrate a variety of Aramaic texts and highlight the roles of a cast of characters including uniquely endowed humans,

---

[20] A. Leo Oppenheim, *The Interpretation of Dreams in the Ancient Near East: With a Translation of an Assyrian Dream-Book*, TAPS 46.3 (Philadelphia: American Philosophical Society, 1956); Frances Flannery-Dailey, *Dreamers, Scribes, and Priests: Jewish Dreams in the Hellenistic and Roman Eras*, JSJSup 90 (Leiden: Brill, 2004).

[21] Devorah Dimant, "Themes and Genres in the Aramaic Texts from Qumran," in *Aramaica Qumranica: Proceedings of the Conference on the Aramaic Texts from Qumran in Aix-en-Provence, 30 June–2 July 2008*, ed. Katell Berthelot and Daniel Stökl Ben Ezra, STDJ 94 (Leiden: Brill, 2010), 15–45; Eibert J. C. Tigchelaar, "Aramaic Texts from Qumran and the Authoritativeness of Hebrew Scriptures: Preliminary Observations," in *Authoritative Scriptures in Ancient Judaism*, ed. Mladen Popović, JSJSup 141 (Leiden: Brill, 2010), 155–71; Florentino García Martínez, "Les rapports avec l'Écriture des textes araméenes trouvés à Qumran," in *Old Testament Pseudepigrapha and the Scriptures*, ed. Eibert J. C. Tigchelaar, BETL 270 (Leuven: Peeters, 2014), 19–40.

famed and faceless angelic beings, pagan kings, and the fabled illicit gargantuan offspring of the fallen watchers and human women.

ENOCH AND ABRAM: THE EVOLUTION OF PATRIARCHS TO DREAMER-ONEIROCRITICS

The revelatory prowess of Enoch looms large in Second Temple Jewish thought and writings in general, and has a particular currency in the world of the Aramaic texts. The origin of the expansive Enochic tradition, however, is to be found in an instance of creative exegesis. Through a playful reading of the allusive phrase "and Enoch walked with God" (ויתהלך חנוך את האלהים) in Gen 5:22 and 24, the early creators of the Enochic tradition discovered an intimation of additional revelation. Rather than signaling his upright character and abrupt departure from the earthly plane—arguably the most natural reading of the text—this phrasing could be read by a clever exegete to imply that Enoch was an otherworldly traveler, dreamer, and repository for divine revelation.[22] The strongest and earliest concentration of the outcomes of this exegetical maneuver is found in the Aramaic booklets of 1 Enoch.[23] Through nearly countless episodes and cycles of vivid revelatory encounters (e.g., dreams, guided journeys, disclosures from celestial writings, etc.), Enoch is associated with special and far-reaching knowledge on topics ranging from the fate of the fallen watchers to the course of human and geopolitical history, to the workings of the cosmos and natural world, and even as far as the eschatological consummation of all things.[24] In view of this burgeoning Enochic revelatory tradition, Enoch's encounters with the divine, many of which are explicitly framed as dreams (e.g., 1 En. 13:8; 83:7; 85:1) or use related terminology (e.g., 1 En. 1:2; 14:14; 83:1–2, 7; 86:1–3; 90:39–40; 93:2), establish him as a reliable source for wisdom, knowledge, and discernment on a host of topics.

While the Qumran finds added important insight into the original Aramaic strata of much of this previously known Enochic literature, they also divulged a

---

[22] For descriptions of the exegetical basis of the Enochic tradition in this phrase, see Devorah Dimant, "The Biography of Enoch and the Books of Enoch," *VT* 33 (1983): 14–29; and James C. VanderKam, *Enoch: A Man for All Generations*, Studies on Personalities of the Old Testament (Columbia: University of South Carolina Press, 1995), 13.

[23] For a survey of the representation of Aramaic Enoch texts at Qumran, see Loren T. Stuckenbruck, "The Early Traditions Related to 1 Enoch from the Dead Sea Scrolls: An Overview and Assessment," in *The Early Enoch Literature*, ed. Gabriele Boccaccini and John J. Collins, JSJSup 121 (Leiden: Brill, 2007), 41–63.

[24] A current and concise synopsis of the content of 1 Enoch may be found in George W. E. Nickelsburg and James C. VanderKam, *1 Enoch: The Hermeneia Translation* (Minneapolis: Fortress, 2012), 1–13.

broader set of Aramaic writings that either enhance Enoch's profile as a dreamer or add the role of oneirocritic, among other proficiencies, to his already impressive resumé.

Adding to the complex of revelations of 1 Enoch, the fragmentary writing Words of Michael (4Q529, 4Q571, 6Q23) provided a new vantage point on the divine-human interchange in Enochic revelatory encounters. By boldly assuming the first-person voice of the archangel Michael, the author of this text imagined the other side of authority for the Enochic tradition, that is, the perspective of an angelic revealer and interlocutor.[25] The topics of Enoch and Michael's exchange are not entirely clear in the remaining text. At least once, the angel refers to visionary revelation involving inscribed otherworldly records: "According to the vision, and I showed him the vision and he said to me in my book of the Great Eternal Lord it is written thus (כחזוא והחזיתה חזוה ואמר לי יָ֯ [בספרי די אֱ הא כתיב עלמא מרא רבי)" (4Q529 1, 5–6). In effect, this achieves a layered authority for the revelation: it derives from a heavenly text, disclosed through a chief heavenly being. As described more fully below, such portrayals of angelic intermediaries indicate a trend for the importance of divine agency achieved by otherworldly beings unlocking revelations.

Twice, Genesis Apocryphon acknowledges Enoch's expertise achieved through dream revelation. In 1QapGen XIX, 25, Abram shares "scribal knowledge and wisdom and truth (ספרא וחכמתא וקושטא)" from the pages of Enochic lore before an audience of Egyptian nobles. Earlier in the narrative, confounded at the miraculous sight of his newborn son (Noah) and suspicious that his paternity might derive from a fallen watcher, Lamech flees to Enoch to find certainty on the matter (1QapGen II, 19–25). Such depictions presuppose Enoch's lofty status and authority achieved primarily through revelatory dreams in the broader Enochic tradition.

While Enoch had already served as the agent delivering petitions and judgments between the fallen watchers and God in the Book of Watchers, his stature and capacity as a dreamer rises specifically into the realm of dream interpretation in the Aramaic Book of Giants, discovered among the Qumran collection in at least ten copies.[26] In a seeming reversal of the traditional *angelus interpres* motif—where divine figures disclose dream meanings to humans (see below)—

---

[25] Enoch is not explicitly named in the available materials, however his identification as the seer is most plausible (J. T. Milik, *The Books of Enoch: Aramaic Fragments from Qumrân Cave 4* [Oxford: Clarendon, 1976], 91; Émile Puech, *Qumrân Grotte 4.XXVII: Textes araméens, deuxième partie: 4Q550–4Q575a, 4Q580–4Q587*, DJD XXXVII [Oxford: Clarendon, 2009], 399–400).

[26] Based on the assessment of Loren T. Stuckenbruck (*The Book of Giants from Qumran: Texts, Translation, and Commentary*, TSAJ 63 [Tübingen: Mohr Siebeck, 1997], 41), these include: 1Q23, 6Q8, 4Q203, 4Q530, 4Q531 (all certain); 2Q26, 4Q532 (both probable); 1Q24, 4Q556, 4Q206 2, 3 (all plausible).

this text portrays the semi-divine, bastard offspring of the fallen watchers and human women turning to a human being, Enoch, for interpretation of a series of nightmares received by the giant brothers 'Ohaya and Hahya. The first trip to consult Enoch occurs after the giant 'Ohaya has a foreboding dream of rinsing text from a tablet (2Q26). The second involves a variation on the traditional *Doppelträume*[27] theme, this time featuring back-to-back dreams by the giants Hahya, envisaging the fiery destruction of a garden, and 'Ohaya, depicting a throne room judgment (4Q530 2 ii + 6 + 7 i + 8–11 + 12 [?], 3–20). In these instances, the giant Mahaway is dispatched to consult Enoch on the meaning of the dream symbolism (6Q8, 1; 4Q530 2 ii + 6 + 7 i + 8–11 + 12 [?], 20–24). While mere shreds of Enoch's interpretations are retained in the surviving texts (4Q530 7 ii, 11), it is evident that the giants' dreams prognosticate their imminent destruction in the flood and eschatological judgement in a future age. With this, the Aramaic texts provide an intriguing view of Enoch's character development from a figure referenced in but a few enigmatic verses in Genesis to a prolific dreamer in his own right, and eventually a sage-oneirocritic par excellence in the Aramaic texts. In this instance, the agency of interpretation is found in the enlightened human figure of Enoch, whose oneirocritical prowess is assumed in the tradition on account of his well-documented prior encounters with angelic beings and his acquisition of otherworldly knowledge.

It is possible to trace a similar trajectory for Abram. While Abram is subject to a series of theophanies in the book of Genesis (e.g., Gen 15:1, 17:1, 18:1), these stories include at best a minimal representation of dreams and have a definite absence of oneirocriticism. The author of Genesis Apocryphon, however, enhanced the portrait of the patriarch in both of these areas. Abram receives at least four revelations in Genesis Apocryphon. To illustrate his portrayal as a dreamer and budding ability as an interpreter, I will focus only on the episode of the dream Abram receives upon his and Sarai's decent into Egypt in an inventive Aramaic retelling of the familiar episode of Gen 12:10–20 in 1QapGen XIX, 14–17.

Whereas the couple's arrival in Egypt was uneventful in Genesis, the author of Genesis Apocryphon spliced a short symbolic dream report into the tale on the eve of their arrival. In this version of the story, Abram receives a frightful dream of a date palm and cedar, the latter of which is under threat of being violently destroyed, until the palm intervenes on the cedar's behalf, stating that the two trees sprout from one root (1QapGen XIX, 16). The symbolism and the impetus for this episode have been discussed extensively.[28] For the present purpos-

---

[27] Alfred Wikenhauser, "Doppelträume," *Biblica* 29 (1948): 100–11.

[28] See Nahman Avigad and Yigael Yadin, *A Genesis Apocryphon: A Scroll from the Wilderness of Judaea* (Jerusalem: Magnes, 1956), 23–24; Manfred R. Lehmann, "1 Q Genesis Apocryphon in the Light of the Targumim and Midrashim," *RevQ* 1 (1958): 249–63; Eva Oßwald, "Beobachtungen zur Erzählung von Abrahams Aufenthalt in

es it is significant that, in similar form to Enoch, Abram's dream profile is rooted in at least two exegetical hints in the text of Genesis. As Kugel and Falk have illustrated, the allusive language of the phrase "Behold! Now I know" (הנה נא ידעתי) in Gen 12:11 could be suggestive to an ancient exegete, taken to imply that Abram received a divine revelation of the couple's impending danger and a potential plan for evading it.[29]

Coupled with this hint, it is possible that the enhanced portrait of Abram in Genesis Apocryphon was occasioned further by a close parallel in Gen 20.[30] In that text, Abram and Sarai are again in a tough spot in a foreign land, with Sarai taken into the royal house after Abram conceals their true relationship. In this instance, King Abimelech of Gerar is compelled to return Sarai to Abram due to a warning within a dream, which communicates that Abram is in fact a "prophet (נביא)" (Gen 20:7).[31] While classical prophecy was open to a number of revelatory and divinatory models, dreams maintained a central role in biblical tradition

---

Ägypten im 'Genesis-Apokryphon,'" *ZAW* 72 (1960): 7–25; H. Lignée, "l'Apocryphe de la Genèse," in *Les textes de Qumran: traduits et annotés*, ed. J. Carmignac, É. Cothenet, and H. Lignée, (Paris: Letouzey et Ané, 1963), 2:207–42; Boudewijn Dehandschutter, "Le rêve dans l'Apocryphe de la Genèse," in *La littérature juive entre Tenach et Mischna: Quelques problèmes*, ed. Willem Cornelis van Unnik, RechBib 9 (Leiden: Brill, 1974), 48–55; Marianne Luijken Gevirtz, "Abram's Dream in the Genesis Apocryphon: Its Motifs and Their Function," *Maarav* 8 (1992): 229–43; Esther Eshel, "The Dream Visions in the Noah Story of the Genesis Apocryphon and Related Texts," in *Prophecy after the Prophets? The Contribution of the Dead Sea Scrolls to the Understanding of Biblical and Extra-Biblical Prophecy*, ed. Kristin De Troyer and Armin Lange, CBET 52 (Leuven: Peeters, 2009), 119–32; and Ariel A. Block, "The Cedar and the Palm Tree: A Paired Male/Female Symbol in Hebrew and Aramaic," in *Solving Riddles and Untying Knots: Biblical, Epigraphic, and Semitic Studies in Honor of Jonas C. Greenfield*, ed. Ziony Zevit, Seymour Gitin, and Michael Sokoloff (Winona Lake: Eisenbrauns, 1995), 13–17.

[29] James Kugel, *Traditions of the Bible: A Guide to the Bible As It Was at the Start of the Common Era* (Cambridge: Harvard University Press, 1999), 256; James Kugel, "Which is Older, Jubilees or the Genesis Apocryphon? An Exegetical Approach," in *The Dead Sea Scrolls and Contemporary Culture: Proceedings of the International Conference Held at the Israel Museum, Jerusalem (July 6–8, 2008)*, ed. Adolfo D. Roitman, Lawrence H. Schiffman, and Shani Tzoref, STDJ 93 (Leiden: Brill, 2011), 257–94; Daniel K. Falk, *The Parabiblical Texts: Strategies for Extending the Scriptures among the Dead Sea Scrolls*, LSTS 63 (London; T&T Clark, 2007), 89.

[30] Several scholars have recently noted how the treatment of Gen 12 in Genesis Apocryphon indicates the author's awareness of the analogous tale in Gen 20. See Moshe J. Bernstein, "Re-Arrangement, Anticipation and Harmonization as Exegetical Features in the Genesis Apocryphon," *DSD* 3 (1996): 37–57; Joseph A. Fitzmyer, *The Genesis Apocryphon of Qumran Cave 1 (1Q20): A Commentary*, 3rd ed., BibOr 18/B (Rome: Pontifical Biblical Institute, 2004), 205; and Falk, *The Parabiblical Texts*, 80–94.

[31] Cf. Ps 105:15.

(e.g., Num 12:6–8, Deut 13:1–3). In view of this, it is possible that the author of Genesis Apocryphon deduced that, since his base text identifies Abram as a prophet, he was a viable candidate for dream revelations. This blend of interpretive outlooks on the traditional text, then, provides a background for the development of Abram's dream life in Genesis Apocryphon.

The characterization of Abram in this Aramaic text also includes at least one instance of dream interpretation, following directly on the heels of Abram's dream of the cedar and date palm. Without the aid of an interpreting angel within the dream or consultation of another party, Abram jolts awake from his nightmare, and the meaning of the dream is immediately apparent: the revelation communicated a plan to ensure the couple's safety in their sojourns by traveling under the guise of siblings (1QapGen XIX, 17–21). As noted by Flannery-Dailey, the ability to interpret one's own dream revelation is a rare feat in ancient Jewish literature.[32] The impact on Abram's characterization here is twofold. First, since the operative cultural understanding of the origins of dreams at this time was that they were of divine import, Abram's proposal to present Sarai as his sister is not made solely in the interests of self-preservation or in the hopes of personal betterment, but, in a way, in line with a divine directive.[33] Second, Abram's innate ability to discern the meaning of the revelation puts him in the league of figures such as Joseph and Daniel, who shared this exceptional, paired endowment.[34] While Abram's evolution into a dreamer and one-time oneirocritic in Genesis Apocryphon is not as expansive as the analogous portrayals of Enoch, or arguably the familiar case of Daniel in the Aramaic tradition, these characters stand out in the Qumran Aramaic corpus for their tandem abilities to receive divine dreams and the ability to promptly discern the meanings of dream revelations without the aid of an external interpreter. These examples indicate that in some dream narratives in the Qumran Aramaic texts, authority of the revelation is rooted in its divine origin while the agency for interpretation is invested in a select cast of characters with privileged knowledge and insight.

INSTANCES OF THE *ANGELUS INTERPRES* MOTIF IN ARAMAIC DREAM EPISODES

---

[32] Flannery-Dailey, *Dreamers, Scribes, and Priests*, 128. See, for example, Add Esth F 10:4–8; *J.W.* 3.351–354.

[33] Beate Ego, "The Figure of Abraham in the Genesis Apocryphon's Re-Narration of Gen 12:20–20," in *Qumran Cave 1 Revisited: Texts from Cave 1 Sixty Years after Their Discovery: Proceedings of the Sixth Meeting of the IOQS in Ljubljana*, ed. Daniel K. Falk et al., STDJ 91 (Leiden: Brill, 2010), 233–43.

[34] For observations in this direction, see Dehandschutter, "Le rêve," 50; Luijken Gevirtz, "Abram's Dream," 239–40; and Falk, *The Parabiblical Texts*, 89.

The figure of an otherworldly interpreting being is a staple in ancient Israelite and early Jewish writings. With a possible background or analogy in the Greek conception of the *oneiros* as well as an identifiable foundation in the Hebrew Scriptures (e.g., Zech 1–8), writers of dream narratives in the Second Temple period appear to have regularly deployed this motif as a way of infusing dream interpretations with authority.[35] This motif functions in several permutations in the Qumran Aramaic texts.

Some Aramaic texts feature a familiar characterization of an *angelus interpres*, such as the New Jerusalem, which utilizes aspects of the referential background of Ezek 40–48, including a guiding angel disclosing a blueprint of a envisioned Jerusalem and its temple for a seer who is technically also unnamed.[36] The presupposition of such a model is that the angelic being within the divine revelation is uniquely positioned as a reliable and authoritative source of otherworldly knowledge.

The most explicit claim to the veracity and authenticity of a dream revelation and interpretation offered by an *angelus interpres* is found in a sprawling (yet fragmentary!) dream of Noah in Genesis Apocryphon. This dream reflects on the deluge, relates the mandates for the geographical inheritance of Noah's sons, and concludes with a generic eschatological outlook (1Q20 XII, 19–XV, 21). Just prior to Noah's awakening from this revelation, the figure states, "I have declared everything to you in truth, and thus it is written concerning you," ([...] עליך כתיב וכן אחויתך בקושט כולא [...]; 1Q20 XV, 20). Not unlike the example from Words of Michael above, this statement couples the angel's authority with the certitude of a heavenly record of a predetermined course of history and human affairs.

In some works, such as the documented cases in the Enochic dreams and journeys of 1 Enoch or Words of Michael, the authority vested in an interpreting angel is enhanced by virtue of their known name and status. Another new Ara-

---

[35] For the background in the Hebrew Scriptures, see Karin Schöpflin, "God's Interpreter: The Interpreting Angel in Post-Exilic Prophetic Visions of the Old Testament," in *Angels: The Concept of Celestial Beings: Origins, Development and Reception*, ed. Friedrich V. Reiterer, Tobias Nicklas, and Karin Schöpflin, DCLY 2007 (Berlin: de Gruyter, 2007), 189–203. For contextualization of early Jewish uses in light of the Greek god-sent messenger motif, see Flannery-Dailey, *Dreamers, Scribes, and Priests*, 64–65, 174, 204.

[36] For discussion of this text and its relation to the book of Ezekiel, see Jörg Frey, "The New Jerusalem Text in Its Historical and Traditio-Historical Context," in *The Dead Sea Scrolls Fifty Years after Their Discovery: Proceedings of the Jerusalem Congress, July 20–25, 1997*, ed. Lawrence H. Schiffman, Emanuel Tov, and James C. VanderKam (Jerusalem: Israel Exploration Society and the Shrine of the Book, Israel Museum, 2000), 800–16; and Armin Lange, "Between Zion and Heaven: The *New Jerusalem* Text from Qumran as a Paratext," in *Biblical Figures in Deuterocanonical and Cognate Literature*, ed. Hermann Lichtenberger and Ulrike Mittman-Richert, DCLY 2008 (Berlin: de Gruyter, 2009), 397–412.

maic text among the Qumran finds, Visions of Amram (4Q543–547), likely also operates from this angle.[37] The dream opens with a courtroom contest between an angel of light and angel of darkness over the scope of their respective domains. Following Amram's vocal interjection over the right of these figures to rule (4Q543 5–9, 1, 4Q544 1, 11), the angel of light transitions into the role of an interpreting figure for the rest of the account. Initially, the otherworldly explanations center on the topic of dualism. However, as the dream unfolds, the dialogue includes revelation on priestly topics, particularly the "mystery (רז)" (4Q545 4, 16) of priestly duties and an endorsement of the priestly genealogy that flows from Amram's forefathers (Levi and Qahat) to his son (Aaron). Given the priestly flavor of this dream dialogue, the identity of the angelic revealer is potentially significant. In the course of their discussion of dualism, the angel of light indicates that his dark counterpart is known by "three name[s]" (תלתת שמה[ ]) (4Q544 3, 2), only one of which is extant in the surviving text: "Melchi-resha" (מלכי רשע) (4Q544 2, 13). In view of this statement and given the parallel nature of the descriptions of the two figures, Milik argued that the text likely also named the angel of light a celestial "Melchizedek" (מלכי צדק), though the name is not extant in the available materials.[38] Far from the oblique reference to Melchizedek, king of Salem, as a "priest to God Most High" in Gen 14:18 or even the suggestive language of Ps 110:4, a host of Second Temple period writers elevated Melchizedek to a high priestly role in the heavenly

---

[37] Duke is likely correct that the texts published as 4QVisAmram[f] (4Q548) and 4QVisAmram[g]? (4Q549) are unlikely to come from the same composition as the more certain manuscripts of Visions of Amram (Robert R. Duke, *The Social Location of the Visions of Amram (4Q543–547)*, StBibLit 135 [New York: Peter Lang, 2010], 35–42).

[38] J. T. Milik, "4Q Visions de 'Amram et une Citation d'Origène," *RB* 79 (1972): 77–97; J. T. Milik, "Milkî-ṣedeq et Milkî-reša' dans les anciens écrits juifs et chrétiens," *JJS* 23 (1972): 95–144. See also the complementary treatments in Paul J. Kobelski, *Melchizedek and Melchireša'*, CBQMS 10 (Washington: Catholic Biblical Association of America, 1981), 27; Florentino García Martínez, "4Q'Amram b, i, 14: ¿Melki-reša o Melki-ṣedeq?" *RevQ* 12 (1985): 111–14; and Maxwell J. Davidson, *Angels at Qumran: A Comparative Study of 1 Enoch 1–36, 72–108 and Sectarian Writings from Qumran*, JSPSup 11 (Sheffield: Sheffield Academic Press, 1992), 264–68; James R. Davila, *Liturgical Works* (Grand Rapids: Eerdmans, 2000), 165; Émile Puech, *Qumrân Grotte 4.XXII: Textes araméens, première partie: 4Q529–549*, DJD XXXI (Oxford: Clarendon, 2001), 327–29; Eric F. Mason, "Melchizedek Traditions in Second Temple Judaism," in *New Perspectives on 2 Enoch: No Longer Slavonic Only*, ed. Andrei A. Orlov, Gabriele Boccaccini, and Jason M. Zurawski, SJS 4 (Leiden: Brill, 2012), 343–60. Dimant, however, maintains that the reconstruction of Melchizedek's name is "speculative and should not be exploited to develop further theories" (Devorah Dimant, "Melchizedek at Qumran and in Judaism: A Response," in *New Perspectives on 2 Enoch: No Longer Slavonic Only*, ed. Andrei A. Orlov, Gabriele Boccaccini, and Jason M. Zurawski, SJS 4 [Leiden: Brill, 2012)], 366).

realm.³⁹ In view of that growing tradition, if Melchizedek was identified in the Aramaic Visions of Amram, the authority of the espoused revelation is not simply achieved by the agency of a generic *angelus interpres*. Rather, it was strategically couched as an authoritative endorsement of the status and roles of the earthly priesthood from the head of an otherworldly priestly order himself.

Finally, in a text known as Four Kingdoms (4Q552, 4Q553, 4Q553a), we find an intriguing variation on otherworldly interpretation of a dream revelation. The motif that mapped the waxing and waning of imperial rules into three or four successive ages represented by dream symbols is well attested in ancient Jewish apocalyptic literature. Likely the most familiar occurrence of this apocalyptic historiographical mechanism is found in the revelations of Dan 2 and 7.⁴⁰ Unlike these instances in the book of Daniel, which rely on additional divine revelation from God (Dan 2:19) or an *angelus interpres* (Dan 7:16) to provide the symbolic equivalents, it seems that at least part of the dream symbolism in Four Kingdoms is explained by the symbolic props of the episode themselves. In this fragmentary text, an unnamed seer beholds "four trees" (ארבעה אילנין) (4Q552 1 ii, 1), which he asks in turn, "What is your name" (מן שמך)? (4Q552 1 ii 1, cf. 6, 11). While only one response is fully extant, it is intriguing that the answer comes from the tree itself. The first tree states, "Babylon" (בבל), to which the seer qualifies, "You are he who rules in Persia" (אָנְתָּה הוא די שליט בפרס) (4Q522 1 ii, 5–6). While talking trees are found in a selection of Israelite fables (e.g., Judg 9:7–15, 2 Kgs 14:9) and are cast in a select few ancient Jewish dream narratives (e.g., 1QapGen XIX, 14–17, 2 Bar 36:7–10), the unique quality of Four Kingdoms is that the dialogue that occurs is of an oneirocritical nature explaining the symbolic tableau. In view of the fragmentary phrase "to me the angel" (לי מלאכא) in 4Q553a 2 ii, 2 and references to the "the angels" (מְלַאֲכִיא; מלאכיא) in 4Q552 1 + 2, 5, 4Q553 2 ii, 1, it is likely that a formal *angelus interpres* and/or angelic figures played a role at some point in the dream depiction. However, the conspicuous absence of such figures from the central interpretive dialogue made way for another type of authoritative interpretation, coming in the form of self-interpreting otherworldly dream symbols.

---

³⁹ Orlov provides a synopsis of early Jewish and Christian sources participating in the development of Melchizedek's otherworldly character (Andrei A. Orlov, "Melchizedek," in *The Eerdmans Dictionary of Early Judaism*, ed. John J. Collins and Daniel C. Harlow [Grand Rapids: Eerdmans, 2010], 931–32).

⁴⁰ The development of this motif by ancient historiographers is treated in now-classic studies by Joseph Ward Swain, "The Theory of the Four Monarchies: Opposition History under the Roman Empire," *CP* 35 (1940): 1–21; David Flusser, "The Four Empires in the Fourth Sibyl and in the Book of Daniel," *IOS* 2 (1972): 148–75; and in a more recent topical excursus in John J. Collins, *Daniel*, Hermenia (Minneapolis: Fortress, 1993), 166–70.

THE POWER AND POLITICS OF DREAMS IN THE FOREIGN COURT

The depiction of a marginalized or exiled Israelite rising through the ranks of a foreign court and excelling in the particular divinatory art of oneirocriticism in the service of a monarch is a well-represented motif in ancient Israelite and early Jewish literature. The Joseph novella in Gen 37–41 provides a classic and memorable case and is one that has been shown to be formative to the analogous depiction of Daniel the dreamer and oneirocritic in the Babylonian court.[41] A variety of Qumran Aramaic texts include scenes of court tales, yet only some of them include instances of dream divination.

In some compositions, dream revelation and divination in royal settings is evident only from glimpses in fragments of narratives that are now largely lost. While little can be said with certainty about the narrative context of the dream in Four Kingdoms, the phrase "and the king said to me" (ואמר לי מלכא) is highly suggestive of a larger framework of a monarch engaging with a human interpreter in a court setting, presumably for the interpretation of the dream account referenced above. Similarly, it is likely that the controversial Aramaic Apocalypse (4Q246)—once commonly called the "Son of God" text—attests to yet another court tale including a dream episode. While the phrases "he fell before the throne" (נפל קדם כרסיא), "wrath is coming to the world, and your years" (עלמא אתה רגז ושניך), and "your vision, and all of it is about to come unto the world" (חזוך וכלא אתה עד ארעא) could fit within a visionary depiction of a heavenly throne room, Milik and subsequent interpreters of this text are likely correct that the scene here is indeed in an earthly court of a human king (4Q246 i, 1–3).[42] In view of the fragmentary remains, texts such as Four Kingdoms and

---

[41] Daniel's orientation around these chapters of Genesis has been noted at intervals. See, for instance, Norman W. Porteous, *Daniel: A Commentary*, OTL (Philadelphia: Westminster John Knox, 1965), 38; Collins, *Daniel*, 39–40; Jan-Wim Wesselius, "The Literary Nature of the Book of Daniel and the Linguistic Character of Its Aramaic," *AS* 3 (2005): 241–83; and Michael Segal, "From Joseph to Daniel: The Literary Development of the Narrative in Daniel 2," *VT* 59 (2009): 123–49. For developments of this motif in other early Jewish writings, see especially Gnuse, "The Jewish Dream Interpreter;" L. M. Wills, *The Jew in the Court of the King: Ancient Jewish Court Legends* (Minneapolis: Fortress, 1990), 75–152; and the recent summary by Sara Raup Johnson, "Court Tales," in *The Eerdmans Dictionary of Early Judaism*, ed. John J. Collins and Daniel C. Harlow (Grand Rapids: Eerdmans, 2010), 489–91. Not all court tale episodes, however, include dream divination, as indicated by the ready examples of Aramaic texts such as Ahiqar and *Jews in the Persian Court* (4Q550).

[42] Milik, *The Books of Enoch*, 60; David Flusser, "The New Testament and Judaism on the First Centuries C.E.: The Hubris of the Antichrist in a Fragment from Qumran," *Immanuel* 10 (1980): 31–37; Joseph A. Fitzmyer, "The Aramaic 'Son of God' Text from Qumran Cave 4 (4Q246)," in *The Dead Sea Scrolls and Christian Origins* (Grand Rap-

Aramaic Apocalypse likely attest to the growing tradition of a foreign king receiving otherworldly revelation, which is only made intelligible when deciphered by a (presumably Jewish) courtier divinely endowed and practiced in the art of oneirocriticism.

Prayer of Nabonidus (4Q242) is another court tale featuring the interactions between a foreign king and Jewish diviner. It features an afflicted Neo-Babylonian king, here Nabonidus, who was transformed into a maddened animalistic state for a period of seven years in Teima (4Q242 1–3, 1–3). By the end of the text, at least in the materials that have survived, Nabonidus is healed, interacts with a local diviner, ascribes greatness and agency to God for his miraculous healing, likely inscribes the account, and confesses the embarrassing inadequacy of his own deities (4Q242 1–3, 4–8). Given its content, Prayer of Nabonidus attests to a previously unknown Second Temple Jewish Nabonidus tradition, which may in some way relate to other known historical and literary traditions about Nabonidus, for example, in the Sippar Cylinder of Nabonidus or material likely behind Dan 4.[43]

While the extant text does not explicitly reference a dream of Nabonidus, the fact that the king beseeched "a diviner" (גזר), specifically "a Jew fr[om the exiles]" ([גלותא בני מ]ן יהודי), suggests that the text either included a dream episode that is now lost or cast a sage character who had the special endowment of oneirocriticism in their divinatory profile, even if it was not explicitly exercised in the text. This determination is made on the basis of several correlated hints and potential analogies with other forms or portrayals of divination. Aramaic Daniel regularly ranks גזרין among courtiers expected to have facility with divination through omens and dreams (Dan 4:7, 5:7, 11). Because of this association, Meyers suggested in broad terms that the individual in Prayer of Nabonidus had some capacity to foretell future destinies.[44] Lexically, while the most basic form of the root *גזר, "to cut," perhaps connotes facility with extispicy (divination through inspection of animal entrails), Jeffers highlighted that oneirocriticism also fits within this semantic domain, since the standard form of lemmatic dream interpretation involved their segmentation (i.e., "cutting") into smaller

---

ids: Eerdmans, 2000), 41–61; Florentino García Martínez, *Qumran and Apocalyptic: Studies on the Aramaic Texts from Qumran*, STDJ 9 (Leiden: Brill, 1992), 164.

[43] The relationship between the ancient Nabonidus traditions has been studied most extensively by Matthias Henze, *The Madness of King Nebuchadnezzar: The Ancient Near Eastern Origins and Early History of Interpretation of Daniel 4*, JSJSup 61 (Leiden: Brill, 1999), 68–73.

[44] R. Meyer, *Das Gebet des Nabonid: Eine in den Qumran-Handschriften wiederentdeckte Weisheiterzählung*, Sitzungsberichte der sächsischen Akademie der Wissenschaften zu Leipzig, Philologisch-historische Klasse 107.3 (Berlin: Akademie Verlag, 1962), 24.

interpretive units.⁴⁵ Finally, Nabonidus's active dream life in other literatures increases the probability that this quality was also a component of his characterization in the Qumran text.⁴⁶

While this lacunous state of Prayer of Nabonidus limits the questions that can be answered with confidence about its cast of characters and narrative setting, the encounter portrays the king as humbled, afflicted, and cast into a social sphere well below his normal standing in the royal court. By virtue of his turning to a Jewish diviner from a marginalized population, the figurehead of a foreign empire is abased, while the Jewish diviner is postured as a channel for authentic and reliable discernment.

CONCLUSION: LITERARY DREAM DIVINATION AS SCRIBAL INNOVATION

The concentration of dream episodes and interpretations found in the Qumran Aramaic texts provides a fresh space to consider the perspectives on revelation in ancient Judaism, at a time when there were certainly competing views on the acceptability of dreams as a medium for divine disclosure. For some in this period, most notably Ben Sira, dreams are not to be trusted—they are the stuff of fools, giving false hope to the simple (Sir 34:1–8).⁴⁷ Other voices, as witnessed for example in a few instances in Josephus, applaud dreamers of the past or even

---

⁴⁵ Ann Jeffers, *Magic and Divination in Ancient Palestine and Syria*, SHCANE 8 (Leiden: Brill, 1996), 30–31.

⁴⁶ In column I lines 4–6 of the Sippar cylinder, Nabonidus is commanded by the deity Marduk to reconstruct the Temple of Sîn (for an introduction and translation, see "The Sippar Cylinder of Nabonidus," translated by Paul-Alain Beaulieu [COS 2.123A:310–13]). In a second Akkadian source, Nabonidus dialogues with Nebuchadnezzar on the topic of a previous astrological revelation (for this text, see Oppenheim, *Interpretation of Dreams*, 250). Daniel 4 might also be kept in mind, as there is the possibility that it is based on an earlier tradition oriented around a dream and sickness of Nabonidus (for this perspective, see Esther Eshel, "Possible Sources of the Book of Daniel," in *The Book of Daniel: Composition and Reception*, ed. John J. Collins and Peter W. Flint, VTSup 83, FIOTL 2 [Leiden: Brill, 2001], 2:387–94).

⁴⁷ It is possible that 11QapocrPs (11Q11) V, 7 also includes a criticism of dreams by deploying them as a metaphor for vanity, though the word חל[ו]ם is far from certain in this crucial phrase. If the reading is, however, retained, Lange proposed that this text, like Ben Sira, may come from a sociocultural environment that rejected dreams as "something negative and illusive" (Armin Lange, "The Essene Position on Magic and Divination," in *Legal Texts and Legal Issues: Proceedings of the Second Meeting of the International Organization for Qumran Studies, Cambridge 1995, Published in Honour of Joseph M. Baumgarten*, ed. Moshe J. Bernstein, Florentino García Martínez, and John Kampen, STDJ 23 [Leiden: Brill, 1997], 404).

claim personal revelation (e.g., *Ant.* 2.86, 10.237, *J.W.* 3.351–354, *Life* 208–210).[48] These are but two heuristic examples of the spectrum of views operative in the wider literature of the mid to late Second Temple era. It was already shown that the Qumranites found strategies to draw scriptural tradition into their contemporary framework through experience or exegesis, although dreams did not figure heavily in their own writings and worldview. The Aramaic texts, however, told a different story. In this domain there was a strong interest in extending ancestral traditions using interpretive strategies that enhanced their revelatory profile. The inclusion of dreams in rewritten versions of already familiar texts and tales (e.g., Genesis) or the creation of dream narratives from more recent eras of Israelite history (i.e., no later than the period of the Babylonian exile) effectively turned up the volume on revelatory activity in the inherited traditions.

To this point, the variables of agency and authority have been measured within the narrative contexts of a cluster of the Aramaic texts. However, there is one figure that is ever-present but hardly visible in this literature: the scribe. In a recent monograph on the development of the Hebrew Bible, Karel van der Toorn emphasizes the evolutionary understandings of "revelation" in ancient scribal settings. He described a revelatory paradigm wherein texts increasingly supplanted oral tradition and experience as the primary means of knowledge exchange:

When the notion of revelation is transferred from the spoken word to the written text, the concept gains a new significance. Applied to a collection of texts, revelation denotes a product rather than an interaction. Since the written text has an objective existence outside its producers and consumers, it is a source of authority by itself. Where before, religious specialists derived their legitimacy from the revelation they possessed in person, they now have to refer to the sum of knowledge laid down in a body of texts. The related changes in the concept of revelation affected the nature and the role of religious experts: revelation became the province of scribes and scholars; the art of interpretation supplanted the gift of intuition.[49]

The scribal innovation of the dream narratives of the Aramaic texts is that they are strategically set in a time past, the common past reflected in Israelite scriptural tradition, and a past in which dream revelation was native to the theological and literary landscapes. When this compositional approach is correlated with the increasing authority attached to, and invested in, written traditions in

---

[48] The richness of dreams in the writings of Josephus of course cannot be captured in a single sentence. See the more complete and incisive treatment of Robert K. Gnuse, *Dreams and Dream Reports in the Writings of Josephus: A Traditio-Historical Analysis*, AGJU 36 (Leiden: Brill, 1996).

[49] Karel van der Toorn, *Scribal Culture and the Making of the Hebrew Bible* (Cambridge: Harvard University Press, 2009), 206–7.

the Second Temple era, the strategy becomes all the more clever. In short, as the authority of written tradition increases, the openness to and acceptability of other forms of revelation seemingly diminishes.[50] By anchoring new ideas and insights within dreams in the past, the writers of the Aramaic texts included fresh revelation within old, and could claim authority for their theological or exegetical expressions using the accepted models of agency operative within the tradition itself. The Aramaic texts, then, may be brought into this conversation as the scribes who crafted them seem to have leveraged the best of both worlds: they at once capitalized on the authority associated with a classical revelatory medium and merged it with written traditions, the authority of which was on the rise.

BIBLIOGRAPHY

Avigad, Nahman and Yigael Yadin. *A Genesis Apocryphon: A Scroll from the Wilderness of Judaea*. Jerusalem: Magnes, 1956.
Bar, Shaul. *A Letter That Has Not Been Read: Dreams in the Hebrew Bible*. Translated by Lenn J. Schramm. HUCM 25. Cincinnati: Hebrew Union College Press, 2001.
Bernstein, Moshe J. "Re-Arrangement, Anticipation and Harmonization as Exegetical Features in the Genesis Apocryphon." *DSD* 3 (1996): 37–57.
Block, Ariel A. "The Cedar and the Palm Tree: A Paired Male/Female Symbol in Hebrew and Aramaic." Pages 13–17 in *Solving Riddles and Untying Knots: Biblical, Epigraphic, and Semitic Studies in Honor of Jonas C. Greenfield*. Edited by Ziony Zevit, Seymour Gitin, and Michael Sokoloff. Winona Lake: Eisenbrauns, 1995.
Collins, John J. *Beyond the Qumran Community: The Sectarian Movement of the Dead Sea Scrolls*. Grand Rapids: Eerdmans, 2010.
———. *Daniel*. Hermenia. Minneapolis: Fortress, 1993.
Davidson, Maxwell J. *Angels at Qumran: A Comparative Study of 1 Enoch 1–36, 72–108 and Sectarian Writings from Qumran*. JSPSup 11. Sheffield: Sheffield Academic Press, 1992.
Davila, James R. *Liturgical Works*. Grand Rapids: Eerdmans, 2000.
Dehandschutter, Boudewijn. "Le rêve dans l'Apocryphe de la Genèse." Pages 48–55 in *La littérature juive entre Tenach et Mischna: Quelques problèmes*. Edited by Willem Cornelis van Unnik. RechBib 9. Leiden: Brill, 1974.
Dimant, Devorah. "The Biography of Enoch and the Books of Enoch." *VT* 33 (1983): 14–29.

---

[50] To trace this trajectory further with respect to subsequent Jewish literature, it seems that, as in the case of the rabbinic "dream book" (b. Ber. 55a–57d), dream revelation as a whole is not entirely discredited or devalued—which would short-circuit the dreams of the authoritative scriptural tradition—they are brought into a hermeneutical framework where new dreams are evaluated in view of scripture and tradition. On this, see Philip S. Alexander, "Bavli Berakhot 55a–57b: The Talmudic Dreambook in Context," *JJS* 46 (1995): 230–48.

———. "Melchizedek at Qumran and in Judaism: A Response." Pages 361–67 in *New Perspectives on 2 Enoch: No Longer Slavonic Only.* Edited by Andrei A. Orlov, Gabriele Boccaccini, and Jason M. Zurawski. SJS 4. Leiden: Brill, 2012.

———. "Themes and Genres in the Aramaic Texts from Qumran." Pages 15–45 in *Aramaica Qumranica: Proceedings of the Conference on the Aramaic Texts from Qumran in Aix-en-Provence, 30 June–2 July 2008.* Edited by Katell Berthelot and Daniel Stökl Ben Ezra. STDJ 94. Leiden: Brill, 2010.

Duke, Robert R. *The Social Location of the Visions of Amram (4Q543–547).* StBibLit 135. New York: Peter Lang, 2010.

Ego, Beate. "The Figure of Abraham in the Genesis Apocryphon's Re-Narration of Gen 12:20–20." Pages 233–43 in *Qumran Cave 1 Revisited: Texts from Cave 1 Sixty Years after Their Discovery: Proceedings of the Sixth Meeting of the IOQS in Ljubljana.* Edited by Daniel K. Falk, Sariana Metso, Donald W. Parry, and Eibert J. C. Tigchelaar. STDJ 91. Leiden: Brill, 2010.

Eshel, Esther. "The Dream Visions in the Noah Story of the Genesis Apocryphon and Related Texts." Pages 119–32 in *Prophecy after the Prophets? The Contribution of the Dead Sea Scrolls to the Understanding of Biblical and Extra-Biblical Prophecy.* Edited by Kristin De Troyer and Armin Lange. CBET 52. Leuven: Peeters, 2009.

———. "Possible Sources of the Book of Daniel." Pages 387–94 in vol. 2 of *The Book of Daniel: Composition and Reception.* Edited by John J. Collins and Peter W. Flint. VTSup 83. FIOTL 2. 2 vols. Leiden: Brill, 2001.

Euting, Julius. "Epigraphische Miscellen. Zweite Reihe." *SPAW* (1887): 407–22, Taf. VI–X.

Falk, Daniel K. *The Parabiblical Texts: Strategies for Extending the Scriptures among the Dead Sea Scrolls.* LSTS 63. London: T&T Clark, 2007.

Finkel, Asher. "The Pesher of Dreams and Scriptures." *RevQ* 4 (1963): 357–70.

Fitzmyer, Joseph A. *The Genesis Apocryphon of Qumran Cave 1 (1Q20): A Commentary.* 3rd ed. BibOr 18/B. Rome: Pontifical Biblical Institute, 2004.

———. "The Aramaic 'Son of God' Text from Qumran Cave 4 (4Q246)." Pages 41–61 in *The Dead Sea Scrolls and Christian Origins.* Grand Rapids: Eerdmans, 2000.

Fitzmyer, Joseph A. and Stephen A. Kaufman. *An Aramaic Bibliography: Part I: Old, Official, and Biblical Aramaic.* Baltimore: Johns Hopkins University Press, 1992.

Flannery-Dailey, Frances. *Dreamers, Scribes, and Priests: Jewish Dreams in the Hellenistic and Roman Eras.* JSJSup 90. Leiden: Brill, 2004.

Flusser, David. "The Four Empires in the Fourth Sibyl and in the Book of Daniel." *IOS* 2 (1972): 148–75.

———. "The New Testament and Judaism on the First Centuries C.E.: The Hubris of the Antichrist in a Fragment from Qumran." *Immanuel* 10 (1980): 31–37.

Frey, Jörg. "The New Jerusalem Text in Its Historical and Traditio-Historical Context." Pages 800–16 in *The Dead Sea Scrolls Fifty Years after Their Discovery: Proceedings of the Jerusalem Congress, July 20–25, 1997.* Edited by Lawrence H. Schiffman, Emanuel Tov, and James C. VanderKam. Jerusalem: Israel Exploration Society and the Shrine of the Book, Israel Museum, 2000.

García Martínez, Florentino. "4Q'Amram b, i, 14: ¿Melki-reša o Melki-ṣedeq?" *RevQ* 12 (1985): 111–14.

———. "Les rapports avec l'Écriture des textes araméenes trouvés à Qumran." Pages 19–40 in *Old Testament Pseudepigrapha and the Scriptures*. Edited by Eibert J. C. Tigchelaar. BETL 270. Leuven: Peeters, 2014.

———. *Qumran and Apocalyptic: Studies on the Aramaic Texts from Qumran*. STDJ 9. Leiden: Brill, 1992.

Gnuse, Robert K. *Dreams and Dream Reports in the Writings of Josephus: A Traditio-Historical Analysis*. AGJU 36. Leiden: Brill, 1996.

———. "The Jewish Dream Interpreter in a Foreign Court: The Recurring Use of a Theme in Jewish Literature." *JSP* 7 (1990): 29–53.

Gray, Rebecca. *Prophetic Figures in Late Second Temple Jewish Palestine: The Evidence from Josephus*. New York: Oxford University Press, 1993.

Henze, Matthias. *The Madness of King Nebuchadnezzar: The Ancient Near Eastern Origins and Early History of Interpretation of Daniel 4*. JSJSup 61. Leiden: Brill, 1999.

Husser, Jean-Marie. *Dreams and Dream Narratives in the Biblical World*. Translated by Jill M. Munro. BibSem 63. Sheffield: Sheffield Academic Press, 1999.

Jassen, Alex P. "Prophecy after 'the Prophets': The Dead Sea Scrolls and the History of Prophecy in Judaism." Pages 577–93 in vol. 2 of *The Dead Sea Scrolls in Context: Integrating the Dead Sea Scrolls in the Study of Ancient Texts, Languages, and Cultures*. Edited by Armin Lange, Emanuel Tov, and Matthias Weigold. 2 vols. VTSup 140. Leiden: Brill, 2011.

Jeffers, Ann. *Magic and Divination in Ancient Palestine and Syria*. SHCANE 8. Leiden: Brill, 1996.

Johnson, Sara Raup. "Court Tales." Pages 489–91 in *The Eerdmans Dictionary of Early Judaism*. Edited by John J. Collins and Daniel C. Harlow. Grand Rapids: Eerdmans, 2010.

Kobelski, Paul J. *Melchizedek and Melchireša'*. CBQMS 10. Washington: Catholic Biblical Association of America, 1981.

Kugel, James. *Traditions of the Bible: A Guide to the Bible As It Was at the Start of the Common Era*. Cambridge: Harvard University Press, 1999.

———. "Which is Older, Jubilees or the Genesis Apocryphon? An Exegetical Approach." Pages 257–94 in *The Dead Sea Scrolls and Contemporary Culture: Proceedings of the International Conference Held at the Israel Museum, Jerusalem (July 6–8, 2008)*. Edited by Adolfo D. Roitman, Lawrence H. Schiffman, and Shani Tzoref. STDJ 93. Leiden: Brill, 2011.

Lange, Armin. "Between Zion and Heaven: The *New Jerusalem* Text from Qumran as a Paratext." Pages 397–412 in *Biblical Figures in Deuterocanonical and Cognate Literature*. Edited by Hermann Lichtenberger and Ulrike Mittman-Richert. DCLY 2008. Berlin: de Gruyter, 2009.

———. "The Essene Position on Magic and Divination." Pages 377–435 in *Legal Texts and Legal Issues: Proceedings of the Second Meeting of the International Organization for Qumran Studies, Cambridge 1995, Published in Honour of Joseph M. Baumgarten*. Edited by Moshe J. Bernstein, Florentino García Martínez, and John Kampen. STDJ 23. Leiden: Brill, 1997.

Lehmann, Manfred R. "1 Q Genesis Apocryphon in the Light of the Targumim and Midrashim." *RevQ* 1 (1958): 249–63.

Levine, Baruch A. "Notes on an Aramaic Dream Text from Egypt." *JAOS* 84 (1964): 18–22.

Lignée, H. "l'Apocryphe de la Genèse." Pages 207–402 in vol. 2 of *Les textes de Qumran: traduits et annotés*. Edited by J. Carmignac, É. Cothenet, and H. Lignée. 2 vols. Paris: Letouzey et Ané, 1963.

Luijken Gevirtz, Marianne. "Abram's Dream in the Genesis Apocryphon: Its Motifs and Their Function." *Maarav* 8 (1992): 229–43.

Machiela, Daniel A. *The Dead Sea Genesis Apocryphon: A New Text and Translation with Introduction and Special Treatment of Columns 13–17*. STDJ 79. Leiden: Brill, 2009.

———. "The Qumran Pesharim as Biblical Commentaries: Historical Context and Lines of Development." *DSD* 19 (2012): 313–62.

Mason, Eric F. "Melchizedek Traditions in Second Temple Judaism." Pages 343–60 in *New Perspectives on 2 Enoch: No Longer Slavonic Only*. Edited by Andrei A. Orlov, Gabriele Boccaccini, and Jason M. Zurawski. SJS 4. Leiden: Brill, 2012.

Meyer, R. *Das Gebet des Nabonid: Eine in den Qumran-Handschriften wiederentdeckte Weisheiterzählung*. Sitzungsberichte der sächsischen Akademie der Wissenschaften zu Leipzig, Philologisch-historische Klasse 107.3. Berlin: Akademie Verlag, 1962.

Milik, J. T. "4Q Visions de 'Amram et une Citation d'Origène." *RB* 79 (1972): 77–97.

———. *The Books of Enoch: Aramaic Fragments from Qumrân Cave 4*. Oxford: Clarendon, 1976.

———. "Milkî-ṣedeq et Milkî-reša' dans les anciens écrits juifs et chrétiens." *JJS* 23 (1972): 95–144.

Najman, Hindy and Nicole Hilton. "What Constitutes Revelation at Qumran?" in *T&T Clark Companion to the Dead Sea Scrolls*. Edited by George J. Brooke and Charlotte Hempel. London: Bloomsbury T&T Clark, forthcoming.

Newsom, Carol. "'Sectually Explicit' Literature from Qumran." Pages 167–87 in *The Hebrew Bible and Its Interpreters*. Edited by William Henry Propp, Baruch Halpern, and David Noel Freedman. Winona Lake: Eisenbrauns, 1990.

Nickelsburg, George W. E. *1 Enoch: A Commentary on the Book of 1 Enoch, Chapters 1–36; 81–108*. Hermeneia. Minneapolis: Fortress Press, 2001.

Nickelsburg, George W. E. and James C. VanderKam. *1 Enoch: The Hermeneia Translation*. Minneapolis: Fortress, 2012.

Niehoff, Maren. "A Dream Which is Not Interpreted is Like a Letter Which is not Read." *JJS* 43 (1992): 58–84.

Nissinen, Martti. "How Prophecy Became Literature." *SJOT* 19 (2005): 153–72.

———. "Spoken, Written, Quoted, and Invented: Orality and Writtenness in Ancient Near Eastern Prophecy." Pages 35–71 in *Writings and Speech in Israelite and Ancient Near Eastern Prophecy*. Edited by Ehud Ben Zvi, and Michael H. Floyd. SBLSymS 10. Atlanta: Society of Biblical Literature, 2000.

Oppenheim, A. Leo. *The Interpretation of Dreams in the Ancient Near East: With a Translation of an Assyrian Dream-Book*. TAPS 46.3. Philadelphia: American Philosophical Society, 1956.

Oßwald, Eva. "Beobachtungen zur Erzählung von Abrahams Aufenthalt in Ägypten im 'Genesis-Apokryphon.'" *ZAW* 72 (1960): 7–25.

Orlov, Andrei A. "Melchizedek." Pages 931–32 in *The Eerdmans Dictionary of Early Judaism*. Edited by John J. Collins and Daniel C. Harlow. Grand Rapids: Eerdmans, 2010.

Perrin, Andrew B. *The Dynamics of Dream-Vision Revelation in the Aramaic Dead Sea Scrolls*. JAJSup 19. Göttingen: Vandenhoeck & Ruprecht, 2015.

Porteous, Norman W. *Daniel: A Commentary*. OTL. Philadelphia: Westminster John Knox, 1965.

Puech, Émile. *Qumrân Grotte 4.XXII: Textes araméens, première partie: 4Q529–549*. DJD XXXI. Oxford: Clarendon, 2001.

———. *Qumrân Grotte 4.XXVII: Textes araméens, deuxième partie: 4Q550–4Q575a, 4Q580–4Q587*. DJD XXXVII. Oxford: Clarendon, 2009.

Rabinowitz, Isaac. "'Pēsher/Pittārōn': Its Biblical Meaning and Its Significance in the Qumran Literature." *RevQ* 8 (1973): 219–32.

Regev, Eyal. *Sectarianism in Qumran: A Cross-Cultural Perspective*. RelSoc 45. Berlin: de Gruyter, 2007.

Schniedewind, William M. "Qumran Hebrew as an Antilanguage." *JBL* 118 (1999): 235–52.

Schöpflin, Karin. "God's Interpreter: The Interpreting Angel in Post-Exilic Prophetic Visions of the Old Testament." Pages 189–203 in *Angels: The Concept of Celestial Beings: Origins, Development and Reception*. Edited by Friedrich V. Reiterer, Tobias Nicklas, and Karin Schöpflin. DCLY 2007. Berlin: de Gruyter, 2007.

Segal, Michael. "From Joseph to Daniel: The Literary Development of the Narrative in Daniel 2." *VT* 59 (2009): 123–49.

Stuckenbruck, Loren T. *The Book of Giants from Qumran: Texts, Translation, and Commentary*. TSAJ 63. Tübingen: Mohr Siebeck, 1997.

———. "The Early Traditions Related to 1 Enoch from the Dead Sea Scrolls: An Overview and Assessment." Pages 41–61 in *The Early Enoch Literature*. Edited by Gabriele Boccaccini and John J. Collins. JSJSup 121. Leiden: Brill, 2007.

———. "Pseudepigraphy and First Person Discourse in the Dead Sea Documents: From the Aramaic Texts to Writings of the *Yaḥad*." Pages 295–326 in *The Dead Sea Scrolls and Contemporary Culture: Proceedings of the International Conference Held at the Israel Museum, Jerusalem (July 6-8, 2008)*. Edited by Adolfo D. Roitman, Lawrence H. Schiffman, and Shani Tzoref. STDJ 93. Leiden: Brill, 2011.

Swain, Joseph Ward. "The Theory of the Four Monarchies: Opposition History under the Roman Empire." *CP* 35 (1940): 1–21.

Taylor, Joan E. "The Classical Sources on the Essenes and the Scrolls Communities." Pages 173–99 in *The Oxford Handbook of the Dead Sea Scrolls*. Edited by Timothy H. Lim and John J. Collins. Oxford: Oxford University Press, 2010.

Thomas, Samuel I. *The "Mysteries" of Qumran: Mystery, Secrecy, and Esotericism in the Dead Sea Scrolls*. EJL 25. Atlanta: Society of Biblical Literature, 2009.

Tigchelaar, Eibert J. C. "Aramaic Texts from Qumran and the Authoritativeness of Hebrew Scriptures: Preliminary Observations." Pages 155–71 in *Authoritative Scriptures in Ancient Judaism*. Edited by Mladen Popović. JSJSup 141. Leiden: Brill, 2010.

van der Toorn, Karel. *Scribal Culture and the Making of the Hebrew Bible*. Cambridge: Harvard University Press, 2009.

VanderKam, James C. *Enoch: A Man for All Generations*. Studies on Personalities of the Old Testament. Columbia: University of South Carolina Press, 1995.

———. "Mantic Wisdom in the Dead Sea Scrolls." *DSD* 4 (1997): 336–53.

Wacholder, Ben Zion. "The Ancient Judaeo-Aramaic Literature (500–164 B.C.E.): A Classification of Pre-Qumranic Texts." Pages 257–81 in *Archaeology and History in the Dead Sea Scrolls: The New York University Conference in Memory of Yigael Yadin*. Edited by Lawrence H. Schiffman. JSPSup 8. Sheffield: JSOT Press, 1990.

Weitzman, Steve. "Why Did the Qumran Community Write in Hebrew?" *JAOS* 119 (1999): 35–45.

Wesselius, Jan-Wim. "The Literary Nature of the Book of Daniel and the Linguistic Character of Its Aramaic." *AS* 3 (2005): 241–83.

Wikenhauser, Alfred. "Doppelträume." *Bib* 29 (1948): 100–11.

Wills, L. M. *The Jew in the Court of the King: Ancient Jewish Court Legends*. Minneapolis: Fortress, 1990.

Vermes, Geza and Martin D. Goodman. *The Essenes According to the Classical Sources*. Sheffield: JSOT Press, 1989.

Zeitlin, Solomon. "Dreams and Their Interpretation from the Biblical Period to the Tannaitic Time: An Historical Study." *JQR* 66 (1975): 1–18.

9
"All the Dreams Follow the Mouth": Dreamers and Interpreters in Rabbinic Literature

Haim Weiss

The encounter between dreamer and dream interpreter is both fascinating and complex.[1] The dreamer must reveal the contents of the dream to another human being, who might be a complete stranger. Oftentimes the dream's contents are enigmatic; they transgress the boundaries of the normative and, as one might expect, cause the dreamer much anxiety. Untrained in the art of dream interpretation, the dreamer may believe that the dream's manifest contents (the dreamtext) provide an unmediated entry into his or her inner world. This perception leads to a fear of the unethical, subversive, and destructive fantasies revealed in the dreams.

The dream interpreter is thus burdened with an enormous responsibility: to create an alternate language that will enable the dreamer to establish new and innovative links between the signifier and the signified, and consequently a new and different understanding of the dream's meaning and of the reality it represents. In other words, the dream interpreter must undo the concrete link the dreamer creates between the image envisioned and its meaning, offering an alternate network of interpretations and creating a discourse reflecting a truth whose value is not measured by the manifest dreamtext, immediately apparent to the dreamer. Moreover, for the sages of the Talmud, the interpretation, and not

---

[1] This article is the result of the session of the Prophetic Texts and Their Ancient Contexts group at the annual meeting of the Society for Biblical Literature in Baltimore, 2013; I would like to thank the organizers of the session for their kind invitation to participate and to all the participants for their valuable remarks. I wish also to thank Galit Hasan-Rokem, Dina Stein and Tzahi Weiss for reading early drafts of this article.

the dream itself, often seems to be the reality-constituting text. To be sure, the interpretation must be adequate to the dream; but multiple, even contradictory interpretations may be adequate to the same dream. This approach gives immense weight to the interpretive effort, domesticating the dream and subjecting its subversive meanings to normative religious and cultural structures. As a result, not only the interpretation, but the interpreter, wields great power.

For the talmudic sages, the interpreter's power was to a large extent a corollary of the great power attributed to language, more precisely to the act of speech.[2] As in the case of magical incantations, language was thought to effect real changes in the world. The sages' complex attitudes towards the interpretation of dreams and towards the interpreters themselves were thus shaped by their fear of the magical and fatalist elements inherent in the interpretive process.

THE BAR-HEDYA STORY

To illustrate the complex relationship between dreamers and interpreters in rabbinic literature, I wish to focus on a few passages from the longest talmudic story of dream interpretation.[3] The story appears in the middle of a long and complex compilation of discussions dedicated to the cultural and religious meaning of dreams. This compilation appears in the Babylonian Talmud at the end of tractate Berakhot; scholars often refer to it as the "Dream Tractate."[4]

---

[2] See Haim Weiss, "'Twenty Four Dream Interpreters Were in Jerusalem': On Dream Interpretation in the Talmudic 'Dream Tractate,'" *Jewish Studies* 44 (2008): 37–77 [Hebrew].

[3] The full story, translated from the original Aramaic (according to MS Oxford 366), is in the appendix to this article. On this story see also: Yitzhak Afik, "Dreams in Rabbinic Literature" (PhD diss., Bar-Ilan University 1991), 178–424 [Hebrew]; Richard Kalmin, *Sages, Stories, Authors, and Editors in Rabbinic Babylonia*, BJS 300 (Atlanta: Scholars Press 1994), 161–80; Haim Weiss, *'All Dreams Follow the Mouth?' A Literary and Cultural Reading in the Talmudic 'Dream Tractate'* (Or-Yehuda: Heksherim Research Center, 2011), 92–172 [Hebrew]; Holger M. Zellentin, *Rabbinic Parodies of Jewish and Christian Literature*, TSAJ 139 (Tübingen: Mohr Siebeck, 2011) 95–136; Holger M. Zellentin, "Jewish Dreams Between Roman Palestine and Sasanian Babylonia: Cultural and Geographic Borders in Rabbinic Discourse (Yerushalmi *Ma'aser Sheni* 57c, 17–24 and Bavli *Berakhot* 58a–b)," in *Borders: Terminologies, Ideologies, and Performances*, ed. Annette Weissenrieder, WUNT 366 (Tübingen: Mohr Siebeck, 2016), 419–57.

[4] For a full description of this dream tractate, see Weiss, *All Dreams*, 9–14, and the bibliography there.

In the story, the two foremost sages of the Babylonian Talmud, Abaye and Rava, appear before an interpreter called Bar-Hedya,[5] presenting to him a series of identical dreams both of them had dreamt and asking for his interpretations. The opening passage is a striking illustration of the complex and intense power play between dreamers and interpreters:

> Bar-Hedya was an interpreter of dreams.
> For those who paid him a zuz (a small fee), he would provide a favorable interpretation, and for those who did not pay him a zuz, he would provide an unfavorable one.
> Abaye and Rava saw a dream. Abaye paid him a zuz. Rava did not pay him a zuz. (b. Ber. 56a)

Bar-Hedya's professional ethics are clearly shown to be dubious, his interpretations favorable or unfavorable in direct relation to his compensation.[6] This has two implications in terms of the resultant power relations. First, the interpreter is free to choose almost any interpretation and the "objective" correspondence between signifier and signified becomes subsidiary. Second, from the moment the interpretation is uttered, it functions as a performative utterance, determining the dreamer's fate in the real world. In fact, in the opening of the story, consulting with the interpreter is portrayed as a way of controlling the future. Paying the interpreter is not only the appropriate thing to do socially speaking, but a wise financial investment likely to pay off tenfold. Not paying the interpreter is not only economically unsound, but potentially fatally dangerous, especially when it comes to the health and well-being of the dreamer's relatives.[7]

The opening of the story is followed by a series of fourteen dreams reported by Abaye and Rava. I shall focus on the third one:

---

[5] On the meaning of this name, see Afik "Dreams," 219; Galit Hasan-Rokem, *Web of Life: Folklore and Midrash in Rabbinic Literature* (Stanford: Stanford University Press 2000), 100 n. 25; Weiss, *All Dreams*, 104.

[6] See also Zellentin, *Rabbinic Parodies*, 105–7.

[7] The Graeco-Roman literature devoted to dreams makes very little mention of payment being rendered. See: Aristophanes, *Vespae* lines 52–54, in *The Complete Greek Drama*, trans. Eugene O'Neill, Jr. (New York: Random House, 1938), 2:611; Juvenal, *Satirae* 6.542–47, in *Juvenal and Perseus*, trans. Susanna Morton Braund, LCL 91 (Cambridge: Harvard University Press, 2004), 284–85; Cicero, *De Divinatione*, 1.58, trans. W. A. Falconer (London: W. Heinemann, 1921). See also R. G. A. van Lieshout, *Greeks on Dreams* (Utrecht: HES Publishers, 1980), 173; Dwora Gilula, "Facetious References to Jews in Roman Literature," *Jerusalem Studies in Jewish Folklore* 9 (1986): 7–37 [Hebrew]; Edward Kortney, *A Commentary on the Satires of Juvenal* (London: Athlone Press, 1980), 332–33.

They said to him, "We saw in the dream that they read us [the verse] 'Your sons and your daughters shall be given to another people'" (Deut 28:32).

He said to Abaye, "You will have many sons and daughters, and you will say, 'Let's give them [in marriage] to my relatives,' but your wife will say, 'Let's give them [in marriage] to my relatives,' until you are compelled [to agree] and they are given to her relatives, and it will seem to you as if they had been given to a foreign people."

He said to Rava, "Your wife will die and your sons and daughters shall be delivered into the hands of another wife," as R. Chiya bar-Abba said, "What is [the meaning of] the verse 'Your sons and your daughters shall be given to another people?' This refers to the father's wife."

As the text makes plain, Abaye and Rava both report the exact same dream.[8] This phenomenon recurs in all fourteen cases. Each time, Abaye and Rava report having dreamt the same dream and narrate it simultaneously, with one voice ("And they said: 'In our dream we saw...'"). That they both report the same dreams calls attention, of course, to the complete dependence of Bar-Hedya's interpretations on his differing compensation.

Shared dreams are a rare but not unheard of phenomenon in the literature of late antiquity. In *City of God*, Augustine describes rare cases in which demons can appear as dream characters to more than one dreamer at the same time.[9] Patricia Cox Miller claims that this type of dream stems from the perception of dreams as independent entities, completely divorced from the dreamer himself. These dreams are created by the gods, or, in a Christian context, by the demons, and therefore may appear to several people simultaneously.[10]

---

[8] For another reading of this segment see Zellentin, *Rabbinic Parodies*, 108–9.

[9] Augustine, *De civitate dei* 18.18, in *Concerning The City of God: Against the Pagans*, trans. Henry Bettenson (Harmondsworth: Penguin Books, 1984). See also Artemidorus, who recounts a situation in which seven women all dreamed of having given birth to a snake. Each woman received a different interpretation contingent upon her own life story. Artemidorus, *Oneirocritica*, 4.67, in *The Interpretation of Dreams: Oneirocritica*, trans. Robert J. White (Park Ridge: Noyes Press, 1975), 212–13. See also Patricia Cox Miller, *Dreams in Late Antiquity: Studies in the Imagination of a Culture* (Princeton: Princeton University Press, 1994), 84.

[10] See Miller, *Dreams,* 52–54; Barbara Tedlock, "Sharing and Interpreting Dreams in Amerindian Nations," in *Dream Cultures: Explorations in the Comparative History of Dreaming*, ed. David Shulman and Guy G. Stroumsa (Oxford: Oxford University Press, 1999), 88–89. Yoram Bilu, in his study of how saint worship was established in the folk culture of Israel, discovered that dreams played a formative role in this process. Dreams in which the saint appeared to various community members were designed to aid in the search for a new place of worship and to grant it legitimacy. Bilu referred to this phenomenon—wherein community members dreamed similar dreams—as an "oneirocommunity" (community of dreamers). See Yoram Bilu, "Oneirobiography and Oneirocommunity in Saint Worship in Israel: A Two-Tier Model for Dream-Inspired Religious Re-

In the above passage, as in many others, the content of the dream is borrowed from the Bible—in this case, from Deut 28: "Your sons and your daughters shall be given to another people, and your eyes shall look and fail with longing for them all day long; and there shall be no strength in your hand." In its original context, the verse is part of a longer passage exhorting the Israelites to obey the Lord on pain of horrific punishment. As Galit Hasan-Rokem has suggested, the use of biblical verses as the subject matter of dreams is potentially subversive. Presenting the verses as dreams in need of interpretation subverts both the biblical text as a sense-giving device and the sages' exclusive exegetical authority.[11] Abaye and Rava were heads of the Babylonian academies of Pumbedita and Mahoza, among the most influential talmudic sages—precisely those who habitually used biblical verses to organize and make sense of reality. Here, however, the relations of authority are reversed. Here, it is they who need the services of an exegete—inferior in erudition and intellect as he may be—in order to understand how a simple biblical verse relates to reality. The manner in which Abaye and Rava narrate their common dreams to Bar-Hedya—together, with one indistinguishable voice, like students reciting to their teacher—portrays them as lacking exegetical and professional authority.[12] Like the verse itself, they are in the interpreter's hands, subject to his every whim. As soon as the biblical verse is taken out of its usual scholarly context, the sages can no longer cope with it. It ceases to function as the sense-making device they normally employ to explain reality; instead, it is an existential riddle. To solve it, they must go to the interpreter, shorn of their usual authority.

Abaye leaves after the fourteenth dream. Rava finds it harder to quit, though he still refuses to pay. His relationship with Bar-Hedya becomes increasingly tense at this point, leading to the following rapid series of dreams and interpretations:

---

vivals," *Dreaming* 10 (2000): 85–101; Yoram Bilu, *The Saints' Impresarios: Dreamers, Healers, and Holy Men in Israel's Urban Periphery* (Haifa: Haifa University Press, 2005), 94 [Hebrew].

[11] For a discussion about the status of the biblical verse within a dream narrative, see Galit Hasan-Rokem, "'A Dream Amounts to the Sixtieth Part of Prophecy': on Interaction Between Textual Establishment and Popular Context in Dream Interpretation by Jewish Sages," in *Studies in the History of Popular Culture*, ed. Benjamin Z. Kedar (Jerusalem: The Zalman Shazar Center for Jewish History, 1995), 45–54 [Hebrew]. In that context see also Dina Stein, "Believing Is Seeing: A Reading of Baba Batra 73a–75b," *Jerusalem Studies in Hebrew Literature* 17 (1999): 9–33, esp. 22 [Hebrew].

[12] Abaye and Rava's inability to interpret these verses in their dreams is even more surprising given the fact that the Talmud attests to Rava's ability to interpret dreams containing verses, see b. Sot. 31a.

He said to him: "I saw that a house had fallen apart and collapsed."
He said to him: "Your wife will die."
He said to him: "Two [of my teeth] broke and fell out."
He said to him: "Two [of your] sons will die."
He said: "I saw two doves flying free."
He said: "You will divorce two wives."

The first three interpretations portend no lesser catastrophes than the death of Rava's wife and two sons and his divorce from two other wives. Rava's interaction with Bar-Hedya here reaches new heights of cruelty—a cruelty due to the interpreter's position of unchecked power, the position of an emperor deciding his subjects' fates with cool detachment. However, these interpretations offer no novel or surprising connections between signifier and signified. The metaphorical association between the house—as the place where women reside and which they represent—and womanliness is prevalent throughout rabbinic literature and has received considerable scholarly attention.[13] The quintessential example of this confluence is the Aramaic word דביתא which means both "house" and "wife."[14]

---

[13] See, for example: Daniel Boyarin, *Carnal Israel: Reading Sex in Talmudic Culture* (Berkeley: University of California Press, 1993), 134–66; Shulamit Valler, *Women and Womanhood in the Stories of the Babylonian Talmud* (Tel-Aviv: Hakiboutz Hameuhad, 1993), 255–64 [Hebrew]; Galit Hasan-Rokem, *Tales of the Neighborhood: Jewish Narrative Dialogues in Late Antiquity* (Berkeley: University of California Press, 2003), 138–39. Curiously, studies predating Freud, which argued that dreams were the result of organic stimuli, identified a connection between dreams about houses and the human body. Scherner, in particular, claimed that such dreams reflected a physiological disorder that needed to be addressed. Freud himself drew an unambiguous connection between dreams about rooms and women and female sexuality, claiming, for instance, that if the dreamer found himself dreaming about walking from room to room, he was dreaming about a brothel or harem. Thus, he proceeded to explain that a dream about ascending and descending a ladder or staircase is without doubt describing sexual intercourse. See Sigmund Freud, *The Interpretation of Dreams*, trans. By James Strachey (London: Allen& Unwin, 1971), 353–56.

[14] See Morris Jastrow, *A Dictionary of the Targumim, The Talmud Babli and Yerushalmi, and the Midrashic Literature* (Ramat-Gan: Bar-Ilan University Press; Baltimore: Johns Hopkins University Press, 1950), 168 s.v. ביתא, 277 s.v. דביתא. The story about the woman who saw the beam of her house breaking seems to be an exception to this rule. (See b. Ma'aś. Š. 55b; Lam. Rab. 1; Gen. Rab.) R. Elazar and his students provide significantly different interpretations of the dream: R. Elazar maintains that the action in the dream symbolizes the woman's actions and predicts that she will give birth imminently, while his students maintain that the symbolic action is to be associated with a man—the woman's husband—and thus explain that the dream foretells his imminent death. The students' interpretation rests on their assumption that it is not the house that symbolizes the man, but rather the beam supporting the entire house. Thus, the house is

The other imagery—the set of teeth as children, the flying doves as a symbol of sexual promiscuity—is also quite familiar from the literature on dream interpretation. Similar images can be found elsewhere in the Talmud and in non-Jewish sources as well, for example the second-century Greek dream interpreter Artemidorus.[15]

The scene's shocking intensity is only heightened by Rava's compulsive urge to keep sharing his dreams despite the terrible consequences, and by his social obtuseness, his refusal to pay Bar-Hedya his meager fee. It is not until he reports his fourth dream that Rava finally come to his senses. In this passage we find a clear illustration of the power of interpretation to shape reality:

> He [Rava] said: "I saw two turnips."
> He [Bar-Hedya] said to him: "You will receive two blows with a cudgel."

---

still associated with the woman, and this interpretation does not depart from the traditional identification of house with wife.

[15] The imagery of teeth as children stems from the assumption that the oral cavity as a whole symbolizes the entire family, while the teeth, which are found in a row that seems to suspend any hierarchical differences, represent the family members, particularly the children. Many different cultures possess dreams recounting teeth falling out, rotting, or being destroyed. The Egyptian Dream Book published by Gardiner, which was dated to the second millennium BCE, presents a dream about a tooth falling out and its interpretation, foretelling the death of an individual subject to the dreamer. See Naphtali Lewis, *The Interpretation of Dreams and Portents* (Toronto: Stevens, 1976), 13. Artemidorus offers a comprehensive commentary on tooth dreams. At the beginning of this discussion, he declares: "Tooth dreams are open to many different interpretations." Following the lead of Aristander of Telmessus, he understands the mouth to represent the home, and therefore he believes that the teeth signify the various family members. His novel addition to this tradition is the extraordinary detail he imparts and the internal hierarchy he establishes between the types of teeth (for instance, molars versus wisdom teeth) based on their relative positions in the oral cavity. See Artemidorus, *Oneirocritica* 1.31. Not only the ancient Near Eastern and Graeco-Roman cultures believed that the loss of teeth signified the death of relatives, as anthropological studies have shown that this interpretation is also dominant among many African tribes. See A. G. O. Hodgson, "Dreams in Central Africa," *Man* 26 (1926): 66–68; J. S. Lincoln, *The Dream in Primitive Cultures* (New York: Johnson Reprint, 1970), 127. The Dagomba of Western Africa interpret this motif as prophesying the death of the dreamer himself. See A. W. Cardinall, "Note on Dreams Among the Dagomba and Moshi," *Man* 27 (1927): 87–88; For another example, see G. H. Hatchell, "Some Dreams from Urwira," *Man* 27 (1927): 88–89. The connection between the figure of the dove and women and womanliness is prevalent throughout ancient literature. As Irit Ziffer demonstrated in her comprehensive study of the dove allegory in antiquity, we find this connection expressed in a variety of ways in ancient Near Eastern, biblical, Graeco-Roman, and early Christian literature. See Irit Ziffer, *O My Dove, That Art in the Clefts of the Rock: The Dove in Antiquity*, Exhibition Catalogue (Tel-Aviv: Tel-Aviv Museum 1998), esp. 95–113 [Hebrew].

[Rava asked:] "And who will hit me?"[16] The next day when he went to the study hall, he found two blind men quarrelling. He went to separate them. One of them slipped away [from him] and landed two blows. He wished to land another one. He [Rava] said: "I saw two [blows] in my dream." So he desisted.

In this dream, Rava sees two turnips, which Bar-Hedya interprets as portending that Rava would receive two blows.[17] The following day, on his way to his study hall (בית מדרש), Rava finds himself in the midst of a bizarre scuffle between two blind men.[18] The text does not say who they are, where they come from, or why they are brawling at the doorstep of Rava's study house. Their entire function is apparently to realize Bar-Hedya's interpretation of the dream—to fashion a situation in which the story's *real* blind character, Rava himself, can suffer the two blows to which Bar-Hedya had condemned him.[19]

---

[16] Rava's unanswered question to Bar-Hedya appears only in MS Oxford 366 (which this article is based upon) and in MS Paris. In the printed editions, as well as in MS Munich 95 and MS Florence, there is no evidence of it.

[17] The turnip, envisioned by Rava in his dream, was a common food in Babylonia and Palestine. See Zohar Amar, *Agricultural Produce in the Land of Israel in the Middle Ages* (Jerusalem: Yad Izhak Ben-Zvi, 2000), 282 [Hebrew]; Azaria Alon, ed., *Plants and Animals of the Land of Israel: An Illustrated Encyclopedia* (Tel-Aviv: Ministry of Defense, 1988), 12–74 [Hebrew]; Shmuel Krauss, *Kadmoniyot Ha-Talmud* (Berlin: Harz, 1929), 1:235–36 [Hebrew]. Two possible associative links can be discerned between the dreamtext and Bar-Hedya's interpretation: the first relates to the turnip's form—turnips have long leaves ending up in a large, round root that is eaten. This shape mirrors that of the cudgel mentioned by Bar-Hedya in his interpretation. The second rests upon the perception of the turnip in mishnaic and talmudic times as cheap food, symbolizing poverty and even danger. Artemidorus also attributes negative import to a plucked turnip. He argues that it symbolizes vain wishes which will never come to fruition because, by analogy, the turnip lacks nutritional value and therefore its consumption is for naught. Furthermore, Artemidorus claims that for people in poor health, seeing a turnip portends imminent surgery. In our context, Artemidorus's next interpretation is of great interest, for he claims that a traveler who sees a turnip in a dream can expect to be injured by iron. He explains that just as the turnip is cut into strips, so too the dreamer's flesh will be cut by iron. Artemidorus, *Oneirocritica* 1.67.

[18] The narrator's compulsion to occasionally report upon the interpretations' fulfillment comes as no surprise. Throughout the entire story, the narrator's underlying radical assumption is that the future is not only revealed by dream interpretation; rather, the dream interpreter, through the power of his words, has the ability to shape the future itself.

[19] Holger Zellentin reads the whole Bar-Hedya story and especially this segment as a perfect example of comical and parodic qualities; see Zellentin, *Rabbinic Parodies*, 97–136 and especially 113–14; Zellentin, *Jewish Dreams*, 426–27. Unlike Zellentin, I do not see parody or satire as the main character of the Bar-Hedya story.

And indeed, Rava takes the two blows; but when the blind man tries to hit him a third time, he protests that his dream predicted only two. The men accept this strange argument as sensible; realizing their (literary) job is done, they leave Rava and vanish.

The power inequality between dreamer and interpreter reaches its apex in this series of dreams, after which Rava finally comes to his senses and pays Bar-Hedya for his interpretations. This leads to a series of four final dreams, in the course of which Bar-Hedya tries to minimize the havoc he has wreaked: he cannot bring the dead back to life, but he can minimize the financial and social damage he has caused. In the framework of these four dreams, I would like to focus on Rava's last dream and its aftermath:

> He [Rava] said to him: "I saw that they were reciting the *Hallel of Egypt* in my dream."
> He [Bar-Hedya] said to him: "A miracle will happen to you."
> Subsequently, Bar-Hedya was about to cross [a river] with Rava on a ferry.
> Bar-Hedya said [to himself]: "Why should I accompany a man who is in need of a miracle?" As he disembarked at the landing, he dropped a book.
> Rava found it and saw written in it, "All the dreams follow the mouth."
> Rava said: "The outcome was in your hands. Just as this man did not spare me, may it be the will [of God] that he be delivered into the hands of the authorities who will not spare him."
> Rava said: "I forgive him for everything except for [the death of] my sons and daughters and the daughter of Rav Chisda [=Rava's wife], for which I do not forgive him."
> Bar-Hedya said: "What am I to do? For the sages have taught that the curse of a wise man, even when undeserved, will come to pass. How much more so [in this case] when I have caused Rava anguish: Let this man arise and go into exile, for exile atones for iniquity."
> He rose and went into exile among the Romans.

This part of the narrative takes a decisive turn. Bar-Hedya is suddenly transformed from an all-powerful dream interpreter who terrorizes his clientele into a terrified, hunted individual whose world has collapsed around him. Living in fear of Rava's curse, the only hope for escape he can think of is going into exile. In contrast, Rava is transformed from a dreamer who is entirely dependent on Bar-Hedya's interpretations into an individual whose status, power, and belief in his own ability have returned. The carnivalesque nature of the narrative comes to an end as the hierarchy returns to its natural order. Rava finally realizes the situation he has placed himself in and reasserts his status and power by utilizing the tools that are rightfully his as a scholar.

The transformative process in this part of the narrative is highlighted by three key words that subvert Bar-Hedya's power: miracle, book, and curse. Each one of them reveals Bar-Hedya's limitations and captures a core aspect of the process that returns Rava to his rightful place: his position as a leading Torah scholar and head of an academy.

In his dream, Rava hears the "Hallel of Egypt"—the prayer in praise of the miracle of the Exodus.[20] Bar-Hedya's interpretation is quite literal: Rava will be the beneficiary of some miracle. Knowing that the interpretation is bound to become a reality, Bar-Hedya is then horrified to hear that Rava plans to ride the same ferry with him: that Rava would be saved by a miracle implies an impending disaster in which Bar-Hedya himself could be hurt.

Bar-Hedya's interpretation of Rava's dream introduces danger into the real world. The interpreter's power is limited: he does not know what the danger is, when it will occur, or who will be hurt. The only information he has is that Rava is protected from the danger while he is not. To escape the fate he had brought upon himself, he leaves the ferry and goes ashore. But as he does this, the secret of his power is exposed. As he leaves the ferry he drops a book—the only mention in rabbinic literature of a dream interpretation book. Rava finds the book and comes upon the sentence: "All the dreams follow the mouth." This statement, which recurs in various other places in the rabbinic literature, is a key to understanding the sages' view of the interpretive process and, consequently, of the complex power play between dreamers and interpreters. According to the statement, the uninterpreted dream has no effect in reality; as long as it has not been subject to the interpreter's verbal interpretation, it is merely a potential waiting to be realized. The dream has no one intrinsic meaning to be *exposed*, but a constructed meaning to be *fashioned* in the course of the interpretive process. The interpreter does not so much *mediate* between dream signifiers and their real-world meaning, but *creates* a new reality through the magical power of speech.

Reading the book at last opens Rava's eyes. He now understands that Bar-Hedya is not merely the interpreter of pre-given meanings but the creator of a new reality—the same reality that has brought such bitter calamity upon him. This newfound comprehension is evident in Rava's immediate reaction to the

---

[20] Rava refers to the Hallel comprising Psalms 113–118. This prayer is recited on various holidays and festivals and is meant to offer praise and gratitude to God for the kindness and miracles he has bestowed. This prayer is discussed on various occasions throughout Tannaitic and Amoraic literature. The most important discussion, for our purposes, is the one in b. Pesaḥ. 117a which addresses the question of when the prayer was established. The sages maintain that the prayer was established by the prophets, while R. Elazar maintains that it was established by the Israelites, after they witnessed the miracle that was performed on their behalf at the Sea of Reeds. For a detailed discussion of both the prayer's history and an overview of the scholarly studies devoted to it, see Shmuel Sprecher, "The *Hallel* Prayer," in *Atara L'Haim: Studies in the Talmud and Medieval Rabbinic Literature in Honor of Professor Haim Zalman Dimitrovsky,* ed. Daniel Boyarin et al. (Jerusalem: Magnes, 2000), 221–30 [Hebrew].

book, which is to set up a new verbal arena in which he would have the edge over Bar-Hedya. Putting to use the linguistic formulae he possesses as a sage, he now puts a curse upon Bar-Hedya: "The outcome was in your hands. Just as this man did not spare me, may it be the will [of God] that he be delivered into the hands of the authorities who will not spare him."

The anxiety Rava's curse induces in Bar-Hedya is pithily expressed by the proverb he utters: "What am I to do? For the sages have taught that the curse of a wise man, even when undeserved, will come to pass." This proverb maintains that a Torah scholar's curse has magical properties, which, like Bar-Hedya's powers, can force reality to conform to the speaker's will. The fate decreed cannot be escaped or changed.[21] Bar-Hedya's use of this proverb to describe the situation he finds himself in adds another layer to the already complex linguistic-cultural thread running through this story. It seems as if Bar-Hedya could only experience reality by wielding powerful linguistic tools; he requires a linguistic mechanism—the proverb—in order to comprehend the transformation he has undergone from curser to cursed. Recognizing that Rava's linguistic power is superior, Bar-Hedya tries to fool fate by escaping it. But as we find at the end of the story, the more he tries to escape his fate, the more his fate catches up with him, until cruel death finally finds him in his city of refuge, Rome (see in the appendix).

Concluding Remarks

The Bar-Hedya narrative, which I presented briefly in this article, is the longest and most complex narrative about dreams in Jewish literature dating from late antiquity. The enormous number of dreams, the vast range of fields and issues addressed, the richness of the symbolism, and the variegated interpretive methodologies all make this narrative a locus classicus for any discussion of the sages' approach to dreams.[22]

Almost the entire Bar-Hedya narrative revolves around a carnivalesque inversion of the power structure in which the two leading Torah scholars of the time, powerful and revered men, Abaye and Rava, are subjected to the whims of an unknown dream interpreter named Bar-Hedya. They are helpless to respond

---

[21] This is also true in a case where the Torah scholar curses himself or those close to him. See Galit Hasan-Rokem, *Proverbs in Israeli Folk Narratives: A Structural Semantic Analysis*, Folklore Fellows Communications 232 (Helsinki: Suomalainen Tiedeakatemia, 1982), 64.

[22] This text's importance is also attested to by the talmudic redactor's decision to place this narrative at the heart of tractate Berakhot's "Dream Tractate;" see Philip S. Alexander, "Bavli Berakhot 55a–57b: The Talmudic Dream Book in Context," *JJS* 46 (1995): 230–48, esp. 232.

to or defend themselves from his interpretations, and they make no attempt to employ their own interpretive authority or knowledge.

This power structure, especially between Bar-Hedya and Rava, seems to lead us inexorably to the borders of the grotesque or absurd. The narrator creates complicated relationships that favors Bar-Hedya and hence is completely open to his abuse. Bar-Hedya may basically do whatever he wishes, as long as he follows his one simple rule about payment. In the face of this boundless power, Rava stands weak and vulnerable, completely incapable of coping with the reality in which he finds himself. The narrative moves back and forth between the polarities of comedy and tragedy: the laughter that springs to the reader's lips upon reading the opening line of the story—"Bar-Hedya was an interpreter of dreams. For those who paid him a *zuz* (a small fee), he would provide a favorable interpretation, and for those who did not pay him a *zuz*, he would provide an unfavorable one"— is immediately replaced by an expression of shock and horror when Bar-Hedya's interpretations and their tragic consequences are revealed.

The narrator seems to have created a story that follows its own internal logic, one that cannot be fully understood from the perspective of the behavioral norms and cultural codes familiar to us from rabbinic scholarly discourse. Not only does the narrative comprise dozens of different dreams, its overall design— the framing narrative which binds all these dreams together into one unitary composition—seems to be dreamlike in character. Thus, a dialogic relationship is established between the overall meaning of the narrative and its parts. Within the narrative, a mirror language comes into being that enables a dialogue between the whole and its parts.[23]

By choosing to portray these two prominent Torah scholars as dreamers instead of as dream interpreters, a more likely role for them in talmudic and midrashic literature, the narrator achieves two goals. He creates a radical narrative, placing at its center the grotesque figure of a corrupt dream interpreter, a feat which would have been almost impossible had the interpreter been a well-known Torah scholar. Furthermore, he is able to set up a confrontation between the sag-

---

[23] To use the terminology popularized by the structuralists in the 1970s and 80s, the narrator employs a mise-en-abyme structure. In this *ars poetica* structure, the literary work examines itself by studying its reflections in the core narrative. However, these reflections create a web of meaning in which the metanarrative not only discovers its reflections in the core narrative, but also has its conflicts and gaps revealed. For the most important theoretical statement on this topic, see Lucien Dàllenbach, *Le récit spéculaire (Essai sur la mise en abyme)* (Paris: Seuill, 1977). On this, see also Moshe Ron, "The Restricted Abyss—Nine Problems in the Theory of *Mise-en-Abyme*," *Poetics Today* 8 (1987): 417–38. For how this concept can be applied to the study of folklore, see Galit Hasan-Rokem, "Representation and Dialogue in Folklore Research: The Poetics and Politics of an Unperformed Festival," *Jerusalem Studies in Jewish Folklore* 19–20 (1998): 459–73, esp. 472–73 [Hebrew].

es and dream interpreters, forcing the sages to address the problematic consequences of prophetic dream interpretation. Since most of the dream interpreters in rabbinic literature were well-known Torah scholars, by having these sages play the unfamiliar role of dreamers, the narrator defamiliarizes the prevailing literary structure and forces his readers to reexamine the struggle for power engendered by the process of dream interpretation. In choosing two of the rabbinic elite as dreamers, the narrator forces the sages to re-examine the entire dream interpretation process, especially its disastrous consequences. From now on, when a sage harms a dreamer, it will no longer be a matter of class, wherein the elite quite naturally causes harm to their subordinates; rather, the sages must now realize that the situation can be subversively reversed: the elite cause harm to their subordinates, the elite can be harmed by the system they created.

Appendix

Text	Translation
בר-הדיא מפשר חלמי הוה מאן דיהיב ליה זוזא מפשר ליה חילמיה לטבא ומאן דלא יהב ליה זוזא מפשר ליה חילמיה לבישא אביי ורבא חזו חלמא אביי יהב ליה זוזא רבא לא יהב ליה זוזא	Bar-Hedya was an interpreter of dreams. For those who paid him a zuz (a small fee), he would provide a favorable interpretation, and for those who did not pay him a zuz, he would provide an unfavorable one. Abaye and Rava saw a dream. Abaye paid him a zuz. Rava did not pay him a zuz.
אמרו ליה חזינן בחילמא דקא קארי לן שורך טבוח לעיניך וגו' לרבא אמ' ליה בבישתא פסיד עיסקך וטבחת תורא ולא אכלת מיניה מצערא דלבך לאביי א"ל בטבא נפיש לך עסקך וטבחו תורא בביתך ולא תיהני למיכל מיניה מחידוה דליבך	They said to him: "We saw in the dream that they read us [the verse] 'Your ox shall be slaughtered before your eyes, etc.'" (Deut 28:31). To Rava, he responded in a negative [fashion]: "Your business will fail and your sorrow will be such that you will slaughter an ox and eat none of it." To Abaye, he responded in a positive [fashion]: "Your business will prosper and grow and you will be so overjoyed that when an ox is slaughtered in your household you will not manage to eat of it.
אמרו ליה חזינן דקא קרינן בחילמא בנים ובנות תוליד וגו' לרבא אמ' ליה בבישתא לאביי א"ל בטיבותא לרבא אמ' ליה בבישתא כדכתי' לאביי אמ' בנך ובנתך נפישן ומנסבן בנתך לנוכרין ומדמיין באפך כדקא אזלן בשביא	They said to him: "We saw in the dream that we were reading [the verse] 'You shall beget sons and daughters [but they shall not be yours; for they shall go into captivity]'" (Deut 28:41). To Rava, he responded in a negative [fashion]; to Abaye he responded positively. To Rava he responded in a negative [fashion] in keeping with the literal meaning of the verse. To Abaye, he said: "You will have many sons and daughters and your daughters will marry foreigners, so that it will seem to you as if they had gone into captivity."
אמרו ליה חזינן בחילמא דקרי לן בניך ובנותיך נתונים לעם אחר לאביי אמ' בנך ובנתך נפישן ואת אמרת לקריבי יהיבנא להו ודביתך אמרה לקריבי יהיבנא להון עד דאכפת לך ויהבינון לקריבהא ומדמיין באפך כדקא משתקלן לעמא נוכראה לרבא א"ל איתתיה מיתא ומסרן בנך ובנתך לידי איתתא אחריתי וכדאמ' ר' חייא בר אבא מאי דכתי' בניך ובנותיך נתונים לעם אחר זו אשת האב	They said to him: "We saw in the dream that they read us [the verse] 'Your sons and your daughters shall be given to another people'" (Deut 28:32). He said to Abaye: "You will have many sons and daughters, and you will say 'Let's give them [in marriage] to my relatives,' but your wife will say 'Let's give them [in marriage] to my relatives,' until you are compelled [to agree] and they are given to her relatives, and it will seem to you as if they had been given to a foreign people." He said to Rava: "Your wife will die and your sons and daughters shall be delivered into the hands of another wife," as R. Chiya bar-Abba said, "What is [the meaning of] the verse 'your sons and your daughters shall be given to another people?' This refers to the father's wife."

אמרו ליה חזינן דקא קארו לן בחילמ' לך אכול בשמחה לחמך לאביי אמ' מרווח עסקך אדאכלת ושתית וקרית פסוקיך מיוקרא דליבא לרבא אמ' מפסיד עסקך אכלת ושתית ואקרייך פסוקיך לפקוחי דעתיך	They said to him: "We saw in the dream that they read us [the verse] 'Go, eat your bread with joy'" (Eccl 9:7). He said to Abaye: "Your business will prosper to the point where you will eat and drink and read your verses out of the joy of the heart." He said to Rava: "Your business will fail, and you will eat and drink and read your verses to better yourself."
אמרו ליה חזינן דקא קרינן בחילמא זרע רב תוציא השדה לאביי א"ל רישיה דקרא לרבא אמ' ליה בסיפא	They said to him: "We saw in the dream that they recited [the verse] 'You shall carry much seed out to the field [but gather little in, for the locust shall consume it]'" (Deut 28:38). He recited the first part of the verse to Abaye. He recited the second part to Rava.
אמרו לי' אקרינן בחלמא וראו כל עמי הארץ כי שם יי' נקרא עליך ויראו ממך לאביי א"ל ריש מתיבתא הוית ודחלי כולי עלמ' מינך לרבא א"ל ביזיונא דמלכא איתבר ולמחר אתי ותפשי לך ואתו כ"ע למימ' לרבא תפסי ליה לדידן על אחת כמה וכמה למחר איתבר ביזיונא דמלכא אתו ותפסו לרבא	They said to him: "In the dream, they read to us [the verse] 'Then all peoples of the earth shall see that you are called by the name of the Lord, and they shall be afraid of you'" (Deut 28:10). He said to Abaye: "You will become the head of an academy, and everyone will stand in awe of you." He said to Rava: "The king's prison will be broken into and on the following day they will seize you. Everyone will say, 'If Rava has been taken into custody, how much more so are we likely to be.'" The next day the king's prison was broken into and they seized Rava.
אמרו ליה אקרינן בחילמ' זיתים יהיו לך לאביי א"ל ברישיה לרבא א"ל בסיפיה	They said to him: "In the dream, they read to us [the verse]: 'You shall have olive trees throughout all your territory, [but you shall not anoint yourself with the oil; for your olives shall drop off.'" (Deut 28:40). He recited the first part of the verse to Abaye. He recited the second part to Rava.
אמרו חזינן חסא דקדח אפום דנא לאביי א"ל מלי עסקך עיף עיסקך כחסא לרבא א"ל מריר עיסקך כחסא	They said: "We saw lettuce growing on the mouth of a jar." He said to Abaye: "Your business will blossom; your business will be doubled like a lettuce." To Rava, he said: "Your merchandise will become bitter like a lettuce."
אמרו ליה חזינן חביתא דתליא בדיקלא לאביי א"ל מלי עיסקך לרבא א"ל חלי ואתו כ"ע ונסבי בלא פשיטי	They said to him: "We saw a cask that was hanging on a date palm." He said to Abaye: "Your business will blossom." To Rava, he said: "It [your merchandise] will become sweet, and everyone will come and take without paying."
אמרו ליה חזינן בישרא אפום דנא לאביי א"ל בסים חמרך וכ"ע זבני מיניה למישתי עם בישרא לרבא א"ל תקיף חמרך ואתו כ"ע למישקל [ח]לא למכוי [למיטוי] בישרא	They said to him: "We saw meat on the mouth of a jar." He said to Abaye: "Your wine will be fragrant and everyone will come to buy it from you to drink with meat." To Rava, he said: "Your wine will sour,[1] and everyone will come to take vinegar to roast the meat."

אמ' ליה חזינן רומני אפום דנא לאביי א"ל עיף עסקך כרומנא לרבא א"ל קוויה עסקך כרומנא	They said to him: "We saw a pomegranate on the mouth of a jar." He said to Abaye: "Your merchandise will double [in price] like a pomegranate." To Rava, he said: "Your merchandise will be tart like a pomegranate."
אמרו ליה חזינן דנא דחמרא דנפל בבירא לאביי א"ל מיתבעי עיסקך כי האי דנפל בבירא לא משתכח לרבא א"ל סרי עיסקך ושדית ליה לבירא	They said to him: "We saw a jar of wine that fell into a pit." He said to Abaye: "Your merchandise will be sought after like that which falls into a pit and cannot be found." To Rava, he said: "Your merchandise will spoil and you will throw it into a pit."
אמרו ליה חזינן דנא דחמרא דסליק לדיקל' לאביי א"ל עדיף עיסקך כדיקלא לרבא א"ל פסיד עיסקך כתמרים	They said to him: "We saw a jar of wine that was lifted into a date palm." He said to Abaye: "Your merchandise will be valuable like a date palm." To Rava, he said: "Your business will fall like dates."
אמרו חזינן פטר חמור דקאי עילוון לאביי אמ' ליה כי הוית ריש מתיבת' קאי עילווך אימורא לרבא א"ל פטר חמור גהיט מתפלך א"ל והא איתי א"ל וו דפטר חמור גהיט עיין רבא וחזא דגהיט וו מופטר חמור דתפילי	They said: "We saw a firstling ass standing next to us." He said to Abaye: "When you become head of the academy, a speaker will stand next to you." To Rava, he said: "[The phrase 'firstling ass'] has been erased from your phylacteries." He said to him: "But I have seen [it]." He said to him: "The vav [in the phrase] 'and firstling ass' has been erased."[1] Rava took a closer look and saw that the vav from [the phrase] 'and firstling ass' in his phylacteries had been erased.
אזל רבא לחודיה לגביה	Rava went to him [Bar-Hedya] by himself.
א"ל חזאן דביתא דאיתבר ונפל א"ל איתתא מיתא	He said to him: "I saw that a house had fallen apart and collapsed." He said to him: "Your wife will die."
א"ל תרי כ[כי] דאיתברו מיניה ונפלו א"ל תרין בנין מיתן ליה	He said to him: "Two [of my teeth][1] broke and fell out." He said to him: "Two [of your] sons will die."
אמ' חזאי תרין יוני דפרקין א"ל תרתין נשין מגרש[ו]ת	He said: "I saw two doves flying free." He said: "You will divorce two wives."
אמ' חזאי תרי רישי לפתות א"ל תרי גולפי בלעת ומאן הוא דלימחיין למחר כי אזל לבי מדרשא אשכח הנהו תרי סגי נהורי דמינצו אזל לפורקינהו אישתמי חד מיניהו ומחינה תרי גולפי בעא למימחייה אחרינא אמ' תרי חזאי בחילמאי ושבקיה	He said: "I saw two turnips." He said to him: "You will receive two blows with a cudgel." [He replied:] "And who will hit me?" [The next day] when he went to the study hall, he found these two blind men quarrelling. He went to separate them. One of them slipped away [from him] and landed two blows. He wished to land another one. He [Rava] said: "I saw two [blows] in my dream." So he desisted.
סוף סוף יהב ליה זוזא	Finally, he paid him a zuz.
א"ל חזאי כותלא חדת' דאיתבר א"ל ניכסי קנית ולא מצטערת בהו	He said to him: "I saw a new wall that fell." He said to him: "You have acquired new properties and you do not regret [having purchased] them."

He said to him: "I saw that my house was being torn down and scattered throughout the world." He said to him: "Your teachings will be disseminated [throughout the world]."	א"ל חזאי דסתרין ביתיה ובדרי בכולי עלמא א"ל ניבדרו שמעתתך
He said to him: "I saw Abaye's villa fall and dust come and cover [me]." He said to him: "Abaye will die and the academy of Pumbedita will come to accept your authority."	א"ל חזאי אפדנא דאביי דנפל ואתא אבקא מכסין א"ל אביי שכיב ואתא מתיבתא דפום בדיתא וסמכי עילווך
He said to him: "I saw that they injured my head and my brains spilled out." He said to him: "Stuffing came out of your pillow."	א"ל חזאי דבזעי ליה לרישיה ונתר מוקריה א"ל אודרא מבי סדיא נפל
He said to him: "I saw that they were reciting the Hallel of Egypt in my dream." He said to him: "A miracle will happen to you." Subsequently, Bar-Hedya was about to cross [a river] with Rava on a ferry. Bar-Hedya said (to himself), "Why should I accompany a man who is in need of a miracle?" As he disembarked at the landing, he dropped a book. Rava found it and saw written in it, "All the dreams follow the mouth." Rava said: "The outcome was in your hands. Just as this man did not spare me, may it be the will [of God] that he be delivered into the hands of the authorities who will not spare him." Rava said: "I forgive him for everything except for [the death of] my sons and daughters and the daughter of Rav Chisda,[1] for which I do not forgive him." Bar-Hedya said: "What am I to do? For the sages have taught that the curse of a wise man, even when undeserved, will come to pass. How much more so [in this case] when I have caused Rava anguish: Let this man arise and go into exile for exile atones for iniquity." He rose and went into exile among the Romans.	א"ל חזינן דקא קריין הלילא דמצרא בחילמא א"ל ניסא מתעביד לך. סוף הוא קא עבר בהדיא במעברא אמ' בר-הדיא בהדי גברא דצריך לניסא למה לי כי סליק לגדאה נפל מיניה סיפרא אשכחיה רבא וחזייה דהוה כתי' ביה כל החלומות הולכין אחר הפה אמ' רבא בדי לך הוה קיימא יהי רעוה כי היכי דלא חס ההוא גברא עילוא לימסר למלכותא דלא ליחסו עילויה אמ' רבא על כל מילי מחילנא ליה בר מבני ובנתי וברתיה דרב חסדא דלא מחילנא ליה אמ' בר-הדיא מאי אעביד דאמור רבנן קללת חכם אפי' בחנם היא באה כ"ש דצערתיה לרב' ליקום ההוא גברא וליגלי דגלות מכפרת עון קם גלה לבי רומאי
He sat at the entrance of the main gate to the king's palace. There was a man in charge of the king's wardrobe. He said to Bar-Hedya: "I saw that my finger was decaying." He said to him: "Give me a zuz." He did not give him one. He said absolutely nothing to him. He said to him: "I saw that two of my fingers were decaying. And then three. And then four. And then my entire hand." He said to him: "What are you in charge of?" He replied: "I am in charge of the king's silk [garments]." He said to him: "The worms (תכלה) have spoiled the king's silk [garments]." Eventually, the story became known in the palace of King Shapur. They brought the keeper of the wardrobe [before the king] and asked him to explain what had happened. He told them exactly what had happened. They said to	יתיב אפיתחא דריש תרעא דמלכא הוה ההוא גברא דהוה מפקיד עילויי גיזא דמלכא א"ל חזאי דנפל תכלא באצבעתיה א"ל הב לי זוזא לא יהב ליה לא אמר ליה ולא מדי א"ל חזאי דנפל תכלא בתרתין אצבעתיה ותו בתלת' ותו בארבע ותו בכוליה ידיה א"ל עילוי מאי מ[י]פקדת א"ל עילוי שיראי דמלכא א"ל נפל תכלתא בשיראי דמלכא סוף אישתמע מילתא בי שבור מלכא אתיוה לריש תרזיא אמרו ליה היכי הוה מעשה אמ' להו הכי והכי הוה אמרו ליה אטו בחמשא זוזי מפסדת שיראי דמלכא קטלוה סוף אתיוה לבר-

הדיא תפשוה להלין ארזי וכפינהו לרישינהו ואסרו חד כרעיה לחדא וחד כרעיה לחדא ושבקוה עד דאיצטליק רישיה אמ' רבא לא מחילנא ליה עד דאיצטליק רישיה מגופיה אזל כל חד וחד וקם בדוכתיה ואיצטליק רישיה ונפל בתריה	him: "For [the lack of] five zuzim, you caused the king's silk [garments] to be ruined." They executed him. Subsequently, they brought Bar-Hedya, took [two] cedars, tied their tops together, and bound one leg to one of the cedars and the other to the other. Then they released the cedars so that [even] his head was split. Rava said: "I did not forgive him until his head was detached from his body." Each [tree] rebounded to its natural position and his head detached [from his body] and fell between them.

Bibliography

Afik, Yitzhak. "Dreams in Rabbinic Literature." PhD diss., Bar-Ilan University, 1991 [Hebrew].
Alexander, Philip S. "Bavli Berakhot 55a–57b: The Talmudic Dream Book in Context." *JJS* 46 (1995): 230–48.
Alon, Azaria, ed. *Plants and Animals of the Land of Israel: An Illustrated Encyclopedia*. Tel-Aviv: Ministry of Defense, 1988 [Hebrew].
Amar, Zohar. *Agricultural Produce in the Land of Israel in the Middle Ages*. Jerusalem: Yad Izhak Ben-Zvi, 2000 [Hebrew].
Aristophanes. "Vespae (Wasps)," Pages 603–663 in vol. 2 of *The Complete Greek Drama*. Edited by Whitney J. Oates and Eugene O'Neill Jr. Translated by Eugene O'Neill, Jr. 2 vols. New York: Random House, 1938.
Artemidorus. *The Interpretation of Dreams: Oneirocritica*. Translated by Robert J. White. Park Ridge: Noyes Press, 1975.
Augustine. *Concerning The City of God: Against the Pagans*. Translated by Henry Bettenson. Harmondsworth: Penguin Books, 1984.
Bilu, Yoram. "Oneirobiography and Oneirocommunity in Saint Worship in Israel: A Two-Tier Model for Dream-Inspired Religious Revivals." *Dreaming* 10 (2000): 85–101.
———. *The Saints' Impresarios: Dreamers, Healers, and Holy Men in Israel's Urban Periphery*. Haifa: Haifa University Press, 2005 [Hebrew].
Blass, Rachel B. *The Meaning of the Dream in Psychoanalysis*. SUNY Series in Dream Studies. New York: State University of New York Press, 2002.
Boyarin, Daniel. *Carnal Israel: Reading Sex in Talmudic Culture*. Berkeley: University of California Press, 1993.
Cardinall, A. W. "Note on Dreams Among the Dagomba and Moshi." *Man* 27 (1927): 87–88.
Cicero. *De Divinatione*. Translated by W. A. Falconer. London: W. Heinemann, 1921.
Dàllenbach, Lucien. *Le récit spéculaire (Essai sur la mise en abyme)*. Paris: Seuill, 1977.
Freud, Sigmund. *The Interpretation of Dreams*. Translated by James Strachey. London: Allen & Unwin, 1971.
Gilula, Dwora. "Facetious References to Jews in Roman Literature." *Jerusalem Studies in Jewish Folklore* 9 (1986): 7–37 [Hebrew].
Hasan-Rokem, Galit. "'A Dream Amounts to the Sixtieth Part of Prophecy': on Interaction Between Textual Establishment and Popular Context in Dream Interpretation by Jewish Sages." Pages 45–54 in *Studies in the History of Popular Culture*. Edited by Benjamin Z. Kedar. Jerusalem: The Zalman Shazar Center for Jewish History, 1995 [Hebrew].
———. "Representation and Dialogue in Folklore Research: The Poetics and Politics of an Unperformed Festival." *Jerusalem Studies in Jewish Folklore* 19–20 (1998): 459–73 [Hebrew].
———. *Proverbs in Israeli Folk Narratives: A Structural Semantic Analysis*. Folklore Fellows Communications 232. Helsinki: Suomalainen Tiedeakatemia, 1982.
———. *Tales of the Neighborhood: Jewish Narrative Dialogues in Late Antiquity*. Berkeley: University of California Press, 2003.

———. *Web of Life: Folklore and Midrash in Rabbinic Literature*. Stanford: Stanford University Press, 2000.
Hatchell, G. H. "Some Dreams from Urwira." *Man* 27 (1927): 88–89.
Hodgson, A. G. O. "Dreams in Central Africa." *Man* 26 (1926): 66–68.
Jastrow, Morris. *A Dictionary of the Targumim, The Talmud Babli and Yerushalmi, and the Midrashic Literature*. Ramat-Gan: Bar-Ilan University Press; Baltimore: Johns Hopkins University Press, 1950.
Jung, Carl Gustav. *Dreams*. Translated by R. F. C. Hull. Princeton: Princeton University Press, 1974.
Juvenal, 'Satires.' Pages 112–532 in *Juvenal and Perseus*. Translated by Susanna Morton Braund. LCL 91. Cambridge: Harvard University Press, 2004.
Kalmin, Richard. *Sages, Stories, Authors, and Editors in Rabbinic Babylonia*. Atlanta: Scholars Press, 1994.
Kortney, Edward. *A Commentary on the Satires of Juvenal*. London: Athlone Press, 1980.
Krauss, Shmuel. *Kadmoniyot Ha-Talmud*. 2 vols. Berlin: Harz, 1929 [Hebrew].
Lewis, Naphtali. *The Interpretation of Dreams and Portents*. Toronto: Stevens, 1976.
van Lieshout, R. G. A. *Greeks on Dreams*. Utrecht: HES Publishers, 1980.
Lincoln, J. S. *The Dream in Primitive Cultures*. New York: Johnson Reprint, 1970.
Miller, Patricia Cox. *Dreams in Late Antiquity: Studies in the Imagination of a Culture*. Princeton: Princeton University Press, 1994.
Ron, Moshe. "The Restricted Abyss—Nine Problems in the Theory of Mise-en-Abyme." *Poetics Today* 8 (1987): 417–438.
Sprecher, Shmuel. "The Hallel Prayer." Pages 221–30 in *Atara L'Haim: Studies in the Talmud and Medieval Rabbinic Literature in Honor of Professor Haim Zalman Dimitrovsky*. Edited by Daniel Boyarin, Shamma Friedman, Marc Hirshman, Menahem Schmelzer, and Israel M. Tashma. Jerusalem: Magnes, 2000 [Hebrew].
Stein, Dina. "Believing Is Seeing: A Reading of Baba Batra 73a–75b." *Jerusalem Studies in Hebrew Literature* 17 (1999): 9–33 [Hebrew].
Tedlock, Barbara. "Sharing and Interpreting Dreams in Amerindian Nations." Pages 87–103 in *Dream Cultures: Explorations in the Comparative History of Dreaming*. Edited by David Shulman and Guy G. Stroumsa. Oxford: Oxford University Press, 1999.
Valler, Shulamit. *Women and Womanhood in the Stories of the Babylonian Talmud*. Tel-Aviv: Hakiboutz Hameuhad, 1993 [Hebrew].
Weiss, Haim. *'All Dreams Follow the Mouth?' A Literary and Cultural Reading in the Talmudic 'Dream Tractate'*. Or-Yehuda: Heksherim Research Center, 2011 [Hebrew].
———. "'Twenty Four Dream Interpreters were in Jerusalem': On Dream Interpretation in the Talmudic 'Dream Tractate.'" *Jewish Studies* 44 (2008): 37–77 [Hebrew].
Zellentin, Holger M. *Rabbinic Parodies of Jewish and Christian Literature*. TSAJ 139. Tübingen: Mohr Siebeck, 2011.
———. "Jewish Dreams Between Roman Palestine and Sasanian Babylonia: Cultural and Geographic Borders in Rabbinic Discourse (Yerushalmi Ma'aser Sheni 57c, 17–24 and Bavli Berakhot 58a–b)." Pages 419–57 in *Borders: Terminologies, Ideologies, and Performances*. Edited by Annette Weisseinrieder. WUNT 366. Tübingen: Mohr Siebeck, 2016.

Ziffer, Irit. *O My Dove, That Art in the Clefts of the Rock: The Dove in Antiquity.* Exhibition Catalogue. Tel-Aviv: Tel-Aviv Museum 1998 [Hebrew].

Contributors

Franziska Ede	Georg-August-Universität Göttingen
Esther J. Hamori	Union Theological Seminary, New York
Koowon Kim	Reformed Theological Seminary, Seoul
Christopher Metcalf	The Queen's College, University of Oxford
Alice Mouton	CNRS—Institut Catholique de Paris
Scott B. Noegel	University of Washington, Seattle
Andrew B. Perrin	Trinity Western University, Langley, British Columbia
Stephen C. Russell	John Jay College of Criminal Justice, City University of New York
Jonathan Stökl	King's College London
Haim Weiss	Ben Gurion University of the Negev

INDEX OF ANCIENT TEXTS

MESOPOTAMIAN SOURCES

ARM 26
1	118
225	148
229	2, 148
232	1
234	128
238	2

CBS 13517	15 n.19

The Cursing of Agade,
2.1.5	118 n.29

Dumuzi's Dream
1.4.3	2 n.2

Erra
v 43	144 n.28

Gilgamesh
	9
i 242–298	9 n.1
i 244–298	141, 151
iv 92–98	113 n.13
vii 162–254	9 n.1

Gudea cylinder A
cylinder	3, 4, 5, 6, 10–15
i 17–23	11
i 20–25	115
i 22–ii 3	115
i 28	11
i 245	115
iv 14–21	11
ix 7–xii 11	11
ix 20	13
v 17–18	11
v 19–vii 8	11
viii 15–ix 4	11
xii 12–13	13
xii 13–19	55 n.42
xii 16–19	12
xx 7–12	13 n.12

Harran Inscriptions of Nabonidus
H2
i 11	112

Rassam Prism [BM 91026]
v 50	113

SAA 2
6	15, 48 n.18, 119 n.32
15	48 n.18

SAA 16
21	119

Sippar cylinder
I 4–6	175 n.46

The Sumerian Sargon Legend
2.1.4	120
2.1.4 3–4	120 n.39
2.1.4 12–15	120 n.39
2.1.12–15	120 n.39

Vulture Stele 113

UGARITIC SOURCES

KTU 1.1
iii 21–24,	114

KTU 1.2
i 14–16	114
i 19–24	114

KTU 1.3		i 35–37	113
iii–1.4	57 n.46	i 40	66 n.17
v 5–9	114	iii 46–49	67 n.21
KTU 1.4		*KTU* 1.17	
iii 4	66 n.17	i 2–16	112
iv 20–24	114	i 15–ii 15	67 n.21
iv 38–39	66 n.17	i 26–34	73 n.43
iv 38–39	73 n.44	vi 46–49	114
vii 25–29	53		
		KTU 1.23	51–52
KTU 1.5		1	52
ii 2–5	49 n.20	39–46	51
iv 6–11	50	30–35	66 n.17,
v 14–15	56		73 n.44
vi 8–9	56		
		KTU 1.27	
KTU 1.6	48	i 44	74 n.45
i 32–36	116		
ii 30–35	48, 56	*KTU* 1.86,	
iii	7, 43–58	44	54
iii 1–2	50		
iii 1–9	47, 49–53	*KTU* 1.100	
iii 2–3	51	75	52 n.30
iii 4–7	51		
iii 4–8	54	**HITTITE SOURCES**	
iii 8	46		
iii 8–9	52, 55	KBo 11.1 (CTH 382)	29, 34
iii 10–13	47, 53–55		
iii 14–19	48 n.15, 55	KBo 17.65+ (CTH 489)	33, 40
iii 14–21	48, 55		
iii 20–21	55	KBo 18.142 (CTH 581),	
iii 22–iv	56	obv. 1–7	29, 35
iii 22–iv 5	48		
iii–iv	56	KBo 24.128 (CTH 570)	
iii–vi	46–56	rev. 1–4	29, 35
iv 1–5	49		
iv 20–21	49	KUB 5.1 (CTH 561)	
		iii 48–50	30, 35
KTU 1.14			
i 20–ii 5	67 n.21	KUB 5.11 (CTH 577)	30, 36
i 26–27	112	i 1–9, 30	36
i 31–35	112		

i 26–29	30, 36		
iv 55–62	30, 36		

EGYPTIAN SOURCES

KUB 5.24+KUB 16.31+ (CTH 577.1)	
ii 12–21 17	

Dream Stele of Thutmose IV	112, 113, 115 n.21

KUB 9.22 (CTH 477) 33, 40	

Famine Stele	113, 115 n.21

KUB 9.27+ (CTH 406)
iv 1–9   32–33, 39
iv 1–9   32–33, 39

Hymn to Osiris, Stele of Amenmose (Paris, Louvre C 286)
l. 16   82 n.77

KUB 14.8 (CTH 378)
rev. 41'–46'   16, 18, 31, 38

Memphis Stele of Amenhotep II
20b–22a   113

KUB 15.1 (CTH 584)   31, 37
i 1–11   31, 37
iii 7'–16'   31, 37

Saqqara
mastaba of Ramesses III   69 n.28
mastaba of Ti   69 n.28
tomb of Khnumhotep   69 n.28
tomb of Niankhkhnum   69 n.28

KUB 15.19 (CTH 590)
obv.? 11'–13'   31, 38

KUB 22.69 (CTH 570)
ii 4'–6'   29–30, 35

HEBREW BIBLE

KUB 27.1 (CTH 712)
iv 46–50   31–32, 38

Genesis	
2:21	70 n.32
5:22	165
5:24	165
12	168 n.30
12:4	69 n.32
12:10–20	167
12:11	168
14:18	172
15:1	167
15:12	69 n.32
15:12–15	69 n.32
17	75
17:1	167
17:7	75 n.51
17:8	75 n.51
17: 9	75 n.51

KUB 30.10 (CTH 373)
obv. 24'–28'   16, 18, 19 n.29, 29, 34

KUB 43.11 (+) KUB 43.12
16–17 n.24

KUB 43.55 (CTH 434)
v 6'–13'   32, 39

17:10	75 n.51	37:3–8	97
17:12	75 n.51	37:4	93–95, 96
17:19	75 n.51	37:4–8	92, 94
18	116 n.22	37:4b	96, 98, 105
18:1	167	37:4b–8	97–98, 105
18:1–15	115 n.22	37:5	93–94
20	76–77 n.57, 170	37:5–8	95–96
20:3	67, 113	37:7	94, 95, 98
20:3–7	68 n.26	37:7–8	96
20:7	168	37:7–9	92
20:8	77 n.61, 113 n.15	37:7–42:6	105
20:17–18	66	37:8	95, 97
21:2	92, 93	37:8b	94, 97, 98, 105
21:6	76–77 n.57	37:9	53 n.34, 92, 96
21:7	92, 93	37:10–13	67
24:2–3	74	37:11	77 n.61
24:9	74	37:19	95
25:22	84 n.81	37:19–20	94, 98
25:22–24	84 n.81	37:20	95
26:1	76–77 n.57	39–41	91, 93, 97
27:41–42	70 n.34	40	100, 101, 102
28:10–22	67	40–41	7, 92, 97, 98, 99–104, 105
28:13	67 n.22, 113, 115 n.21		
28: 14	67 n.22	40:5a	102
28:18	74 n.45	40:5b	102, 103
29:30–31	92, 93	40:6	99
30:23–24	92	40:7	99
31:10	73 n.44	40:8	76 n.57, 101, 102, 115
31:10–13	162	40:8	100, 101
31:12	73 n.44, 115 n.21	40:8a	99, 100
31:24	68 n.26	40:9–11	100, 149
31:28	68 n.26	40:12	103
31:34–35	84 n.81	40:12–13	101
32	115–16 n.22	40:12–15	149
32:29	92, 93	40:16	100, 101
34	76	40:16–17	149
37	3, 7, 91, 91–98, 99, 105	40:18	103
		40:18–19	149
37–41	173	40:20	68 n.26
37–45	7, 91–92, 98, 105	40:22	67, 100, 101
37:2	68	41	100, 101, 103
37:3	93–94	41:1–8	101
37:3–4	92, 93–94, 97	41:8	4, 67, 99, 100 n.20
37:3–4a	98	41:9–12	101, 102

41:11	102	Leviticus	
41:11b	102, 103	12	75 n.51
41:12	101, 102, 103	15:16–18	63
41:14	101	18	83 n.80
41:15	76 n.57, 101	19:23	80 n.73
41:15	99	21:16–18	139
41:16	67, 102, 103	26:41	80
41:24b	99		
41:28	77–78 n.61	Numbers	
41:33	103	1:3	69 n.29
41:38–39	102, 103	12	84–85 n.81, 150
42–45	91, 95, 98, 99, 105	12:6	149
42:6	95, 96	12:6–8	136, 169
42:6	97 n.16, 98	12:12	85 n.81
42:6–9	95	22:8	119 n.35
42:9	97 n.16, 98	22:13, 21	113 n.15
42:9–10	96		
43:26	96, 105	Deuteronomy	
43:28	96, 105	7:14–15	71
45	96	10:16	80
45:3–4	96	13	134, 142, 150
45:4	96	13:1–3	169
45:4–7*	98 n.18	13:2–4	136
45:5	98 n.18	13:2–6	162
45:15	96, 98	18	134, 142, 150
45:15b	105	21:17	74 n.46
46:1	112	28	187
46:1–5	91	28:1–24	71
46:3	115 n.21	28:10	197
47:29	74	28:31	196
49:3	74 n.46	28:32	186, 196
49:4	73 n.44	28:38	197
49:24	64 n.13	28:40	197
50:19–21*	98 n.18	28:41	196
		30:6	80
Exodus			
4:24–26	76	Joshua	
6:12	80 n.73	4:7	72 n.42
17:14	72 n.42	4:23–24	72 n.42
23:25–26	71	7:26	72 n.42
32:33	72 n.42	8:29	72 n.42
35:21	82 n.77	10:27	72 n.42
36:2	82 n.77		

Judges	
4:4	62 n.5
6:36–40	3
7:9–15	2
7:14	76 n.57
9:7–15	174
13:2–3	62 n.6

1 Samuel	
1	114
1–3	123, 127
1–8	126
1:1	114
2	111, 125
2–3	122
2:10	127 n.67
2:11	122, 123
2:12–26	123 n.48
2:13–14	122
2:15–16	122
2:18	122, 123
2:19	127 n.68
2:22	114
2:22–25	122
2:27–33	123
2:27–36	123, 125 n.59
2:30	121 n.40
3	3, 7, 109–28
3:1	122, 123
3:1, 7	126
3:1, 7, 21	126
3:1–6	118
3:1a	121, 123 n.45
3:1b	125
3:2–6	125
3:2b	126 n.61
3:3	112
3:4	124
3:4–8	121
3:6	124
3:7	126
3:7–10	118
3:8	124
3:8b	121
3:9	121, 126
3:10	113, 124
3:11	122 n.43
3:11–16	118
3:12	122 n.42
3:13	122 n.42
3:15	112
3:15–16	124
3:15–17	118
3:16	124
3:17	119, 124
3:17–30	118
3:18	121, 122 n.43
3:20–4:1a	124 n.50
4:11	112 n.7
4:18	121 n.40
5:7	112 n.7
5:8	112 n.7
5:10	112 n.7
5:11	112 n.7
5:16–2 Sam 5:8	126 n.66
6:3	112 n.7
6:7–9	50 n.22
8:10	126 n.63
9	126
11:6–7	119 n.36
13:13	121 n.40
14:24	119 n.36
14:26–28	119 n.36
15	111, 117, 125, 126, 127, 128
15:1	126
15:10	126
15:12	73 n.44
15:13	126
15:16	126
15:18	127
15:19	127
15:23	126
15:26	126
15:27–28	127
26:12	70 n.32

Cited Texts

2 Samuel
5:20	126 n.60
6:8	126 n.60
7:4	126
7:13	121 n.40
7:16	121 n.40
7:25–26	121 n.40
8:3	73 n.44
9–1 Kgs 2	126 n.66
12:9	126
13:6	82 n.76
14:27	73 n.43
18:18	73
24:11	126

1 Kings
2:4	121 n.40
3:4–5	112
3:5–14	69
3:6	121 n.40
3:7	69
8:25	121 n.40
9:4	121 n.40
11:4	69
12:8	69 n.31
22:16	119

2 Kings
14:9	174
21:12	122 n.42

Isaiah
8:3	62 n.6
29:10	70 n.32
38:10	70
38:16	65, 70
43:25	79 n.69
56:5	73 n. n.43–44
57:8	73 n.44
65:17	78 n.64

Jeremiah
3:16	78
4:4	80
5:31	73 n.44
6:10	80 n.73
9:25	80
17:1	81
19:3	122 n.42
23	152
23:16	81 n.74
23:26	78
23:28	78 n.65
25:11–12	146
26:2	119 n.35
29:10	146
31:33	81, 81 n.75
42:4	119 n.35
44:21	78 n.64
50:15	73 n.44

Ezekiel
11:19	81 n.75
14:20	69 n.31
16:17	74 n.44
21:24	73 n.44
36:26	81 n.75
40–48	170
44:7	80

Joel
3:1	71 n.36

Habakkuk
2:1–2	162

Zechariah
1–8	170
9:17	81–82 n.76

Psalms

31:12	78 n.64
51:11–12	79 n.69
73:20	43 n.1
78:7	114
78:8	114
78:17	114
78:18	114
78:19	114
78:34	114
78:35	114
78:41	114
78:56	114
78:60	114
110:4	174
113–118	192 n.20
126:1	43 n.1, 65 n.14, 66 n.19
127:3	71

Proverbs

3:3	81 n.75
7:3	81 n.75

Job

4:12–13	70 n.32
5:24–25	68 n.25
7:14	69 n.30
11:12	81–82 n.76
15:10	69, 69 n.30
18:7–19	73 n.42
20:8	43 n.1
29:20	69 n.30
32:4	70 n.32
32:6	69, 70 n.32
33:15	70 n.32
33:15–16	78 n.61
39:3–4	65, 70
40:16	74 n.46
42:13	69
42:16	69 n.30

Song of Songs

4:9	81 n.76
5:2	79 n.66

Ecclesiastes

5:2, 6	43 n.1
9:7	201

Daniel

book	7
1	141 n.14
1–6	103, 137 n.8
1:2–4	140
1:3	139
1:3–4	150
1:10	69
1:15, 17	69 n.31
1:17	139–40
1:20	145
2	4, 99, 100, 103, 134, 137 n.8, 138, 140 n.19, 141 n.23, 147–150
2–6	137 n.8, 150
2–7	157, 165
2–12	140
2:1	68 n.26
2:1–3	147
2:3	67
2:4	147
2:4	101 n.23
2:5	99
2:6–7	101 n.23
2:7–9	147
2:9	101 n.23
2:10–11	147
2:13–15	147
2:16	76 n.57, 101 n.23, 147
2:19	78 n.61, 172
2:24	101 n.23
2:25–26	101 n.23
2:27–29	100
2:30	79
3:31–4:34	140

4	4, 103, 141, 143, 174, 175 n.46	9	146
4–5	134, 140–43	9–12	143–47
4–6	140	9:20–12:13	162 n.15
4:1	141	9:20–27	146
4:3–4	101 n.23	10–12	146
4:5–24	140	10:9	69 n.32
4:6	101 n.23		
4:7	174	1 Chronicles	
4:11	174	2:19	62 n.4
4:15	101 n.23, 141	4:4	62 n.4
5	103, 142 n.19, 142, 143, 146	13:3	112 n.7
5:2	146 n.32		
5:7	101 n.23		
5:8	101 n.23		
5:11	142		
5:11, 14	101 n.23		
5:12	101 n.23, 142		
5:14	142		
5:15	101 n.23		
5:15–17	101 n.23		
5:16	103		
5:20–21	68 n.26		
6–7	134		
7	141 n.23		
7–8	143–47		
7–12	103, 139, 146 n.32, 150		
7:1	143 n.27		
7:13	143 n.27		
7:16	101 n.23, 144, 172		
8	162 n.15		
8–12	134		
8:1	143 n.27		
8:2	143 n.27		
8:2	143 n.27		
8:13	143 n.27		
8:15	143 n.27		
8:15–16	143		
8:16	143 n.27, 145		
8:18	69 n.32		
8:26	143 n.27		
8:27	143 n.27		

NEW TESTAMENT

Matthew
27:19   70 n.34

Acts
2:17   71 n.36

Romans
2:27–29   81 n.75

2 Corinthians
3:3   81 n.75

OTHER SECOND TEMPLE LITERATURE
Apocrypha, Pseudepigrapha, and Deuterocanonical Books

2 Baruch
36:7–10   172

Ben Sira
34:1–8   175

1 Enoch
book   163 n.17, 165
1:2   165
13:8   165
14:14   165
83:1–2   165

83:7 165
85:1 165
86:1–3 165
90:39–40 165
93:2 165

Jubilees
14:1–17 162 n.15
27:1 70 n.34
27:21–25 162 n.15
32:1–2 162 n.15
32:16–20 162 n.15
35:6 70 n.34
39:16–18 162 n.15
40:1–5 162 n.15

Tobit
1:4 68 n.27
1:22 68 n.27

Elephantine
CIS 2.137 163

Qumran

1Q20
XII, 19–XV, 21 170

1Q20
XV, 20 170

1QapGen
XIX, 14–17 167, 172
XIX, 16 167
XIX, 17–21 169

1Q23 166 n.26

1Q24 166 n.26

1QapGen
II, 19–25 166

1QapGen
XIX, 25 166

1QH[a]
VI, 18 161 n.14
X, 17 161 n.14
XII, 11 161 n.14
XII, 19 161 n.14
XII, 21 161 n.14
XXII, 19 161
XXII, 21 161

1QM
X, 10 161 n.14
XI, 8 161 n.14

1QpHab
II, 7–10 160 n.10
VII, 1–5 160

2Q26 166 n.26, 171

4Q203 166 n.26

4Q206 2, 3 166 n.26

4Q242 174
1–3, 1–3 174
1–3, 4–8 174

4Q246 173
i, 1–3 174

4Q529 166

4Q530 166 n.26

4Q530
2 ii + 6 + 7 i +8–11 +12 [?], 3–20 167
2 ii + 6 + 7 i + 8–11 +12 [?], 20–24 167

4Q530
7 ii, 11 167

4Q531 166 n.26

4Q532 166 n.26

4Q543
5–9, 1 171

4Q543–547 174

4Q544		4QNarrative and Poetic	
1, 11	171	Composition[b] (4Q372)	
4Q545		1 7	161 n.14
4, 16	171	4QpapApocalypse (4Q489)	
4Q552	172		163
4Q552		4QpapPseudo–Ezek[e] (4Q391)	
1 + 2, 5	173		162
4Q552		4QpapUnclassified[d] (4Q517)	
1 ii, 1	172	15 1	161 n.14
1 ii, 6	172	4QpapUnclassified[e] (4Q518)	
1 ii, 11	172	2 1	161 n.14
1 ii, 5–6	172	4QpapVision[b] (4Q558)	163
4Q553	172	4QPseudo–Ezek[a–d] (4Q385,	
2 ii, 1	173	4Q385b, 4Q386, 4Q388)	162
4Q553a	172	4Q(Reworked) Pent[b] (4Q364)	
2 ii, 2	172	4b–e ii 21–26	162
4Q556	166 n.26	4QVisAmram[f] (4Q548)	171 n.37
4Q571	166	4QVisAmram[g]? (4Q549)	171 n.37
4QCurses (4Q280)		4QVision and Interpretation	
2 7	161 n.14	(4Q410)	161 n.14, 162
4QEoch[c]	163 n.17	4QVision[a] (4Q557)	163
4QH[d] (4Q430)		4QVision[d] (4Q575)	163
1 6	161 n.14	6Q8	166 n.26
4QInstruction[c] (4Q417)		1	167
1 i 16	161 n.14		
1 i 22	161 n.14	6Q23	166
4QMysteries[b] (4Q300)		11QapocrPs (11Q11)	
1 a ii 2, 3	161 n.14	V, 7	175 n.47
1 a ii 2, 6	161 n.14	11QT[a] [11Q19]	
1 a ii 8, 1	161 n.14	LIV, 8–15	162
4QNarrative and Poetic		CD	
Composition[a] (4Q371)		II 12	161 n.14
1a–b 4	161 n.14	VI, 7–8	160 n.10

Q544
2, 13	171
3, 2	171

GREEK AND ROMAN SOURCES

Aeschylus
Choephori
32–36	70 n.34
526–54	70 n.34

Persae
176–230	70 n.34

Prometheus Bound
788	81 n.75

Aristophanes
Vespae
52–54	189 n.7

Artemidorus of Daldis
Oeirocritica 14
1.31	189 n.15
1.67	190 n.17
2.69	14 n.15
4.67	186 n.9
4.71–72	14 n.15

Augustine
De civitate dei
18.18	186 n.9

Cicero
De Divinatione
I.58	185 n.7

Epidaurus, stela at 79

Euripides,
Iphigeneia at Tauris
42–45	70 n.34

Herodotus
Histories
1.209	70 n.34
6.131	70 n.34

Hippocrates
On Regimen	79–80

Homer
Iliad
1.62–63	22 n.38
1.62–64	18, 23
2.1–40	18
2.80–82	22
5.1–5	68 n.27
12.230–243	22
20.232	69 n.27
24.171–187	22 n.38
24.217–224	22
24.308–321	22 n.38

Odyssey 6, 10, 18–23
2.146–156	21
2.146–176	20
2.181–182	22
4.795–837	20
4.809	21 n.33
15.160–165	21
15.160–178	20
19.257–260	20 n.31
19.308–316	20 n.31
19.535–69	4
19.535–553	70 n.34
19.535–569	19
20.87–90	20
20.92–94	22 n.38
20.102–104	22 n.38
23.173–206	20

Josephus
Against Apion
1:206–207	70 n.34

Antiquities
2.86	176

3.54	62 n.4	Tacitus	
10.237	178	*Historiae*	
13.311–313	160 n.3	4:83	118 n.24
15.373–379	160 n.2		
16.8.1	62 n.4, 68 n.27	**RABBINIC SOURCES**	
17.345–348	160		
17.349–353	70 n.34	**Babylonian Talmud**	

Jewish War
		B. Bat.	
1.78–80	160 n.3	12b	81–82 n.76
2.111–113	160	Berakhot,	
3.351–354	178	4	7–8
		55a–57d	177 n.50
Life		56a	185
208–210	178	56a–56b	183–202

Juvenal		ʿErub	
Satirae		29b	83 n.79
6.542–47	187 n.7		
		Maʿaś. Š.	
Passio Sanctarum Perpetuae et		55b	188 n.14
Felicitatis			
		Pesaḥ.	
4	70 n.34	117a	192 n.20
Pindar		Sot.	
Olympian Odes		31a	187 n.12
13.60–82	22 n.38		
		Midrash	
Plato		Exodus Rabbah	
Timaeus	79–80	48:3	62 n.4
		Genesis Rabbah	190 n.14
Plutarch		42:3	76 n.55
De Iside		46:4	76 n.55
28	118 n.24	47:10	76 n.56
		48:2	76 n.56
Pseudo–Philo		55:4	76 n.55
Liber antiquitatum biblicarum		59:8	74 n.47
9.10	70 n.34		
		Lamentations Rabbah	
Sophocles		1	188 n.14
Elektra			
417–20	70 n.34	**Targum**	
		1 Chron 2:19	62 n.4
		1 Chron 4:4	62 n.4

CAIRO GENIZA
Mosseri
VI.5 133 n.1

www.ingramcontent.com/pod-product-compliance
Lightning Source LLC
Chambersburg PA
CBHW021705230426
43668CB00008B/732